Student Learning Guide

to accompany

Miller

ECONOMICS TODAY: THE MICRO VIEW

Eighth Edition

Robert W. Pulsinelli
Western Kentucky University

Roger LeRoy Miller
University of Texas at Arlington

HarperCollins*CollegePublishers*

Student Learning Guide to accompany Miller, ECONOMICS TODAY: THE MICRO VIEW, Eighth Edition

 For information, address HarperCollins College Publishers, 10 E. 53rd St., New York, N.Y. 10022

ISBN: 0-06-501468-5

94 95 96 97 9 8 7 6 5 4 3 2

ACKNOWLEDGEMENTS

Many thanks to my daughter Elizabeth and my colleague Mel Borland who offered valuable proofreading services.

Typing and computer services were provided by Mrs. Paula Newby. I wish to thank her for her excellent work, patience, and understanding.

Robert W. Pulsinelli

To all the uncles and aunts
of my youth.

CONTENTS

PART SEVEN: PRODUCTIVE FACTORS, POVERTY, AND THE ENVIRONMENT

PART EIGHT: GLOBAL ECONOMICS

TO THE STUDENT

This *Student Learning Guide* is designed to help you read and understand Roger LeRoy Miller's textbook, *Economics Today*, Eighth Edition. Lesson one in economics is that nothing is free; a price must be paid for every activity that is performed and for every good or service that is obtained. The price that you must pay to learn economics certainly includes the course tuition and the costs of your textbook and this *Student Learning Guide*. The price for learning economics also includes the time and effort that it will take you to read and think about this discipline. But the benefits are, potentially, enormous.

If you really learn economics you will achieve your immediate objective, which is (presumably) to make a good grade. More importantly--for the long run--if you learn to think like an economist, you will gain some very crucial insights into human behavior. You should never forget that economics is, first and foremost, a study of human behavior. An understanding of human behavior is a necessary prerequisite to attaining your personal goals and to fulfilling any goals that you might have of helping other people. Good intentions are not enough; if you really want to help people you must understand how they are likely to respond to specific policies. And economics has proven to be an invaluable aid in understanding human motivation.

HOW THIS STUDENT LEARNING GUIDE CAN HELP YOU

This student guide can help you to maximize your learning, subject to constraints on the amount of time that you can allot to this course. There are at least five specific ways in which you can benefit from this guide.

(1) The *Student Learning Guide* can help you decide what topics are the most important. Because there are so many topics analyzed in each chapter (in *all* principles of economics textbooks) many students become confused about what is essential and what is not. You can't learn everything; the Student Guide can help you concentrate on the crucial topics in each chapter.

(2) If you are forced to miss a class or two (we strongly recommend that you attend class regularly, but we realize that emergencies do arise), you can use this *Learning Guide* to help you learn the material discussed in your absence.

(3) There is a good chance that the questions you are required to answer in this *Learning Guide* are representative of the types of questions that you will be asked during examinations.

(4) You can use this *Learning Guide* to help you review for exams.

(5) Finally, this *Learning Guide* can help you decide whether you really do understand the material. Don't wait until exam time to find out!

Ultimately, the way to learn economics is by reading your textbook and *thinking about the theories*. You should try to express the analysis in your own words and to apply the theory to real world circumstances. This *Learning Guide* can't teach you to think like an economist--you'll have to learn to do that on your own. It can , however, provide feedback on your progress; if you can answer the questions and solve the problems, then you will know that you are on the right path.

THE CONTENTS OF THE STUDENT LEARNING GUIDE

Economics is considered to be a rather difficult subject because (a) it is theoretical in nature, (b) it uses a specialized jargon, or vocabulary, and (c) it takes (most people) much time and effort to learn. We who are economists, however, believe that our discipline is exciting and provides tremendous insights into human behavior. Your text and this student learning guide have been written for the precise purpose of helping you to learn economics. We always try to keep you, the student, in mind; we leave the task of trying to impress your teacher to other texts.

Before we indicate to you how we think you can best utilize this learning guide to achieve your goals we want to indicate to you what it contains. Most chapters include the following sections.

1. PUTTING THIS CHAPTER INTO PERSPECTIVE

In this section we attempt to show you where the particular chapter fits into the big picture and, on occasion, offer you advice about how to study the chapter and on what ideas to concentrate.

2. LEARNING OBJECTIVES

Here we list approximately ten things that you should be able to do after you have completed the chapter.

3. CHAPTER OUTLINE

This section presents a sentence outline for the chapter; it provides you with a quick overview of the contents of the chapter and it includes only the most important topics.

4. KEY TERMS

Section (4) is a list of the most important terms used in the text chapter; these terms are crucial to your understanding and each is defined in the glossary at the end of its student learning guide chapter.

5. KEY CONCEPTS

This is a list of the most important theoretical concepts used in the chapter; these too are explained in the end-of-chapter glossary.

6. COMPLETION QUESTIONS

This set of short answer "fill-in-the-blank" questions is intended to test your knowledge of key terms, key concepts, and facts. Some will require an application of the theoretical concepts contained in the text.

7. TRUE-FALSE QUESTIONS

This is another objective test to help you see if you understand the main issues in the chapter. We also explain what is wrong with each false statement. We believe that this will be very helpful to you.

8. MULTIPLE-CHOICE QUESTIONS

The numerous multiple-choice questions in each chapter are another objective test to help you decide whether or not you need to spend more time and effort on the chapter at hand.

9. WORKING WITH GRAPHS

Because graphs are so central to the study of economics, we decided to allocate an entire section (in those chapters where applicable) devoted to helping you interpret graphs. We believe that if you can master graphical analysis, the rest of economics will follow easily. The questions appearing in this section are the actual questions that we pose to our students in the classroom; teachers know that if students cannot answer such questions there is no point in moving on.

10. PROBLEMS

This section requires you take pencil in hand and solve specific problems that depend on your knowledge of the chapter's contents. Often students believe that they understand certain concepts, but then they cannot solve related problems. By working on these questions you will see the concepts in another light, and a deeper understanding will emerge.

11. CASE STUDY

Here we apply chapter concepts to real life situations, in an attempt to show you how useful and interesting economics can be.

12. ANSWERS

We have placed the answers to the student learning guide at the end of each chapter, and not at the end of the book. We believe that you will find this convenient.

13. CHAPTER GLOSSARY

Because economics vocabulary is so important, we decided to add it to the student guide. And we have placed it where it is the most useful: at the end of the relevant chapter, not at the end of the book.

You should be aware that *some of the questions are preceded by an asterisk* (*). These questions are more difficult or go beyond the text or are controversial or may be useful to later chapters. Some may not even have a definitive answer. You can ignore them or accept the challenge.

HOW TO USE THIS LEARNING GUIDE

What follows is a recommended strategy for improving your grade. It may seem like an awful lot of work, but the payoffs will be high. Try the whole program for the first three or four chapters. If you feel you can skip some steps safely, then try doing so and see what happens. After all, only you can know your capabilities and individual circumstances. We do urge you, however, to give this approach a chance.

For each chapter we recommend that you follow the sequence of steps below.

1. Read the introduction, the learning objectives, the sentence outline, and the list of key terms in this *Learning Guide*; follow any study suggestions offered in the introduction.

2. Read the Chapter Summary in your text at the end of the chapter.

3. Read about half the textbook chapter (unless it is very long), being sure to underline only the most important points (which you should be able to recognize after having read two chapter outlines). Put a check mark by that material that you don't understand.

4. If you find the textbook chapter easy to understand, you might want to finish reading it. Otherwise, rest for a sufficient period (you can be the judge of how long it takes you to be refreshed) before you read the second half of the chapter. Again be sure to underline only the most important points and to put a checkmark by the material you find difficult to understand.

5. After you have completed the entire textbook chapter, take a break. Then read only what *you* have underlined, throughout the entire chapter.

6. Now concentrate on the difficult material, by which you have left checkmarks. Reread this material and *think about it;* you will find that it is very exciting to figure out difficult material on your own.

7. Read each of the chapter preview questions in the textbook and write out your answers. After you have finished, compare your answers to the answers to those questions provided by your author at the end of the chapter.

8. Find the comparable chapter in this *Learning Guide* and answer the completion questions, the true-false questions, the multiple choice questions, the problems, and the working with graphs questions. Compare your answers with the answers provided at the back of the *Learning Guide* chapter. Make a note of the questions you have missed and find the page(s) in your textbook upon which these *Learning Guide* questions are based. If you still don't understand--ask your teacher or your student helper. (If you decided that *my* answers are wrong, then by all means write and tell me.)

9. Re-read the learning objectives in this *Learning Guide* and decide if you are able to achieve each of these objectives.

10. Before your examination, study your class notes. Then review the chapter outline in the text and write out your answers to the text preview questions; compare your answer with answers at the end of the text chapter. Re-read the *Learning Guide* outline, then re-do the completion questions, the true-false questions, the multiple choice questions, and the problems. Compare your answer with the answer at the back of the chapter in this guide. Identify your problem areas and re-read the relevant pages in the book. Think through the answers on your own. If you still can't understand the analysis, ask your teacher or your student assistant for help. (Be sure to let your teacher know that you have tried to answer the questions on your own.)

    If you have followed the strategy outlined above, you should feel sufficiently confident and be relaxed to do well on your exam.

SOME HELP WITH YOUR TEXT--READING DESCRIPTIVE GRAPHS AND TABLES

While its true "a picture is worth a thousand words," it is only true that pictures are helpful when they are understood. In your text, *Economics Today*, there are numerous descriptive graphs usually showing information about the economy over time. There are also a number of tables that present information about, say, the composition of unemployment. Although we are aware that the common tendency is to skip over graphical presentations, we suggest that you avoid this pitfall. The presentation of information in the charts and tables is important and merits your careful attention. Below we outline some of the things you should remember when interpreting the descriptive charts and tables in Economics Today.

STEPS IN READING GRAPHS

1. **Read the titles, captions, and legends carefully.** The *title* tells you what the chart is about. The *captions* are printed along the horizontal and vertical axes of the chart. For example, a time line showing unemployment will have the years as the caption for the horizontal axis and the unemployment rate as the caption for the vertical axis. The *legend* is the explanation of what the chart is about. It is a short summary, in most cases, of what is presented in the chart.

2. **Study the format of the chart.** Look at the intervals on each axis. In virtually all cases involving descriptive charts, the horizontal and vertical axes are measured differently. You need to examine the range of data on both the horizontal and vertical axes.

3. **Look at the configuration of the line, bars, or pie chart.** Decide what the significance is. For example, if you are looking at the line showing unemployment over time, what does it show happened in the 1930s? In the 1980s? Think about why differences exist.

STEPS IN READING TABLES

1 **Read carefully each table's title, caption, and legend.** In the case of tables, the captions usually define the rows and the columns. The captions for a table on unemployment rates might have different classes of workers, such as male and female. These different classes of workers would have their own unemployment rates shown for different years.

2. **Look at each column row carefully.** All tables are organized horizontally and vertically. In examining each table, look for differences and similarities in the data. Tables are constructed to permit such comparisons.

INTERPRETING BAR CHARTS

Bar charts are used in a number of places in *Economics Today*. They can be easily interpreted. Below we duplicate a typical bar chart, one in which the percentage of annual total national output (income) accounted for by taxes for eight countries is presented.

Figure 5.3

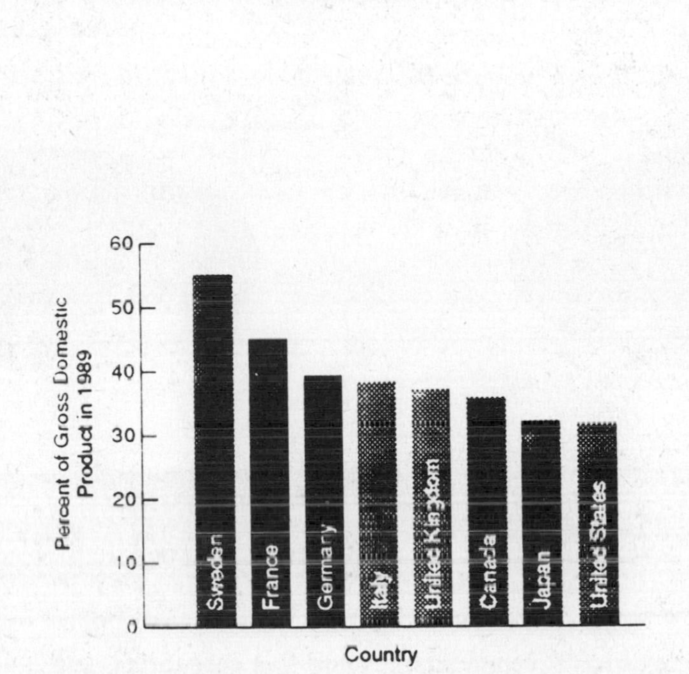

Here the different categories are nations and they are listed across the horizontal axis. The percentage values are listed on the vertical axis. Vertical bars are constructed above each category--each nation with its bar's height corresponding to the average percentage of that nation's annual income paid in taxes. The bars represent that actual percentage for each nation at the time the information was gathered. Notice that the percentage for each country is relative to its own annual income, so that differences in total national income across different ratios is thereby taken into consideration.

INTERPRETING PIE CHARTS

Another way to look at percentages for categories is by using a pie chart. Below we examine a typical pie chart taken out of your textbook. It shows the percentage of federal and state and local tax revenue generated from various sources.

Figure 5.4

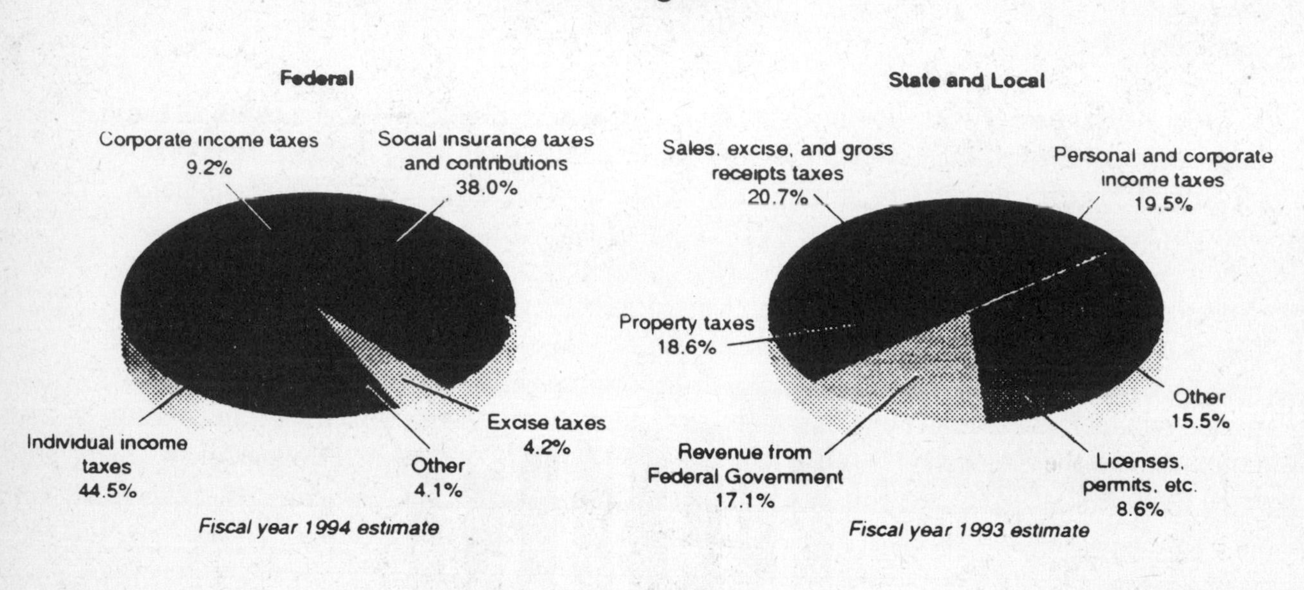

The pie chart divides such revenue sources into five categories, and indicates quite readily the relative importance of each source. For example, at the federal level individual income taxes are clearly the most important revenue source; at the state and local level three separate categories contribute near equally to revenues.

There is no real difference between a pie chart and a bar chart; they are both effective ways to present categorical information. What determines the size of the slice of the pie or the length of the bar is the relative frequency for that category within the data set.

STUDY SKILLS FOR ECONOMICS TODAY

Every student has a different way to study. We give several study hints below that we think will help any student to better master the textbook *Economics Today*. These skills involve outlining, marking, taking notes, and summarizing. You may not need to use all of these skills. Nonetheless, if you do improve your ability to use them, you will be able to understand more easily the information in *Economics Today*.

MAKING AN OUTLINE

An outline is simply a method for organizing information. The reason an outline can be helpful is because it shows how concepts relate to each other. Outlining can be done as part of your reading or at the end of your reading, or as a rereading of each section within a chapter before you go on to the next section. Even if you do not believe that you need an outline, our experience has been that the mere fact of actually *physically* writing an outline for a chapter helps most students to improve greatly their ability to not only retain the material in *Economics Today*, but to master it and thereby obtain a higher grade in the class, with less effort.

In order to make an effective outline you have to be selective. Outlines that contain all the information in the text are not very useful. Your objective in outlining is therefore is to identify main concepts and to subordinate details to those main concepts. Therefore, your first goal is to *identify the main concepts in each section*. Often the large first-level headings within your textbook are sufficient as identifiers of the major concepts within each section. You may decide, however, that you want to make a heading say something else that is more meaningful to you. In any event, your outline should consist of several levels written in a standard outline format. The most important concepts are assigned a roman numeral; the second most important a capital letter, the third most important, numbers; and the fourth most important, lower-case letters. Consider an example taken from Chapter 2 of your textbook.

I. Scarcity

A. Scarcity is not a shortage, nor does it mean the same thing as poverty.

B. Scarce resources are inputs used in production, sometimes called factors of production.

1. Land
2. Labor
3. Capital
4. Entrepreneurship

C. Goods are anything from which people derive satisfaction.

1. Economic goods are produced from scarce resources.
2. Services are intangible goods--tasks performed for someone else.

If you'll compare the outline that we just did for the first part of Chapter 2, you will see that it mirrors more or less the headings in the text. Even if in fact you make an outline that is basically the headings in the text, you will still be studying more efficiently than you would be otherwise. As we stated above, the process of physically writing the words will help you master the material.

MARKING A TEXT

From first grade through high school you typically did not own your own textbooks. They were made available by the school system. You were told not to mark in them. Now that you own your own text for a course, your learning can be greatly improved by marking your text. There is a trade-off here. The more you mark up your textbook, the less you will receive from your bookstore when you sell it back at the end of the semester. The benefit is a better understanding of the subject matter, and the cost is the reduction in the price you receive for the resale of the text. Additionally, if you want a text that you can mark with your own notations, you necessarily have to buy a new one or a used one that has no markings. Both carry a higher price tag than a used textbook with markings. Again there is a trade-off.

Different Ways of Marking The most commonly used form of marking is to underline important points. The second most commonly used method is to use a highlighter, or marker, in yellow or some other transparent watercolor. Marking also includes circling, numbering, using arrows, brief notes or any other system that allows you to remember things when you go back to skim the pages in your textbook prior to an exam.

Why Marking is Important Marking is important for the same reason that outlining is--it helps you to organize better the information in the text. It allows you to become an *active* participant in the mastery of the material. Researchers have shown that the physical act of marking, just like the physical act of outlining, helps you better retain the material. The better the material is organized in your mind, the more you will remember. There are two types of readers--passive and active. The active reader outlines and/or marks. Active readers typically do better on exams. Perhaps one of the reasons that active readers retain more is because the physical act of outlining and/or marking requires greater concentration. It is through greater concentration that more is remembered.

Points to Remember When Marking

1. **Read one section at a time before you do any extensive marking.** You can't mark a section until you know what is important and you can't know what is important until you read the whole section.

2. **Don't overmark.** Just as an outline cannot contain everything that is in a text (or in a lecture) marking can't be of the whole book. Don't fool yourself into thinking you've done a good job just because each page is filled with up with arrows, asterisks, circles, and underlining. When you go back to review the material you wont remember what was important. The key word is *selective* activity. Mark each page in a way that allows you to see the most important points at a glance. You can follow up your marking by writing out more in your subject outline.

SUMMARIZATION

At the end of each section or set of sections in your text, *Economics Today*, there is something called *Concepts in Brief*. These are summary points. You will also find approximately ten summary points at the end of each chapter. You might ask yourself, then, why you should be interested in making your own summary points? The answer is again that the more active you are as a reader, the better you will master the material.

Summarization helps you in your reading comprehension. It is the final step in reviewing the book. There is probably nothing else you can do that works as well to help you remember what your textbook has to say.

The importance of summarization is that the notes you make are in your own words, not in the words of the author. While it wouldn't hurt you to actually write down the *Concepts in Brief* and the point-by-point chapter summary for every relevant chapter prior to the exam, you will spend your time much more efficiently by writing the summaries *in your own words*. This allows you to process the information into your own memory by being required to think about it. You also have to make it part of your vocabulary. Whenever you cannot state important economic concepts in your own words, you probably haven't understood the concepts necessary to master the material. Indeed, summary notes are a good way to determine whether you actually understood something. Don't simply make a mechanical listing of quotes taken right out of the textbook. Rather, you should make summary notes using complete sentences with correct grammar. This forces you to develop your ideas logically and clearly. Also, summary notes written in this manner can be more easily remembered.

Be Brief Your notes should condense the information in the text into statements that summarize the concepts. It is when you force yourself to make the statements brief that you best learn the material. By making only brief summary notes, you have to think about the essence of each concept and present it in a form that is compact enough to remember. You should typically have no more than a one-paragraph summary for each important topic in the chapter.

What Format to Use? The authors find that using 5 x 8 cards is the best way to take summary notes. Don't fill up each note card. You need to leave room to make additional notes later on when you are reviewing for the final exam. That is to say, leave margins for further notes and study markings. Additionally, if you leave enough room, you can integrate your notes that you take during lectures on to these summary note cards.

Another reason to place your summary notes on 5 x 8 cards is because in so doing you have a set of flash cards that you can use in studying for a final exam.

HOW TO STUDY AND TAKE FINAL EXAMS

There is basically one reason why you have purchased this study guide to *Economics Today*--to improve your grade. By using this study guide assiduously, you will have the confidence to take your midterms and final examinations and to do well. The *Student Learning Guide*, however, should not just be used a day before each exam. Rather, it is most helpful if you use it at the time you read the chapter. That is to say, after you have read the chapter you should directly go to the appropriate chapter in the *Learning guide*. This is a systematic review technique; it is the most effective study technique you can use.

Besides learning the concepts in each chapter as well as possible, there additional strategies for taking exams. You need to know in advance what type of exam you are going to take--essay or objective or both. You need to know which reading materials and lectures will be covered. For both objective and essay exams (but more importantly for the former) you need to know if there is a penalty for guessing incorrectly. If there is, your strategy will be different: you will usually only mark what you are certain of. Finally, you need to know how much time will be allowed for the exam.

FOLLOW DIRECTIONS

Students are often in a hurry to start an exam so they take little time to read the instructions. The instructions can be critical, however. In a multiple-choice exam, if there is no indication that there is penalty for guessing, then you should never leave a question unanswered. Even if there only remains a few minutes at the end of the exam, you should guess for those questions about which you are uncertain.

Additionally, you need to know the weight given to each section of an exam. In a typical multiple-choice exam, all questions have equal weight. In some exams, particularly those involving essay questions, different parts of the exam carry different weights. You should use these weights to apportion your time accordingly. If an essay part of an exam accounts only 20% of the total points on the exam, you should not spend 60% of your time on the essay.

You need to make sure you are answering the question in the correct manner. Some exams require a No. 2 pencil to fill in the dots on a machine-graded answer sheet. Other exams require underlining or circling. In short, you have to look at the instructions carefully.

Lastly, check to make sure that you have all of the pages of the examination. If you are uncertain, ask the instructor or the exam proctor. It is hard to justify not having done your exam correctly because you failed to answer all of the questions. Simply stating that you didn't have them will pose a problem for both you and your instructor. Don't take a chance. Double check to make sure.

STRATEGY FOR OBJECTIVE EXAMINATIONS

The most important point to discover initially with any objective test is if there is a penalty for guessing. If there is none, you have nothing to lose by guessing. In contrast, if a half a point is subtracted for each incorrect answer, then you probably should not answer any question for which you are purely guessing.

Students usually commit one of the two errors when they read objective exam questions: (1) they read things into the questions that don't exist, or (2) they skip over words or phrases.

Most test questions include key words such as:

- all
- always
- never
- only

If you miss these key words you will be missing the "trick" part of the question. Also you must look for questions that are only *partly* correct, particularly if you are answering true/false questions.

Never answer a question without reading all of the alternatives. More than one of them may be correct. If more than one of them seems correct, make sure you select the answer that seems most correct.

Whenever the answer to an objective question is not obvious, start by the process of elimination. Throw out the answers that are clearly incorrect. Even with objective exams in which there is a penalty for guessing, if you can throw out several obviously incorrect answers, then you may wish to guess among the remaining ones because your probability of choosing the correct answer is high.

Typically, the easiest way to eliminate incorrect answers is to look for those that are meaningless, illogical, or inconsistent. Often test answers put in choices that make perfect sense and are indeed true, but they are not the answer to the question under study.

A FEW HINTS ABOUT WRITING ESSAY EXAMS

Although essay exams are not the most commonly used in principles of economics courses, some of you may have to take them. If you do, you should be prepared. One way of being prepared is to practice writing timed essays. Find out in advance how much time you will have for each essay question, and then practice writing an answer to a sample essay question during that time period. This is the only way you will develop the skills needed to pace yourself for an essay exam. Do your timed essay practice without using the book, since most essay exams are closed book.

Usually you can anticipate certain exam questions. You do this by going over the major concept headings, either in your lecture notes or in your text. Search for the themes that tie the materials together and then think about questions that your instructor might ask you. You might even list possible essay questions as a review device then write a short outline for each of those most likely questions.

As with objective exams you need to read the directions to the essay very carefully. Unlike objective exams an essay requires that you carefully present your ideas. It is best to write out a brief outline *before* you start writing. The outline should present your thesis in one or two sentences, then your supporting argument. It is important to stay on the subject. Both of the authors of this *Study Guide* have graded many essay exams. We can tell you from first hand experience that no instructor likes to read answers to unasked questions.

Finally, make a strong attempt to **write legibly.** Speaking from experience, we can tell you that it is easier to be favorably inclined to a student's essay if we don't have to reread it five times to decipher the handwriting.

Robert W. Pulsinelli
Roger LeRoy Miller

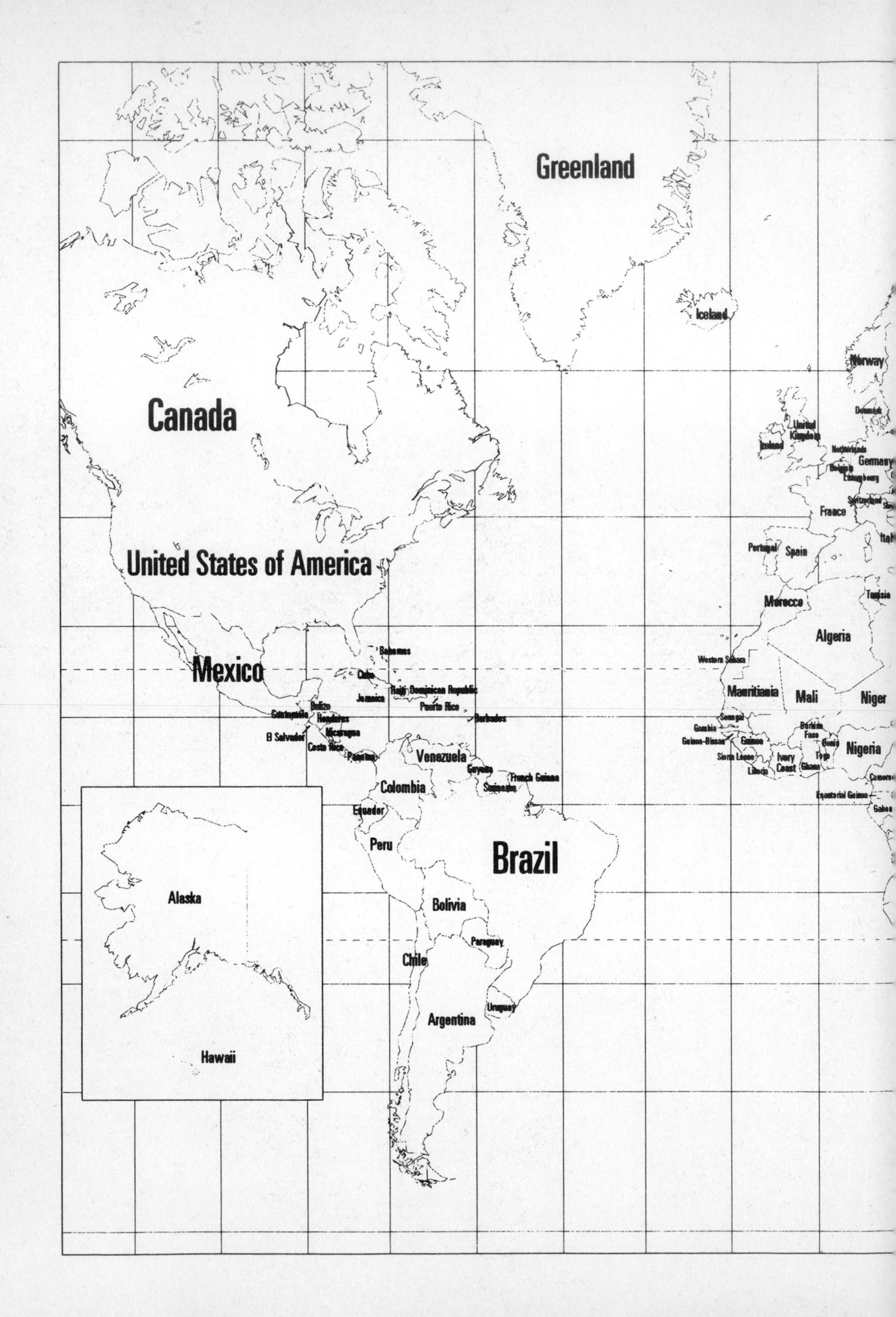
Greenland
Iceland
Norway
Canada
United Kingdom
Ireland
Netherlands
Germany
Belgium
Luxembourg
France
Switzerland
Portugal
Spain
United States of America
Morocco
Tunisia
Algeria
Western Sahara
Bahamas
Mexico
Cuba
Haiti
Dominican Republic
Jamaica
Puerto Rico
Belize
Guatemala
Honduras
Barbados
El Salvador
Nicaragua
Costa Rica
Panama
Venezuela
Guyana
French Guiana
Suriname
Colombia
Ecuador
Mauritania
Mali
Niger
Senegal
Gambia
Guinea-Bissau
Guinea
Burkina Faso
Benin
Sierra Leone
Liberia
Ivory Coast
Ghana
Togo
Nigeria
Equatorial Guinea
Gabon
Alaska
Hawaii
Peru
Brazil
Bolivia
Paraguay
Chile
Argentina
Uruguay

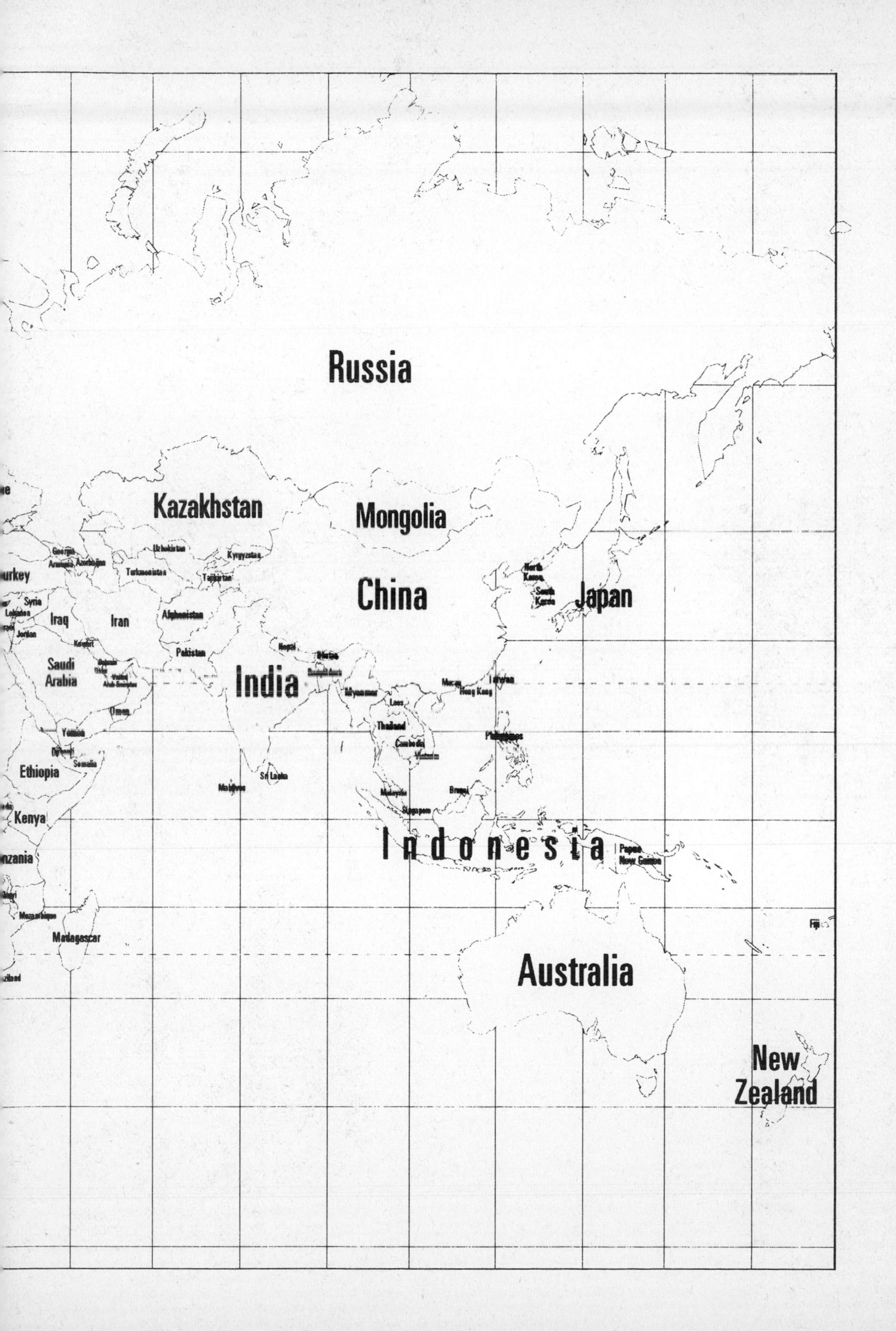
Russia
Kazakhstan
Mongolia
Georgia
Armenia
Azerbaijan
Uzbekistan
Kyrgyzstan
Turkmenistan
Tajikistan
Syria
Iraq
Iran
Afghanistan
Jordan
Kuwait
China
North Korea
South Korea
Japan
Pakistan
Nepal
Bhutan
Saudi Arabia
India
Macau
Taiwan
Hong Kong
Myanmar
Oman
Laos
Yemen
Thailand
Cambodia
Philippines
Somalia
Ethiopia
Sri Lanka
Maldives
Malaysia
Brunei
Singapore
Kenya
Indonesia
Papua New Guinea
Mozambique
Madagascar
Fiji
Australia
New Zealand

CHAPTER 1

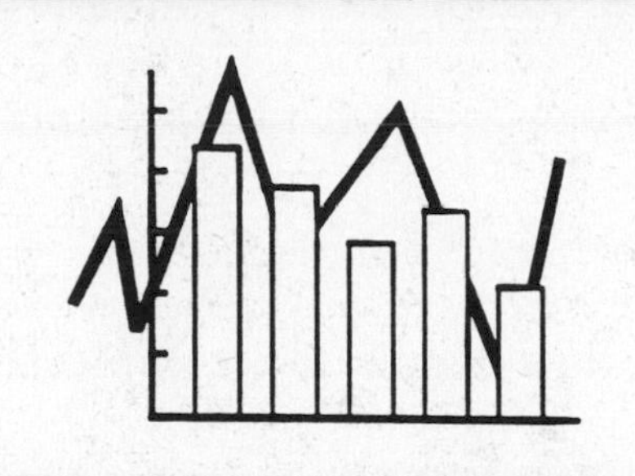

THE NATURE OF ECONOMICS

PUTTING THIS CHAPTER INTO PERSPECTIVE

The aim of Chapter 1 is to help you begin to get a feel for what economics is all about. Chapter 1 defines economics and introduces you to the theory of economic behavior. Economists are concerned with how people do in fact behave in the economic arena *and not* with how people themselves describe their actions, motivations, and beliefs. We contend that people act in ways that promote their own (sometimes broadly- defined) self-interest, and that they respond predictably to economic incentives.

By combining this theory of human behavior with the concept of marginal analysis and the "other things constant" assumption, economists are able to (1) generate numerous insights and testable theories about behavior, (2) explain widely disparate social phenomena, and (3) predict how people are likely to behave under numerous circumstances.

Although an understanding of Chapter 1 cannot possibly turn you into an economist, it can certainly begin to give you a feel for "the economic way of thinking." It is a good idea to re-read this chapter every three or four weeks, just to reinforce the important perspective that it provides.

LEARNING OBJECTIVES

After you have read this chapter you should be able to

1. define economics.
2. distinguish between microeconomics and macroeconomics.
3. recognize the rationality assumption.
4. recognize elements of an economic model, or theory.
5. recognize substitution options.
6. distinguish between substitution options in consumption and substitution options in production.
7. apply the concepts of substitution options.

8. distinguish between positive economics and normative economics, and be able to classify specific statements under each category.

CHAPTER OUTLINE

1. Economics, a social science, is defined as the study of how people make choices to satisfy their wants.
   a. Wants are all the things that people would consume if they had unlimited income.
   b. Because wants are enormous and people cannot satisfy all their wants, individuals are forced to make choices about how to spend their income and how to allocate their time.

2. Economics is broadly divided into microeconomics and macroeconomics.
   a. Microeconomics studies decision making undertaken by individuals (or households) and by firms.
   b. Macroeconomics studies the behavior of the economy taken as a whole; it deals with such economywide phenomena as unemployment, the price level, and national income.

3. Economists assume that individuals are motivated by self-interest and respond predictably to opportunities for gain.
   a. The rationality assumption is that individuals act *as if* they were rational.
   b. Self-interest often means a desire for material well-being, but it can also be defined broadly enough to incorporate goals relating to love, friendship, prestige, power, and other human characteristics.
   c. By assuming that people act in a rational, self-interested way, economists can generate testable theories concerning human behavior.

4. Economics is a Social Science.
   a. Economists develop models, or theories, which are simplified representations of the real world.
   b. Such models help economists to understand, explain, and predict economic phenomena in the real world.
   c. Like other social scientists, economists usually do not perform laboratory experiments; they typically examine what already has occurred in order to test their theories.
   d. Economic theories, like all scientific theories, are simplifications--and in that sense they are "unrealistic."
   e. Economists, as do all scientists, employ assumptions; one important economic assumption is "all other things being equal."
   f. Models or theories are evaluated on their ability to predict, and not on the realism of the assumptions employed.
   g. Economic models relate to behavior, not thought processes.

5. An important tenet of economics is that there are substitution options for practically anything.

a. Substitution options for consumption exist when *a given level of satisfaction* can be obtained from more than one bundle of goods and services.
b. Substitution options for production exist when *a given level of output* can be obtained from more than one combination of inputs.

6. Consumers are believed to pick that substitution option in consumption that has the lowest cost to them; producers are believed to select that substitution option in production that has the lowest cost to them.

7. Economists maintain that the unit of analysis is the individual; members of a group are assumed to pursue their own goals rather than the group's objectives.

8. Positive economics is objective and scientific in nature, and deals with testable *if this, then that* hypotheses.

9. Normative economics is subjective and deals with value judgements, or with what *ought* to be.

KEY TERMS

Aggregates
Ceteris paribus (other things being equal)
Economics
Macroeconomics
Microeconomics
Models (or theory)
Wants
Substitution options for consumption
Substitution options for production

KEY CONCEPTS

Normative economics
Positive economics
Rational behavior
Self-interest

COMPLETION QUESTIONS

Fill in the blank or circle the correct term.

1. Because it is impossible to have all that we want, people are forced to make ________________.

2. Economics is a (natural, social) science.

3. Economics is the study of how people make ____________ to satisfy their ________________.

4. Microeconomics deals with (individual units, the whole economy).

5. A nation's unemployment level is analyzed in (microeconomics, macroeconomics).

6. (Macroeconomics, Microeconomics) studies the causes and effects of inflation.

7. Economists maintain that a member of a group usually attempts to make decisions that are in (her own, the group's) interest.

8. The rationality assumption is that individuals (believe, act as if) they are rational.

9. Economic models are (simplified, realistic) representations of the real world.

10. The *ceteris paribus* assumption enables economists to consider (one thing at a time, everything at once).

11. Substitution options in consumption (are, are not) the same as variety of choices.

12. Economists maintain that substitution options in consumption are (rare, common).

13. Substitution options in consumption imply that consumers choose among options of (equal, unequal) value.

14. Substitution options in production exist for producers or consumers who choose options that generate (equal, unequal) outputs.

15. Producers tend to select those substitution options in production that are (cheaper, of higher output).

16. Economists take the (individual, group) as the unit of analysis.

17. Economic statements that are testable and are of an "if/then" nature are (positive, normative).

TRUE-FALSE QUESTIONS

Circle the **T** if the statement is true, the **F** if it is false. Explain to yourself why a statement is false.

T F 1. Economics is the study of how people think about economic phenomena.

T F 2. The economists' definition of self-interest includes only the pursuit of material goods.

T F 3. Macroeconomics deals with aggregates, or totals, of economic variables.

T F 4. When economists attempt to predict the number of workers a firm will employ, they are studying macroeconomics.

T F 5. Economists maintain that people respond in a predictable way to economic incentives.

T F 6. The rationality assumption is that individuals attempt, quite consciously, to make rational economic decisions, and will admit to it.

T F 7. It is justifiable to criticize theories on the realism of the assumptions employed.

T F 8. Households cannot be thought of as producers.

T F 9. Because economics is a science, economists do not make normative statements.

T F 10. Producers select that substitution option in production that has the highest output.

MULTIPLE CHOICE QUESTIONS
Circle the letter that corresponds to the best answer.

1. Economics is
   a. a natural science.
   b. nonscientific.
   c. a social science.
   d. usually studied through lab experiments.

2. Wants include desires for
   a. material possessions.
   b. love.
   c. power.
   d. All of the above

3. Which of the following areas of study is concerned, primarily, with microeconomics?
   a. the steel industry
   b. inflation
   c. the national unemployment rate
   d. national income determination

4. Macroeconomics analysis deals with
   a. the steel industry.
   b. how individuals respond to an increase in the price of gasoline.
   c. inflation.
   d. how the price of energy affects Ms. Boulware.

5. Economists maintain that Mr. Smith will usually make decisions that promote the interests of
   a. his gender.
   b. himself.
   c. his class.
   d. his race.

6. Economic models
   a. use unrealistic assumptions.
   b. are seldom tested in laboratories.
   c. are concerned with how people behave, not with how they think.
   d. All of the above

7. An economic model is justifiably criticized if
   a. its assumptions are not realistic.
   b. it cannot be tested in a controlled, laboratory experiment.
   c. it fails to predict.
   d. All of the above

8. Which of the following is true regarding substitution options in production?
   a. They exist only for producers.
   b. They exist for producers and households.
   c. They are rare.
   d. They exist only at the profit-maximizing output level.

9. Substitution options in production compare
   a. options of the same cost.
   b. options of the same output level.
   c. combinations of inputs with the same profit.
   d. combinations of different levels of consumer satisfaction.

10. Producers will pick that substitution option in production which has
   a. the lowest cost.
   b. the highest cost.
   c. the greatest output level.
   d. the lowest quality.

11. Substitution options in consumption compare
   a. equal levels of satisfaction for consumers.
   b. equal levels of output for consumers.
   c. different levels of satisfaction for consumers.
   d. equal levels of satisfaction for different people.

12. Which of the following is not true?
   a. Substitution options in production compare different combinations of inputs that generate the same output.
   b. Substitution options in consumption compare different combinations of consumer goods that generate the same level of satisfaction to different people.
   c. Producers select that substitution option in production that has the lowest cost.
   d. Consumers select that substitution option in consumption that has the lowest cost.

13. Which of the following is a normative economics statement?
    a. If price rises, people will buy less.
    b. If price rises, people will buy more.
    c. If price rises the poor will be injured; therefore price should not be permitted to rise.
    d. If price rises people will buy less; therefore we ought to observe that quantity demanded falls.

14. Which of the following is a positive economics statement?
    a. Full employment policies should be pursued.
    b. If minimum wage rates rise, then unemployment will fall.
    c. We should take from the rich and give to the poor.
    d. The government should help the homeless.

15. Normative economics statements
    a. are testable hypotheses.
    b. are value-free.
    c. are subjective, value judgements.
    d. can be scientifically established.

MATCHING

Choose the item in Column (2) that best matches an item in Column (1).

(1)	(2)
a. normative economics	f. nonscientific value judgements
b. macroeconomics	g. objective, scientific hypotheses
c. least cost production	h. study of individual behavior
d. positive economics	i. study of economic aggregates
e. microeconomics	j. substitution option

CASE STUDY

Economists were surprised to discover that most people, when interviewed immediately after purchasing gasoline, did not have any idea what they just paid per gallon. Non-economists use this as evidence against the notion that people are rational.

Economists maintain that price (cost) is an important determinant of consumer behavior, yet, apparently people don't even consider price! How can economists predict consumer behavior if consumers don't even know what price is?

Interestingly, it was discovered that at the *end of the month*, those gasoline stations that charged the highest prices sold the least gasoline, and those that charged the lowest prices sold the most gasoline.

Apparently, although most people didn't know the price per gallon, nevertheless *as a group*, consumers bought more of that gasoline (given quality) that was sold at a cheaper price. Consider this apparent contradiction then answer the following questions.

1. Which consumers are more likely to know the price of gasoline: owners of cab companies and fleets of automobiles, or casual drivers?

2. Is it rational for the typical buyer of gasoline to drive around to every gas station to check price each time she buys -- or should she form a buying habit and do business with the same station (and check prices only occasionally)?

3. Why might it be rational for some buyers *knowingly* to pay a higher price and be a regular customer at a higher-priced station? (Hint: consider emergencies).

ANSWERS TO CHAPTER 1

COMPLETION QUESTIONS

1. choices
2. social
3. choices; wants
4. individual wants
5. macroeconomics
6. macroeconomics
7. her own
8. act as if
9. simplified
10. one thing at a time
11. are not
12. common
13. equal
14. equal
15. cheaper
16. individual
17. positive

TRUE AND FALSE QUESTIONS

1. F Economics is the study of how people make choices to satisfy their wants.
2. F Economists have a broader definition of self-interest; wants include power, friendship, love, and so on.
3. T
4. F The example is about microeconomics.
5. T
6. F That assumption is merely that people act as if they are rational.
7. F All theories employ unrealistic hypotheses; what matters is how they predict.
8. F Households can be thought of as combining goods and time to produce outputs such as meals.
9. F Economists, like other scientists, can and do make normative statements.
10. F Producers select that option which, given an output level, has the lowest cost of production.

MULTIPLE CHOICE QUESTIONS

1.c; 2.d; 3.a; 4.c; 5.b; 6.d; 7.c; 8.b; 9.b; 10.a;
11.a; 12.b; 13.c; 14.b; 15.c.

MATCHING

a and f; b and i; c and j; d and g; e and h

CASE STUDY

1. People who spend *much* money on gasoline are more likely to know its price.
2. It is rational to form habits and to check price only occasionally, because people value their time too.
3. You might knowingly trade with a higher-priced gasoline station because you can get to know and trust the owner who can then be relied upon to fix or tow your car in an emergency -- at a reasonable price.

GLOSSARY TO CHAPTER 1

Aggregates Total amounts or quantities; aggregate demand, for example, relates to the total quantity demanded within a nation.

***Ceteris paribus* assumption** The assumption that all things are held equal, or constant, except those under study.

Macroeconomics The study of the behavior of the economy as a whole, including such economywide phenomena as unemployment, the price level, and national income.

Microeconomics The study of decision making undertaken by individuals (or households) and by firms.

Models, or theories Simplified representations of the real world used to make predictions or to better understand the real world.

Normative economics Analysis involving value judgments about economic policies; relates to whether things are good or bad. A statement of what ought to be.

Positive economics Analysis that is strictly limited to making either purely descriptive statements or scientific predictions; for example, *If A, then B.* A statement of *what if.*

Rationality assumption An assumption in economics in which people are assumed to behave in a reasonable way and would not intentionally make decisions that would leave them worse off.

Substitution options in consumption Choices available to a consumer in which different combinations of goods and services (each combination having the same level of satisfaction to the consumer) have different costs.

Substitution options in production Choices available to a consumer or producer in which different combinations of inputs (each combination generating the same output level) have different costs.

Wants Wants are the things that people would consume if they had unlimited income.

CHAPTER 2

SCARCITY AND THE WORLD OF TRADE-OFFS

PUTTING THIS CHAPTER INTO PERSPECTIVE

Chapter 1 defined wants and stressed that no one can satisfy all his or her wants. Chapter 2 starts with this notion and builds upon it. People want more things--both material and nonmaterial (such as love, friendship, and affection)--than their individual and collective resources permit. Because we cannot have everything that we want, scarcity forces us to make choices. We are all faced with trade-offs; if we have more of good A, we must give up other goods. Hence the important concept of opportunity cost emerges. This concept is one of the most useful and universally applied concepts in economics, and you will do well to learn it now. As this chapter shows, the opportunity cost concept helps to decide which resource combinations are efficient, and which are not.

Resources that produce goods and services that satisfy wants are scarce, hence choices, trade-offs, and opportunity costs emerge when we consider resource allocation. Chapter 2 lists and defines resources and indicates how resources must be allocated for efficiency to exist.

LEARNING OBJECTIVES

After you have studied this chapter you should be able to

1. define scarcity, resources, land, labor, capital, entrepreneurship, goods, services, resource allocation, opportunity costs, production possibilities curve, technology, efficiency, inefficient point, law of increasing costs, specialization, absolute advantage, comparative advantage, and division of labor.

2. distinguish between a free good and an economic good.

3. determine the opportunity cost of an activity, when given sufficient information.

4. determine the least-cost combination of inputs, given sufficient information.

5. draw production possibilities curves under varying assumptions, and recognize efficient and inefficient points relating to such curves.

6. determine a person's absolute advantage and comparative advantage, given sufficient information.

CHAPTER OUTLINE

1. Because individuals or communities do not have the resources to satisfy all their wants, scarcity exists.
   a. If society can get all that it wants of good A when the price of good A is zero, good A is not scarce.
   b. If the price of good B is zero, and society cannot get all that it wants of good B, then B is scarce.
   c. Because resources, or factors of production, are scarce, the outputs they produce are scarce.
      i. Land, the natural resource, includes all the gifts of nature.
      ii. Labor, the human resource, includes all productive contributions made by individuals who work.
      iii. Capital, the man-made resource, includes the machines, buildings, and tools used to produce other goods and services.
      iv. Entrepreneurship includes the functions of organizing, managing, assembling, and risk-taking necessary for business ventures.
   d. Goods include anything from which people derive satisfaction, or happiness.
      i. Economic goods are scarce.
      ii. Non-economic goods are not scarce.
      iii. Services are intangible goods.
   e. Economists distinguish between wants and needs; the latter are objectively undefinable.

2. Because of scarcity, choice and opportunity costs arise.
   a. Due to scarcity, people trade off options.
   b. The production possibilities curve (PPC) is a graph of the trade-offs inherent in a decision.
      i. When the marginal cost of additional units of a resource or good remains constant, the PPC curve is a straight line.
      ii. When the marginal cost of additional units of a resource or good rises, the PPC curve is bowed outward.
      iii. A point on a PPC is an efficient point; points inside a PPC are inefficient; points outside the PPC are unattainable (impossible), by definition.
   c. People have an economic incentive to specialize in that endeavor for which they have a comparative advantage.
   d. The process of division of labor increases output and permits specialization.

3. Economic growth can be depicted through PPCs.
   a. There is a trade off between present consumption and future consumption.
   b. If a nation produces fewer consumer goods and more capital goods now, then it can consume more goods in the future than would otherwise be the case.

KEY TERMS

Resources
Land
Labor
Capital
Entrepreneurship
Goods
Services
Resource allocation
Technology
Specialization
Division of labor
Inefficient point
Law of increasing cost
Production possibilities curve

KEY CONCEPTS

Efficiency
Absolute advantage
Comparative advantage
Opportunity cost
Least-cost combination

COMPLETION QUESTIONS

Fill in the blank or circle the correct term.

1. The factors of production include ________________, ________________, ________________, and ______________.

2. People tend to specialize in those activities for which they have a(n) (comparative, absolute) advantage.

3. When people choose jobs that maximize their income, they are specializing according to their ________________ advantage.

4. If at a zero price quantity demanded exceeds quantity supplied for a good, that good is a(n) ______________________; if at a zero price quantity supplied exceeds quantity demanded for a good, that good is a(n) ________________________________.

5. The ____________________________________ of good A is the highest valued alternative that must be sacrificed to attain it.

6. If the marginal cost of additional units of a good remains constant, the production possibilities curve will be (linear, bowed outward); if the marginal cost of additional units of a good rises, the production curve will be (linear, bowed outward).

7. Because specialized resources are more suited to specific tasks, the extra cost of producing additional units of a specific good will (rise, fall).

8. If an economy is inefficient, its actual output combination will lie (inside, outside) the production possibilities curve.

TRUE-FALSE QUESTIONS

Circle the **T** if the statement is true, the **F** if it is false. Explain to yourself why a statement is false.

T F 1. Most people's needs exceed their wants.

T F 2. Because resources are scarce, the goods that they produce are also scarce.

T F 3. For most activities no opportunity cost exists.

T F 4. If a production possibilities curve is linear, the marginal cost of a good rises with its production.

T F *5. If labor's productivity falls, the production possibilities curve will shift outward.

T F 6. At any given moment in time it is impossible for a nation to be inside its production possibilities curve.

T F *7. The cost to society of lowering the speed limit is zero.

T F 8. People have little incentive to specialize in jobs for which they have a comparative advantage.

T F 9. Economic growth shifts the production possibilities curve outward.

T F 10. If the price to a specific user is zero, the good must be a free good.

MULTIPLE CHOICE QUESTIONS

Circle the letter that corresponds to the best answer.

1. Because of scarcity
   a. people are forced to make choices.
   b. opportunity costs exist.
   c. people face trade-offs.
   d. All of the above.

2. Which of the following is not considered to be "land"?
   a. bodies of water
   b. fertility of soil
   c. capital
   d. climate

3. Which of the following words does not belong with the others?
   a. opportunity cost
   b. free good
   c. scarcity
   d. economic good

4. Which statement concerning a production possibilities curve is not true?
   a. A trade-off exists along such a curve.
   b. It is usually linear.
   c. Points inside it indicate inefficiency.
   d. A point outside it is currently impossible to attain.

*5. Which of the following will cause the production possibilities curve to shift outward?
   a. a reduction in the size of the labor force
   b. an increase in the quantity of labor
   c. an inefficiency that is corrected
   d. a decrease in the size of the capital stock

6. The production possibilities curve is bowed outward because
   a. the relative cost of producing a good rises.
   b. of the law of decreasing relative costs.
   c. all resources are equally suited to the production of any good.
   d. All of the above.

*7. When nations and individuals specialize
   a. overall living standards rise.
   b. trade and exchange increase.
   c. people become more vulnerable to changes in tastes and technology.
   d. All of the above

8. When a nation expands its capital stock, it is usually true that
   a. it must forego output of some consumer goods in the present.
   b. the human capital stock must decline.
   c. fewer consumer goods will be available in the future.
   d. no opportunity cost exists for doing so.

9. Ms. Boulware is the best lawyer and the best secretary in town.
   a. She has a comparative advantage in both jobs.
   b. She has an absolute advantage in both jobs.
   c. She has a comparative advantage in being a secretary.
   d. All of the above

MATCHING

Choose the item in Column (2) that best matches an item in Column (1).

(1)	(2)
a. absolute advantage	i. production possibilities curve
b. efficiency	j. specialization
c. trade-offs	k. capital
d. comparative advantage	l. ability to produce at a lower cost
e. resource	m. specializing in one's comparative advantage
f. scarce good	n. society cannot get all it wants at at a zero price
g. inefficiency	o. highest-valued foregone alternative
h. opportunity cost	p. inside PPC

WORKING WITH GRAPHS

1. Given the following information, graph the production possibilities curve in the space provided and then use the graph to answer the questions that follow.

Combination (points)	Autos (100,000 per year)	Wheat (100,000 tons per year)
A	16	0
B	14	4
C	12	7
D	9	10
E	5	12
F	0	13

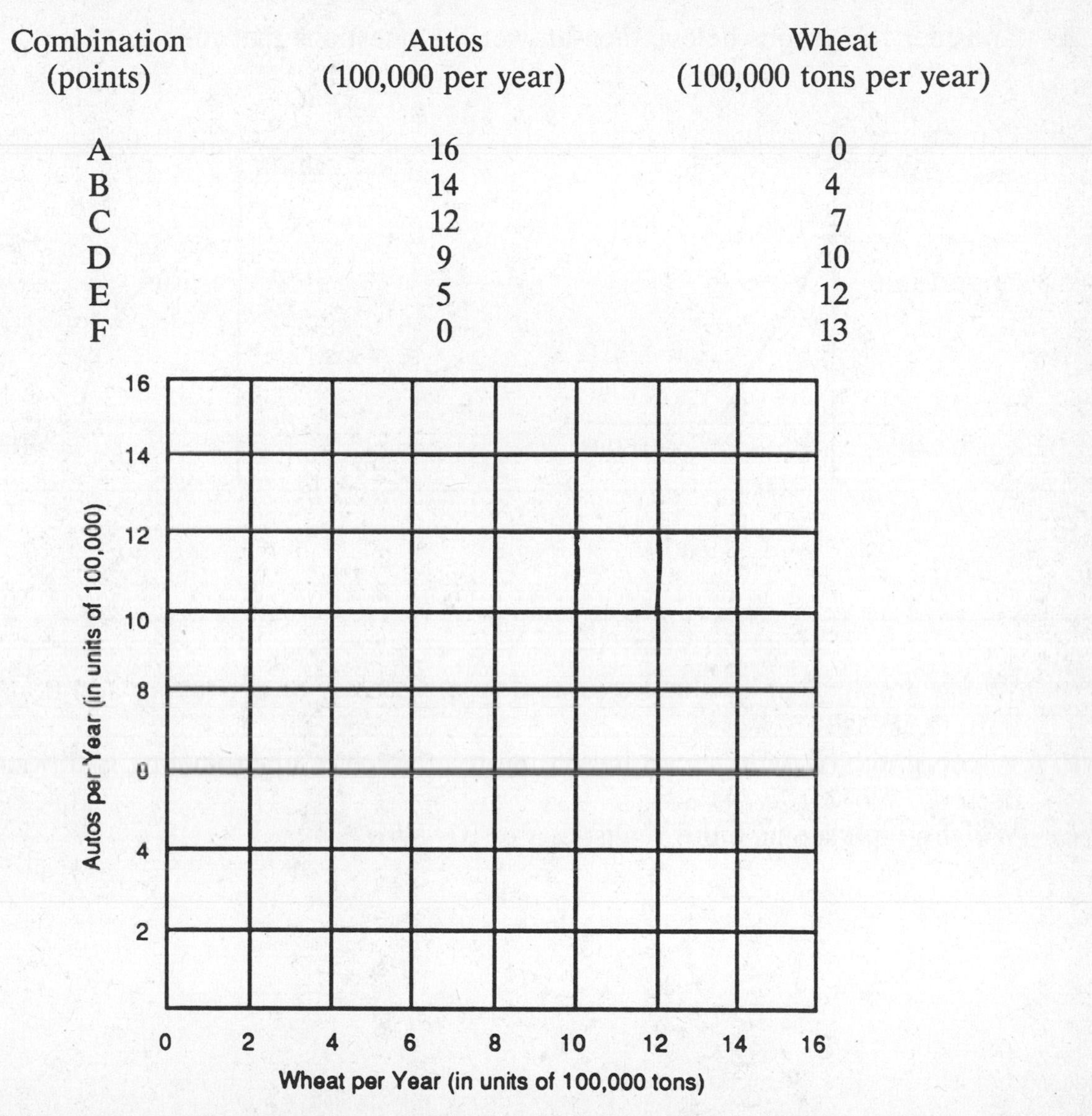

a. If the economy is currently operating at point C, what is the opportunity cost of moving to point D? to point B?

b. Suppose that the economy is currently producing 1,200,000 autos and 200,000 tons of wheat per year. Label this point in your graph with the letter G. At point G the economy would be suffering from what? At point G we can see that it is possible to produce more wheat without giving up any auto production, or produce more autos without giving up any wheat production, or produce more of both. Label this region in your graph. This region appears to contradict the definition of a production possibilities curve. What is the explanation for this result?

c. Suppose a new fertilizer compound is developed that will allow the economy to produce an additional 150,000 tons of wheat per year if no autos are produced. Sketch in a likely representation of the effect of this discovery, assuming all else remains constant.

d. What sort of impact (overall) will this discovery have on the opportunity cost of more wheat production at an arbitrary point on the new production possibilities curve as compared to a point representing the same level of output of wheat on the original curve?

2. Consider the graphs below, then answer the questions that follow.

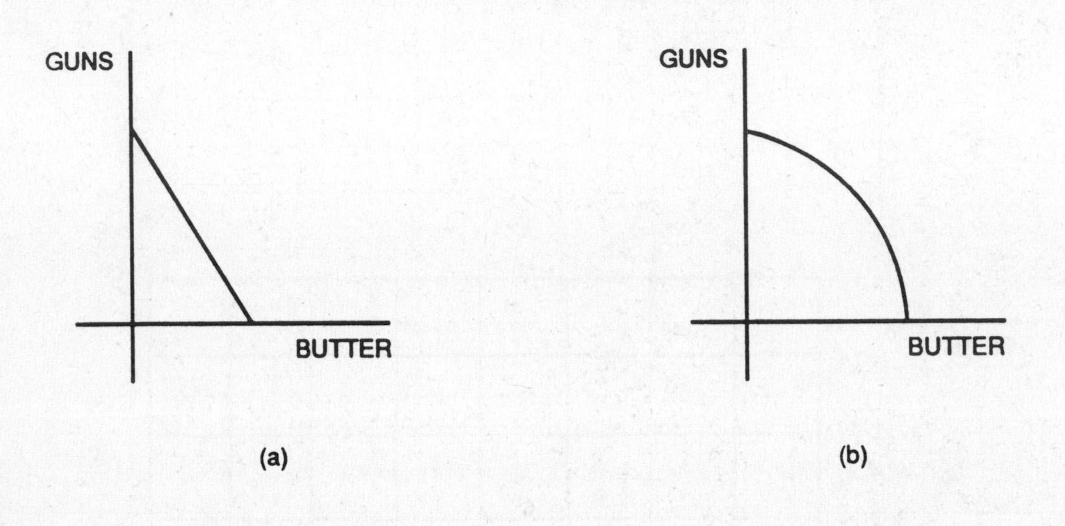

a. Which graph, a or b, shows constant relative costs of producing additional units of butter? Why?
b. Which graph, a or b, shows increasing relative costs of producing additional units of butter? Why?
c. Which graph seems more realistic, a or b? Why?

3. Graph the probable relationship between
   a. Income and the amount of money spent on housing.
   b. Annual rainfall in New York City and the annual value of ice cream sales in New Orleans.
   c. Number of vegetarians per 10,000 people and meat sales per 10,000 people.

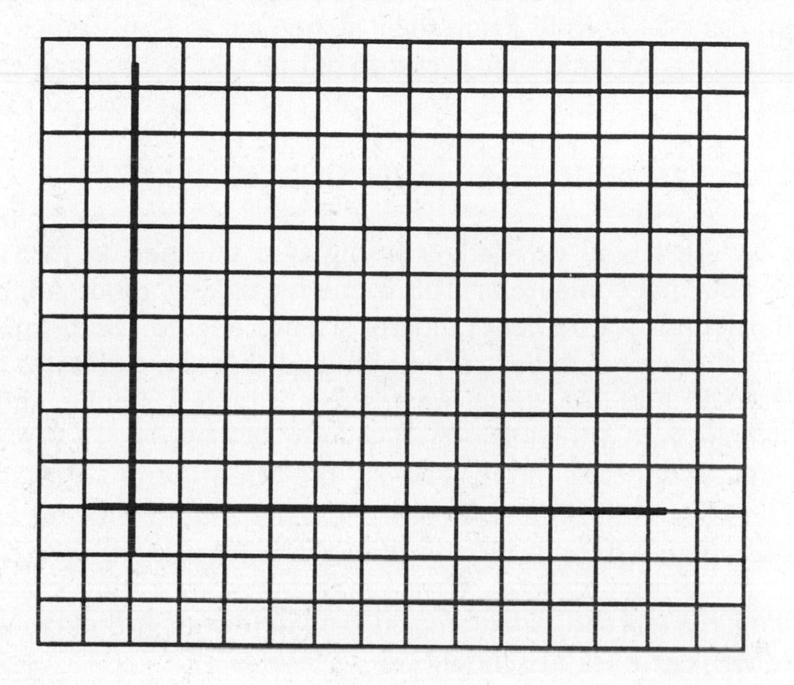

PROBLEMS

1. If a *nation* wants to increase its future consumption it must forego some present consumption because it must allocate some resources to the production of capital goods. Suppose *you* want to increase your future consumption, given a fixed lifetime income, what can you do?

*2. Assume that, given its resource base, an economy is able to produce output combinations A, B, C, and D. Society values combination A at $10,000, combination B at $20,000, combination C at $30,000, and combination D at $15,000.
   a. What is the opportunity cost of producing combination A?
   b. What is the opportunity cost of producing combination B?
   c. What is the opportunity cost of producing combination C?
   d. What is the opportunity cost of producing combination D?

e. If the community wanted to maximize the value of its output, given its resource base, which combination should it produce?
f. If the community wants to minimize the opportunity cost of its output, which combination would it choose?

3. Assume that Ms. Gentile values her time at $50 per hour because she has the opportunity to do consulting, and that Joe College values his time at $2 per hour. Assume that it costs $400 to fly from their hometown to San Francisco, and that the flight takes 6 hours. Assume that it costs $200 to take a bus, and that the bus trip takes 24 hours.
   a. What is the cheaper way to get to San Francisco for Ms. Gentile? Why?
   b. Which transportation is cheaper for Joe College? Why?

*4. Suppose you have a friend currently working as a salesperson in a local computer store that sells personal computers. This friend is thinking about going back to school full-time to finish up work on her computer science degree. She explains to you that she earns $15,000 per year in her current job and that she estimates tuition will cost $1,600 per year. In addition she estimates fees, supplies, books, and miscellaneous expenses associated with attending school will run $800 per year. She wants to attend a university that is located directly across the street from the store where she currently works. She claims that she pays $350 per month for rent and utilities and that she spends about $200 per month on food.

   Using what you have learned, calculate and explain to your friend the opportunity cost to her of another year back at school.

5. The Hughes family consists of Mr. Hughes, Mrs. Hughes, and their son, Scotty. Assume that Mr. Hughes can earn $30 per hour any time he chooses, Mrs. Hughes can earn $5 per hour, and the family values homemaker activities at $6 per hour.
   a. Because the family requires money to purchase goods and services, who will probably work in the marketplace?
   b. Who will probably do the housework?
   c. If the family must pay $3 per hour to have its lawn mowed, who will be assigned that work?
   d. If Scotty can now earn $4 per hour on a job, who now might mow the grass?
   e. If wage rates in the marketplace for Mrs. Hughes rise to $7 per hour, what is the family likely to do?

CASE STUDY

Over the past twenty years the percentage of women in the labor force has increased dramatically. In recent years divorce rates, and the number of women and children officially classified as living in poverty have increased also. Some people maintain that higher percentages of women in the labor force reflect the fact that "times are tougher and it now takes two people to support a family." Others maintain that the feminist movement is the main reason for some of these changes. Almost everyone sees higher divorce rates and higher poverty rates for women and children as a serious social problem and increased human misery.

Consider, however, that over the past twenty years real (inflation-adjusted) wage rates have increased in the United States, and that therefore the opportunity cost for women staying out of the labor force has risen.

1. How might increasing female percentages in the labor force be accounted for by rational family decision-making processes?

2. Is it more rational for women to opt for divorce now than it was twenty years ago?

3. If women *choose* divorce, work, and income that is *officially* considered to be at poverty levels, are their lives necessarily worse?

ANSWERS TO CHAPTER 2

COMPLETION QUESTIONS

1. land, labor, capital, entrepreneurship
2. comparative
3. comparative
4. economic good; free noneconomic good
5. opportunity cost
6. linear; bowed outward
7. rise
8. inside

TRUE-FALSE QUESTIONS

1. F Wants vastly exceed needs for everyone.
2. T
3. F An opportunity cost exists for all activities.
4. F A linear PPC implies a constant relative cost.
5. F The PPC will shift inward.
6. F All a nation need be is inefficient to be inside the PPC.
7. F If people drive more slowly they suffer opportunity costs for their time.
8. F People can earn more money in jobs for which they have a comparative advantage.
9. T
10. F An individual user *may* pay a zero price for an economic good--and he or she will probably waste it.

MULTIPLE CHOICE QUESTIONS

1.d; 2.c; 3.b; 4.b; 5.b; 6.a; 7.d; 8.a; 9.b;

MATCHING

a and l; b and m; c and i; d and j; e and k; f and n; g and p; h and o

WORKING WITH GRAPHS

1. See the following graph.

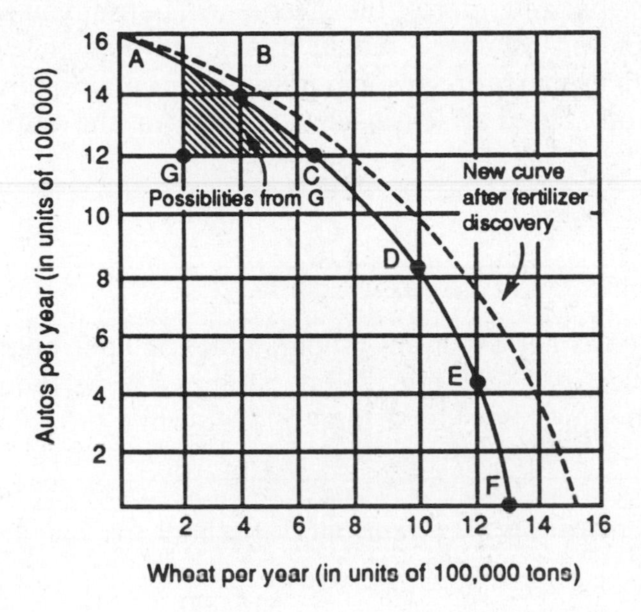

a. The move from C to D "costs" 300,000 autos--that is, the economy must give up 300,000 autos (1,200,000 - 900,000) to make such a move. The move from C to B "costs" 300,000 tons of wheat. Notice that in both cases there are gains (C to D involves 300,000 more tons of wheat and C to B means 200,000 more autos are produced), but we measure opportunity costs in terms of movements along a production possibilities curve and what has to be given up to make the choice reflected in the move.
b. See the preceding graph. Remember, the production possibilities curve shows all possible combinations of two goods that an economy can produce by the efficient use of all available resources in a specified period of time. Since point G is not on the production possibilities curve, the statement contained in this portion of the question does not contradict the definition of the curve. Point G is inside the curve, which implies available resources are not being used efficiently.
c. See the preceding graph.
d. It will lower the opportunity cost of additional wheat production.

2. a. Panel a shows constant relative costs because the PPC is linear.
b. Panel b shows increasing costs because the PPC is bowed out.
c. Panel b is more realistic because it is likely that the production of guns and butter require specialized resources.

3. a. The graph should be upward sloping from left to right.
b. There should be no systematic relationship between these two variables.
c. The graph should be downward sloping from left to right.

PROBLEMS

1. If you have a fixed lifetime income and you want to increase your future consumption--for retirement, say--then you will have to save more out of your current income. The principal and interest that accrue will permit you to purchase more goods in the future than you otherwise would have been able to. Note that by doing so you--as an individual--must forego some present consumption in order to increase your future consumption. In that sense what is true for the nation is also true for an individual.

2. a. $30,000 c. $20,000 e. C
   b. $30,000 d. $30,000 f. C

3. a. plane; flying costs her $400 plus 6 hours times $50 per hour, or $700, while taking a bus would cost her $200 plus 24 hours times $50 per hour, or $1400.
   b. bus; taking the bus costs him a total of $248 while the total cost of flying is $412 to him.

4. The opportunity cost of another year back at school for your friend is as follows:

Foregone salary	$15,000
Tuition costs	1,600
Expenses associated with school	800
Total opportunity costs	$17,400

5. a. Mr. Hughes
   b. Mrs. Hughes or Scotty
   c. Scotty
   d. The family (or perhaps Scotty) will hire someone to mow the lawn.
   e. Mrs. Hughes may enter the labor force and the family may hire someone to do housework.

CASE STUDY

1. As the opportunity cost for staying at home rises, more women will enter the labor force and substitute their work at home with (a) appliances and/or (b) hired domestic workers.
2. If they now can earn more money in the labor force the opportunity cost to them of staying in an unhappy marriage rises.
3. Assuming that they are adults, who know the consequences of divorce, if women voluntarily choose to divorce and work at a wage rate that is near or below the "official" poverty level, all things considered they are probably better off. Otherwise they would have stayed home and traded off material goods for unhappiness.

GLOSSARY TO CHAPTER 2

Absolute advantage The ability to produce a good or service at an "absolutely" lower cost, usually measured in units of labor or resource input required to produce one unit of the good.

Capital All manufactured resources, including buildings, equipment, machines, and improvements to land.

Comparative advantage The ability to produce a good or service at a lower opportunity cost.

Consumption goods Goods that are bought by households to be used up, such as food, clothing, and movies.

Division of labor The segregation of a resource into different specific tasks; for example, one automobile worker puts on bumpers, another doors, and so on.

Economic goods Any goods or services that are scarce.

Economic system The institutional means through which resources are used to satisfy human wants.

Efficiency The situation where a given output is produced at minimum cost. Or alternatively the case where a given level of inputs is used to produce the maximum output possible.

Entrepreneurship The fourth factor of production, involving human resources that perform the functions of raising capital, organizing, managing, assembling other factors of production, and making basic business policy decisions. The entrepreneur is a risk taker.

Goods Anything from which individuals derive satisfaction or happiness and thus is valued.

Inefficient point Any point that does not lie on the production possibilities frontier, where resources are being used inefficiently.

Labor Productive contributions of humans who work, which involve both thinking and doing.

Land The natural resources that are available without alteration or effort on the part of humans. Land as a resource includes location, original fertility and mineral deposits, topography, climate, water, and vegetation.

Law of increasing relative costs The opportunity cost of additional units of a good generally increases as society attempts to produce more of that good. It is what causes the bowed-out shape of the production possibilities curve.

Least-cost combination The level of input use that produces a given level of output at minimum cost.

Opportunity cost The highest valued alternative that must be sacrificed to attain something or satisfy a want.

Production possibilities curve (PPC) A curve representing all possible combinations of total output that could be produced assuming (a) a fixed amount of productive resources of a given quality and (b) the efficient use of those resources.

Resource allocation The assignment of resources to specific uses. More specifically, it means determining what will be produced, how it will be produced, and for whom it will be produced.

Resources Inputs used to produce goods and services. (Also called factors of production).

Scarcity A situation in which the necessary ingredients for producing those things that people desire are insufficient to satisfy all wants.

Services Things purchased by consumers that do not have physical characteristics. Examples of services are those purchased from doctors, lawyers, dentists, repair personnel, and so on.

Specialization The division of productive activities among persons and regions so that no one individual or one area is totally self-sufficient. An individual may specialize, for example, in law or medicine. A nation may specialize in the production of coffee, computers, or cameras.

Technology Society's pool of applied knowledge concerning how goods and services can be produced.

CHAPTER 3

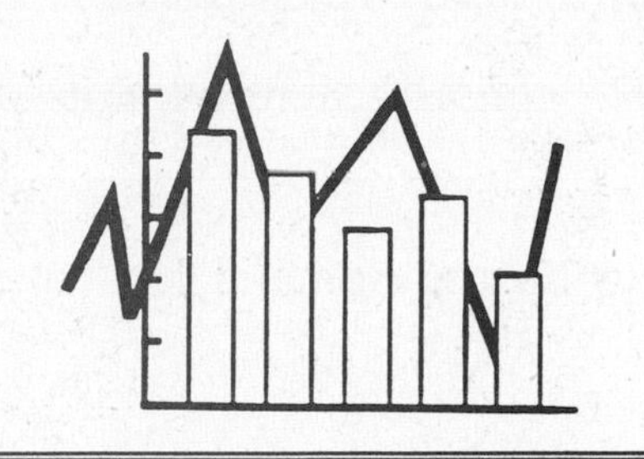

DEMAND AND SUPPLY

PUTTING THIS CHAPTER INTO PERSPECTIVE

This chapter is one of the most important chapters in the text. To students who take the time to study it, the returns are exceptionally high. Chapter 3 analyzes the economist's most indispensable tools: demand and supply. Specifically, in this chapter you will study (a) demand and supply, (b) how demand and supply determine equilibrium (or market-clearing) price, and (c) how periods of surpluses or shortages result if price is not at the equilibrium level.

It is important that you master the material in this chapter, because you will be applying and reapplying these same tools and principles to many different situations. When presented with a problem, the economist will first try to express the problem in terms of the concepts of demand and supply and then proceed to economic analysis proper. It is with this thought in mind that an anonymous writer once noted: "You can make even a parrot into a learned economist--all it must learn are the two words *supply* and *demand*."

Mastering Chapter 3, however, will require some time. Many pitfalls to understanding economics can be avoided if you learn and understand the key definitions in this chapter. Unless you learn to use these key concepts in the same way economists do, communication will be impossible. You simply must learn the jargon of economics before you can move on to theoretical analysis. You must understand *exactly* what demand and supply mean; *exactly* what quantity demanded and quantity supplied mean; *exactly* what a change in demand and a change in supply mean; *exactly* what a surplus and a shortage mean. A universal confusion exists for students and others about the distinction between a change in demand (or supply) and a change in quantity demanded (or quantity supplied). Similarly, unless you know exactly what a shortage or a surplus is, you will be continually misinterpreting economic events.

LEARNING OBJECTIVES

After you have studied this chapter you should be able to

1. define demand schedule, quantity demanded, supply schedule, quantity supplied, equilibrium, posted-offer pricing, bargaining, shortage, and surplus.

2. graph demand and supply curves from demand and supply schedules.

3. state the law of demand and state two reasons why we observe the law of demand.

4. enumerate five nonprice determinants of demand and five nonprice determinants of supply.

5. predict the effects of a change in the price of one good on the demand for (a) a substitute good, and (b) a complementary good.

6. recognize, from graphs, the difference between a change in demand and a change in quantity demanded and the difference between a change in supply and a change in quantity supplied.

7. determine from a supply curve and a demand curve what the equilibrium price and the equilibrium quantity will be.

8. explain how markets eliminate surpluses and shortages.

CHAPTER OUTLINE

1. The *law of demand* states that at higher prices a lower quantity will be demanded than at lower prices, *other things being equal.*
   a. For simplicity, things other than the price of the good itself are held constant.
   b. Buyers respond to changes in *relative*, not *absolute*, *prices*.
   c. The law of demand is accounted for by the *substitution effect* and the *income effect*.
      i. The substitution effect is the tendency of people to substitute in favor of cheaper commodities and away from more expensive commodities.
      ii. The real-income effect is the change in people's purchasing power that occurs when, other things constant, the price of one good that they purchase changes.

2. The *demand schedule* for a good is a set of pairs of numbers showing various possible prices and the quantity demanded at each price, for some time period.
   a. Demand must be conceived of as being measured in constant quality units.
   b. A *demand curve* is a graphic representation of the demand schedule and it is negatively sloped, reflecting the law of demand.
   c. A market demand curve for a particular good or service is derived by summing all the individual demand curves for that product.

3. The determinants of demand include all *nonprice* factors that influence the quantity purchased.
   a. When deriving a demand curve, nonprice determinants of demand are held constant. When such nonprice determinants do change, the original demand curve shifts to the left or to the right.
   b. The major *determinants of demand* are consumers' income, tastes and preferences, changes in their expectations about future relative prices, the price of substitutes and complements for the good in question, population, and age composition of the population.

c. A change in demand is a shift in the demand curve, whereas a change in *quantity demanded* is a movement along a given demand curve.

4. Supply is the relationship between price and the quantity supplied, other things being equal.
   a. There is a direct, or positive, relationship between price and quantity supplied.
      i. As the relative price of a good rises, producers have an incentive to produce more of it.
      ii. As a firm produces greater quantities in the short run, the cost of producing additional units rises, and therefore a firm requires a higher relative price before it will increase output.
   b. A *supply schedule* is a set of numbers showing prices and the quantity supplied at those various prices.
   c. A *supply curve* is the graphic representation of the supply schedule; it is positively sloped.
   d. By summing individual supply curves for a particular good or service we derive that good or service's market supply curve.
   e. The major *determinants of supply* are the prices of resources (inputs) used to produce the product, technology, taxes and subsidies, price expectations of producers, and the number of firms in an industry.
   f. Any change in the determinants of supply (listed in part e) causes a change in supply and therefore leads to a shift in the supply curve.
   g. A change in price, holding the determinants of supply constant, causes a movement along--but not a shift in--the supply curve.

5. By graphing demand and supply on the same coordinate system, equilibrium can be found at the intersection of the two curves.
   a. *Equilibrium* is a situation in which the plans of buyers and of sellers exactly coincide, so that there is neither excess quantity supplied nor excess quantity demanded; at the equilibrium price, quantity supplied equals quantity demanded.
   b. At a price below the equilibrium price, quantity demanded exceeds quantity supplied, and *excess demand*, or a *shortage*, exists.
   c. At a price above the equilibrium price, quantity supplied exceeds quantity demanded, and an *excess supply*, or a *surplus*, exists.
   d. Seller competition forces price down, and eliminates a surplus.
   e. Buyer competition forces price up, and eliminates a shortage.

KEY TERMS

Other things being equal (*ceteris paribus*)
Demand schedule
Demand curve
Quantity demanded
Supply schedule
Supply curve
Equilibrium quantity
Equilibrium price
Posted-offer pricing
Bargaining

KEY CONCEPTS

Law of demand
Relative price
Absolute, or nominal, price
Substitution effect
Real-income effect
Constant-quality units
Normal goods
Inferior goods
Nonprice determinant of demand
Increase and decrease in demand
Substitutes
Complements
Law of increasing costs
Nonprice determinants of supply
Equilibrium
Shortage, or excess quantity demanded
Surplus, or excess quantity supplied

COMPLETION QUESTIONS

Fill in the blank or circle the correct term.

1. A ______________________________ relates various possible prices to the quantities demanded at each price, and a ______________________________ relates various prices to the quantities supplied at each price.

2. A change in quantity demanded is a (movement along, shift in) the demand curve; and a change in demand is a ______________________________ the demand curve.

3. At the intersection of the supply and demand curves, the quantity supplied equals the quantity demanded, and at that price a(n) ____________________ exists; at a price above that intersection, quantity supplied exceeds quantity demanded and a(n) __________ exists; at a price below that intersection, quantity demanded exceeds quantity supplied, and a(n) ____________ exists.

4. The law of demand is that, other things being equal, more is bought at a (lower, higher) price and less is bought at a ________________ price.

5. Two reasons for the law of demand are the ____________________ and the ______________________; for these reasons there is a(n) (direct, inverse) relationship between price and quantity demanded, and demand curves will be (positively, negatively) sloped.

6. When the nonprice determinants of demand change, the entire demand curve shifts; the five major nonprice determinants of demand are ____________________, ____________________, ____________________, ____________________, and ______________.

7. If the demand for pizza rises, given the supply, then the equilibrium price of pizza will (rise, fall) and the equilibrium quantity will ___________.

8. The supply schedule relates prices to quantities supplied; in general, as price rises, quantity supplied ____________. Therefore a(n) (direct, inverse) relationship exists, and the supply curve is (positively, negatively) sloped.

9. The supply curve is positively sloped because as price rises, producers have an incentive to produce (less, more) and because as producers increase output, the extra cost of producing additional units (rises, falls) in the short run.

10. When the determinants of supply change, the entire supply curve will shift; five major determinants of supply are ____________, ____________, ____________, ____________, and ____________.

11. Videocassettes and videocassette players are (substitutes, complements); if the price of videocassette players rises, then the demand for video cassettes will ____________.

12. When the price of peaches rises, the demand for pears rises; peaches and pears are (substitutes, complements).

13. Analogy: An excess quantity supplied is to a surplus as a(n) ____________ is to a shortage.

14. A rise in demand causes the demand curve to shift to the (left, right); an increase in quantity demanded is a movement (up, down) the demand curve.

15. By convention, economists plot (price, quantity) on the vertical axis and (price, quantity) on the horizontal axis.

16. Bargaining for low cost items is more important in countries where the opportunity cost of time is (low, high).

TRUE-FALSE QUESTIONS

Circle the **T** if the statement is true, the **F** if it is false. Explain to yourself why a statement is false.

T F 1. A demand schedule relates quantity demanded to quantity supplied, other things being constant.

T F 2. A change in the quantity demanded of cigarettes results from a change in the price of cigarettes.

T F 3. A graphical representation of a demand curve is called a demand schedule.

T F 4. An increase in price leads to a leftward shift in demand and a rightward shift in supply.

T F 5. The real income effect helps to account for an upward sloping supply curve.

T F 6. Buyers tend to substitute relatively lower-priced goods for relatively higher-priced goods, according to the real income effect.

T F 7. As producers increase output in the short run, the extra cost of additional units of output tends to rise.

T F 8. If the price of tennis racquets rises, the demand for tennis balls will tend to rise also.

T F 9. If the price of butter rises, the demand for margarine will rise.

T F 10. If price is below the equilibrium price a shortage exists.

MULTIPLE CHOICE QUESTIONS

Circle the letter that corresponds to the best answer.

1. A demand schedule
   a. relates price to quantity supplied.
   b. when graphed, is a demand curve.
   c. cannot change.
   d. shows a direct relationship between price and quantity demanded.

2. If the price of milk rises, other things being constant,
   a. real income falls for milk drinkers.
   b. buyers will substitute milk for other beverages.
   c. the demand for milk will fall.
   d. the demand for cola drinks will fall.

3. Which of the following will *not* occur if the price of hamburgers falls, other things being constant?
   a. Real incomes will rise for hamburger eaters.
   b. People will substitute hamburgers for hot dogs.
   c. The demand for hot dogs will rise.
   d. The quantity demanded for hamburgers will increase.

4. If the price of good A rises and the demand for good B rises, then A and B are
   a. substitutes.
   b. complements.
   c. not related goods.
   d. not scarce goods.

*5. Recently some cities in North Carolina passed a law that limited showers to 4 minutes, with a possible 30-day jail sentence for violators. Which of the following statements is probably true for those cities?
   a. A surplus of water existed.
   b. The price of water was too high.
   c. A shortage of water would exist regardless of how high its price got.
   d. The price of water was below the equilibrium price.

6. If the supply of gasoline rises, given its demand, then
   a. the relative price of gasoline will rise.
   b. the equilibrium price of gasoline will rise.
   c. the equilibrium quantity of gasoline will increase.
   d. the equilibrium price and equilibrium quantity of gasoline will increase.

7. If income falls and the demand for steak falls, then steak is a(n)
   a. substitute good.
   b. complement good.
   c. normal good.
   d. inferior good.

Consider the graphs below when answering questions 8 and 9.

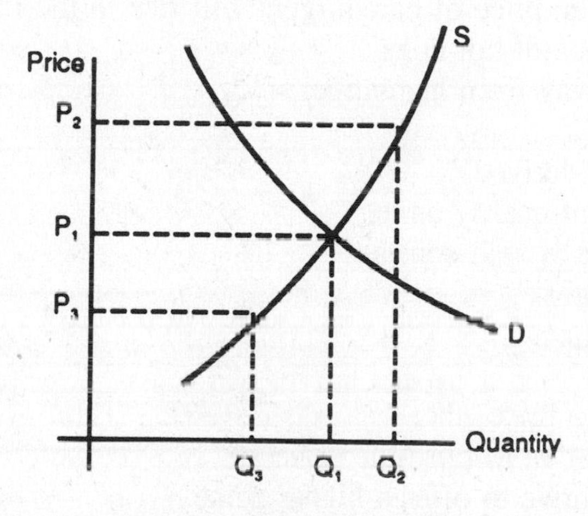

8. Given the figure above,
   a. the equilibrium price is P_1, the equilibrium quantity is P_2.
   b. the equilibrium quantity is P_1.
   c. the equilibrium price is P_3, the equilibrium quantity is Q_1.
   d. the equilibrium quantity is Q_1, the equilibrium price is P_1.

9. Which of the following is *not* true?
   a. A shortage exists at P_2.
   b. The equilibrium price is P_1.
   c. An excess quantity demanded exists at P_3.
   d. The market-clearing price is P_1.

10. If the demand for hamburgers rises, given the supply, then
   a. the supply of hamburgers will rise because price rises.
   b. the equilibrium price of hamburgers will fall and the equilibrium quantity will rise.
   c. the equilibrium quantity and the equilibrium price of hamburgers will rise.
   d. the quantity supplied of hamburgers will decrease.

*11. If a shortage exists at some price, then
   a. sellers can sell all they desire to sell at that price.
   b. sellers have an incentive to raise the price.
   c. buyers cannot get all they want at that price.
   d. All of the above

12. Which of the following will lead to a rise in supply?
   a. an increase in the price of the good in question
   b. a technological improvement in the production of the good in question
   c. an increase in the price of labor used to produce the good in question
   d. All of the above

*13. Which of the following probably will **NOT** lead to a fall in the demand for hamburgers?
   a. a modest decrease in income
   b. an expectation that the price of hamburgers will rise in the future
   c. a decrease in the price of hot dogs
   d. a change in tastes away from hamburgers

14. When a demand curve is derived,
   a. quantity is in constant-quality units.
   b. the price of the good is held constant.
   c. money income changes.
   d. consumer tastes change.

*15. If a surplus exists at some price, then
   a. sellers have an incentive to raise the price.
   b. buyers have an incentive to offer a higher price.
   c. sellers cannot sell all they wish to at that price.
   d. seller inventories are falling.

MATCHING

Choose the item in Column (2) that best matches an item in Column (1).

(1)	(2)
a. excess quantity demanded	k. real income effect
b. supply curve	l. law of increasing relative cost
c. demand curve	m. population increases
d. bread and butter	n. raw material prices rise
e. eyeglasses and contact lenses	o. community money income falls
f. demand shifts to the left	p. market clearing price
g. supply shifts to the left	q. surplus
h. equilibrium price	r. complements
i. equilibrium quantity rises	s. substitutes
j. excess quantity supplied	t. shortage

WORKING WITH GRAPHS

1. Use the demand schedule below to plot the demand curve on the following coordinate system. Be sure to label each axis correctly.

Price per bottle of shampoo	Quantity demanded of bottles of shampoo per week (in thousands)
$6	8
$5	10
$4	12
$3	14
$2	16
$1	18

7
6
5
4
3
2
1
2 4 6 8 10 12 14 16 18 20

2. Use the supply schedule below to plot the supply curve on the coordinate system in problem 1.

Price per bottle of shampoo	Quantity supplied of bottles of shampoo per week (in thousands)
$6	18
$5	15
$4	12
$3	9
$2	6
$1	3

3. Using the graphs from problems 1 and 2, indicate on the graph the equilibrium price and the equilibrium quantity for bottles of shampoo. What is the equilibrium price? the equilibrium quantity?

4. Continuing with the same example, assume that the government puts a price ceiling at $3 per bottle of shampoo. What is the quantity demanded at that price? the quantity supplied? Does a surplus or a shortage exist at that price?

5. Consider the two graphs below, in panels a and b.

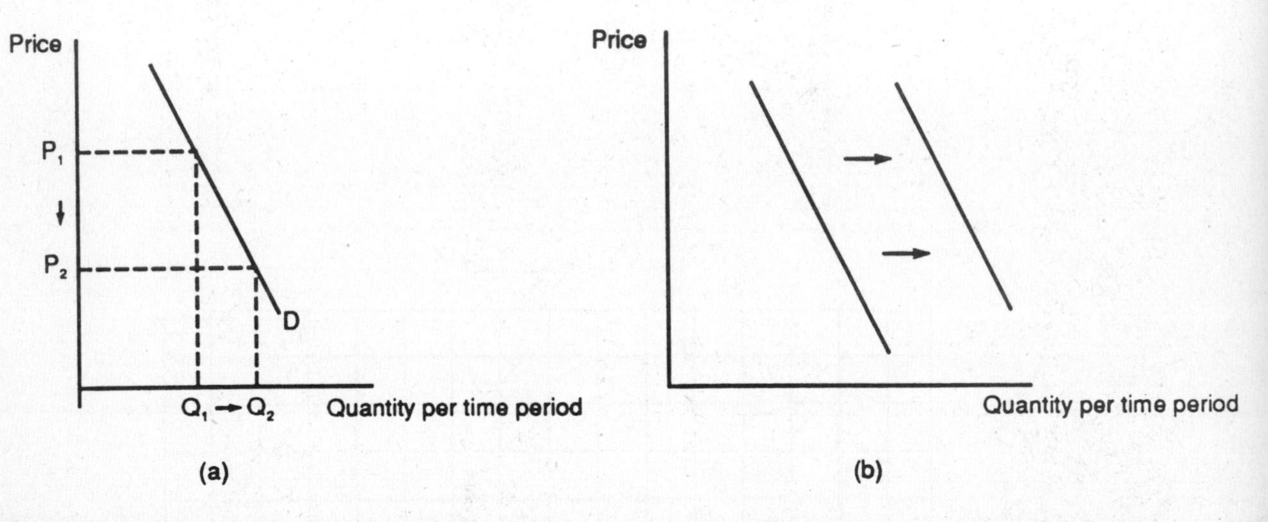

Which panel shows an increase in quantity demanded? Which shows a rise in demand?

6. Distinguish between a fall in supply and a decrease in quantity supplied, graphically, using the space below. Use two panels.

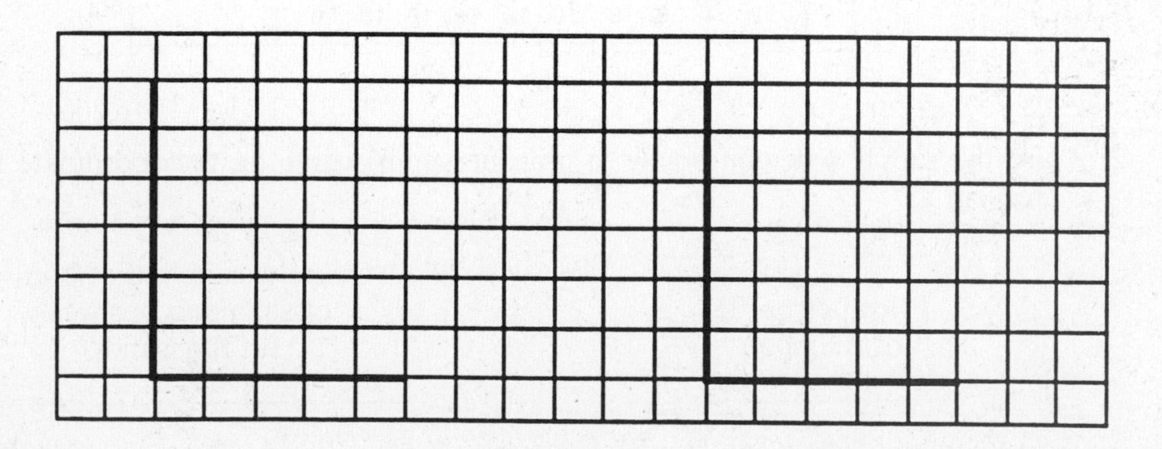

7. Consider the graphs below in panel (a). Then show, in panel (b), the new equilibrium price (label it P_1) and the new equilibrium quantity (label it Q_1) that results due to a change in tastes in favor of the good in question.

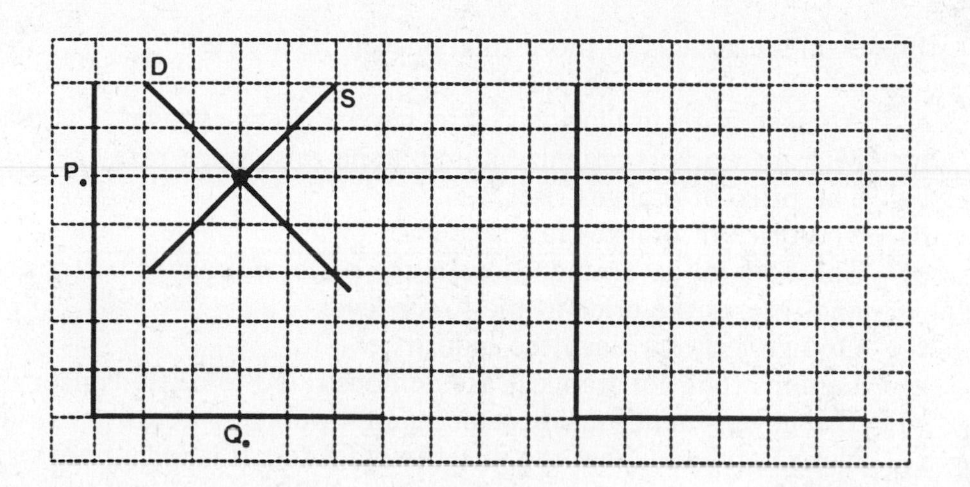

PROBLEMS

1. In the table below, monthly demand schedules for turkey are indicated. Assume that column 2 represents quantities demanded in October, column 3 represents November, and column 4 represents December.

(1)	(2)	(3)	(4)
Price per pound	Q_d	Q_d	Q_d
5 cents	10,000		16,000
10 cents	8,000		14,000
15 cents	6,000		12,000
20 cents	4,000		10,000
25 cents	2,000		8,000

Fill in column 3 yourself. What happens to the demand for turkey in November? Why?

2. List the nonprice determinants of demand that will lead to a decrease in demand. Be specific.

3. List the nonprice determinants of supply that will lead to a rise in supply. Be specific.

*4. Concerning oranges, indicate whether each event leads to (i) a rightward shift in demand, (ii) a leftward shift in demand, (iii) an increase in quantity demanded, (iv) a decrease in quantity demanded, (v) a rightward shift in supply, (vi) a leftward shift in supply, (vii) an increase in quantity supplied, (viii) a decrease in quantity supplied.

(Note: some events may lead to more than one of the above.)

_____ a) An early frost in Florida destroys some orange groves.
_____ b) Migrant workers organize a union and raise wage rates.
_____ c) The price of oranges rises.
_____ d) The price of oranges falls.
_____ e) The Federal government lowers the price of oranges below equilibrium and freezes the price at the lower level.
_____ f) Orange growers leave the industry.
_____ g) Lemons (but not oranges) are demonstrated to cause cancer in lab rats.
_____ h) The government subsidizes orange growers at 3 cents per orange.
_____ i) News is released that the government forecast is for a poor orange crop this year.
_____ j) The price of lemons rises (assume now that orange growers can also grow lemons).

*5. For each of the statements a through j in the previous question, decide whether the equilibrium price will rise, fall, or be unaffected.

a) _________ f) _________
b) _________ g) _________
c) _________ h) _________
d) _________ i) _________
e) _________ j) _________

***CASE STUDY**

College professors are excited by ideas and love to debate profound philosophical issues. For many, the topic that seems to really get their blood boiling is the campus parking problem. It seems that a parking shortage exists at many colleges, and faculty senates all over the country provide a forum for endless debate of various solutions. Faculty members think that their employers have a "duty" to provide parking for them; students think that parking should be provided for them, because they are crucial to the university. Administrators, in their heart of hearts, believe that they are what make universities important; hence they lay claim to special parking privileges.

1. Draw a probable demand curve for campus parking, with the number of parking spaces on the horizontal axis and the price of parking permits on the vertical axis. Why is such a curve likely to be negatively sloped? (Clue: Are there substitutes for parking one's car on campus?)

2. Draw a probable supply curve on the same coordinate system as in problem (1). Why is such a curve likely to be (at least slightly) upward sloping?

3. Label the equilibrium price P_e and label a price P_1 at which a shortage exists. The price P_1 is the one suggested to exist on many college campuses.

4. How can the parking shortage be eliminated? Why? How will a higher price allocate parking spaces? Is such a solution fair?

ANSWERS TO CHAPTER 3

COMPLETION QUESTIONS

1. demand curve or schedule, supply curve or schedule
2. movement along; shift in
3. equilibrium; surplus; shortage
4. lower, higher
5. substitution effect, real-income effect; inverse, negatively
6. income, tastes and preferences, prices of related goods, expectations about future relative prices, population
7. rise, rise
8. increases; direct, positively
9. more, rises
10. prices of inputs, technology, taxes and subsidies, price expectations, number of firms in industry
11. complements; fall
12. substitutes
13. excess quantity demanded
14. right; down
15. price, quantity
16. low

TRUE AND FALSE

1. F A demand schedule relates quantity demanded to price.
2. T
3. F A graphical representation of a demand schedule is a demand curve.
4. F An increase in price leads to a decrease in quantity demanded and an increase in quantity supplied.
5. F The real income effect helps to account for a negatively sloped demand curve.
6. F ... according to the *substitution* effect.
7. T
8. F ... the demand for tennis balls will tend to *fall*, because they are complements.
9. T
10. T

MULTIPLE CHOICE QUESTIONS

1.b; 2.a; 3.c; 4.a; 5.d; 6.c; 7.c; 8.d; 9.a; 10.c;
11.d; 12.b; 13.b; 14.a; 15.c.

MATCHING

a and t; b and l; c and k; d and r; e and s; f and o; g and n; h and p;
i and m; j and q

WORKING WITH GRAPHS

1. See graphs.
2. See graphs.

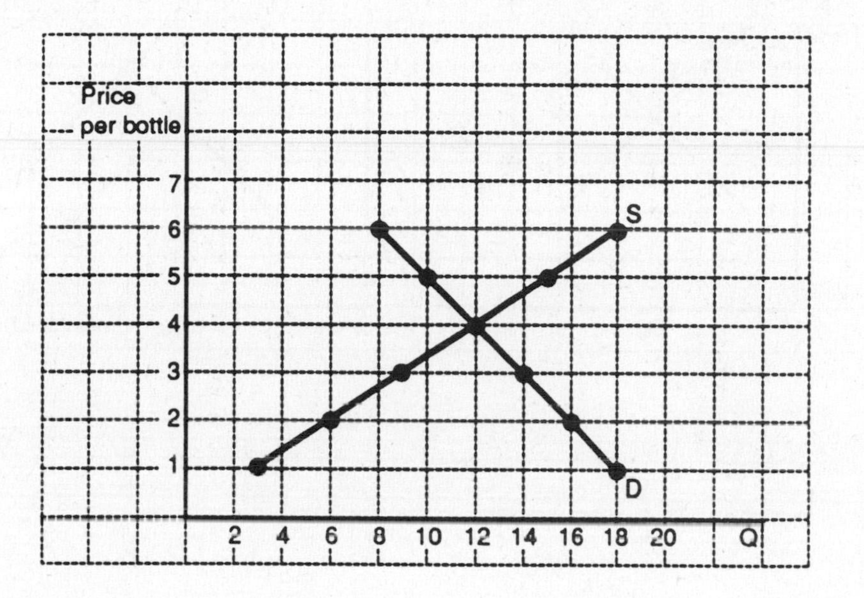

3. $4; 12 bottles
4. 14 bottles; 9 bottles; shortage
5. Panel (a); Panel (b)

6.

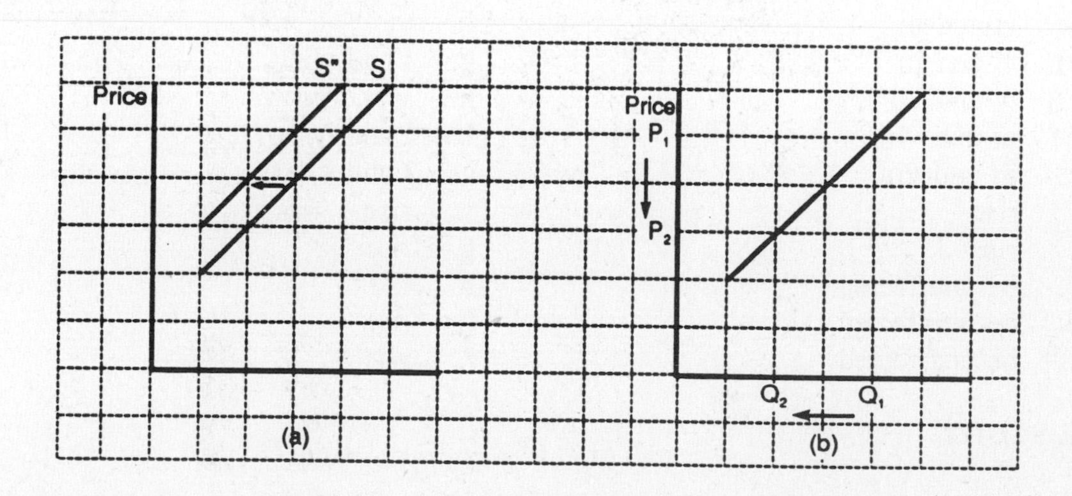

(a) A decrease in supply

(b) A decrease in quantity supplied

7.

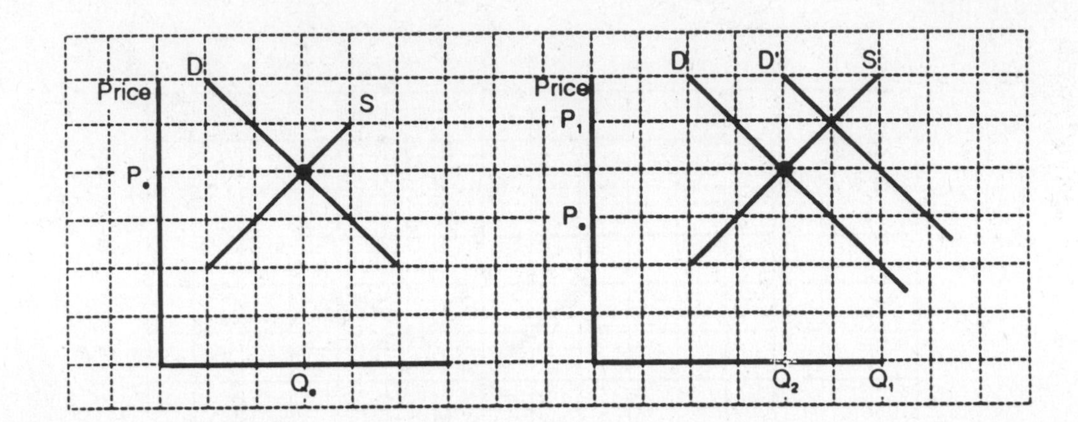

PROBLEMS

1. Rises; due to Thanksgiving
2. Income falls for a normal good or rises for an inferior good; change in tastes occurs away from the good; price of a substitute falls or price of a complement rises; expectations exist that the good's future relative price will fall; decrease in population occurs.
3. Reduction in the price of inputs; decrease in a sales tax on the good or increase in the (per unit) subsidy of the good; expectation that the future relative price will rise; increase in the number of firms in the industry.
4. a. vi and iii
   b. vi and iii
   c. iv and vii
   d. iii and viii
   e. iii and viii
   f. vi
   g. i and vii
   h. v and iii
   i. i and iv
   j. i and vi
5. a. rise
   b. rise
   c. be unaffected
   d. be unaffected
   e. be unaffected
   f. rise
   g. rise
   h. fall
   i. rise
   j. rise

CASE STUDY

1. See graphs, question 3. As the price of parking permits rises, faculty and students will find substitutes. They will join car pools, walk, ride bicycles, park off-campus, and so on.
2. If price rises to sufficiently high levels the administration will find it profitable to increase the quantity supplied of parking places. In the short run this may be accomplished by laying out parking lots more efficiently, re-painting lines, allocating some spaces specifically to economy cars, and so on. In the long run more lots can be paved or parking

specifically to economy cars, and so on. In the long run more lots can be paved or parking structures can be constructed.

3. See graphs.

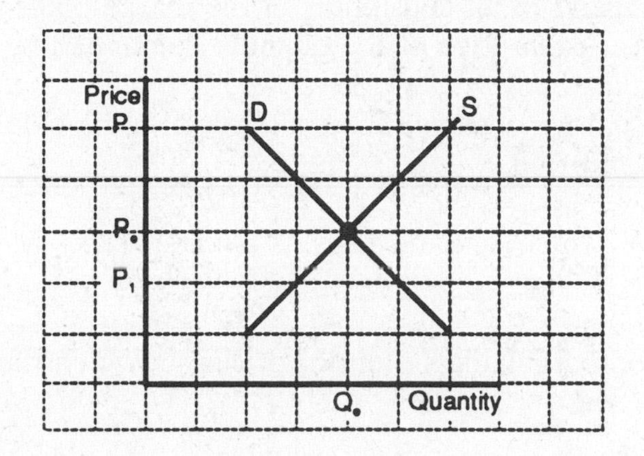

4. The shortage can be eliminated by allowing the price of parking permits to rise from P_1 to P_e. This price rise will lead to a decrease in the quantity demanded and to an increase in the quantity supplied of parking places. Parking spaces will be allocated according to the highest bidders. Whether or not this is a "fair" way to allocate parking spaces is a normative issue and therefore depends on one's value judgements.

GLOSSARY TO CHAPTER 3

Bargaining The process of establishing price through a series of offers and counter offers.

Complements Two goods are complements if both are used together for consumption or enjoyment. The more you buy of one, the more you buy of the other. For complements, a change in the price of one causes an opposite shift in the demand for the other.

Demand A schedule of how much of a good or service people will purchase at each different possible price during a specified time period.

Demand curve A graphic representation of the demand schedule. A negatively sloped line showing the inverse relationship between the price and the quantity demand.

Equilibrium A situation where quantity supplied equals quantity demanded at a particular price.

Inferior good Those goods for which demand falls as income rises.

Market-clearing, or equilibrium price The price that clears the market, where quantity demanded equals quantity supplied; the price at which the demand curve intersects the supply curve.

Market demand The demand of all consumers in the marketplace for a particular good or service. The summing at each price of the quantity demanded by each individual.

Money price That price that we observe today in terms of today's dollars. Also called the *absolute*, *nominal*, or *current* price.

Normal good A good for which demand rises as income rises. Most goods are normal goods.

Poster-offer pricing A non-bargaining system of pricing in which the price of the good is labeled for one and all to see.

Purchasing power The value of your money income in buying goods and services. If your money income stays the same but the price of one good that you are buying goes up, your effective purchasing power falls.

Real-income effect The change in people's purchasing power that occurs when, other things being constant, the price of one good that they purchase changes. When that price goes up, real income, or purchasing power, falls; and when that price goes down, real income, or purchasing power, increases.

Relative price The price of a commodity expressed in terms of the price of another commodity or the (weighted) average price of all other commodities.

Shortage A situation in which quantity demanded is greater than quantity supplied at a price below the market-clearing price.

Subsidy A negative tax; a payment to a producer (or consumer) from the government, usually in the form of a cash grant.

Substitutes Two goods are substitutes when either one can be used for consumption. The more you buy of one, the less you buy of the other. For substitutes, the change in the price of one causes a shift in demand for the other in the same direction as the price change.

Substitution effect The tendency of people to substitute in favor of cheaper commodities and away from more expensive commodities.

Supply A schedule showing the relationship between price and quantity supplied, other things being equal, for a specified period of time.

Supply curve The graphic representation of the supply schedule; a line (curve) showing the supply schedule, which slopes upward (has a positive slope).

Surplus A situation in which quantity supplied is greater than quantity demanded at a price above the market-clearing price.

CHAPTER 4

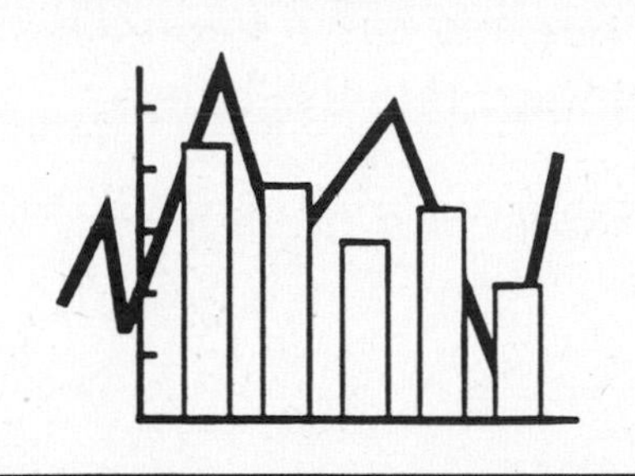

EXTENSIONS OF DEMAND AND SUPPLY ANALYSIS

PUTTING THIS CHAPTER INTO PERSPECTIVE

In Chapter 3 you learned how the forces of supply and demand, with buyers and sellers transacting voluntarily, determine market-clearing or equilibrium price. Sellers compete with sellers for sales, and buyers compete with buyers for goods and services. If price is above equilibrium, a surplus exists and seller competition forces price down toward equilibrium; if price is below equilibrium, a shortage exists and buyer competition forces price up toward equilibrium. Prices adjust until surpluses and shortages are eliminated.

Because resources are scarce, outputs are scarce and somehow scarce outputs must be allocated (or rationed) to people. Under voluntary exchange, when supply and demand forces are unrestricted, goods and services are allocated to the highest bidders. In effect, goods and services go to those customers who are willing to give up more of *other* goods and services.

In this chapter you learn that (a) it takes time for price adjustments to eliminate surpluses and shortages; (b) when governments disallow prices from falling or rising, then prolonged surpluses and prolonged shortages arise, respectively; (c) if price is not allowed to allocate goods to the highest bidder then some other rationing system must--and will--emerge to determine how a specific good will be allocated.

LEARNING OBJECTIVES

After you have studied this chapter you should be able to

1. define price controls, price ceiling, price floor, non-price rationing devices, black market and rent control.

2. predict what happens to equilibrium price and equilibrium quantity when supply increases or decreases relative to demand, and when demand increases relative to supply.

3. predict what happens to the relative price of a good or resource if it becomes more or less scarce.

4. give examples of indirect price increases.

5. differentiate between the causes of short-run and long-run (prolonged) shortages.

6. explain how labor shortages eventually disappear, given wage rate flexibility.

7. recognize various methods of rationing goods and services.

8. recognize, from graphs, how a black market emerges.

9. enumerate several consequences of rent control.

10. recognize several consequences of government quantity restrictions.

CHAPTER OUTLINE

1. In a price system (free enterprise) voluntary exchange typically determines price; buyers and sellers transact with a minimum amount of governmental interference.
   a. Under a system of voluntary exchange the terms of exchange (the terms, usually price, under which trade takes place) are set by the forces of supply and demand.
   b. Markets reduce transactions costs (all the costs associated with exchanging, including such costs associated with gathering information and enforcing contracts).
   c. Under voluntary exchange *both* buyers and sellers are presumed to benefit--otherwise the transactions would not continue.

2. Changes in demand and/or supply lead to changes in the equilibrium price and the equilibrium quantity.
   a. If demand shifts to the right (left), given supply, then the equilibrium price rises (falls) and the equilibrium quantity rises (falls).
   b. If supply shifts to the right (left), given demand, then the equilibrium price falls (rises) and the equilibrium quantity rises (falls).
   c. When both supply and demand change, it is not always possible to predict the effects on the equilibrium price and the equilibrium quantity.

3. Prices and wage rates aren't always perfectly flexible.
   a. If prices are inflexible, published prices will not change very much, but such hidden price rises as a quality reduction might occur.
   b. Markets do not always move to equilibrium (given a change in demand or supply) immediately; hence shortages can emerge in the short run.
   c. Short-run labor shortages could arise if employers are reluctant to bid wage rates up and it takes time for people to learn new skills.

4. Price reflects relative scarcity and performs a rationing function.
   a. If an input or output becomes less scarce (more scarce) its relative price will fall (rise).
   b. If governments prevent price from rising, via a price control or ceiling, then goods cannot (legally) be allocated to the highest bidder and prolonged shortages result; other forms of rationing emerge.

c. During prolonged shortages such non-price rationing devices as cheating, long lines, first-come first-served, political power, physical force, and other non-market forces arise to answer the for whom question.
d. Governments also interfere in markets by putting price floors on price; for example, governments impose minimum wage rates.

5. Rent controls are governmentally imposed price ceilings on rental apartments, which lead to predictable results.

6. Governments also impose quantity restrictions on market transactions.
   a. Some goods, such as certain drugs and human organs are outright illegal to trade.
   b. Licensing arrangements, in effect, restrict the quantity of some goods and services.
   c. An import quota is a quantity restriction that prohibits the importation of more than a specified quantity of a particular good in a one-year period.

KEY TERMS

Price ceiling
Transactions costs
Price floor
Import quota
Black market

KEY CONCEPTS

Price controls
Voluntary exchange
Rent control
Terms of exchange

COMPLETION QUESTIONS

Fill in the blank or circle the correct term.

1. Resources are scarce; therefore none of us can have all we want at a (zero, positive) price and there will be various ways in which people will _______________ for resources.

2. If demand shifts to the left, given supply, then the equilibrium price will (rise, fall) and the equilibrium quantity will _________.

3. If supply shifts to the right, given demand, then the equilibrium price will _________ and the equilibrium quantity will _________.

4. If both demand and supply shift to the right then the equilibrium price (will rise, will fall, is indeterminate) and the equilibrium quantity (will rise, will fall, is indeterminate).

5. If both demand and supply shift to the left, then the equilibrium price (will rise, will fall, is indeterminate), and the equilibrium quantity (will rise, will fall, is indeterminate).

6. If the demand for good A or resource A rises relative to its supply, it has become relatively (less scarce, more scarce) and its relative price will (rise, fall); if the demand for good or resource B falls relative to its supply, then it has become relatively ______________, and its relative price will _________.

7. If the published price of good A remains constant, but its quality falls, then its relative price has really (risen, fallen). If the published price of good A remains constant, but people have to wait in line to get it, then the price of good A has really _____________, because people have an opportunity cost for their _______________.

8. If the demand for a labor skill rises relative to its supply, that skill becomes (less scarce, more scarce) and its relative price will (rise, fall); this leads to a(n) (decrease, increase) in the number of people willing to learn that skill.

9. Price performs a(n) _______________ function; inputs or outputs go to the ____________ bidders, if people are free to exchange voluntarily in markets; if such economic freedoms do not exist, then other (price, nonprice) determinants will allocate goods and services.

*10. Price controls that put a price ceiling on goods and services create (surpluses, shortages); and price floors create (surpluses, shortages).

11. If governments place price (floors, ceilings) on goods, then black markets might emerge.

12. Rent control is a form of price (floor, ceiling); rent control (increases, reduces) the future supply of apartment construction; (increases, reduces) tenant mobility, (improves, deteriorates) the quality of the existing stock of apartments, and hurts _______________.

13. By prohibiting the sale and use of certain drugs, the government causes the supply of such drugs to shift to the (left, right), makes such drugs (more, less) scarce, and causes their relative price to (rise, fall).

14. Import quotas, licensing arrangements, and outright bans on specific goods are forms of government (price, quantity) restrictions.

15. An import quota tends to (lower, raise) price to consumers.

TRUE-FALSE QUESTIONS

Circle the **T** if the statement if true, the **F** if it is false. Explain to yourself why a statement is false.

T F 1. If supply shifts to the left, given demand, then the equilibrium price and the equilibrium quantity will rise.

T F 2. If demand shifts to the left, given supply, then the equilibrium price and the equilibrium quantity will fall.

T F 3. If both supply and demand shift to the right, then equilibrium price and equilibrium quantity are indeterminate.

T F 4. If the supply of good A increases relative to its demand, then good A is now more scarce, and its relative price will rise.

T F 5. If published price is constant, but it takes consumers longer to wait in lines, price has really risen.

T F 6. If markets are flexible and no market restrictions exist, then surpluses and shortages won't occur, even in the short run.

T F 7. Minimum wage laws are a form of price ceiling.

T F 8. Rent controls help the poor who are looking for apartments, because rents are lower.

T F 9. Black markets, in effect, cause price to rise for certain buyers.

T F 10. If an import quota is imposed on sugar, the domestic supply of sugar curve will shift to the left.

MULTIPLE CHOICE QUESTIONS

Circle the letter that corresponds to the best answer.

1. Because resources are scarce,
   a. buyers compete with buyers for outputs.
   b. the for whom question must be answered.
   c. people cannot have all they want at a zero price.
   d. All of the above

2. If markets are free and prices are flexible,
   a. equilibrium price cannot be established.
   b. shortages and surpluses eventually disappear.
   c. shortages and surpluses can't arise.
   d. equilibrium quantity cannot be established.

3. If demand shifts to the right (given supply), then equilibrium
   a. quantity will rise.
   b. price is indeterminate.
   c. price and equilibrium quantity are indeterminant.
   d. price will fall.

4. If supply shifts to the right (given demand), then equilibrium
   a. quantity will rise.
   b. price will rise.
   c. price and equilibrium quantity will fall.
   d. price and equilibrium quantity rises.

5. If both supply and demand shift to the left, then equilibrium
   a. price is indeterminate and equilibrium quantity rises.
   b. price is indeterminate and equilibrium quantity falls.
   c. price falls and equilibrium quantity falls.
   d. price falls and equilibrium quantity is indeterminate.

6. If the demand for good A falls relative to its supply, then
   a. good A is now relatively more scarce.
   b. good A is now relatively less scarce.
   c. the relative price of good A will rise.
   d. the actual price of good A will rise, even if A is not price flexible.

7. If the demand for good B rises relative to it supply, then
   a. good B is now relatively more scarce.
   b. the relative price of good B will rise.
   c. the actual price of good B will rise, even if good B is price inflexible.
   d. All of the above

8. If the demand for good A rises relative to its supply, and markets are price-flexible, then
   a. no shortage of A can exist in the long run.
   b. no shortage of A can exist in the short run.
   c. the published price of A remains constant; but its actual price falls.
   d. the published price of A remains constant, but its actual price rises.

9. If the demand for good A rises relative to its supply, and markets are price-inflexible, then
   a. a shortage can exist in the short run.
   b. a shortage can exist in the long run.
   c. the published price of A might remain constant, but its actual price rises.
   d. All of the above

10. If the demand for economists falls relative to their supply, then
    a. more college students will major in economics.
    b. some economists will change professions.
    c. a shortage of economists will result, in the long run.
    d. All of the above

11. Which of the following can influence how a society allocates a specific good?
    a. Price system that allocates to the highest bidder
    b. Political power
    c. Religion
    d. All of the above

12. Prolonged shortages arise if
    a. demand increases relative to supply.
    b. price floors are set by governments.
    c. prices are not allowed to rise to equilibrium.
    d. buyers are allowed to compete for goods.

13. Black markets may arise if
    a. price ceilings exist.
    b. price floors exist.
    c. governments do not intervene in the market.
    d. equilibrium price is too low.

14. Rent controls
    a. are a form of price floor.
    b. help the homeless who need apartments.
    c. make tenants less mobile.
    d. reduce litigation in society.

*15. If an import quota on good A were imposed, then
    a. the relative price of good A would rise.
    b. the domestic supply of good A would shift to the left.
    c. domestic substitutes for good A would arise.
    d. All of the above

MATCHING

Choose the item in Column (2) that best matches an item in Column (1).

(1)	(2)
a. price floor	e. buyer competition
b. price ceiling	f. rent control
c. scarce resources	g. minimum wage law
d. non-price rationing	h. black market, long lines

WORKING WITH GRAPHS

1. Consider the graphs below, then answer the questions that follow.

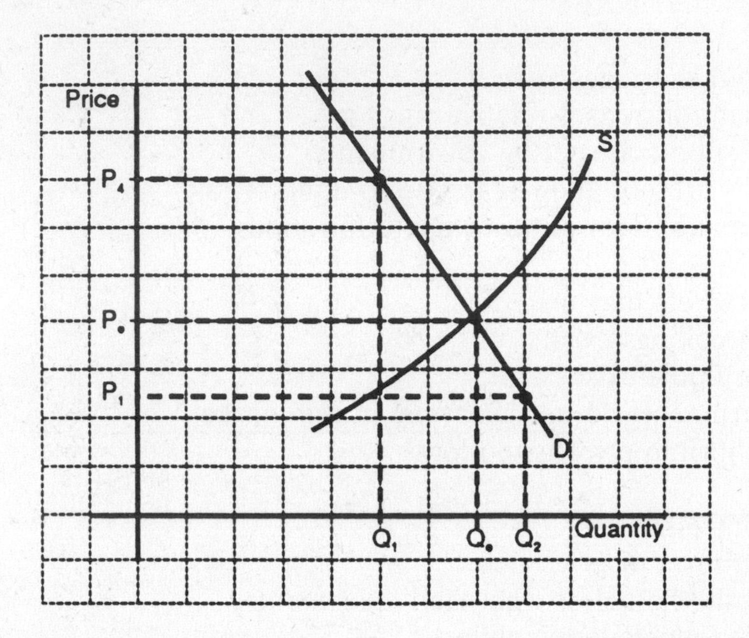

a. The market-clearing price is ___________?
b. If the government imposes a price ceiling at P_1, what will be the quantity supplied? The quantity demanded? What exists at that price?
c. Given the quantity that will be forthcoming at the permitted price of P_1, what will the actual or black market price be?
d. Other than via a black market transaction, how can the actual price paid by buyers exceed the permitted price, P_1.
e. If price had been permitted to rise to equilibrium, what would be the quantity supplied by sellers? Is that amount greater or lesser than the quantity at P_1? Why?

2. Consider the following supply and demand curves for labor, and then answer the questions.

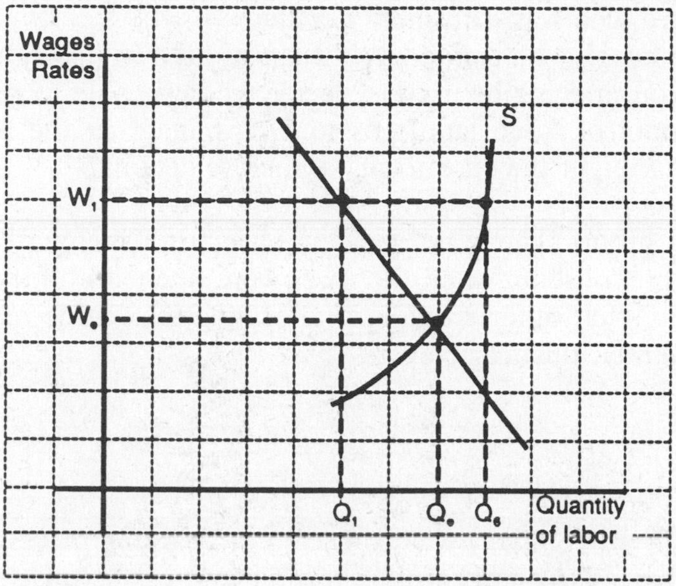

   a. What is the equilibrium wage rate? The equilibrium quantity of labor?
   b. If the government sets a minimum wage rate at W_1, what is the quantity of labor demanded by employers? The quantity of labor supplied by workers? What exists at the minimum wage rate?
   c. Is there a shortage or surplus of *jobs*? How might such jobs be allocated (that is, how will employers go about deciding who gets the jobs)?

3. During September of 1989, the then "drug Czar" William T. Bennett, Director of the Office of National Drug Control Policy, and Nobel Prize winning economst Milton Friedman debated the case for the prohibition of drugs in various letters to the editor, in the *Wall Street Journal*. Bennett, who favors prohibition, maintained that if drugs were legalized price would fall, and therefore, the total amount of drug usage in the U.S. would rise. Friedman, who favors legalization of drugs (to adults) maintained that, once legalized, the demand for drugs would fall because (1) the appeal to people who want the excitement of doing something "taboo" would disappear, and (2) addicts who have only a $2 a day habit have less of an incentive to get other people hooked on drugs (to support their own habit) than if they had a $200 a day habit.

   a. Is Bennett correct when he says that once legalized, price will fall? Why?
   b. If the demand for drugs shifts to the left, and the supply of drugs to the right, what happens to the price of drugs?
   c. If the demand for drugs shifts to the left (Friedman) and the supply of drugs shifts to the right (Bennett), what happens to the equilibrium quantity?
   d. How does your answer to (c) help you decide whether drug usage will rise or fall if drugs are legalized? What information is necessary to resolve this issue?

PROBLEMS

1. In a 1950s movie entitled "Under the Yum-Yum Tree" Jack Lemmon played a lecherous landlord who was extremely wealthy.
   a. How do you imagine he created a shortage of his own luxury apartments, and what criteria do you imagine he used to decide who was able to rent such apartments?
   b. Does rent control force landlords to discriminate in the selection of tenants? What criteria might they use to make such selections?

2. In 1979 the rock group "The Who" gave a concert in Cincinnati, and 11 people died outside Riverfront Coliseum when the gates were opened and the crowd rushed in to get choice seats. What other method of allocating the scarce resource "choice seats" would have prevented this tragic event?

CASE STUDY

In California, 1984, an oil company was convicted of charging prices that were above the legally-set price, and forced to charge, for a short time, prices below market prices to atone. Customers were then faced with a choice between (1) waiting in line for low-priced gasoline or (2) not waiting and purchasing gasoline of a similar quality at a higher price across the street. Two economists surveyed customers who chose each of those options.

1. What kinds of people waited in line for the lower-priced gasoline?

2. What kinds of people frequented the higher-priced gasoline stations?

ANSWERS TO CHAPTER 4

COMPLETION QUESTIONS

1. zero, compete
2. fall, fall
3. fall, rise
4. is indeterminate, will rise
5. is indeterminate, will fall
6. more scarce, rise; less scarce, fall
7. risen; risen, time
8. more scarce, rise; increase
9. rationing or allocating; highest; nonprice
10. shortages; surpluses
11. ceilings
12. ceiling; reduces; reduces, deteriorates, landlords and low income apartment hunters
13. left, more, rise
14. quantity
15. raise

TRUE-FALSE QUESTIONS

1. F The equilibrium quantity falls.
2. T
3. F Equilibrium quantity rises.
4. F Good A is now less scarce, and its relative price will fall.
5. T
6. F No, surpluses and shortages can exist--in the short run.
7. F They are a price floor.
8. F That group is hurt because they will be discriminated against, and because the housing stock diminishes.
9. T
10. T

MULTIPLE CHOICE QUESTIONS

1.d; 2.b; 3.a; 4.a; 5.b; 6.b; 7.d; 8.a; 9.d; 10.b;
11.d; 12.c; 13.a; 14.c; 15.d.

MATCHING

a and g; b and f; c and e; d and h

WORKING WITH GRAPHS

1. a. P_e
   b. Q_1; Q_2; shortage
   c. P_4
   d. quality deterioration, long lines that increase opportunity costs
   e. Q_e; greater; a higher price induces sellers to produce more.

2. a. W_e; Q_e
   b. Q_1; Q_6; surplus of labor, or unemployment
   c. shortage; family influence, political power, bribes, racial or gender preference

3. a. He is correct, because the supply curve will shift to the right as the costs and risks of drug-dealing fall.
   b. falls; Therefore Bennett is right.
   c. It is impossible to predict the net effect on the equilibrium quantity.
   d. The real issue is an empirical one; Will supply rise by more than demand falls, or vice versa?

PROBLEMS

1. a. He set rents far below the market-clearing levels, and many people wanted his apartments; he rented only to "lovely young ladies."
   b. Yes; gender, beauty, race, number of children, age, ability to pay, pets, and so on.
2. Instead of "first-come first-served seating", ticket sellers could have raised the price of choice seats and used assigned seating. Shortly thereafter, the city of Cincinnati passed a resolution that outlawed first-come first-served seating.

CASE STUDY

1. People who had low opportunity costs for their time: teenagers, homemakers, senior citizens, low income people.
2. People who had high opportunity costs for their time: professionals, business executives, high income people.

GLOSSARY TO CHAPTER 4

Black market A market in which goods are traded at prices above their legal maximum prices.

Nonprice rationing devices All those methods used to ration scarce goods that are price controlled. Whenever the price system is not allowed to work there will exist nonprice rationing devices to ration the affected goods and services.

Price ceiling A legal maximum price that can be charged for a particular good or service.

Price controls Government mandated controls on either minimum or maximum prices that can be charged for goods and services.

Price floor A legal minimum price below which a good or service cannot be sold. Legal minimum wages are an example.

Rent control Price ceilings placed on rents in particular municipalities.

Terms of exchange The terms under which the trading takes place. Usually the terms of exchange are given by the price at which a good is traded.

Transactions costs All of the costs associated with exchanging, including the informational costs of finding out price and quality, service record, durability, etc., of a product, plus the cost of contracting and enforcing that contract.

Voluntary exchange The act of trading, usually done on a voluntary basis in which both parties to the trade are subjectively better off after the exchange.

CHAPTER 5

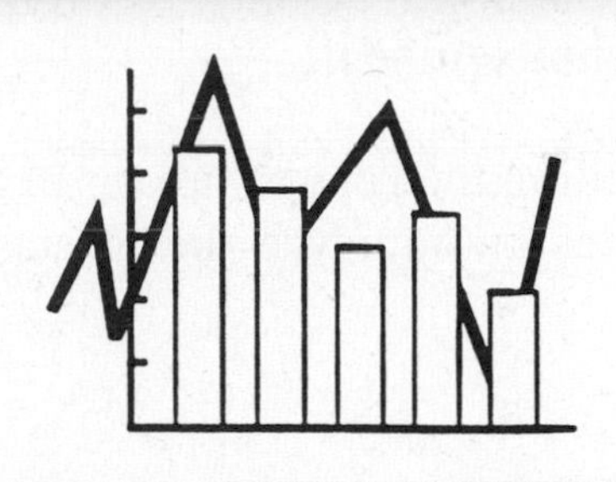

THE PUBLIC SECTOR

PUTTING THIS CHAPTER INTO PERSPECTIVE

To date you have learned that scarcity is a human condition, that economists study how resources are allocated to satisfy wants, and that there are many potential determinants of how resources are allocated in specific societies. In Chapter 5 we analyze how governments influence resource allocation--or more specifically, how individuals and groups use the institution of government to influence resource allocation.

It is important to master this chapter because our overall goal is to understand how resources are allocated in the American economy. The role of the government in our economy has grown tremendously since World War II; some maintain that it is nearly as important as the price system in determining resource allocation in the United States. Another reason why this chapter is important is because it analyzes the public choice model. This model is a relatively recent invention, and because of its predictive and explanatory power it has gained much influence.

It is generally agreed that the price system is an efficient resource allocator. Typically the value of output will be maximized (opportunity costs will be minimized) if the price system is permitted to allocate resources to satisfy wants. Nevertheless, the resource allocation that results from a price system is not always efficient. In this chapter you learn that if externalities exist, then the price system will transmit *incorrect* signals, and resource misallocation will result as the economy overproduces or underproduces specific goods and services. Similarly, because of the "free rider" problem, the price system will underproduce public goods. For these reasons the government has an *economic* function to perform; it can help to correct resource misallocation by providing the correct signals to economic agents.

The government has important *political* functions to perform also; it affects the output of merit and demerit goods and it redistributes income if the political process decides that the income distribution that results from the price system is unfair.

Because the government plays an important role in resource allocation in modern economies, it is crucial to analyze the public choice model, which attempts to explain why specific political decisions are made. It is one thing to state what a government *should* do to promote efficiency, and quite another to determine what decision will actually result from the political process. We owe this distinction to the public choice model.

It is impossible to analyze the public sector without understanding the role of taxes. In this chapter we distinguish between marginal and average tax rates and analyze the effects of raising tax revenues through various types of tax systems.

LEARNING OBJECTIVES

After you have studied this chapter you should be able to

1. define antitrust legislation, monopoly, spillover or externality, third parties, market failure, subsidy, private goods, public goods, principle of mutual exclusivity, exclusion principle, free-rider problem, merit good, demerit good, transfer payment, transfers in kind, collective decision making, theory of public choice, incentive structure, government goods, majority rule, proportional rule, marginal and average tax rates, value-added tax, consumption tax.

2. enumerate the five economic functions of government.

3. predict whether a specific good will be overproduced, underproduced, or produced in just the right amount if resources are allocated by the price system.

4. identify which graph takes into account an externality and which does not.

5. list the two ways in which a government can correct for negative externalities.

6. identify the three ways in which a government can correct for positive externalities.

7. list four characteristics of public goods that distinguish them from private goods.

8. recognize differences and similarities between market and collective decision making.

9. distinguish between a marginal and an average tax rate.

10. calculate the tax burden for individuals with different incomes, given different tax structures.

CHAPTER OUTLINE

1. The government provides many economic functions that affect the way in which resources are allocated.
   a. A legal system that defines and enforces property rights is crucial to the American capitalistic economy.
   b. Because a competitive price system transmits correct signals, an important role for government is to promote competition.

c. If a benefit or cost associated with an economic activity *spills over* to *third parties*, the price system will misallocate resources; a proper role for government is to correct such externalities.
   i. If a negative externality exists, the price system will over-allocate resources to that industry; the government can correct this by taxing or regulating such activities.
   ii. If a positive externality exists, the price system will under-allocate resources to that industry; the government can correct this by financing additional production, by providing special *subsidies*, or by regulation.
d. A price system will underallocate resources to the production of *public goods*.
   i. Characteristics of public goods include:
      (1) They are usually indivisible.
      (2) They can be used by more people at no additional cost.
      (3) Additional users of public goods do not deprive others of any of the services of the good.
      (4) It is difficult to charge individual users a fee based on how much they themselves consume of the public good.
   ii. Because public goods must be consumed collectively, individuals have an incentive to take a *free ride* and not pay for them.
   iii. Because the price system underproduces public goods, the proper role of government is to ensure their production.
e. In recent years the government has taken on the economic role of ensuring economywide stability: full employment, price stability, and economic growth.

2. The government provides political functions that also affect resource allocation.
   a. Governments subsidize the production of *merit goods* and tax or prohibit the production of *demerit goods*.
   b. By combining a progressive tax structure with *transfer payments*, the government attempts to redistribute income from higher to lower income groups. (Although many "loopholes" frustrate such a policy.)

3. In recent years *public choice theory* has been developed to analyze the behavior of voters, regulators, politicians, and government bureaucrats.
   a. There are similarities between decision making in the market sector and in the public sector.
      i. Individuals in both sectors are assumed to act (usually, not always) so as to pursue their own, not society's, self-interest.
      ii. A scarcity constraint exists in both sectors.
      iii. Individuals compete for resources in both sectors.
      iv. Although individuals in each sector face a different incentive structure, people in each sector behave in predictable ways.
   b. There are also dissimilarities between decision making in the market sector and in the public sector.
      i. Government (or political) goods are usually provided at a zero cost to consumers.
      ii. Governments can legally use force to achieve economic objectives.

iii. In the private sector, dollar votes can express proportional intensity of wants; in the public sector the typical majority rule system permits only an all-or-nothing vote preference or arrangement.

4. Governments tax in order to obtain revenues to finance expenditures.
   a. The marginal tax rate is the change in the tax payment divided by the change in income.
   b. The average tax rate equals the total tax payment divided by total income.

5. There are three main types of taxation systems.
   a. Under a *proportional taxation* system, as a person's income rises, the percentage of income paid (rate of taxation) in taxes remains constant.
   b. Under a *progressive taxation* system, as a person's income rises, the percentage of income paid in taxes rises.
   c. Under a *regressive taxation* system, as a person's income rises, the percentage of income paid in taxes falls.

6. A value added tax assesses a tax on the difference between what the firm sells its final product for and the value of the goods that it bought and used to produce the final product.

7. The federal government imposes income taxes on individuals and corporations, and it collects social security taxes and other taxes.
   a. The most important tax in the U.S. economy is the personal income tax; recently some have proposed a consumption tax, which taxes people based on what they actually spend.
   b. The difference between the buying and selling price of an asset, such as a share of stock or a plot of land, is called a capital gain if a profit results, and a capital loss if it doesn't.

8. The corporate income tax is a moderately important source of revenue for the various governments in the U.S. economy.
   a. Corporate stockholders are taxed twice: once on corporate income and again when dividends are received or when the stock is sold.
   b. The incidence of corporate taxes falls on people--consumers, workers, management, and stockholders--not on such inanimate objects as "corporations."

9. An increasing percentage of federal tax receipts is accounted for each year by taxes (other than income) levied on payrolls, such as Social Security taxes and unemployment compensation.

10. In general, there are two distinct types of government expenditures.
    a. Resource-using government expenditures are the purchase by governments of goods and services that divert economic resources from the private sector.
    b. Pure transfers, on the other hand, merely tax one group and extend purchasing power to another, without diverting resources from the private sector.

11. Major sources of revenue for states and local governments are sales and excise taxes.

12. Federal government outlays are made mostly for defense, income security, and Social Security; state and local government expenditures allocate more funds to education than to other categories.

13. Today many nations pursue an industrial policy, which attempts to alter the growth rates of specific sectors within the economy.

KEY TERMS

Antitrust legislation
Monopoly
Subsidy
Expenditures
Merit good
Demerit good
Transfer payment
Collective decision making
Resource-using government expenditures
Value added tax
Consumption tax

KEY CONCEPTS

Spillover or externality
Third parties
Market failure
Principle of mutual exclusivity
Exclusion principle
Private goods
Public goods
Marginal tax rate
Average tax rate
Transfers in kind
Theory of public choice
Majority rule
Proportional rule
Proportional taxation
Progressive taxation
Regressive taxation

COMPLETION QUESTIONS

Fill in the blank or circle the correct term.

1. The five economic functions of federal government in our capitalistic system are ____________________, ____________________, ____________________, ____________________, ____________________.

2. If there are disputes in an economic arena, the ________________ often acts as a "referee" to help settle the dispute.

3. Antitrust legislation, in theory, is supposed to (decrease, promote) competition in the private sector.

4. If externalities are an important result of an economic activity, then the price system is (inefficient, efficient).

5. If Mr. Johnson buys an automobile from General Motors, then those people not directly involved in the transaction are considered ______________.

6. Pollution is an example of a (negative, positive) externality.

7. When there are spillover costs, a price system will (under, over) allocate resources to the production of the good in question.

8. If third parties benefit from a transaction, then (negative, positive) externalities exist, and the price system will allocate resources (inefficiently, efficiently).

9. Positive and negative externalities are examples of market ___________.

10. A government can correct negative externalities by imposing taxes and by _______________ the industry or firms in question.

11. A government can correct positive externalities by _______________, _______________, _______________.

12. If a positive externality exists for good B, a price system will produce too _____________ of good B.

13. Public goods have four distinguishing characteristics. They are usually _______________; they can be used by more people at ___________ additional cost; additional users (do, do not) deprive others of the services of a public good; it is very (easy, difficult) to charge individuals based on how much they used the public good.

14. A free rider has an incentive to (pay, not pay) for a public good.

15. Demerit goods are goods for which society wants to (decrease, increase) production.

16. The public choice model assumes that even though regulators and bureaucrats are (like, unlike) the rest of us, they face a (similar, different) incentive system.

17. The public choice model assumes that politicians, bureaucrats, and regulators pursue (society's, their own) self-interest.

18. Many government, or political, goods are provided to consumers at a (zero, positive) price; but the opportunity cost to society of providing government goods is (zero, positive).

19. If the price of an asset rises after its purchase, the owner receives a _______________ gain; if the price falls, the owner suffers a _______________ loss.

20. The marginal tax rate applies only to the (first, last) tax bracket.

21. The corporate income tax is paid by one or more of the following groups: _______________, _______________, and _______________.

TRUE-FALSE QUESTIONS

Circle the **T** if the statement is true, the **F** if it is false. Explain to yourself why a statement is false.

T F 1. In the U.S. economy the government plays only a minor role in resource allocation, because the country is capitalistic.

T F 2. Governments provide a legal system, but this important function is not considered an economic function.

T F 3. One aim of antitrust legislation is the promotion of competition.

T F 4. If externalities, or spillovers, exist, then a price system misallocates resources, so that inefficiency exists.

T F *5. If a negative externality exists, buyers and sellers are not faced with the true opportunity costs of their actions.

T F 6. If a positive externality exists when good A is produced, a price system will underallocate resources into the production of good A.

T F 7. One way to help correct for a negative externality is to tax the good in question, because that will cause the price of the good to fall.

T F 8. A price system will tend to overallocate resources to the production of free goods, due to the free rider problem.

T F 9. Scarcity exists in the market sector, but not in the public sector.

T F 10. If third parties are hurt by the production of good B and they are not compensated, then too many resources have been allocated to industry B.

T F 11. Deciding what is a merit good and what is a demerit good is easily done and does not require value judgments.

T F 12. The public choice model assumes that regulators and bureaucrats are mostly concerned with the public's--not their own--self-interest.

T F 13. The largest source of receipts for the federal government is the individual income tax.

T F 14. In a progressive tax structure, the average tax rate is greater than the marginal tax rate.

T F 15. Positive economics confirms that a progressive taxation system is more equitable than a regressive taxation system.

T F 16. In the United States the tax system that yields the most revenue to all governments combined is the corporate tax.

T F 17. When corporations are taxed, consumers and corporate employees are also affected.

MULTIPLE CHOICE QUESTIONS
Circle the letter that corresponds to the best answer.

1. Which of the following is not an economic function of government?
   a. income redistribution
   b. providing a legal system
   c. ensuring economywide stability
   d. promoting competition

2. A price system will misallocate resources if
   a. much income inequality exists.
   b. demerit goods are produced.
   c. externalities exist.
   d. All of the above

*3. Which of the following does not belong with others?
   a. positive externality
   b. negative externality
   c. demerit good
   d. public good

4. The exclusion principle
   a. does not work for public goods.
   b. does not work for private goods.
   c. causes positive externalities.
   d. makes it easy to assess user fees on true public goods.

5. Which of the following statements concerning externalities is true?

   a. If a positive externality exists for good A, A will be overproduced by a price system.
   b. If externalities exist, then resources will be allocated efficiently.
   c. Efficiency may be improved if the government taxes goods for which a positive externality exists.
   d. The output of goods for which a positive externality exists is too low, from society's point of view.

6. Which of the following is *not* a characteristic of public goods?
   a. indivisibility
   b. high extra cost to additional users
   c. exclusion principle does not work easily
   d. difficult to determine how each individual benefits from public goods

7. Market failure exists if
   a. Mr. Smith cannot purchase watermelons in his town.
   b. buyers and sellers must pay the true opportunity costs of their actions.
   c. third parties are injured and are not compensated.
   d. the government must provide merit goods.

*8. Which of the following will properly correct a negative externality that results from producing good B?
   a. subsidizing the production of good B
   b. letting the price system determine the price and output of good B
   c. forcing buyers and sellers of good B to pay the true opportunity costs of their actions.
   d. banning the production of good B

9. Merit and demerit goods
   a. are examples of public goods.
   b. are examples of externalities.
   c. indicate market failure.
   d. are not easily classified.

10. Which of the following characterizes collective, but not market, decision making?
   a. the legal use of force
   b. a positive price is charged to users
   c. intensity of wants is easily revealed
   d. proportional rule

11. People who work in the public sector
   a. are more competent than other workers.
   b. are less competent than other workers.
   c. face a different incentive structure than many workers in the private sector.
   d. would behave in the same way if they worked for a small private business.

*12. If the government taxes group A and gives to group B, then economic incentives for
   a. group A may be reduced.
   b. group B may be reduced.
   c. both may change so as to reduce output.
   d. All of the above.

13. If Mr. Ayres loves good A, he can convey the intensity of his wants if good A is
   a. a private good.
   b. a public good.
   c. not subject to the exclusion principle.
   d. expensive.

14. The free rider problem exists
    a. for private goods.
    b. for goods that must be consumed collectively.
    c. only if people can be excluded from consumption.
    d. All of the above

15. In a progressive tax structure,
    a. the marginal tax rate exceeds the average tax rate.
    b. equity exists.
    c. the average tax rate rises as income falls.
    d. All of the above

16. Which of the following statements is true?
    a. Under a regressive tax structure the average tax rate remains constant as income rises.
    b. If upper-income people pay more taxes than lower income people, equity must exist.
    c. The U.S. income tax is slightly progressive.
    d. At very high income levels, the Social Security tax and employee contribution become progressive.

17. The tax incidence of the corporate income tax falls on
    a. corporate stockholders.
    b. corporate employees.
    c. consumers of goods and services produced by corporations.
    d. All of the above

18. Which of the following statements about the Social Security tax is *not* true?
    a. It is a progressive tax.
    b. It came into existence in 1935.
    c. It is imposed on employers and employees.
    d. It is a payroll tax.

19. If Mr. Romano faces a 90 percent marginal tax rate,
    a. the next dollar he earns nets him ninety cents.
    b. his total tax payments equal 90 percent of his total income.
    c. he has a strong incentive to not earn extra money.
    d. his average tax rate must be falling.

*20. A proportional tax system
    a. is unfair.
    b. cannot be consistent with people's ability to pay such taxes.
    c. means that upper income people pay smaller percentages of their income in taxes than do lower income people.
    d. requires upper income people to pay more tax dollars than lower income people pay.

MATCHING

Choose the item in Column (2) that best matches an item in Column (1).

(1)	(2)
a. antitrust legislation	g. pollution
b. spillover	h. externality
c. positive externality	i. national defense
d. negative externality	j. alcohol
e. government good	k. monopoly
f. demerit good	l. flu shots

PROBLEMS

1. Complete the following table for three taxes and then indicate what type of tax each is.

Income	Tax 1		Tax 2		Tax 3	
	Tax paid	Average tax rate	Tax paid	Average tax rate	Tax paid	Average tax rate
$ 1,000	$ 30	______	$ 10	______	$ 100	______
3,000	90	______	60	______	270	______
6,000	180	______	180	______	480	______
10,000	300	______	400	______	700	______
15,000	450	______	750	______	900	______
20,000	600	______	1200	______	1000	______
30,000	900	______	2100	______	1200	______

2. Suppose the above table had a fourth tax as shown below. Find the average and marginal tax rates and explain what type tax it would be.

Income	Tax paid	Average tax rate	Marginal tax rate
$ 1,000	$ 30	______	______
3,000	120	______	______
6,000	300	______	______
10,000	500	______	______
15,000	600	______	______
20,000	700	______	______
30,000	900	______	______

3. One important purely economic function of government is to promote competition, which presumably makes the price system more efficient. During the 1970s the OPEC oil cartel was able to restrict output dramatically, which permitted the cartel to charge much higher prices and earn higher profits. How did consumers, businesses, and other governments react to the higher relative price of oil? Were such actions rational, from the point of view of the individuals involved? Did such decisions lead to a misallocation of resources from *society's* point of view? (Hint: the OPEC price was artificially high because the cartel reduced output and repressed competition.)

4. In the text five economic functions of the government and two political functions were analyzed. Place each of the following governmental activities in one (or more) of these seven categories in the space provided at the far right of each letter.

   a) Providing aid to welfare recipients ________
   b) Passing antitrust laws ________
   c) Subsidizing the arts ________
   d) Prohibiting the sale and possession of drugs ________
   e) Providing national defense ________
   f) Enforcing a progressive tax structure ________
   g) Enforcing contracts ________
   h) Providing public education to children ________
   i) Prosecuting fraud ________
   j) Providing funds for AIDS research ________
   k) Creating jobs to reduce unemployment ________

WORKING WITH GRAPHS

*1. Consider the graph below, then answer the questions. Assume S represents industry supply and S' includes pollution costs to society as well as industry private costs.

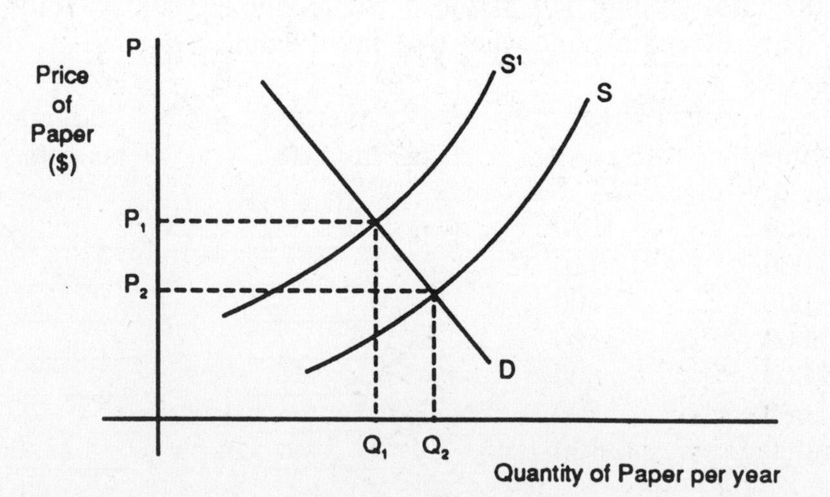

a. If no governmental intervention takes place, what will be the market equilibrium price? The market equilibrium quantity?

b. At the market equilibrium quantity (Q_2), which is higher: private costs or social costs?

c. From *society's* point of view, what is the price that reflects the true opportunity costs of paper? From that same point of view, what is the optimal quantity of paper?

d. Considering your answers in the above three questions, will a price system produce too little, or too much paper.

e. Does a negative externality or a positive externality exist?

*2. Consider the graphs below, then answer the questions that follow. Assume that D represents private market demand and that D' represents benefits that accrue to third parties as well as private benefits.

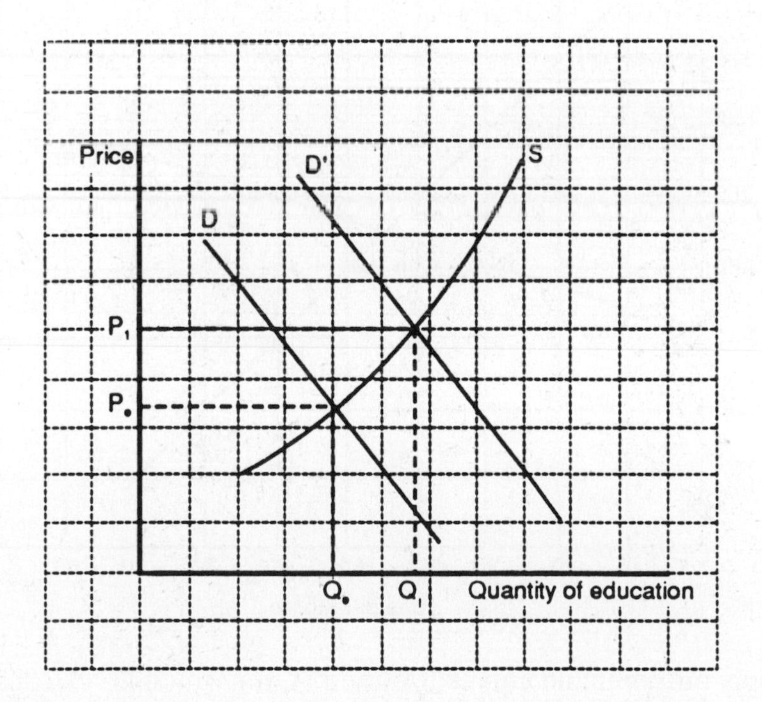

a. If no government intervention occurs, what will be the market equilibrium price? The market equilibrium quantity?

b. At the market equilibrium quantity, which is greater, private benefits or social benefits?

c. From *society's* point of view, what is the optimal price and the optimal quantity of education?

d. In this example, does the price system provide too much, or too little education?

e. Is there a positive externality or a negative externality for this good?

*3. Suppose you know the demand and supply of fertilizer locally, and you have graphed them as shown in the graphs that follows. The fertilizer plant that operates in your town is also producing pollution. This pollution is a constant amount per unit of output (proportional to output) at the plant. If the government decides to try to combat the pollution problem by imposing a $20-per-ton tax on fertilizer produced, show graphically what will happen to the fertilizer market. Will the level of pollution in your town be reduced? If so, by how much? If not, can you offer a solution to the pollution problem?

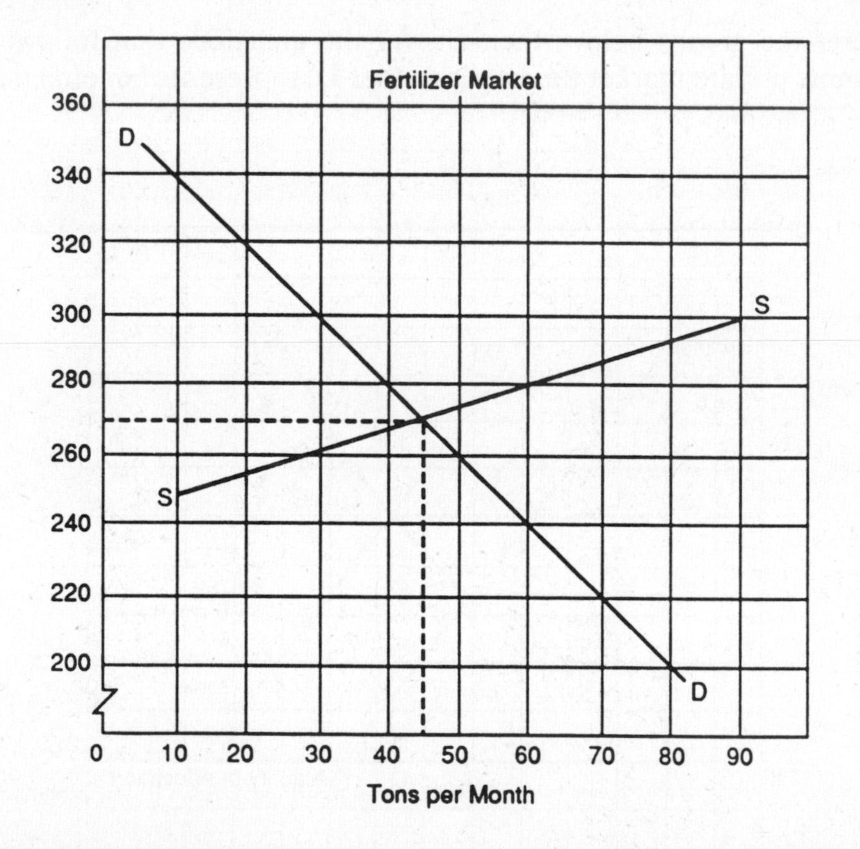

*4. a. Draw supply and demand curves for good A, for which no externalities exist, and indicate the optimal quantity of output, the price that reflects the opportunity cost to buyers and sellers of that good, and whether the price system has over-, or under-, or properly allocated resources into industry A.

b. Draw private supply and demand curves for good B, for which negative externalities exist. Draw another curve on that coordinate system which reflects negative externalities. Indicate the optimal output quantity and price from society's point of view, and compare them to the output quantity and price that would result from a price system.

c. Draw private supply and demand curves for good C, for which positive externalities exist. Draw another curve which reflects the positive externalities associated with good C. Indicate the optimal price and output quantity of good C from society's point of view, and compare them to the output quantity and price that result from the price system.

CASE STUDY

Approximately 6 percent of dairy farmers who own over one-third of the dairy cows obtain about one-third of the benefits of the dairy subsidy program. The largest dairy cooperative receives about $400-500 million in subsidy payments per year. The average American taxpayer pays about $20-$22 of his or her federal income taxes to cover the cost of the dairy subsidy program. Additionally the average household consumer pays between $8 and $25 more per year for milk, because of the artificially high price created by subsidies and restrictions on milk output.

1. According to the public choice model, why do price subsidies for dairy farmers exist?

2. Why don't taxpayers join together to fight milk subsidies?

3. Why don't consumer groups join together to fight milk subsidies?

ANSWERS TO CHAPTER 5

COMPLETION QUESTIONS

1. providing a legal system, promoting competition, correcting externalities, providing public goods, ensuring economywide stability
2. government
3. promote
4. inefficient
5. third parties
6. negative
7. over
8. positive, inefficiently
9. failure
10. regulating
11. subsidizing production, financing production, regulation
12. little
13. indivisible; zero; do not; difficult
14. not pay
15. decrease
16. like, different
17. their own
18. zero; positive
19. capital; capital
20. last
21. stockholders, consumers, employees

TRUE-FALSE QUESTIONS

1. F Even in capitalist countries the government plays a major role.
2. F It is an economic function because by enforcing contracts government can promote trade and commerce.
3. T
4. T
5. T
6. T
7. F A tax will cause the price of the good to *rise*, which is a movement in the correct direction.
8. F The free rider problem deals with goods that are *scarce*, but for which the exclusion principle does not work well.
9. F Scarcity exists in the public sector too; after all, the government uses and allocates scarce goods.
10. T
11. F Whether or not a good is a merit good is very difficult business.
12. F The public choice model assumes that bureaucrats and regulators are just like the rest of us.
13. T

14. F For average taxes to rise with income (a progressive tax) the marginal tax rate must exceed the average tax rate.
15. F "Equitable" requires normative statements.
16. F No, the personal income tax does so.
17. T

MULTIPLE CHOICE QUESTIONS

1.a; 2.c; 3.c; 4.a; 5.d; 6.b; 7.c; 8.c; 9.d; 10.a;
11.c; 12.d; 13.a; 14.b; 15.a; 16.c; 17.d; 18.a; 19.c; 20.d

MATCHING

a and k; b and h; c and l; d and g; e and i; f and j

PROBLEMS

1. Tax 1: 3 percent; 3 percent; 3 percent; 3 percent; 3 percent; 3 percent; 3 percent; proportional

   Tax 2: 1 percent; 2 percent; 3 percent; 4 percent; 5 percent; 6 percent; 7 percent; progressive

   Tax 3: 10 percent; 9 percent; 8 percent; 7 percent; 6 percent; 5 percent; 4 percent; regressive

2. ATR: 3 percent; 4 percent; 5 percent; 5 percent; 4 percent; 3.5 percent; 3 percent

   MTR: 3 percent; 4.5 percent; 6 percent; 5 percent; 2 percent; 2 percent; 2 percent

   The average tax rate for this tax initially rises and then falls, as does the marginal tax rate. As a result, this tax is progressive up to an income of $6,000, proportional from there to $10,000, and regressive for levels of income above $10,000. Thus this tax is a combination of all three types of taxes as income varies. Can you graph the ATR and MTR for this tax? Can you think of any taxes that might behave in this manner?

3. Consumers joined car pools, drove less often, bought smaller cars, and endured less comfortable temperatures at home; businesses invested in the production of such oil substitutes as solar energy, nuclear energy, shale oil, coal, etc.; governments subsidized the production of gasohol and shale oil, etc. Such actions were rational because they were responses to a perceived increase in the relative price of oil and its distillates. From society's point of view, such actions led to a misallocation because the lack of competition caused the price system to transmit an incorrect signal. The signal was that oil had become more scarce--but the signal was induced by an artificial restriction of supply.

4. a. redistribution
   b. promoting competition
   c. providing merit goods
   d. discouraging demerit goods
   e. providing public goods
   f. redistribution
   g. providing legal systems
   h. correcting positive externality
   i. providing legal system
   j. correcting negative externality
   k. stabilizing economy

WORKING WITH GRAPHS

1. a. P_2; Q_2
   b. social costs
   c. P_1; Q_1
   d. too much
   e. negative

2. a. P_e; Q_e
   b. social benefits
   c. P_1; Q_1
   d. too little
   e. positive

3. The supply curve after the tax is imposed shifts to S_1--that is, upward by $20 at each quantity. The equilibrium quantity falls from 45 tons per month to below 40 tons per month as a result. Thus the quantity of fertilizer produced has declined by more than 10 percent. This means that the output of pollution has declined by more than 10 percent, because the output of pollution is a constant per unit of output of fertilizer.

   The result of the analysis should not be extended in a general fashion without regard to other possible effects that a tax of this nature might have. We might also wish to consider other factors before imposing a pollution tax. Among these factors are the effects of the increased price of the fertilizer, the likely reduction in employment as a result of the reduced quantity of fertilizer produced, and the ability of alternative methods of pollution control to achieve the same results.

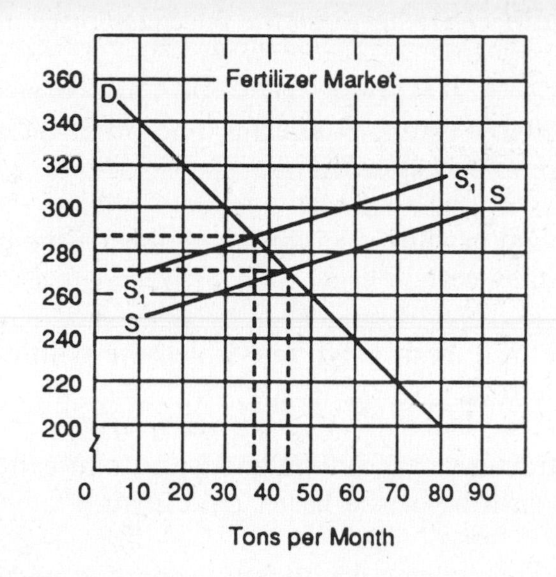

4. a. The market price and the equilibrium quantity are at the socially optimal values because no externalities exist; resources are allocated properly into industry A.
   b. The *new* curve you draw, which reflects a negative externality, should be a supply curve that lies to the left of (above) the original curve, labeled S_1. The optimal price-quantity combination exists where S_1 intersects the demand curve; the socially optimal price is higher than the market price, and the socially optimal quantity is lower than the market quantity.
   c. The new curve should be a demand curve, D', that lies to the right of (above) the original demand curve. The socially optimal price-output combination is where D' intersects the supply curve; price will be higher and output will be higher than the market price-output combination.

CASE STUDY

1. The benefits to such a program can be concentrated to a small number of people, and the costs be allocated to many, each of whom endures a small share.
2. They perceive, rationally, that the opportunity costs of their time outweigh any benefits.
3. Same as (b).

GLOSSARY FOR CHAPTER 5

Antitrust legislation The enactment of laws that restrict the formation of monopolies and that regulate certain anticompetitive business practices.

Average tax rate The total tax payment divided by total income. It is the proportion of total income paid in taxes.

Capital gain The positive difference between the purchase price and the sale price of an asset. If a share of stock is bought for $5 and then sold for $15, the capital gain is $10.

Capital loss The negative difference between the purchase price and the sale price of an asset.

Collective decision making How voters, politicians, and other interested parties act, and how these actions influence nonmarket decisions.

Consumption tax A tax system in which taxes are paid only on the income that individuals actually spend, not on what they earn.

Demerit good The opposite of a merit good; one which the political process has decided is socially undesirable, e.g., heroin.

Exclusion principle A characteristic of public goods; no one can be excluded from the benefits of a public good, even if he or she hasn't paid for it.

Free-rider problem A problem associated with public goods in which individuals presume that others will pay for the public goods, so that, individually, they can escape paying for their portion without a reduction in production occurring.

Government failure Occurs any time government action does not create an economically efficient situation, given the constraints of the real world.

Government, or political, goods Goods (and services) provided by the public sector; they can be either private or public goods.

Incentive structure The system of rewards and punishments facing individuals with respect to their own actions.

Majority rule A collective decision-making system in which group decisions are made on the basis of 50.1 percent of the vote. In other words, whatever more than 50 percent of the population votes for, the entire population has to take.

Marginal tax rate The change in the tax payment divided by the change in income, or the percentage of additional dollars that must be paid in taxes. The marginal tax rate is applied to the last tax bracket of taxable income.

Market failure A situation in which an unfettered market leads to either an under- or overallocation of resources to a specific economic activity. Spillovers, or externalities, are cases of market failure.

Merit good A good that has been deemed socially desirable via the political process, e.g., museums.

Monopoly A firm that has great control over the price of a good. In the extreme case, a monopoly is the only seller of a good or service.

Principle of mutual exclusivity Stated briefly, when I use a private good, my use excludes the possibility of your using it simultaneously. You and I cannot eat the same apple.

Private goods Goods that can only be consumed by one individual at a time. Private goods are subject to the principle of mutual exclusivity.

Progressive taxation A tax system in which, as one earns more income, a higher percentage of the additional dollars is taxed. The marginal tax rate exceeds the average tax rate as income rises.

Proportional rule A decision-making system in which actions are based on the proportion of the "votes" cast and are in proportion to those votes cast. In a market system, if 10 percent of the dollar votes are cast for blue cars, 10 percent of the people get to buy blue cars.

Proportional taxation A tax system in which, as the individual's income goes up, the tax bill goes up in exactly the same proportion. Also called a *flat rate tax*.

Public goods Goods for which the principle of mutual exclusivity does not apply; they can be jointly consumed by many individuals simultaneously at no additional cost and with no reduction in the quality or quantity of the public good.

Regressive taxation A tax system in which, as more dollars are earned, the percentage of tax paid on them falls. The marginal tax rate is less than the average tax rate as income rises.

Resource-using government expenditures Those expenditures by the government that involve the use of land, labor, capital, or entrepreneurship. To be contrasted with pure transfers in which the government taxes one group and pays some of those taxes to another without demanding any services in return.

Spillover, or externality A situation in which a benefit or a cost associated with an economic activity spills over to third parties.

Subsidy Negative tax; payment to producers or consumers of a good or service. For example, farmers often get subsidies for producing wheat, corn, or peanuts.

Tax bracket A specified interval of income to which a specific and unique marginal tax is applied.

Tax incidence The distribution of tax burdens among various groups in society.

Transfer payments Money payments made by governments to individuals for which no services or goods are concurrently rendered. Examples are welfare, Social Security, and unemployment insurance benefits.

Transfers in kind Payments for which no goods or services are rendered concurrently, which are in the form of actual goods and services, such as food stamps, low-cost public housing, and medical care.

User charge system A system of distributing government, or political, goods and services whereby the consumer pays more or less directly for those goods and services by specific taxes according to use or specific fees according to use.

Value added tax (VAT) A tax assessed on the value added by a firm. The value added is the value of the products that firms sell minus the value of the materials that it bought and used to produce those products.

CHAPTER 6

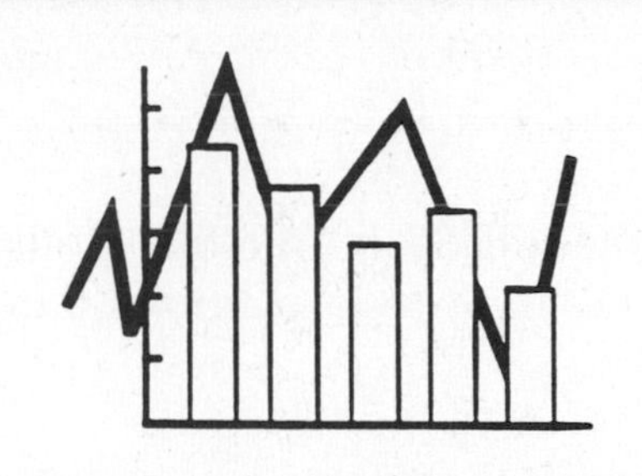

CONVERGING ECONOMIC SYSTEMS

PUTTING THIS CHAPTER INTO PERSPECTIVE

Our concern is with how the different economic systems answer the three fundamental questions facing all societies: *what* to produce, *how*, and *for whom*.

Under market capitalism private property rights to goods and services, including labor, are extended to individuals who make voluntary exchanges as buyers and sellers. Governments enforce such property rights.

The main characteristics of the command socialist economy model analyzed in this chapter are (1) government control over the (large-scale) means of production (capital), (2) central planning to help decide *what* to produce and *how* to produce, and (3) wide-scale governmental redistribution of income to help answer the *for whom* question. You should be aware that even in communist nations very small business enterprises are permitted, that workers have some options concerning where to work, and that individuals can own consumer durable goods.

Despite many years of central planning experience, communist, or command socialist, economies have not lived up to their economic promise; problems still abound in such economies. One major problem is the enormous administrative task involved in planning a modern economy; even sophisticated computers haven't been able to make a dent in the problem. Planners haven't been able to get around the problem of issuing specific orders or rules for production plans; enterprise directors and workers often find it advantageous to follow the letter, rather than the spirit, of the rules. Finally, such economies have an enormous incentive problem; it is not easy to get people to be productive and innovative if they are not rewarded sufficiently. It is not surprising, therefore, that communist economies have collapsed in Russia and in Eastern Europe.

In Chapter 6 we describe the economic systems of Russia, the People's Republic of China, and various other countries.

LEARNING OBJECTIVES

After you have studied this chapter you should be able to

1. define command socialism, communism, market capitalism, property rights, price system, least-cost combination, mixed economy, and privatization.

2. list five characteristics of a command socialism.

3. compare market capitalism with command socialism.

4. describe how market capitalism answers the three fundamental economic questions.

5. recognize the least-cost combination of inputs.

6. recognize the main elements of recent economic reforms in the Russian and Chinese economic systems.

CHAPTER OUTLINE

1. In its theoretical form market capitalism has the following attributes:
   a. Private property rights are enforced by a judicial system.
   b. Prices are set by the forces of supply and demand.
   c. Resources flow to their most profitable use.
   d. Risk-taking in the business sphere, and the costs and benefits to doing so, are undertaken by individuals and not by the state.
   e. "What", "how", and "for whom" are determined by market forces.

2. An alternative form of economic system is command socialism; in its purest form it has the following attributes:
   a. Restricted private property rights exist, with respect to the major factors of production.
   b. Prices are (mostly) set by the state, not by the forces of supply and demand.
   c. The mobility of labor and other resources is severely restricted; a centralized planning authority allocates resources.
   d. "What", "how", and "for whom" are determined by the government.
   e. Economic risk-taking is done by the state, not by individuals.
   f. Taxation is used to redistribute income.

3. Under capitalistic nations the price, or market, system answers the three economic questions.
   a. The forces of supply and demand determine "What, and how much to produce"; market price must be sufficiently high to make a good profitable for producers to produce.
   b. Profit maximization via the price system assures that the "How" question is answered so that the least-cost combination of resources will be used to produce outputs.
   c. Under such a system "For Whom" is answered by the distribution of money income; those with high money incomes get more goods than those with low money incomes.
      i. The quantity, quality, and type of the various human and nonhuman resources that a person owns determines his or her money income.
      ii. A specific good or service is allocated to the highest bidders; hence the market rations each output to specific individuals.

   d. Under capitalism voluntary exchanges in markets take place; as such, resources (inputs) are allocated to businesses, and goods and services (outputs) are allocated to households.

4. Real-world economies are comprised of elements from both pure market capitalism and pure command socialism; they are mixed economies. In the past many predicted that the two economic systems would converge, becoming more like the command socialist economy; the recent collapse of the Soviet Union and Eastern-bloc economic systems has changed this notion. Today it appears that convergence will be toward the mixed economy model that exists in the United States.

5. In the main, the economy of the People's Republic of China has been modeled after the Soviet system. Recently, however, Mainland China's system is becoming closer to the United States' model.
   a. Traditional economic reforms in China consist mainly of transferring economic power from the central government to the local governments.
   b. In 1978, reforms were instituted in the agricultural and foreign economic sectors; state purchase prices of agricultural goods were raised, land leases to peasants were instituted, and private enterprises were encouraged; farm productivity increased dramatically.
   c. Pricc rcforms were not carried out in the state-controlled industrial sector, however, and that sector lagged behind.
   d. In 1984 another reform was instituted: decision-making powers of individual (state-owned) enterprises were extended.

6. Many prople agree that the virtual collapse of the economies of the Communist Bloc in 1989-1990 has settled the question as to whether a command economy can outperform the mixed economies which are predominately market-oriented.

7. Russia and its former satellite countries are now moving from centrally planned economies toward market capitalism via privatization--at least apparently; such a change inevitably causes short-run problems with higher prices and more unemployment.

8. North Korea has had a truly centrally planned economy for over 40 years. It has not been successful economically and in recent years it has been making small moves toward opening its economy for foreign investment.

9. Israel is, and always has been, a highly socialistic country. It has not done well economically and depends on aid from the United States.

10. Sweden has been called a welfare state--a blend of capitalism and socialism. While it has been a successful economy, recent stagnation has led to privatization of a good deal of the economy--with the usual attendant problems during the transition period.

11. While most Latin American countries are classified as capitalistic, in practice the state has had vast control in these economies. Since 1985 many of these countries have experimented with privatization. The most successful seems to be Mexico; Chile and

Argentina also seem to have had some moderate success.

12. Economists maintain that people in different countries behave differently largely because they face different incentive structures.

13. The world has discovered recently that although in theory a command economy is better equipped to solve ecological problems than capitalistic economies are, in practice the Soviet Union was an ecological disaster.

KEY TERMS

Command socialism
Communism
Market capitalism
What, how, for whom

KEY CONCEPTS

Privatization
Least cost combination
Resource allocation
Voluntary exchange

COMPLETION QUESTIONS

Fill in the blank or circle the correct term.

1. Under pure command socialism, economic decisions are made by (a central authority, many individuals); the closer we go to a pure capitalist system, the (less, more) political centralization there is.

2. One of the important features of a socialist economy is that the nonlabor means of production are owned by the ______________; another is that there is an attempt to distribute income (less, more) evenly; because of these factors, economic incentives (are, are not) a problem.

3. The forces that determine relative rewards from production in a socialist state are set by the (market, government).

4. In its purest form, command socialism has the following attributes: ______________, ______________, ______________, ______________, ______________, and ______________.

5. In its purest form, market capitalism has the following attributes: ______________, ______________, ______________, ______________, and ______________.

6. Resource allocation involves answering the three basic questions of ______________, ______________, and ______________ goods and services will be produced.

7. Real world economies are ______________ economies, because they have elements of both ________________ and ________________ economies.

8. Under ______________ individuals have vast, government-protected private property rights.

9. Central planning is important under ________________.

10. Under (planning, a price system) resources will be more likely allocated such that the least-cost combination will be chosen by producers.

*11. Under capitalism specific goods and services are allocated to the (highest bidders, rich).

12. Markets (reduce, increase) transaction costs.

*13. Technological improvements in communication have (reduced, increased) market transactions costs over time.

14. In recent years China has become (less, more) de-centralized; farmers have gained (less, more) control over economic decisions.

15. In 1989-90 command socialism was demonstrated to be an obvious economic (failure, success).

TRUE-FALSE QUESTIONS

Circle the **T** if the statement is true, the **F** if it is false. Explain to yourself why a statement is false.

T F 1. Under command socialism, producers must follow the commands of many individuals, through the market.

T F 2. Under command socialism, all factors of production are owned by the state.

T F 3. In real world socialist economies, no wage rate differentials exist.

T F 4. In command socialist economies, economic risk-taking is undertaken mostly by individual enterprises.

T F 5. In the real world, economies are a mixture of capitalistic and socialistic economies.

T F 6. In China, recent price reforms have been successful in the industrial sector, but reforms have not yet been carried out in the agricultural sector.

T F 7. Privatization is relatively painless for formerly command economies.

T F 8. Although Sweden has been a relatively successful economic system, recent stagnation has led to some privatization.

MULTIPLE CHOICE QUESTIONS
Circle the letter that corresponds to the best answer.

1. In socialist economies,
   a. all factors of production are owned by the state.
   b. no wage differentials exist.
   c. an economic plan is developed by decision makers.
   d. households do not own durable goods.

*2. In recent years the Russian economy is moving toward
   a. less income inequality.
   b. more privatization.
   c. more government control of industry.
   d. dramatic increases in private property rights.

*3. Which of the following is *not* a key attribute of an actual socialist system?
   a. The government owns the major productive resources.
   b. No form of private property exists.
   c. Relative rewards for production are set by the state.
   d. Wage differentials induce production.

4. In the Russian economy recently there have been plans for
   a. restructuring the economy.
   b. reforming the price system.
   c. increasing incentives via more income inequality.
   d. All of the above.

5. Under market capitalism
   a. income inequality is too extreme.
   b. a price system allocates resources.
   c. central planning plays a huge role.
   d. what to produce is determined, in theory, by the government.

6. As of the early 1990s, Russian economic reforms have
   a. been extremely successful.
   b. not been particularly successful.
   c. transformed the Soviet economy into market capitalism.
   d. None of the above

7. In recent years privatization is becoming important in
   a. Russia.
   b. Sweden.
   c. Mexico.
   d. All of the above

MATCHING

Choose the item in column (2) that best matches an item in column (1).

(1)	(2)
a. market capitalism	f. transfer property rights from government to private sector
b. command socialism	g. fundamental economic questions
c. privatization	h. governmental resource allocation
d. what, how, for whom	i. voluntary exchange
e. least cost combination	j. efficient resource allocation

PROBLEMS

*1. Under a pure capitalistic system, consumer sovereignty helps to answer *what*, *how* and *for whom*.
   a. Explain how *for whom* is affected if *what* changes, for example if tastes change in favor of tiddlywink matches and away from professional football.
   b. Explain how *for whom* is affected if *how* changes because unions increase wage rates relative to other factors of production.
   c. Explain how a change in *for whom* (taxing some and giving to others) might change *what* to produce.

*2. Assume that, given its resource base, an economy is able to produce output combinations A, B, C, and D. Society values combination A at $10,000, combination B at $20,000, combination C at $30,000, and combination D at $15,000.
   a. What is the opportunity cost of producing combination A?
   b. What is the opportunity cost of producing combination B?
   c. What is the opportunity cost of producing combination C?
   d. What is the opportunity cost of producing combination D.
   e. If the community wanted to maximize the value of its output, given its resource base, which combination should it produce?
   f. If the community wanted to minimize the opportunity cost of its output, which combination would it choose?

CASE STUDY

How should developed countries help the Communist Bloc countries which have renounced the command economy system in favor of a more capitalistic, market-oriented, approach? Answers from different ends of the political spectrum will, of course, differ. Free market economists are in agreement that aid in the form of financial gifts and bailouts should be minimal and short-lived. Instead, they believe that those countries can achieve increased living standards in the long run only if they protect private property rights and permit foreign investments. Consumers in advanced nations can also receive benefits if they open their markets (i.e., reduce trade barriers) to the changing nations. "Trade, not aid" would seem to them to be a better permanent solution.

1. How can those economies produce goods and services that advanced countries will buy if their economies are devastated?

2. How will consumers in advanced economies benefit by opening their markets to ex-communist countries? Will everyone in advanced economies benefit?

ANSWERS TO CHAPTER 6

COMPLETION QUESTIONS

1. a central authority; less
2. state; more; are
3. government
4. restricted private property rights, prices mostly set by the state, restricted mobility of resources, what, how, and for whom answered by government, economic risk-taking assumed by the state, taxation used to redistribute income
5. private property rights, prices set by supply and demand, resources flow to most profitable use, risk-taking assumed by individuals, what, how, and for whom determined by market forces
6. what, how, for whom
7. mixed, market, planned
8. market capitalism
9. command socialism
10. a price system
11. highest bidders
12. reduce
13. reduced
14. more, more
15. failure

TRUE-FALSE QUESTIONS

1. F Commands are set by a centralized government.
2. F Labor is not completely owned by the state.
3. F They exist, and in some cases are quite large.
4. F It is assumed by the state.
5. T
6. F Just the opposite is the case.
7. F Prices and unemployment typically rise in the short run.
8. T

MULTIPLE CHOICE QUESTIONS

1.c; 2.b; 3.b; 4.d; 5.b; 6.b; 7.d

MATCHING

a and i; b and h; c and f; d and g; e and j

PROBLEMS

1. a. The incomes of football players will fall; incomes of those people who are dexterous and have the skills required of tiddlywinks competition will rise. Thus a change in

tastes (*what*) redistributes income from one group to another, and so *for whom* changes.

b. If wage rates rise relative to the price of capital and land, then producers will increase their demand for nonlabor resources; nonlabor resources will be substituted for labor. Income will be redistributed from some newly laid-off laborers to people who own property or are skillful at designing and producing capital. Thus a change in *how* leads to changes in *for whom*.

c. To the extent that people with low incomes have tastes different than people with high incomes, then *what* is produced will be affected.

2. a. $30,000 c. $20,000 e. C
 b. $30,000 d. $30,000 f. C

CASE STUDY

1. All economies (and all individuals) have a comparative advantage in producing something; also, if they permit multi-national companies to invest in their countries they will be able to export saleable goods.
2. Consumers will pay lower prices for imported goods and services; hence their living standards will rise. However, those businesses and laborers that are replaced by imported goods will be harmed--at least in the short run.

GLOSSARY TO CHAPTER 6

Command socialism An economy in which there is virtually no private property, such that the state owns virtually all the factors of production. Decisions about what and how much, by whom, and for whom are decided by command from a central authority.

Communism A theoretical economic political system as outlined by Karl Marx in which the state withers away and we observe "from each according to his ability, to each according to his need."

Least-cost combination The combination of input use that produces a given level of output at minimum cost.

Market An abstract concept concerning all of the arrangements that individuals have for exchanging with one another. Thus, we can speak of the labor market, the automobile market, and the credit market.

Market system A system in which individuals own the factors of production and decide individually how to use them; a system with completely decentralized economic decision making.

Mixed system An economic system in which the decision about how resources should be used is made partly by the private sector and partly by the government or public sector.

Price system An economic system in which (relative) prices are constantly changing to reflect changes in supply and demand for different commodities. The prices of those commodities are signals to everyone within the system about what is relatively scarce and what is relatively abundant.

Property rights The right of an owner to use and to exchange property.

Resource allocation The assignment of resources to specific uses. More specifically, it means determining what will be produced, how it will be produced, and for whom it will be produced.

Resources Inputs used to produce goods and services. (Also called factors of production).

Scarcity A situation in which the necessary ingredients for producing those things that people desire are insufficient to satisfy all wants.

Services Things purchased by consumers that do not have physical characteristics. Examples of services are those purchased from doctors, lawyers, dentists, repair personnel, and so on.

Socialism An economic system in which the state owns the major share of productive resources except labor. Also, socialism usually involves the redistribution of income.

Technology Society's pool of applied knowledge concerning how goods and services can be produced.

Terms of exchange The terms under which the trading takes place. Usually the terms of exchange are given by the price at which a good is traded.

Transactions costs All of the costs associated with exchanging, including the informational costs of finding out price and quality, service record, durability, etc., of a product, plus the cost of contracting and enforcing that contract.

Voluntary Exchange The act of trading, usually done on a voluntary basis, in which both parties to the trade are subjectively better off after the exchange.

CHAPTER 19

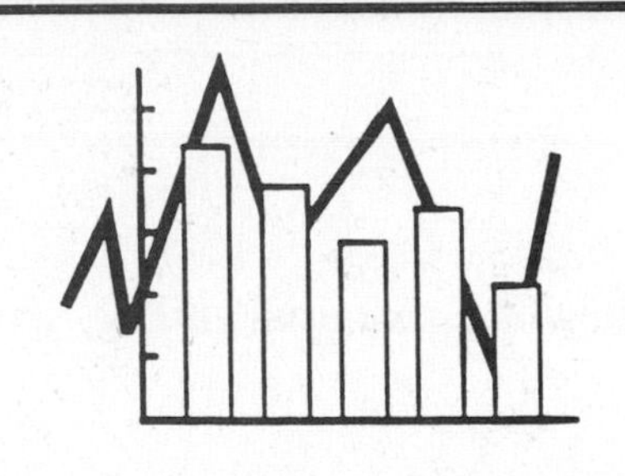

CONSUMER CHOICE

PUTTING THIS CHAPTER INTO PERSPECTIVE

Chapter 19 analyzes consumer choice. The body of this chapter is concerned with the traditional, or classical, theory of consumer behavior, which is referred to as utility analysis. In the appendix to this chapter (which is analyzed separately immediately following this section), the more modern approach to the study of consumer behavior--indifference curve analysis--is presented.

Your understanding of Chapter 19 and its appendix will be aided immeasurably by your learning to distinguish between an ordinal measure and a cardinal measure. (See footnote 1, Chapter 8, in the text.) In this chapter we deal with utility as something that can be measured cardinally. The analysis in the appendix, however, requires only that utility be measured ordinally--a less stringent, and therefore more analytically powerful, requirement.

You are also well-advised to study carefully the distinction between total utility and marginal utility--and how they are related. As long as marginal utility is positive, total utility will rise; if marginal utility is rising, total utility will rise at an *increasing* rate; if marginal utility is constant, total utility will rise at a constant rate (the total utility curve would be linear); if marginal utility falls, then total utility will rise at a *decreasing* rate. Memorize, and then learn, how "marginal" and "total" are related now, because we shall return to these concepts often.

Equally important is the relationship between marginal utility and average utility (or "average" and "marginal" anything); marginal pulls and tugs average. Thus, if marginal is above average, then average will rise; if marginal is below average, then average will fall; if marginal equals average, then average will remain constant. The relationship between marginal and average is also a recurring thread in this text; learn it now, once and for all.

Another important (and recurring) topic is the concept "marginal utility per dollar's worth," which in equation form is MU/P, or marginal utility divided by price. Play around with this ratio; convince yourself that given MU, changes in price lead to changes in marginal utility per dollar's worth of a good. Also, learn exactly what the inequality $MU_1/P_1 > MU_2/P_2$, and *exactly* what the inequality $MU_1/P_1 < MU_2/P_2$ means, and learn what such an inequality implies about consumer optimization behavior.

Time spent now on the concepts stressed here will pay handsome dividends in the future. If you really master these concepts, then the more difficult analysis that lies ahead in later chapters will be much easier.

LEARNING OBJECTIVES

After you have studied this chapter you should be able to

1. define utility, util, marginal utility, marginal analysis, diminishing marginal utility, and consumer optimum.

2. distinguish between total utility and marginal utility, and answer questions that require an understanding of how they are related.

3. distinguish between marginal utility and average utility, and answer questions that require an understanding of how they are related.

4. apply the concept of diminishing marginal utility to the law of demand.

5. predict what happens to the marginal utility per dollar's worth of a good when (a) its price changes, other things being constant and (b) more or less is consumed, other things being constant.

6. predict what a consumer will do if the marginal utility per dollar's worth of good A is greater (less) than the marginal utility per dollar's worth of good B.

7. predict how a change in price generates an income effect, and a substitution effect.

8. answer questions that require an understanding of how economists can explain the diamond-water paradox.

CHAPTER OUTLINE

1. *Utility analysis* is the study of consumer decision making based on utility maximization.
   a. A *util* is an artificial unit by which *utility* is measured.
   b. *Total utility* is the sum of all the utils derived from consumption; *marginal utility* is the change in total utility due to a one-unit change in the quantity of a good consumed.
   c. Economists maintain that economic decisions are made by comparing the marginal benefit of an activity with its marginal cost.
   d. When relative price changes, it is the *marginal* buyers who respond, not the average buyers.
   e. As long as marginal utility is positive, total utility will rise.
   f. If marginal utility becomes negative--the good becomes a nuisance--total utility will fall.

2. The principle of *diminishing marginal utility* states that as more of any good or service is consumed, eventually its extra benefit declines.

3. Consumers are assumed to optimize their consumption choices; the consumer attempts to maximize total utility subject to such constraints as income and relative prices.

4. When relative price changes, the *consumer optimum* is affected and the consumer reacts consistently and predictably.
   a. A consumer is optimizing when she allocates all of her money income in such a way that the marginal utility per dollar's worth of goods and services purchased is equated.
   b. If the relative price of a good falls, consumers will substitute it for the now relatively more expensive substitutes.
   c. If the price of a good falls, given money income and given the prices of all other goods, a consumer's real income rises and she normally will purchase more of that good whose price has fallen.

5. The "law" of diminishing marginal utility can account for the law of demand; because the marginal benefit falls to consumers as they consume more per unit of time, price must fall to induce them to purchase more.

6. The *diamond-water paradox* is that diamonds are unessential to life and have a high relative price, while water is essential to life yet has a low relative price.
   a. The total utility of water to humans far exceeds the total utility of diamonds to humans; but the *marginal utility* of water is relatively low and the marginal utility of diamonds is high.
   b. The price of a good, therefore, reflects its value on the margin--not its total or average value.

KEY TERMS

Utility
Util
Marginal utility
Total utility

KEY CONCEPTS

Utility analysis
Marginal analysis
Diminishing marginal utility
Diamond-water paradox
Substitution effect
Income effect
Consumer optimum
Rule of equal marginal utility per dollar spent
Marginal utility per dollar's worth

COMPLETION QUESTIONS

Fill in the blank or circle the correct term.

1. The want-satisfying power that a good or service possesses is referred to as __________________.

2. The ________________ is an artificial unit by which utility is measured.

3. The change in total utility due to a one-unit change in quantity consumed is called _________________; ________________ analysis is the study of what happens when small changes take place relative to the status quo.

4. When relative price changes, the (average, marginal) buyer responds; economists maintain that (average, marginal) analysis is the key to understanding human behavior.

5. If marginal utility is positive, total utility must (fall, rise); if marginal utility is negative, total utility must______; if marginal utility falls (but is positive) then total utility must (fall, rise) at a decreasing rate.

6. Economists maintain that as more of a good or service is consumed, per unit of time, its marginal benefit (falls, rises); therefore before buyers will purchase more and more of a good, its price must (fall, rise).

7. The consumer optimum exists when consumers__________ their total utility, subject to such constraints as ______________ and relative price; in order to optimize, a consumer should allocate his income so that the marginal utility per dollar's worth of each good or service he purchases is ____________.

8. Assume a consumer is in consumer optimum and then the price of good A rises, other things being constant. It is now true that the marginal utility per dollar's worth of good A is (less, greater) than the marginal utility per dollar's worth of other goods; the consumer will now feel (richer, poorer) and probably spend (more, less) on good A; furthermore, the consumer will tend to substitute (A for other goods, other goods for A).

9. Although the (marginal, total) utility of water is greater than that of diamonds, the (marginal, total) utility of diamonds is higher; the price of a good reflects its (marginal, average, total) utility.

TRUE-FALSE QUESTIONS

Circle the **T** if the statement is true, the **F** if it is false. Explain to yourself why a statement is false.

T F *1. Economists today maintain that utility can be measured cardinally.

T F 2. Economists maintain that decisions are made on the margin; hence the concept of "margin" is usually more important than that of "average."

T F *3. Positive economics permits economists to say that person 1 gets more utility from ice cream than does person 2.

T F 4. If total utility rises at a decreasing rate, then marginal utility must be falling.

T F 5. If marginal utility is less than average utility, then average utility must rise.

T F 6. Economists typically assume that as a person consumes more of any good, that good's total utility must fall.

T F 7. If the MU of good X/price of good X exceeds the MU of good Y/price of good Y, the consumer can increase her total utility by substituting good X for good Y.

T F 8. The law of diminishing marginal utility implies the law of demand, assuming consumers wish to optimize.

T F 9. When the price of hamburgers falls, other things constant, everyone's real income will rise.

T F 10. When the price of butter falls, other things constant, people will tend to substitute butter for margarine.

T F 11. Because price reflects average utility rather than total utility, diamonds are more expensive than water.

MULTIPLE CHOICE QUESTIONS

Circle the letter that corresponds to the best answer.

1. If marginal utility is positive, but falling, then total utility
   a. falls.
   b. falls at a decreasing rate.
   c. rises.
   d. rises at a decreasing rate.

*2. Which of the following words is most unlike the others?
   a. marginal
   b. average
   c. incremental
   d. extra

3. When the relative price of good A rises, the
   a. average buyer is affected.
   b. marginal buyer is affected.
   c. total buyer is affected.
   d. marginal utility of good A falls.

4. As more of good A is consumed per week, over broad ranges
   a. the marginal utility of good A falls.
   b. the total utility of good A rises.
   c. the total utility of good A rises at a decreasing rate.
   d. All of the above

5. If marginal utility is negative, then
   a. total utility falls.
   b. total utility rises at a decreasing rate.
   c. total utility must be negative.
   d. None of the above.

6. Which of the following helps to explain the law of demand?
   a. the law of diminishing marginal utility
   b. the substitution effect
   c. the income effect
   d. All of the above

7. Consumer optimizing requires that the consumer
   a. maximize income.
   b. maximize total utility, subject to an income constraint.
   c. maximize marginal utility, subject to an income constraint.
   d. maximize average utility, subject to an income constraint.

8. If the marginal utility per dollar's worth of good A exceeds that of good B for Mr. Capra, then he
   a. is optimizing.
   b. will substitute good A for good B.
   c. will substitute good B for good A.
   d. is minimizing, not maximizing.

9. If the price of good A rises, other things being constant, then
   a. the marginal utility of good A falls.
   b. the marginal utility of good A rises.
   c. the marginal utility per dollar's worth of good A falls.
   d. the relative price of good A falls.

10. If the price of steak rises, other things constant,
    a. everyone's real income will rise.
    b. everyone's money income will rise.
    c. the real income of steak buyers will rise.
    d. the real income of steak buyers will fall.

11. If the price of steak rises, other things constant,
    a. a real income effect will induce people to purchase less steak.
    b. people will substitute hamburgers for steak.
    c. the quantity demanded for steak will fall.
    d. All of the above

12. Diamonds have a higher price than water because
    a. people are shallow and shortsighted.
    b. price reflects total, not marginal, utility.
    c. price reflects marginal, not total, utility.
    d. the total utility of diamonds is greater, but the marginal utility of water is greater.

WORKING WITH GRAPHS

1. Use the information given below to complete the table.

Hamburgers consumed per month	Total utility (in utils)	Marginal utility (in utils)
0	0	______
1	5	______
2	14	______
3	22	______
4	28	______
5	33	______
6	36	______
7	35	______
8	32	______

a) Fill in the marginal utility column in the above chart.

b) Graph the total and marginal utility curves on the graph provided below. (Plot the marginal utilities at the midpoint between quantities.)

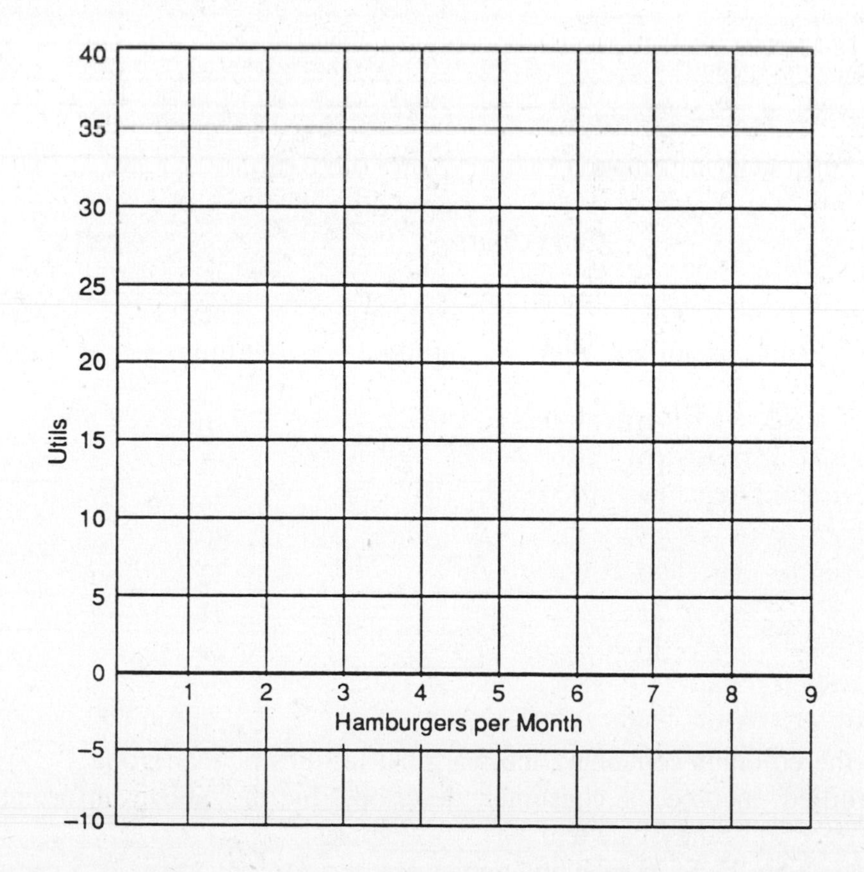

c) At what quantity does diminishing marginal utility set in?

2. Consider the graphs below; then answer the questions that follow.

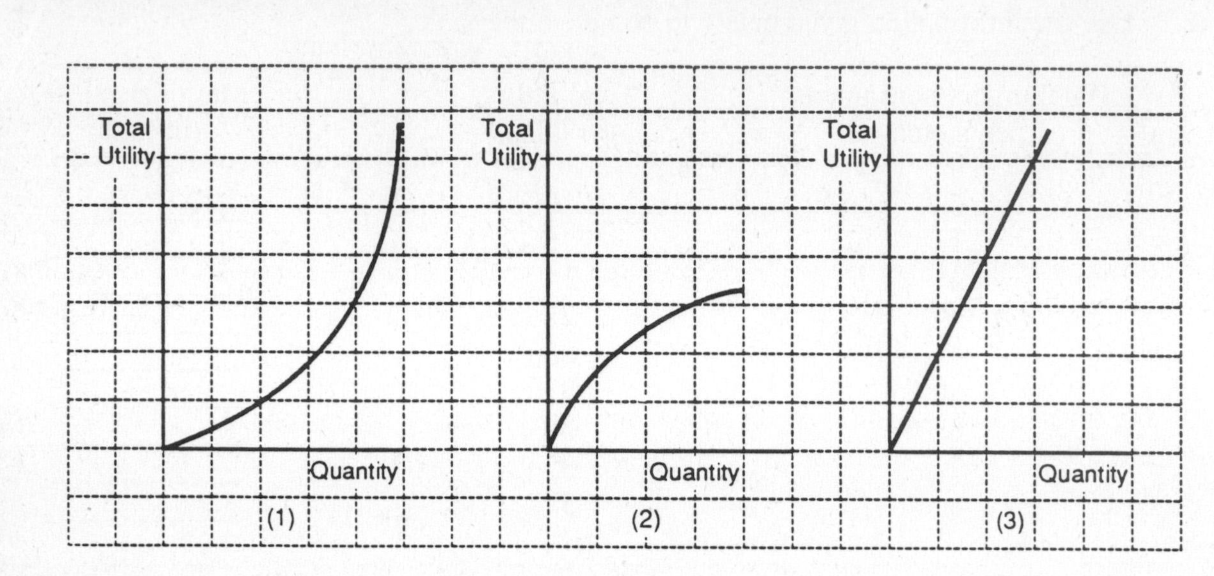

a. Which panel indicates constant marginal utility?
b. Which panel indicates increasing marginal utility?
c. Which panel indicated decreasing marginal utility?

PROBLEMS

*1. Consider the following information.

Quantity Consumed per week	Candy Bars: Total utility	Candy Bars: Marginal utility	Apples: Total utility	Apples: Marginal utility
0	0	______	0	______
1	10	______	15	______
2	18	______	24	______
3	25	______	30	______
4	29	______	32	______
5	31	______	31	______
6	30	______	29	______

a. Complete the columns containing the marginal utilities of each good.
b. With unlimited income, a consumer described by the above information would consume________ candy bars and ________ apples.
c. If candy bars cost 25 cents each and apples are two for a quarter (12.5 cents each) and the consumer has $1.50 to spend on candy and apples, what quantity of candy bars and apples will put the above consumer into an equilibrium situation?

d. Now suppose the consumer suffers a loss of income and has 20 cents to spend. In addition, the price of candy bars is now 10 cents and the price of apples is 2 cents. What quantities of each will put the consumer in equilibrium?

2. Mr. Smith does not believe that economists are correct when they say that diminishing marginal utility is the rule for most goods. He claims that *increasing* marginal utility is the rule: as he consumes more and more of any good, his marginal utility rises.

   Assume that Mr. Smith spends his income one dollar at a time, and that he can purchase one dollar's worth of any good. Assume further that he wishes to maximize his total utility.

   On what good does Mr. Smith spend his first dollar? The second? The third? What predictions can you make about his behavior? Do most people behave that way? Does anyone?

3. Conduct the same analysis that you did in question (2) above for Mrs. Smith, who claims that for her *constant* marginal utility is the rule.
   a. How do your answers differ from those in question (2)?
   b. Can you think of *anything* for which diminishing marginal utility does not occur eventually, *per unit of time*?

ANSWERS TO CHAPTER 19

COMPLETION QUESTIONS

1. utility
2. util
3. marginal utility; marginal
4. marginal; marginal
5. rise; fall; rise
   falls; fall
6. 6
7. maximize, income; equal
8. less; poorer, less; other goods for A
9. total, marginal; marginal

TRUE-FALSE QUESTIONS

1. F They need only to assume that it can be measured ordinally.
2. T
3. F Interpersonal utility comparisons require normative judgments.
4. T
5. F If marginal is less than average, average will fall
6. F They assume that its *marginal utility* falls.
7. T
8. T
9. F Only hamburgers buyers will experience an increase in real income.
10. T
11. F Price reflects marginal utility.

MULTIPLE CHOICE QUESTIONS

1.d; 2.b; 3.b; 4.d; 5.a; 6.d; 7.b; 8.b; 9.c; 10.d;
11.d; 12.c

WORKING WITH GRAPHS

1. a. 0; 5; 9; 8; 6; 5; 3; 1; -3

   b.

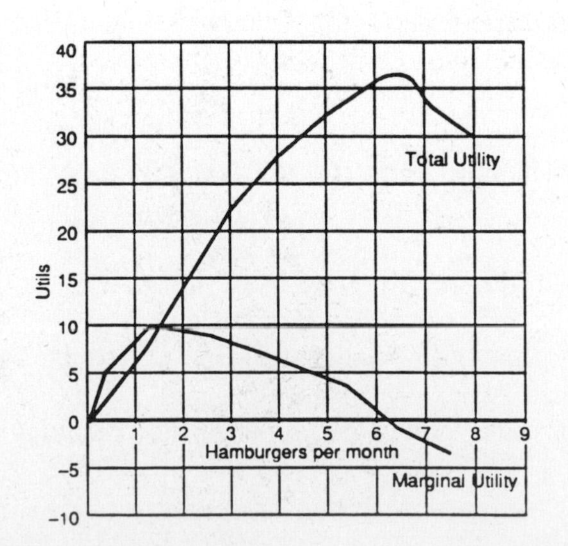

   c. with the third hamburger consumed each month

b. with the third hamburger consumed each month

2. a. 3
   b. 1
   c. 2

PROBLEMS

1. a. marginal utility of candy bars: 0, 10, 8, 7, 4, 2, -1; marginal utility of apples: 0, 15, 9, 6, 2, -1, -2
   b. 5, 4
   c. 4 candy bars and 4 apples
   d. 1 candy bar and 4 apples. Note that the consumer has 2 cents left over, cannot purchase another candy bar, and will not purchase another apple, since the additional apple has a negative marginal utility (total utility declines).

2. Mr. Smith will spend every dollar of his income on the same good--that which gives him the highest marginal utility per dollar's worth of his first dollar spent. Only drug addicts, perhaps, behave that way.

3. a. The answers are the same as in (2) above.
   b. Given the qualifications in the question, its difficult to think of any good for which that is not the case.

GLOSSARY TO CHAPTER 19

Consumer optimum A choice of a set of goods and services that maximizes the level of satisfaction for each consumer, subject to limited income.

Diminishing marginal utility The principle stating that as more of any good or service is consumed, its extra benefit declines. Otherwise stated, there are smaller and smaller increases in total utility from the consumption of a good or service as more is consumed during a given time period.

Marginal utility The change in total utility due to a one-unit change in the quantity of a good consumed.

Util Representative unit by which utility is measured.

Utility The want-satisfying power that a good or service possesses.

Utility analysis The analysis of consumer decision making based on utility maximization.

APPENDIX E

MORE ADVANCED CONSUMER CHOICE THEORY

In Appendix E the more modern, but more difficult, theory of consumer demand is analyzed. Here we assume that utility *cannot* be measured cardinally; instead it can be measured only ordinally. In other words, people can only rank one combination of goods and services as being more preferable to, less preferable to, or equally preferable to another combination of goods. Another way to think of this is to realize that 30 utils is preferable to 15 utils, but 30 utils are not necessarily *twice* as preferable as 15 utils (as would be the case if utility were cardinally measurable).

In this appendix we introduce the indifference curve, explore its properties, and develop an indifference map. Then a budget line is constructed, and its properties are explored. By graphing an indifference map and a budget line, a more sophisticated analysis of the consumer optimum position is possible.

Then we turn to some of the fun topics. We show what happens to consumer optimum when income, and then price, changes; next we derive a price-consumption line; finally we derive a demand curve using the indifference curve-budget line model.

LEARNING OBJECTIVES

After you have studied Appendix E you should be able to

1. define indifference curve, budget constraint, income consumption curve, normal good, inferior good, and price consumption curve.

2. draw an indifference curve based on data presented in a table.

3. answer questions that require a proper interpretation of an indifference curve and of an indifference map.

4. recognize properties of indifference curves.

5. interpret the meaning of the slope of an indifference curve and the slope of a budget line.

6. recognize the consumer optimum combination of goods, given an indifference map and a budget line.

7. interpret and sketch an income consumption curve and a price consumption curve.

8. predict what happens to a budget line when each price changes and when income changes.

Appendix E OUTLINE

1. This appendix presents a more rigorous and more formal analysis of consumer behavior.
   a. An *indifference curve* is the set of consumption alternatives which yield the same total amount of satisfaction.
   b. Indifference curves have important properties.
      i. Indifference curves are negatively sloped.
      ii. Indifference curves are never linear; they are convex with respect to the origin.
   c. The slope of an indifference curve is referred to as the *marginal rate of substitution*, which is the change in the quantity of one good that just offsets a one-unit change in the consumption of another good, so that total satisfaction remains constant.

2. An *indifference map* is a set of indifference curves; higher indifference curves represent higher levels of satisfaction (because they permit more consumption of *both goods*), and lower indifference curves represent less preferred combinations of goods.

3. A *budget constraint* represents the set of opportunities facing a decision maker.
   a. The budget line is derived assuming a fixed money income and a given set of relative prices.
   b. The slope of a budget line is (the negative of) the ratio of the prices of the relevant goods.
   c. The position of a budget line depends on the level of nominal income; if nominal income changes, a parallel shift in the budget line results.

4. *Consumer optimum* exists at that point (combination of goods and services) where the slope of the indifference curve equals the slope of the budget line; at that point the consumer is maximizing utility.

5. If nominal and relative prices are held constant and *income is increased*, an income consumption curve can be derived.

6. A *normal good* is one for which the quantity demanded increases as income increases; an *inferior good* is one for which the quantity demanded decreases as income increases.

7. A *price consumption curve* is the set of consumer optimum combinations of two goods that results when the price of one good changes, holding money income and the price of the other good constant.

8. A demand curve can be derived from the indifference map-budget line model; as the price of one good changes, other things being constant (the price of the other good and money income), consumer optimum changes so as to indicate an inverse relationship between price and quantity demanded.

9. Even if people had identical preferences for good weather vs. bad weather, wages would be higher in bad weather areas (other things being constant). Because people do have different preferences for good weather over bad weather, such wage differences will be magnified.

KEY TERMS

Income consumption curve
Price consumption curve
Budget Line
Normal good
Inferior good

KEY CONCEPTS

Indifference curve
Indifference map
Marginal rate of substitution
Budget constraint
Consumer optimum

COMPLETION QUESTIONS

Fill in the blank or circle the correct term.

1. A curve that indicates combinations of goods and services that yield an equal level of satisfaction is called a(n) ________________ curve; such a curve is (positively, negatively) sloped.

2. Ignoring its sign, the slope of an indifference curve (falls, rises) as we move down the curve; a set of indifference curves is called an indifference ____________.

3. If indifference curve B lies below indifference curve A, it is (less, more) preferred; if indifference curve C lies above indifference curve A, indifference curve C permits a consumer to consume (less, more) of both goods.

4. A budget constraint line is derived holding relative _____________ constant and holding nominal _______________ constant; the slope of a budget constraint line is determined by _________________, and the position of such a line depends on _____________________.

5. Consumer optimum exists where the budget constraint line is _____________ to a(n) ____________________ curve; at such a point the (lowest, highest) indifference curve is achieved.

6. If income falls, other things being constant, the budget line ________________; if a good is normal, then a reduction in income will lead to a(n) (decrease, increase) in its quantity demanded; if a decrease in income leads to an increase in the quantity demanded of good A, then good A is a(n) _____________ good.

7. If the price of one good changes, the slope of an indifference curve (remains constant, changes); if the price of one good changes, the slope of a budget constraint line (remains constant, changes); if nominal income changes, the slope of a budget constraint line (remains constant, changes).

8. Along a price consumption curve which relates the combinations of good A and good B that a consumer will purchase, the price of good A falls while the price of good B (rises, falls, remains constant) and nominal income (rises, falls, remains constant).

9. If people have identical preferences for good weather over bad weather, wages in bad-weather areas will be (lower, higher) than wages in good-weather areas; if some strongly prefer good weather, while others are largely indifferent, then wage differentials in good vs. bad weather areas will be (smaller, larger).

TRUE-FALSE QUESTIONS

Circle the **T** if the statement is true, the **F** if it is false. Explain to yourself why a statement is false.

T F 1. Along an indifference curve, a consumer has the same level of marginal utility.

T F 2. Indifference curves are negatively sloped.

T F 3. Indifference curves are usually linear.

T F 4. The slope of the budget constraint curve is referred to as the marginal rate of substitution.

T F 5. Points below a budget constraint line are not attainable goods combination for a consumer.

T F 6. If indifference curve 3 lies above indifference curve 2, it is less preferable to the consumer.

T F 7. Indifference curves that lie entirely above a budget constraint line are unattainable for the consumer.

T F 8. If nominal income changes, then the slope of an indifference curve changes.

T F 9. If nominal income changes, then the slope of a budget constraint line changes.

T F 10. If relative prices change, then the slope of a budget constraint line changes, but the slope of an indifference curve is unaltered.

T F 11. Consumer optimum is attained where the budget constraint line is tangent to an indifference curve.

T F 12. If income falls and the quantity demanded for good A rises, then good A is an inferior good.

T F 13. Along an income consumption curve, prices remain constant.

T F 14. Along a price consumption curve, relative prices change, but money income is constant.

MULTIPLE CHOICE QUESTIONS

Circle the letter that corresponds to the best answer.

1. Along an indifference curve,
   a. total utility stays the same.
   b. marginal utility stays the same.
   c. average utility stays the same.
   d. All of the above

2. In indifference curve analysis, if combination A is preferred to combination B and combination B is preferred to combination C, then
   a. A is on a higher indifference curve than B or C.
   b. C is on a lower indifference curve than A or B.
   c. A, B, and C are on different indifference curves.
   d. All of the above

3. Indifference curves
   a. are upward sloping.
   b. are linear.
   c. are convex with respect to the origin.
   d. indicate objective, not subjective, valuations of a consumer.

4. As we move down an indifference curve, the marginal rate of substitution
   a. remains constant.
   b. remains constant, but total utility rises.
   c. changes.
   d. changes, but total utility rises.

5. The negative of the slope of a(n) _________ is the marginal rate of substitution.
   a. production possibilities curve
   b. budget constraint line
   c. income consumption curve
   d. indifference curve

6. Where consumer optimum is reached,
   a. the slope of the budget constraint line equals the slope of an indifference curve.
   b. the ratio of relative prices equals the marginal rate of substitution.
   c. the consumer attains the highest indifference curve, given the budget constraint line.
   d. All of the above

7. The slope of the budget constraint line
   a. reflects the relative prices of the two goods in question.
   b. reflects the consumer's income.
   c. varies as nominal income varies.
   d. always equals the slope of the indifference curve.

8. If income rises, other things being constant, then
   a. an indifference curve shifts outward.
   b. a parallel, rightward shift in the budget constraint line occurs.
   c. the slope of the budget constraint line falls.
   d. the slope of the budget constraint line rises.

9. Which of the following is least like the others?
   a. normal good
   b. inferior good
   c. free good
   d. economic good

10. When a price consumption curve is derived,
    a. the relative price of both goods changes.
    b. the relative price of only one good changes.
    c. money income changes.
    d. consumer optimum is not attained.

11. When an income consumption curve is derived,
    a. relative prices remain constant.
    b. income changes.
    c. consumer optimum exists at each point along such a curve.
    d. All of the above

12. When the price of good A rises, other things being constant,
    a. the indifference map does not change.
    b. the slope of the budget constraint line changes.
    c. a new consumer optimum is reached, where less of good A is purchased.
    d. All of the above

WORKING WITH GRAPHS

1. Suppose that a consumer is faced with the choice of only two goods: food and entertainment. After some consideration, the consumer provides the following information about various combinations of food and entertainment per month to which she is indifferent, given some particular level of satisfaction.

Units of entertainment per month	Units of food per month
35	7
20	11
10	15
5	20
3	30
2	45

a. Use this information and the following grid to plot this consumer's indifference curve for entertainment and food for a given level of satisfaction. Label the curve I.

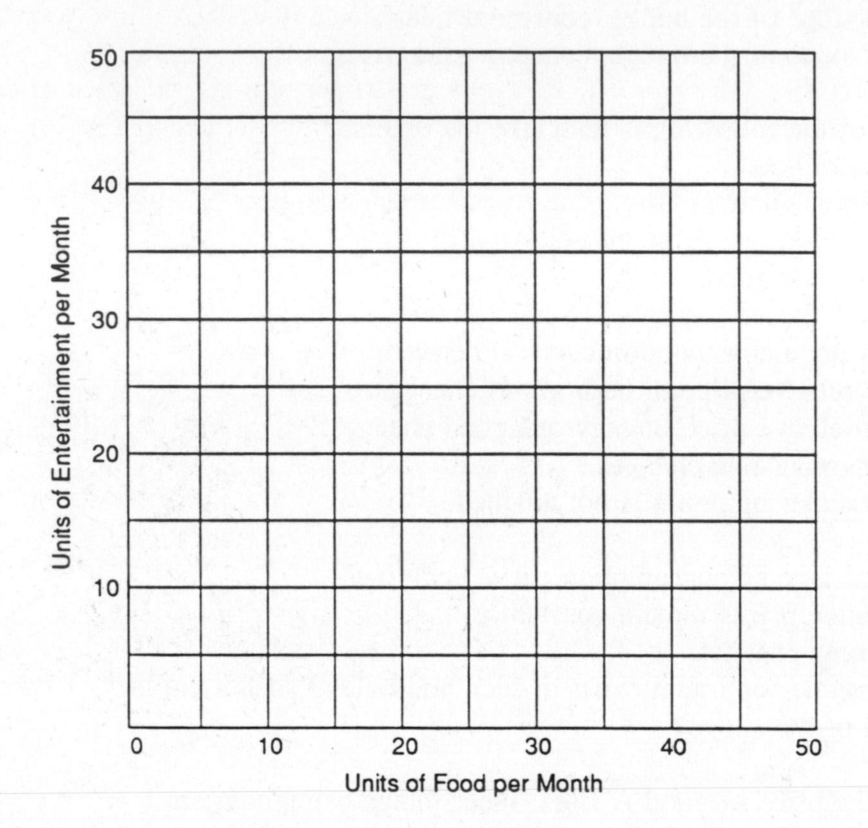

Suppose the consumer is asked to provide the same type of information for some higher level of satisfaction. In this case the consumer supplies the information given below.

Units of entertainment per month	Units of food per month
40	11
30	15
25	18
15	25
10	35
7	45

b. Use this new information and the grid above to plot this additional indifference curve. Label this curve II.

2. Suppose that the consumer in problem 1 has a monthly income of $400 and that the price of entertainment is $10 per unit and the price of food is $20 per unit.
   a. Plot the consumer's budget line on the above grid and label it BL1.
   b. Given the consumer's indifference map and the above prices and income, what combination of entertainment and food will put the consumer at an optimum point?
   c. Suppose that the price of food drops to $10 per unit but the price of entertainment and the consumer's income remain unchanged. Draw the new budget line in the above grid and label it BL2.
   d. After the change in part (c), which combination of entertainment and food will put the consumer at an optimum point?

3. Draw a price-consumption curve for each of the following combinations of goods.
   a. Hot dogs and hot dog buns with the price of buns changing.
   b. Coke and Pepsi with the price of Pepsi changing.
   c. Potatoes and guitar strings with the price of guitar strings changing.

ANSWERS TO APPENDIX E

COMPLETION QUESTIONS

1. indifference; negatively
2. falls; map
3. less; more
4. prices, income; relative prices, income
5. tangent, indifference; highest
6. shifts inward (parallel); decrease; inferior
7. remains constant; changes; remains constant
8. remains constant, remains constant
9. higher, larger

TRUE-FALSE QUESTIONS

1. F Total utility stays the same, not marginal
2. T
3. F A linear indifference curve implies a constant marginal rate of substitution.
4. F The slope of the budget line reflects relative prices.
5. F They are attainable, but not optimal.
6. F It is more preferable if it lies above 2.
7. T
8. F Indifference curves are independent of income.
9. F Slope stays the same, but the budget line shifts.
10. T
11. T
12. T
13. T
14. T

MULTIPLE CHOICE QUESTIONS

1.a; 2.d; 3.c; 4.c; 5.d; 6.d; 7.a; 8.b; 9.c; 10.a;
11.d; 12.d

WORKING WITH GRAPHS

1. a. see graph below; b. see graph below

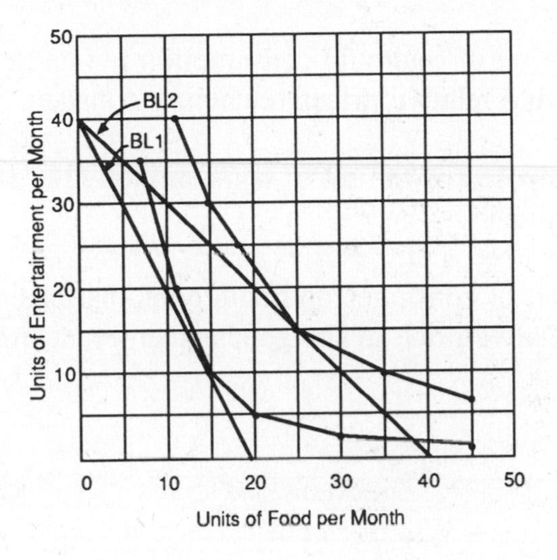

2. a. see graph above; b. 10 units of entertainment per month and 15 units of food per month; c. see graph above; d. 15 units of entertainment per month and 25 units of food per month.

3.

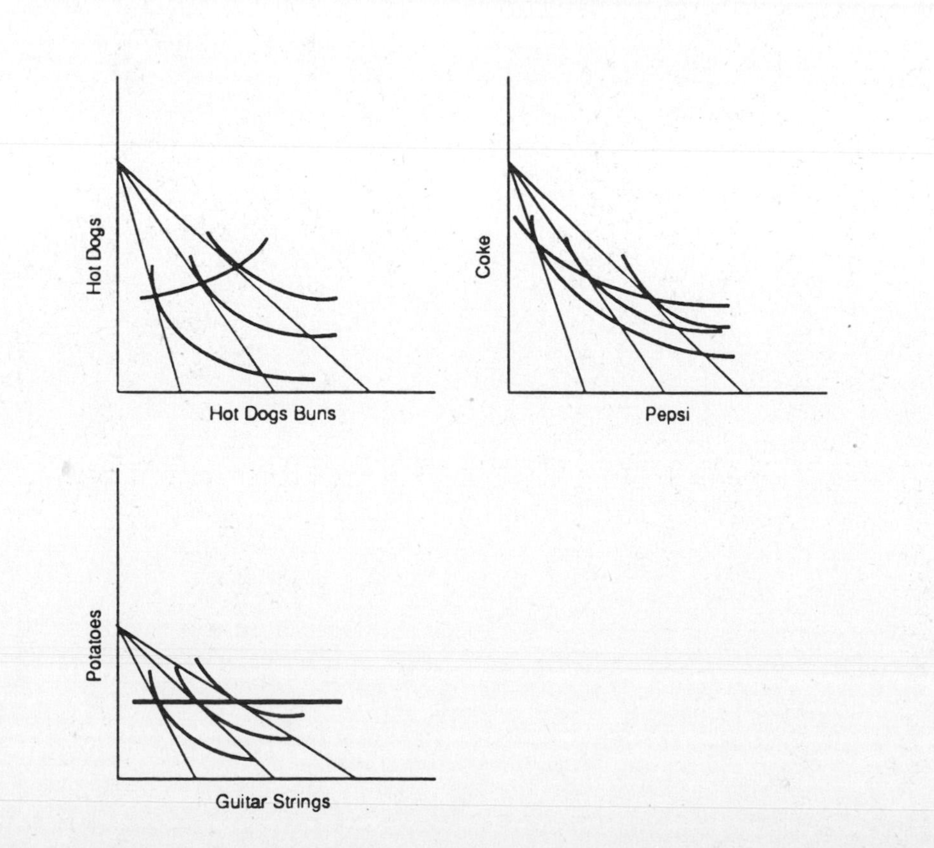

GLOSSARY TO APPENDIX E

Budget constraint The resource constraint imposed on households and firms at any point in time; it represents the set of opportunities facing each decision maker.

Income-consumption curve The set of optimum consumption points that would occur if income were increased, nominal and relative prices remaining constant.

Indifference curve A curve composed of the set of consumption alternatives, each yielding the same total amount of satisfaction.

Price-consumption curve The set of consumer optimum combinations of two goods that the consumer would choose as the relative price of the goods changes, while money income remains constant.

CHAPTER 20

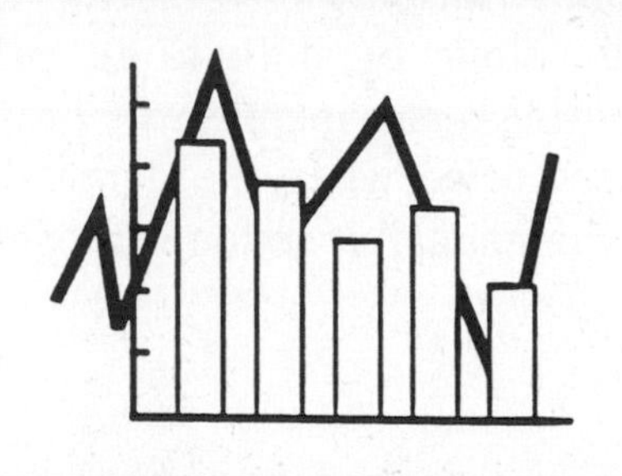

DEMAND AND SUPPLY ELASTICITY

PUTTING THIS CHAPTER INTO PERSPECTIVE

Chapter 20 is the second chapter in Part Five, in which the micro-economics portion of this text begins. You have already analyzed supply and demand in Chapter 3; this chapter is concerned with demand and supply elasticity.

The law of demand posits an inverse relationship between price and quantity demanded, other things being constant. Knowing that quantity demanded will rise if price falls and that quantity demanded will fall if price rises, other things being constant, is useful information--to be sure. But the concept of price elasticity of demand goes one step further; it is concerned with how responsive quantity demanded is to changes in price. If price rises, will quantity demanded fall by a little or a lot? If price falls, will quantity demanded rise by just a little bit, or by a great amount?

Price elasticity of demand is defined as the percentage change in quantity demanded divided by the percentage change in price. Because of the law of demand, the price elasticity of demand coefficient (number) will always be negative. By convention, therefore, economists ignore the sign; and if the coefficient is greater than one, less than one, or equal to one, we refer to a good (in the relevant price range) as being price elastic, price inelastic, or unitary price elastic, respectively.

Price elasticity of demand is a very useful concept. If you are in business and you know the price elasticity of demand coefficient for your good, you can raise your total revenues (and perhaps profits) by raising or lowering your sales price, depending on whether the elasticity coefficient is less than or greater than one. If you are in charge of raising revenues for a government, you would be well-advised to tax only those goods for which at current prices the price elasticity of demand coefficient is quite low. Many other issues, in this chapter and throughout the remainder of this text, will revolve around the value of the price elasticity of demand coefficient.

In Chapter 20 we analyze how price elasticity of demand coefficients can be measured; we also analyze cross elasticities of demand, income elasticities of demand, and the price elasticity of supply.

There are several pitfalls that you should be careful to avoid. Many students think in terms of whether a *good* is price elastic or inelastic; instead you should realize that for each good (given a linear demand curve) there are ranges of price elasticity and price inelasticity. For that reason you should always be careful to specify the *price range* when analyzing price elasticity of demand. Another problem arises for students in confusing slope with elasticity; as the text points out, along a linear demand curve (which has a constant slope by definition), price elasticity varies greatly. Finally, many students believe that a business can increase its profits by raising selling price; but as the text indicates, if a firm raises price when the demand is highly price elastic at the current price, its total revenues will fall dramatically; so too, probably, will its profits.

LEARNING OBJECTIVES

After you have studied this chapter you should be able to

1. define price elasticity of demand, elastic demand, unitary elastic demand, inelastic demand, perfectly inelastic demand, perfectly elastic demand, cross elasticity of demand, income elasticity of demand, price elasticity of supply, perfectly elastic supply, and perfectly inelastic supply.

2. calculate price elasticity of demand in two ways, given the relevant information.

3. predict what will happen to a firm's total revenues if the firm changes price, given price elasticity of demand.

4. classify an elasticity coefficient as indicating whether demand is price elastic, unitary elastic, or price inelastic, in the relevant price range.

5. distinguish between slope and elasticity.

6. recognize from a graph whether the demand for a good is perfectly elastic or perfectly inelastic in the specified price range.

7. identify the determinants of price elasticity of demand.

8. calculate the cross elasticity of demand coefficient, and determine from the sign of that coefficient whether or not the goods in question are substitutes or complements.

9. calculate income elasticity of demand from relevant information and distinguish price elasticity of demand from income elasticity of demand.

10. calculate price elasticity of supply, identify the determinants of price elasticity of supply, and recognize a graph of a perfectly elastic supply curve and a perfectly inelastic supply curve.

11. predict where most of the burden of a sales tax falls, depending on the elasticity of demand relative to the elasticity of supply.

CHAPTER OUTLINE

1. Elasticity measures quantity responsiveness to price changes.
   a. *Price elasticity of demand* is defined as the percentage change in quantity demanded divided by the percentage change in price.
      i. Because of the law of demand, the price elasticity of demand is always negative; by convention the sign is ignored.
      ii. Price elasticity of demand relates percentage changes, not absolute changes.
   b. There are two ways to calculate the price elasticity of demand.
      i. Price elasticity of demand may be calculated by dividing the change in quantity demanded over the original quantity demanded by the change in price over the original price; this method yields a different elasticity over the same range of the demand curve, depending on whether price rises or falls.
      ii. In order to get consistent results over the same range of a demand curve, it is possible to calculate price elasticity by using average values for base price and base quantity.

2. If the calculated price elasticity of demand for a good is greater than one, the demand is called *elastic*; if it is equal to one, the demand is called *unitary elastic*; if it is less than one, the demand is called *inelastic*.

3. Elasticity is related to a firm's *total revenues*.
   a. In the range of price elastic demand, if a firm lowers price its total revenues will rise; if it raises price its total revenues will fall.
   b. In the range of unitary price elastic demand, small changes in price leave the firm's total revenues unaltered.
   c. In the range of price inelastic demand, if a firm lowers price its total revenues will fall; if it raises price its total revenues will rise.
   d. Along a linear demand curve (which has a constant slope, by definition), a good has a price elastic, a unitary elastic, and a price inelastic range; therefore slope and elasticity are different concepts.
   e. There are two extreme price elasticities of demand.
      i. *Perfectly inelastic demand* indicates no change in quantity demanded as price changes; such a demand curve is vertical at the given quantity.
      ii. *Perfectly elastic demand* indicates that even a slight increase in price will lead to a zero quantity demanded; such a demand curve is horizontal at the given price.

4. There are three major determinants of the price elasticity of demand.
   a. The closer the substitutes for a particular good, and the more available they are, the greater will be its price elasticity of demand.
   b. The higher the percentage of total expenditures that people allocate to a good, the higher will be that good's price elasticity of demand.
   c. The longer any price change persists, the greater the price elasticity of demand; the distinction between the short-run and long-run consumer adjustment period varies with the good in question.

5. *Cross elasticity of demand* is defined as the percentage change in the quantity demanded of one good (holding its price constant) divided by the percentage change in the price of a related good.
   a. If the sign of the cross elasticity of demand is positive, the two goods are *substitutes*.
   b. If the sign of the cross elasticity of demand is negative, the two goods are *complements*.

6. *Income elasticity of demand* is defined as the percentage change in the quantity demanded for a good (holding its price constant) divided by the percentage change in money income.

7. *Price elasticity of supply* is defined as the percentage change in quantity supplied divided by the percentage change in price.
   a. One extreme is *perfectly elastic supply*, where a slight decrease in price leads to a zero quantity supplied; such a supply curve is horizontal at the given price.
   b. Another extreme is *perfectly inelastic supply*, where quantity supplied is constant, regardless of what happens to price; such a supply curve is vertical at the given quantity.
   c. The longer the time for adjustment, the more price elastic is the supply curve.
   d. Empirical evidence indicates that short-run elasticities for goods are considerably smaller than long-run elasticities.

8. Governments tax specific goods in order to raise revenues or to discourage consumption; a per unit sales tax shifts the supply curve upward.
   a. The burden of a tax falls partly on buyers, and partly on sellers, depending on the relative price elasticity of demand and the price elasticity of supply.
   b. In general, if the demand for a good is price inelastic and its supply is relatively elastic, then the burden of a sales tax will fall mostly on buyers.
   c. The burden of a sales tax will fall entirely on buyers if demand is perfectly price inelastic or if supply is perfectly price elastic.
   d. The burden of a sales tax will fall entirely on sellers if demand is perfectly price elastic or if supply is perfectly price inelastic.

9. The market demand for crack cocaine is not perfectly inelastic because (a) not all users are completely addicted (some are marginal users) and (b) crack addicts have budget constraints.

10. A 10 percent luxury tax induced higher income people to find substitutes for such goods; they bought used (but not old) luxury items.

KEY TERMS

Elastic demand
Unitary elasticity of demand
Inelastic demand
Substitutes
Complements

KEY CONCEPTS

Price elasticity of demand
Perfectly inelastic demand
Perfectly elastic demand
Income elasticity of demand
Cross elasticity of demand
Price elasticity of supply
Total revenue test for elasticity of demand

COMPLETION QUESTIONS

Fill in the blank or circle the correct term.

1. Price elasticity of demand is a measure of buyer _______________ to price changes.

2. Price elasticity of demand is defined as the percentage change in ______________ divided by the percentage change in _____________; the problem with this measure is that we get (the same, a different) numerical value when we move up, as opposed to down, the same range of the demand curve.

3. In order to correct for the problem in question 2 above, the ______________ value method of calculating the price elasticity of demand can be used.

4. Assume a 1 percent change in price. If quantity demanded changes by less than 1 percent then we say that in that range the demand for the good is ________________; if quantity demanded changes by 1 percent then in that range demand is ________________; if quantity demanded changes by more than 1 percent then in that range demand is ________________.

5. If price falls and total revenues rise, then in that range demand was price ________________; if price falls and total revenues remain constant, then in that range demand was price ________________; if price falls and total revenues fall, then in that range demand was price ________________.

6. If price rises and total revenues fall, then demand was price ______________; if total revenues rise, then demand was price ________________; if total revenues remain constant, then demand was ________________.

7. Elasticity and slope are (the same, different) concepts.

8. A demand curve that exhibits zero responsiveness to price changes is ___________; such a demand curve is (horizontal, vertical) at the given quantity; a demand curve in which even the slightest increase in price will lead to a zero quantity demanded is ________________; such a demand curve is (horizontal, vertical) at the given price.

9. The determinants of price elasticity of demand are ________________, ________________, and ________________.

10. Cross elasticity of demand is defined as the percentage change in the ______________ of one good, holding its ______________ constant, divided by the percentage change in the ______________ of another good.

11. If the cross elasticity of demand is positive, then the two goods are ________________; if it is negative, the two goods are ________________.

12. The income elasticity of demand is defined as the percentage change in ________________ for a good, holding its ________________ constant, divided by the percentage change in ________________.

13. The price elasticity of supply measures the responsiveness of the ________________ of a good to a change in its price; a supply curve in which a slight decrease in price leads to a zero quantity supplied is ________________; if quantity supplied remains constant no matter what happens to price, the supply curve is ________________.

14. If demand is perfectly price inelastic or if supply is perfectly price (elastic, inelastic), then the burden of a sales tax will fall entirely on (buyers, sellers).

15. If demand is perfectly price (elastic, inelastic), or if supply is perfectly price inelastic, the burden of a sales tax will fall entirely on (buyers, sellers).

16. The market demand for crack cocaine (is, is not) perfectly inelastic because (not all, all) users are addicts, and because addicts (have, don't have) budget constraints.

TRUE-FALSE QUESTIONS

Circle the **T** if the statement is true, the **F** if it is false. Explain to yourself why a statement is false.

T F 1. Price elasticity of demand measures the responsiveness of price to changes in quantity demanded.

T F 2. Because of the law of demand, price elasticity of demand will always be a negative number.

T F 3. Price elasticity of demand deals with absolute, not relative values.

T F 4. When price elasticity of demand is found by the average value approach, price elasticity is the same whether price rises or falls over a given demand curve range.

T F 5. If the price elasticity of demand is 3, then over the relevant price range, demand is price inelastic.

T F 6. If price falls and total revenues rise, then over that price range demand is price inelastic.

T F 7. If a demand curve for good A is very steep, the demand for good A is price elastic.

T F 8. If a firm discovers that at current prices the price elasticity of demand is 1/2, the firm will raise prices if it wants to maximize profits.

T F *9. The price elasticity of demand for McDonald's hamburgers is less than the price elasticity of demand for hamburgers.

T F 10. If the demand for good A is perfectly price elastic, its demand curve is vertical at that price.

T F *11. If the demand for good A is perfectly price inelastic, good A violates the law of demand.

T F *12. A demand curve which exhibits constant price elasticity of demand must be linear.

T F 13. The less time people have to respond to a price change, the higher is the price elasticity.

T F 14. If the cross elasticity of demand for goods A and B is negative, A and B are complements.

T F 15. Income elasticity of demand is calculated for a horizontal shift in the demand curve, given price.

T F 16. If supply is perfectly inelastic, the curve will be horizontal at the given quantity.

T F 17. If the demand for good A is perfectly price inelastic, the burden of a sales tax will fall entirely on buyers.

T F 18. If the supply of good A is perfectly price elastic, the burden of a sales tax will fall entirely on buyers.

T F 19. The market demand for crack cocaine is perfectly price inelastic.

T F 20. Buyers ignored the 1990 luxury tax because only wealthy people were affected.

MULTIPLE CHOICE QUESTIONS

Circle the letter that corresponds to the best answer.

1. Price elasticity of demand measures responsiveness of
   a. quantity demanded to changes in price.
   b. quantity demanded to changes in income.
   c. price to changes in quantity demanded.
   d. price to changes in demand.

2. If the price elasticity of demand is 1/3, then
   a. demand is inelastic.
   b. demand is inelastic over that price range.
   c. demand is elastic.
   d. demand is elastic over that price range.

3. Which of the following is *not* true concerning the price elasticity of demand?
   a. Its sign is always negative, due to the law of demand.
   b. It is a unitless, dimensionless number.
   c. It equals the percentage change in price divided by the percentage change in quantity demanded.
   d. It measures the responsiveness of quantity demanded to changes in price.

4. If price elasticity of demand is calculated using the original price and quantity, then over a given range in the demand curve price elasticity of demand
   a. differs depending on whether price rises or falls.
   b. is the same, regardless of whether price rises or falls.
   c. is equal to 1.
   d. rises as price falls.

5. If price falls by 1 percent and quantity demanded rises by 2 percent, then the price elasticity of demand
   a. is inelastic over that range.
   b. is 1/2.
   c. is elastic over that range.
   d. cannot be calculated from this information.

6. If price rises and total revenue rises, then the price elasticity of demand over that range is
   a. elastic.
   b. inelastic.
   c. unitary elastic.
   d. equal to 1.

7. If price falls and over that price range demand is price inelastic, total revenues will
   a. remain constant.
   b. fall.
   c. rise.
   d. fall, then rise.

8. Over a linear demand curve, price elasticity of demand
   a. remains constant as price falls.
   b. remains constant as price rises.
   c. rises as price falls.
   d. falls as price falls.

*9. If the demand for good A is perfectly inelastic,
  a. quantity demanded does not change as price changes.
  b. the law of demand is violated.
  c. the demand curve is vertical at the given quantity.
  d. All of the above

*10. If the demand for good A is perfectly elastic,
  a. quantity demanded does not vary with price.
  b. the demand curve is horizontal.
  c. the demand curve is vertical.
  d. the demand curve is positively sloped.

11. Which of the following is *not* a determinant of the price elasticity of demand?
  a. existence and closeness of substitutes
  b. importance of the good to the consumer
  c. price elasticity of supply
  d. length of time allowed for adjustment to a price change

12. If the cross elasticity of demand between good A and good B is positive, the goods are
  a. substitutes.
  b. complements.
  c. unrelated.
  d. necessities.

13. If the cross elasticity between good A and good B is -10, then A and B are
  a. close substitutes.
  b. near substitutes.
  c. strongly complementary.
  d. mildly complementary.

14. Baseballs and baseball bats are
  a. substitutes.
  b. complements.
  c. not related goods.
  d. necessities.

15. When the income elasticity of demand for good A is calculated,
  a. the price of good A varies.
  b. income changes which lead to horizontal shifts in the demand curve for good A are measured.
  c. a movement along the demand curve for good A is measured.
  d. All of the above

*16. Analogy: A movement along a demand curve is to price elasticity of demand as a shift in the demand curve is to
a. an increase in demand.
b. changes in taxes or subsidies.
c. income elasticity of demand.
d. substitutes and complements.

17. At current prices for salt, salt is highly price
a. elastic.
b. inelastic.
c. cross elastic.
d. unitary elastic.

18. Which of the following goods is probably the most highly income elastic?
a. salt
b. food
c. alcoholic beverages
d. private education

19. A perfectly inelastic supply curve
a. shows great quantity supplied responsiveness to price changes.
b. is horizontal at the given price.
c. indicates zero quantity supplied responsiveness to price changes.
d. is a normal situation.

20. If the supply of good B is perfectly elastic and price falls, quantity supplied will
a. remain unchanged.
b. rise.
c. fall.
d. fall to zero.

21. If price rises, the quantity supplied will be greater the
a. longer the time that elapses.
b. more income elastic is the good.
c. higher the price elasticity of demand for the good.
d. All of the above

22. If a sales tax is instituted on good A, the burden will fall on
a. both buyers and sellers, usually.
b. buyers only, if the demand curve is perfectly inelastic.
c. buyers only, if the supply curve is perfectly elastic.
d. All of the above

23. Regarding the demand for crack cocaine,
a. individual addicts have perfectly inelastic demand curves.
b. the market demand is perfectly inelastic.
c. marginal users are responsive to price changes.
d. individual addicts do not have budget constraints.

MATCHING

Choose the item in column (2) that best matches an item in column (1).

(1)	(2)
a. perfectly inelastic demand	h. elasticity coefficient less than 1
b. perfectly elastic demand	i. horizontal supply curve
c. perfectly inelastic supply	j. complementary or substitute goods
d. perfectly elastic supply	k. quality of substitutes
e. determinant of price elasticity	l. horizontal demand curve
f. cross price elasticity of demand	m. vertical demand curve
g. price inelastic	n. vertical supply curve

WORKING WITH GRAPHS

1. Analyze the graphs below and then answer the questions that follow. Assume that a per unit sales tax has been placed on the good in question.

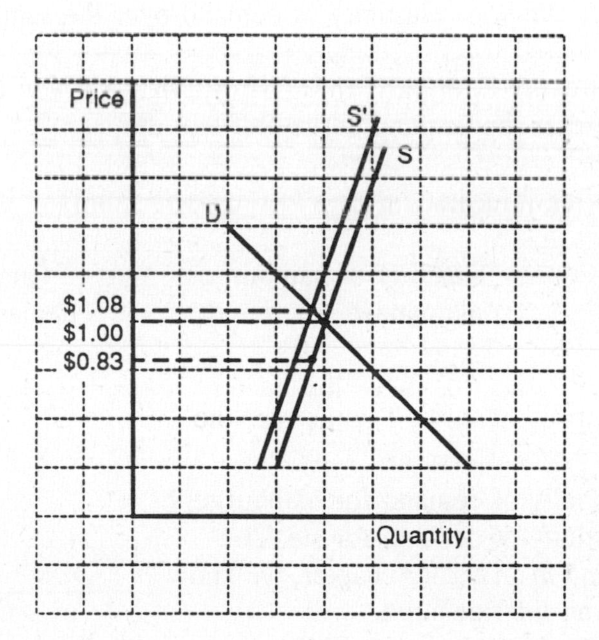

a. What is the original equilibrium price?
b. What is the value of the per unit sales tax?
c. What is the new equilibrium price?
d. What is the per unit burden on buyers?
e. What is the after-tax price per unit received by the sellers?
f. What is the per unit burden on sellers?

PROBLEMS

1. Suppose you are given the following data on the market demand and supply for CD's in a small record store. (Use the average elasticity measure.)

Price	Quantity demanded (per week)	Quantity supplied (per week)
$4.00	50	10
4.50	45	15
5.00	40	25
5.50	35	35
6.00	30	45

a. What is the equilibrium price for CD's?
b. What is the price elasticity of demand over the price range $4.50 to $5? Over the range $5.50 to $6?
c. What is the price elasticity of supply over the same two ranges of price?
d. Now suppose that most students in the area are working for the minimum wage and that the minimum wage has gone up. As a result, at each price, two more CD's per week are demanded. Calculate the price elasticity of demand over the same ranges as in part (b).
e. After comparing your answers from parts (b) and (d), what can you conclude about the price elasticity of demand as the demand curve shifts to the right?

2. Suppose we have the following information for a low-income family:

	Income per month	Quantity of hamburger demanded per month	Quantity of steak demanded per month
Period 1	$750	8 lbs.	2 lbs.
Period 2	950	5 lbs.	4 lbs.

a. What is the income elasticity of demand for hamburger?
b. What is the income elasticity of demand for steak?
c. From our study of demand in an earlier chapter, we know __________ is a normal good, whereas __________ is an inferior good.

3. Suppose the price of color print film has recently risen by 10 percent due to an increase in the cost of the silver that is used to make film. As a result, less film is being sold in the camera store where you work. You do some checking and find that camera sales are down by 4 percent. What is the cross-price elasticity of cameras and film? Are these two goods complements or substitutes?

CASE STUDY

High prestige private American universities (and state universities as well) charge different prices to different students, even though they provide the same service to students. By charging tuition (giving scholarships) based solely on "need" (essentially, the income and wealth of the students' parents), such universities are pricing according to the price elasticity of demand.

1. Is the demand for an education at a high prestige university likely to be less price elastic for high income parents, or for low income parents? Why?
2. How would a revenue-maximizing university charge tuition to students?

ANSWERS TO CHAPTER 20

COMPLETION QUESTIONS

1. responsiveness
2. quantity demanded, price; a different
3. average
4. price inelastic; unitary elastic; price elastic
5. elastic; unitary elastic; inelastic
6. elastic; inelastic; unitary elastic
7. different
8. perfectly inelastic; vertical; perfectly elastic; horizontal
9. closeness of available substitutes; importance of the good in consumer budgets; length of time to respond
10. quantity demanded, price, price
11. substitutes; complements
12. quantity demanded, price, money income
13. quantity supplied; perfectly elastic; perfectly inelastic
14. elastic, buyers
15. elastic, sellers
16. is not, not all, have

TRUE-FALSE QUESTIONS

1. F It measures quantity responsiveness to price change.
2. T
3. F It deals with relative values.
4. T
5. F It is price elastic because the coefficient exceeds 1.
6. F It must have been price elastic.
7. F Slope and elasticity are different concepts.
8. T
9. F It is greater, because there are more substitutes for *McDonald's* hamburgers than for hamburgers.
10. F It is horizontal at that price.
11. T
12. F A linear demand curve has ranges of elasticity, unitary elasticity, and inelasticity.
13. F Elasticity increases over time because substitutes become more readily available over time.
14. T
15. T
16. F It will be vertical, at the given quantity.
17. T
18. T
19. F Even individual addicts have budget constraints; moreover, marginal users will be price responsive.
20. F They responded by buying used luxury goods.

MULTIPLE CHOICE QUESTIONS

1.a; 2.b; 3.c; 4.a; 5.c; 6.b; 7.b; 8.d; 9.d; 10.b;
11.c; 12.a; 13.c; 14.b; 15.b; 16.c; 17.b; 18.d; 19.c; 20.d;
21.a; 22.d; 23.c

MATCHING

a and m; b and l; c and n; d and i; e and k; f and j; g and h

WORKING WITH GRAPHS

a. $1.00
b. 25 cents
c. $1.08
d. 8 cents
e. 83 cents
f. 17 cents

PROBLEMS

1. a. $5.50
   b. 1.12; 1.77
   c. 4.75; 2.88
   d. 1.07; 1.67
   e. As the demand curve shifts to the right, for any price range, demand becomes less elastic--or, alternatively stated, more inelastic.

2. a. -1.96
   b. 2.83
   c. steak; hamburger

3. -0.43; complements

CASE STUDY

1. Demand is less price elastic for high income parents, who will view other universities as inferior substitutes for high prestige universities.
2. The same way that the prestigious universities do; it would, however, give fewer 100% tuition scholarships, unless long-run profit considerations required that minority or low income students who are very likely to be successful in the future be advertisements for *that* school.

GLOSSARY TO CHAPTER 20

Cross elasticity of demand The percentage change in the quantity demanded of one good (holding its price constant) divided by the percentage change in the price of a related good.

Elastic demand A demand relationship in which a given percentage change in price will result in a larger percentage change in quantity demanded. Total revenues and price are inversely related in the elastic portion of the demand curve.

Income elasticity of demand The percentage change in quantity demanded for any good, holding its price constant, divided by the percentage change in money income; the responsiveness of the quantity demanded to changes in income, holding its relative price constant.

Inelastic demand A characteristic of a demand curve in which a given change in price will result in a less-than-proportionate change in the quantity demanded. Total revenue and price are directly related in the inelastic region of the demand curve.

Perfectly elastic demand A demand curve that has the characteristic that even the slightest increase in price will lead to a zero quantity demanded.

Perfectly elastic supply A supply curve characterized by a reduction in quantity supplied to zero when there is the slightest decrease in price.

Perfectly inelastic demand A demand curve that exhibits zero responsiveness to price changes; that is, no matter what the price is the quantity demanded remains the same.

Perfectly inelastic supply The characteristic of a supply curve for which quantity supplied remains constant, no matter what happens to price.

Price elasticity of demand The responsiveness of the quantity demanded of a commodity to changes in its price. The price elasticity of demand is defined as the percentage change in quantity demanded divided by the percentage change in price.

Price elasticity of supply The responsiveness of the quantity supplied of a commodity to a change in its price. Price elasticity of supply is defined as the percentage change in quantity supplied divided by the percentage change in price.

Unitary elasticity of demand A demand relationship in which the quantity demanded changes exactly in proportion to the change in price. Total revenue is invariant to price changes in the unit elastic portion of the demand curve.

CHAPTER 21

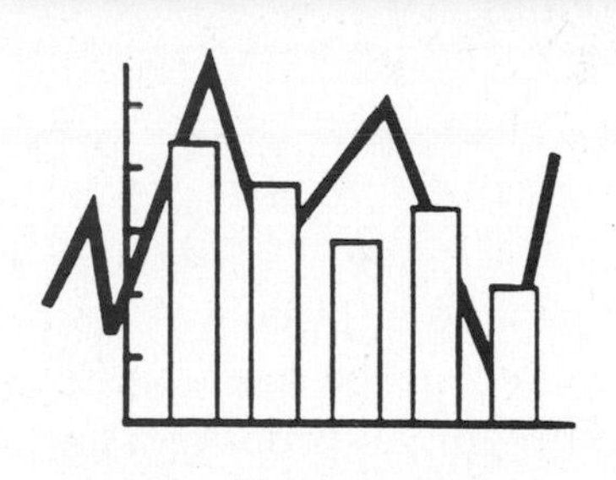

THE FINANCIAL ENVIRONMENT: THE STOCK MARKET AND GLOBAL CAPITAL MARKETS

PUTTING THIS CHAPTER INTO PERSPECTIVE

Chapter 21 is the third chapter in Part Five, and it introduces you to the various forms of business organization and provides some background information that will be helpful in Part Five. The very interesting and timely issue of corporate takeovers is also analyzed.

Corporate takeovers come about because a separation of ownership and control exists in large corporations, enabling managers to place their own interests above those of the shareholders. Economists refer to this as the principal-agent problem; also the problems of asymmetric information, adverse selection, and moral hazard are related to financial transactions. In this chapter you will learn the colorful jargon used in discussing takeovers: corporate raider, white knight, hostile takeover, friendly takeover, golden parachute, poison pill, greenmail, and junk bonds.

LEARNING OBJECTIVES

After you have studied this chapter you should be able to

1. define financial capital, proprietorship, partnership, corporation, unlimited liability, limited liability, dividends, limited partnership, S corporation, share of stock, bond, reinvestment, asymmetric information, adverse selection, moral hazard, principal-agent problem, separation of ownership and control, collateral, incentive compatible, random walk theory, inside information, corporate raider, white knight, hostile takeover, friendly takeover, golden parachute, poison pill, greenmail, and junk bonds.

2. state the distinctions among proprietorships, partnerships, and corporations.

3. state the advantages and disadvantages of proprietorships, partnerships, and corporations.

4. recognize how owners can reduce the principal-agent problem that arises from the separation of ownership and control.

5. recognize how asymmetric information can contribute to a moral hazard problem and an adverse selection problem.

6. enumerate the three principal methods of corporate financing.

7. list the advantages and disadvantages of corporate takeover activities.

8. list advantages and disadvantages of a globalized economy.

CHAPTER OUTLINE

There are three basic forms into which U.S. businesses have chosen to organize: proprietorship, partnership, and corporation.

1. A proprietorship is owned by a single individual who makes the business decisions, receives all the profits, and is legally responsible for all the debts of the firm.
   a. Advantages: a proprietorship is easy to form and dissolve; all decision-making powers reside with the sole proprietor; a proprietorship is taxed only once.
   b. Disadvantages: the proprietorship faces unlimited liability for debts of the firm and has limited ability to raise funds; the business normally ceases to exist with the death of the proprietor.

2. A partnership is owned by two or more who share profits or losses.
   a. Advantages: partnerships are easy to form, experience relatively low costs of monitoring job performance, permit more specialization than sole proprietorships, and are only taxed once.
   b. Disadvantages: partnerships face unlimited liability and more difficulty in decision-making (relative to proprietorship); dissolution of the partnership is usually necessary when a partner dies or leaves the partnership.

3. A corporation is a legal entity that may conduct business in its own name, just as an individual does. The owners of the corporation are its shareholders.
   a. Advantages: shareholders enjoy limited liability; a corporation continues to exist even if some owners cease to remain owners; a corporation has the ability to raise large sums of money for investments.
   b. Disadvantages: owners are subject to double taxation because corporations pay taxes on profits and shareholders pay taxes on dividends received; ownership and control are separated in a corporation.
      i. Professional managers, who may have little or no ownership in the firm, may pursue their own, not shareholder-owner, interests.
      ii. Shareholders may experience high costs to monitor the behavior of professional managers.

4. Limited partnerships and S corporations are hybrids of the other business forms.
   a. A limited partnership is a firm which contains some partners who are granted limited liability and some general partners who face unlimited liability.
   b. An S corporation is a firm that is exempt from most of the burden of double taxation; disadvantages include a limited number of owners (35), less than full exemption from corporate taxation in some states, quick taxation of profits (retained earnings are taxed), and limitations on the extent to which S corporation losses can offset members' personal income for taxation purposes.

5. Stocks, bonds, and reinvestment of retained earnings or depreciation reserves are the most important sources of corporate financing.
    a. From the investor's point of view, stocks offer the highest risk (and, therefore, the highest potential rate of return), and the greatest control over the firm's decisions.
    b. Bonds are relatively safer (and yield a correspondingly lower rate of return) and provide little control over decision-making.

6. When financial transactions take place, asymmetric information may exist.
    a. If asymmetric information exists *before* a transaction takes place, adverse selection exists; borrowers who are the worse credit risks know better than lenders that they are poor risks, and such borrowers can outbid other borrowers for funds.
    b. If asymmetric information exists *after* a transaction, moral hazard may exist; after borrowing funds the borrowers may be able to use the money to make investments riskier than was otherwise expected by the lender.
    c. A moral hazard problem arises *within* a firm; because modern business is characterized by a separation of ownership (stockholders) and central (management) a principal-agent problem exists; management has an incentive to pursue its own, and not stockholder, interest.
    d. In order to reduce the problems that arise from asymmetric information, various countermoves have evolved.
        i. Lenders can reduce the problem of *adverse selection* in general ways.
            (a) Lenders can purchase information from independent businesses who rate the credit worthiness of borrowers.
            (b) Lenders can require borrowers to put up collateral.
        ii. Lenders can reduce the problem of *moral hazard* by requiring an incentive compatible contract, which assures that borrowers also place a good deal of their own assets at risk; such a scheme makes the interests of borrowers and lenders more closely aligned.
        iii. The market for corporate control has evolved in order to reduce the principal-agent problem resulting from the separation of ownership and control that exists in modern corporations.
            (a) Critics of corporate takeovers maintain that the buying and selling of major corporations benefits only the main actors in the deal; management is distracted from its main business, and stockholders can be hurt.
            (b) Proponents of corporate takeovers argue that such actions force existing managers to be more concerned with profit maximization or to turn corporations over to managers who are; as a result, resources are allocated more efficiently and stockholders benefit.
            (c) In recent years "junk bonds" (relatively risky bonds that offer high rates of return) have been issued to finance corporate takeovers; whether junk bonds are beneficial or not is a controversial topic.
            (d) The evidence seems to be that corporate takeovers have benefitted the stockholders of both the acquired and the acquiring firms.

7. Technological advances in computers, telecommunications, and travel, along with an increased decentralization and opening of economies, have helped to make the world a global economy; as is always the case in economics, a trade-off exists.
8. Leading the way toward a globalized economy is worldwide financial integration.

a. Legal and technological changes have blurred the distinctions among financial institutions and between financial and non-financial institutions.
b. Multinational corporations with a wide array of financial services operate worldwide.
c. Markets for U.S. government securities, interbank lending and borrowing, foreign exchange trading, and common stock are now operating continuously, in vast quantities, around the clock and around the world; along with technological and legal changes, the U.S. trade deficit has helped to spur such markets.

9. One problem with integrated financial markets is that a financial crisis in one economy is immediately transferred into another; when the U.S. stock market plummeted in 1987, the stock markets in Sidney, London, Hong Kong, and Tokyo, and many other cities, followed suit.

KEY TERMS

Proprietorship
Partnership
Corporation
Unlimited liability
S corporation
Limited partnership
Dividends
Share of stock
Bond
Corporate raider
White knight
Golden parachute
Greenmail
Junk bond
Poison pill
Collateral

KEY CONCEPTS

Unlimited liability
Limited liability
Separation of ownership and control
Moral hazard
Adverse selection
Reinvestment
Hostile takeover
Friendly takeover
Corporate takeover market
Asymmetric information
Random walk
Inside information
Incentive compatible

COMPLETION QUESTIONS

Fill in the blank or circle the correct term.

1. The three major forms of U.S. business organizations are ___________, ___________, and ___________; hybrid business organizations include ___________ and ___________.

2. While the highest percentage of U.S. firms are (proprietorships, partnerships, corporations), the highest percentage of total business revenue is attributed to ___________.

3. A ______________ is a legal entity that may conduct business in its own name, just as an individual does; its owners are called (shareholders, bondholders), and such owners enjoy (unlimited, limited, partially limited) liability.

4. The income that corporations earn is taxed (once, twice).

*5. When transactions take place ______________ information may exist; if such a situation exists before the transaction occurs, the ______________ problem exists; if it exists after the transaction exists then the ______________ problem exists.

6. Because modern corporations are characterized by a separation of ownership and ______________, a ______________ hazard problem exists.

7. Lenders can reduce the problem of adverse selection by purchasing information regarding a borrower's ______________; lenders can also require borrowers to put up ______________.

8. Lenders can reduce the moral hazard problem by requiring a(n) ______________ contract, which requires borrowers to assume part of the ______________.

9. A separation of ownership and control could lead to the ______________ problem, which is resolved in part by the evolution of the market for ______________.

10. The three main sources of corporate finance are ______________, ______________, and ______________; of these a ______________ denotes ownership in the corporation and a ______________ is a legal claim against the firm, entitling the owner to receive a fixed annual coupon, plus a lump sum at ______________.

11. Because professional managers usually own a very small percentage of the firms they manage, a separation of ownership and ______________ exists; this separation can lead to a situation in which managers can maximize (their own; shareholders') interests; this, in turn, can lead to corporate takeovers by specialists called ______________.

12. In order to discourage outsiders from taking over the management of their company, current managers use various tactics, such as ______________, ______________, or ______________. In recent years ______________ bonds have been used to finance corporate takeovers; such bonds often have relatively (low, high) chances of being paid off, and therefore offer a correspondingly (low, high) interest rate to lenders.

TRUE-FALSE QUESTIONS

Circle the **T** if the statement is true, the **F** if it is false. Explain to yourself why a statement is false.

T F 1. Corporations are the most common form of business organization in the United States.

T F 2. Proprietorships account for the highest percentage of total business revenues in the United States.

T F 3. Proprietorships and partnerships face unlimited liability for the debts of their firms.

T F 4. The main advantage of corporations is that they offer limited liability to shareholders.

T F 5. Corporate shareholders are taxed twice on the corporation's earnings.

T F 6. A separation of ownership and control often exists in large corporations.

T F 7. In large corporations managers can possibly pursue their own, not shareholders', interests.

T F 8. To the extent that current managers face hostile takeovers, they need to be concerned with shareholders' interests.

T F 9. The adverse selection problem results due to asymmetric information after a transaction.

T F 10. Borrowers who do not intend to repay loans might be able to outbid honest borrowers for the funds.

T F 11. Stocks offer a higher risk and return, relative to bonds, but bonds offer investors greater control over the firm's decisions.

T F 12. Reinvestment of retained earnings and depreciation reserves are the most important sources of corporate finance.

T F 13. In a limited partnership at least one partner must face unlimited liability.

T F 14. The principal-agent problem implies that management will pursue the public's interest, not stockholder interests.

T F 15. When lenders insist that borrowers put up collateral they are trying to avoid the principal-agent problem.

T F 16. Golden parachutes, poison pills, and greenmail necessarily harm the stockholders of the company being acquired.

T F 17. The evidence is clear that junk bonds are harmful to those who purchase them and to the acquired company.

T F 18. Globalization of markets benefits everyone.

MULTIPLE CHOICE QUESTIONS

Circle the letter that corresponds to the best answer.

1. Which of the following is *not* true, concerning a proprietorship?
   a. Most U.S. firms are proprietorships.
   b. They are easy to form and to dissolve.
   c. They offer limited liability.
   d. The owner is taxed only once on business income.

2. Which of the following is a disadvantage of a proprietorship?
   a. Unlimited liability for the firm's debts.
   b. Limited ability to raise funds.
   c. The firm ends with the death of the proprietor.
   d. All of the above

3. Which of the following is *not* true, concerning partnerships?
   a. There are fewer partnerships than proprietorships in the United States.
   b. They permit more effective specialization than proprietorships.
   c. Business income is taxed only once.
   d. Partners have limited liability for the firm's debts.

4. Which of the following is an advantage of partnerships?
   a. Partners have unlimited liability.
   b. They enjoy reduced cost in monitoring job performance.
   c. They must be dissolved if one partner dies.
   d. All of the above

5. A corporation
   a. is a legal entity that conducts business in its own name.
   b. permits unlimited liability to shareholders.
   c. must be dissolved if a majority stockholder dies.
   d. has severely limited abilities to attract financial resources.

*6. Which is most unlike the others, with respect to taxation?
   a. proprietorship
   b. partnership
   c. corporation
   d. S corporation

7. Regarding asymmetric information:
   a. if it exists before a transaction, adverse selection may occur.
   b. it exists only after the transaction.
   c. it presents a problem that cannot be reduced.
   d. if it exists after a transaction, adverse selection may occur.

8. Which of the following helps to reduce the problem of asymmetric information?
   a. Require borrowers to put up collateral.
   b. Purchase information regarding the credit rating of borrowers.
   c. Require an incentive compatible contract.
   d. All of the above

*9. Which of the following is *not* an example of a problem resulting from asymmetric information?
   a. moral hazard problem
   b. junk bond problem
   c. adverse selection problem
   d. principal-agent problem

*10. Which of the following has *not* evolved to solve a problem resulting from asymmetric information?
   a. market for corporate control
   b. incentive compatible contracts
   c. globalized stock markets
   d. credit rating agencies

11. Shareholders
   a. are the owners of corporations.
   b. are less at risk than are bondholders.
   c. are subject to unlimited risk.
   d. have less control over firm decisions than do bondholders.

12. In a large corporation
   a. ownership is usually concentrated in a few hands.
   b. separation of ownership and control is unlikely.
   c. managers may try to maximize their own (not shareholders') wealth.
   d. shareholders usually are hurt by hostile takeovers.

*13. Which of the following problems is most unlike the others?
   a. moral hazard
   b. principal-agent
   c. adverse selection
   d. asymmetric information

14. Analogy: Incentive compatible contracts are to the moral hazard problem as ________________ is to the principal-agent problem.
   a. the development of credit rating agencies
   b. the development of the corporate takeover market
   c. requiring borrowers to put up collateral
   d. separation of ownership and control

15. Corporate takeovers
    a. generally benefit stockholders of the acquiring company.
    b. generally benefit stockholders of the acquired company.
    c. make managers more responsive to stockholder interests.
    d. All of the above

16. Junk bonds
    a. are relatively risky.
    b. pay relatively low interest rates.
    c. are harmful to stockholders when used to finance corporate takeovers.
    d. are too risky to people who purchase them.

MATCHING

Choose the item in column (2) that best matches an item in column (1).

(1)	(2)
a. greenmail	h. corporate debt
b. share of stock	i. poison pill
c. bond	j. limited liability
d. separation of ownership and control	k. total revenues minus total costs
e. total profits	l. corporate ownership
f. corporation	m. principal-agent problem
g. asymmetric information	n. adverse selection

CASE STUDY

Frank R. Lichtenberg, who teaches at Columbia Business School, has analyzed productivity trends in more than 17,000 manufacturing plants in the United States. He found that during the 1980's, the merger/acquisition/leveraged buyout heyday, the extent to which firms diversified decreased; and that reduced diversification led to increased worker productivity. In other words, the conglomerate wave of the 1960s (which was due partly to vigorous antitrust enforcement which discouraged firms from buying firms in their own industries) led to decreased productivity, and the merger trend reversed that problem.

1. How might you account for Lichtenberg's findings?

2. Do his studies favor corporate takeovers or not? Why?

ANSWERS TO CHAPTER 21

COMPLETION QUESTIONS

1. proprietorships, partnerships, corporations; limited partnerships, S corporations
2. proprietorships, corporations
3. corporation; shareholders, limited
4. twice
5. asymmetric; adverse selection; moral hazard
6. control, moral
7. credit rating; collateral
8. incentive, risk
9. principal-agent, corporate control (or takeovers)
10. stocks, bonds, reinvestment; stock, bond, maturity
11. control; their own; corporate raiders
12. poison pills, greenmail, golden parachutes; junk; low, high

TRUE-FALSE QUESTIONS

1. F Proprietorships account for about 70 percent of total business organizations.
2. F Corporations do.
3. T
4. T
5. T
6. T
7. T
8. T
9. F Before a transaction.
10. T
11. F Stocks also give investors greater control than bonds.
12. T
13. T
14. F It implies that managers pursue their own interests.
15. F They are trying to prevent the adverse selection problem.
16. F They may well help shareholders because management might now consider shareholders' interests more fully.
17. F All the evidence is not in yet.
18. F All consumers benefit, but some businesses and workers will lose to the competition.

MULTIPLE CHOICE

1.c; 2.d; 3.d; 4.b; 5.a; 6.c; 7.a; 8.d; 9.b; 10.c;
11.a; 12.c; 13.c; 14.b; 15.d; 16.a

MATCHING

a and i; b and l; c and h; d and m; e and k; f and j; g and n

CASE STUDY

1. Apparently conglomerates induced firms to expand into industries in which they had no expertise; the merger period has induced managers to stay in areas in which they have a comparative advantage.
2. His data seem to support corporate takeovers; apparently takeovers and mergers tend to concentrate, rather than diversity, a firm's business.

GLOSSARY TO CHAPTER 21

Adverse selection The problem that arises in financial markets when borrowers that are the worst credit risks are most likely to receive loans.

Asymmetric information Information that is possessed by one side of a transaction only. If, for example, sellers have relatively more information than buyers, they will be at an advantage.

Bond A legal claim against a firm entitling the owner of the bond to receive a fixed annual coupon payment, plus a lump sum payment at the bond's maturity date; bonds are issued in return for funds lent to the firm.

Corporate raiders People or firms that specialize in seeking out corporations that are potential targets for takeovers.

Corporation A legal entity that may conduct business in its own name just as an individual does; the owners of a corporation, called shareholders, own shares of the firm's profits and enjoy the protection of limited liability.

Dividends Portion of a corporation's profits paid to the firm's owners.

Financial capital The money available to purchase capital goods such as plant and equipment.

Golden parachute A guarantee to the existing managers of a firm that if they are ousted as a result of a takeover they will receive lucrative severance payments.

Greenmail Payment by a target firm of a substantial premium for shares held by a corporate raider, in return for the raider's agreement to cease attempts at a takeover.

Hostile takeover Purchase of a firm that is opposed by the target firm's current management, sometimes because it appears likely they will lose their jobs if the takeover is successful.

Incentive compatible A situation in which an individual has no incentive to change.

Inside information Information about what is happening in a corporation that only "insiders" know and is not available to the general public.

Junk bonds Risky bonds offering high coupon yields, sometimes issued by corporate raiders to finance takeovers.

Limited liability A legal term meaning that the responsibility, or liability of the owners of a corporation is limited to the value of their ownership shares in the firm.

Limited partnership A firm in which some partners, called limited partners, are granted limited liability; at least one general partner, responsible for managing the partnership, must accept unlimited liability.

Moral hazard A problem that occurs because of asymmetric information after a transaction occurs. In financial markets, a person to whom money has been lent may indulge in more risky behavior, thereby increasing the probability of default on the debt.

Partnership A business owned by two or more co-owners, or partners, who share the responsibilities and profits of the firm, and who are individually liable for all of the debts of the partnership.

Poison pill In general, any maneuver by the management of a target firm that makes the firm either unattractive to a potential raider, or prohibitively expensive.

Principal-agent problem The conflict of interest that occurs when agents--managers of firms--pursue their own objectives to the detriment of the principals'--owners of the firm-- goals.

Proprietorship A business owned by one individual who makes the business decisions, receives all of the profits, and is legally responsible for all of the debts of the firm.

Random walk theory A theory that indicates that successive prices are independent of each other in security markets. In other words, there are no predictable trends in prices, so today's prices cannot be used to predict future prices.

Reinvestment Profits or depreciation reserves used to purchase new capital equipment.

S corporation A type of corporation in which the owners are largely exempt from the double taxation of corporate income.

Separation of ownership and control A situation that exists in corporations in which the owners--shareholders--are different from those who control the operation of the corporation--the managers. The goals of these two groups often are different.

Share of stock A legal claim to a share of a corporation's future profits; if it is common stock, it incorporates certain voting rights regarding major policy decisions of the corporation; if it is preferred stock, its owners are accorded preferential treatment in the payment of dividends.

Unlimited liability A legal term meaning that the personal assets of the owner(s) of a firm may be used to pay off the debts of the firm.

White knight A buyer of a firm that is willing to execute a "friendly" takeover, typically one that retains the management of the acquired firm.

CHAPTER 22

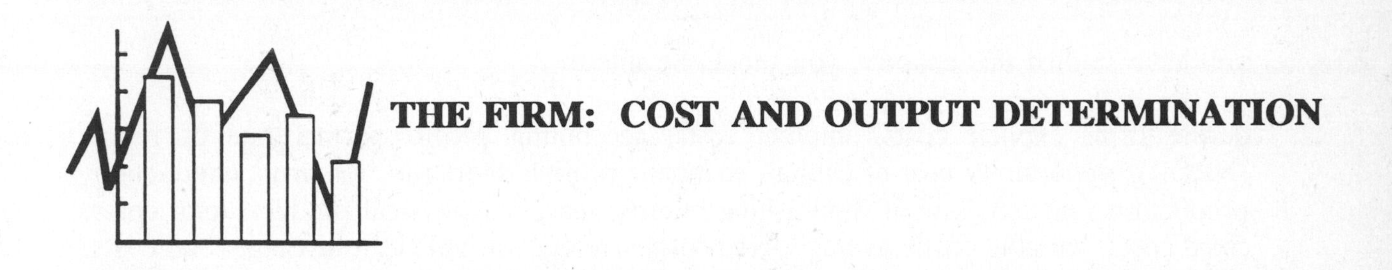

THE FIRM: COST AND OUTPUT DETERMINATION

PUTTING THIS CHAPTER INTO PERSPECTIVE

Chapter 22 is the first chapter in Part Six. It is an important chapter because the material it contains is essential to the remaining five chapters in Part Six.

Chapter 19 analyzed consumer behavior in detail, and it provided the ingredients for a proper understanding of demand. Chapter 22 lays the foundation for supply because it analyzes business costs of production. Many economists refer to microeconomics--the second major topic of this text--as "price theory." The modern theory of price is that market price is determined by supply and demand; because supply is intimately related to a firm's cost of production, this chapter is obviously important.

In this chapter we analyze again the relationship between "average" and "marginal" concepts; more specifically, Chapter 22 analyzes the relationship between marginal cost and average cost. As expected, marginal cost pulls and tugs average cost: if marginal cost is above average cost, then average cost will rise; if marginal cost is below average cost, then average cost will fall; if marginal cost equals average cost, then average cost remains constant. If you truly understand this, then you can easily see why the marginal cost curve intersects the average variable cost curve and the average total cost curve at their minimum points.

In this chapter we also introduce the law of diminishing returns. It is important to understand that this law is a purely technological statement; it indicates what happens to output when inputs are changed in a specific way. By itself the law has nothing to do with costs or profits--each of which, after all, is denominated in money. The law, however, does have *implications* for firm production costs (and therefore for profits), and you should concentrate on how the law accounts for the upward sloping portion of the marginal cost, the average variable cost, and the average total cost curves. Pay particular attention to the marginal cost curve; it is the most important because, as we stress again and again, economic decisions are made on the margin. The profit maximizing firm will compare the marginal cost of producing another unit of output with the marginal benefit of doing so.

Chapter 22 also makes the important distinction between accounting profits and economic profits; it also distinguishes between long-run and short-run cost curves. Note well that it is the law of diminishing returns that determines the shape of the short-run average cost curve, and that it is the existence (or lack thereof) of economies or diseconomies of scale that determines the shape of the long-run average cost curves.

LEARNING OBJECTIVES

After you have studied this chapter, you should be able to

1. define firm, explicit costs, implicit costs, accounting profit, normal rate of return (NROR), opportunity cost of capital, economic profits, short run, long run, production, production function, law of diminishing returns, marginal physical product, total costs, fixed costs, variable costs, average fixed costs, average variable cost, average total costs, marginal costs, planning horizon, long-run average cost curve, planning curve, economies of scale, constant returns to scale, diseconomies of scale, minimum efficient scale.

2. distinguish between accounting profits and economic profits.

3. distinguish between explicit costs and implicit costs.

4. distinguish between the firm's short run and its long run.

5. apply the law of diminishing returns to account for the shape of the firm's short-run marginal cost curve, average total cost curve, and average variable cost curve.

6. classify firm costs as fixed or variable costs.

7. calculate average total cost, average variable cost, average fixed cost, and marginal cost, given sufficient information.

8. apply the concepts of economies of scale, diseconomies of scale, and constant returns to scale to predict the shape of a firm's long-run average cost curve.

9. list reasons for economies of scale and for diseconomies of scale.

10. recognize reasons for a declining number of airline companies in recent years.

CHAPTER OUTLINE

1. A *firm* is an organization that brings together different factors of production, such as labor, land, capital, and entrepreneurial skill, to produce a product or service which it is hoped can be sold for a profit.
   a. *Accounting profits* equal total revenues minus explicit costs.
   b. The opportunity cost of capital, or the normal rate of return to invested capital, is the rate of return that must be paid to an investor to induce him or her to invest in a business.
   c. There is also an opportunity cost to labor; single-owner proprietors, after all, could earn wages elsewhere.
      i. There is an opportunity cost to all inputs.
      ii. Economic profits equal total revenues minus the opportunity cost of all inputs; stated differently, total profits equal total revenues minus the sum of explicit and implicit costs.

2. It is widely assumed by economists that the goal of the firm is to maximize total profits.

3. The short run is defined as that time period in which a firm cannot alter its current size of plant; the long run is that time period in which all factors of production can be varied.

4. *Total costs* are identical to total *fixed costs* plus total *variable costs*.
   a. Total fixed costs do not vary with output.
   b. Total variable costs are the sum of all those costs that vary with output.
   c. There are several short-run average cost curves.
      i. Average total costs equal total costs divided by output.
      ii. Average variable costs equal total variable costs divided by output.
      iii. Average fixed costs equal total fixed costs divided by output.
   d. *Marginal cost* equals the change in total cost divided by the change in output.
   e. When marginal cost is above average cost, average cost rises; when marginal cost is below average cost, average cost falls; when marginal cost equals average cost, average cost remains constant.
   f. The marginal cost curve intersects the average total cost curve and the average variable cost curve at their *minimum points*.

5. The *production function* is a relationship between inputs and outputs; it is a technological, not an economic, relationship.
   a. The law of *diminishing returns* comes into play when the firm increases output in the short run.
   b. The marginal physical product is the change in total product that occurs when a variable input is increased and all other inputs are held constant.
   c. The law of diminishing returns implies that the marginal physical product of labor eventually falls.

6. Diminishing marginal product causes the marginal cost curve, the average total cost curve, and the average variable cost curve to rise.

7. In the *long run* all inputs are variable, and long-run cost curves must take this into account.
   a. The *long-run average cost curve* is the locus of points representing the minimum unit cost of producing any given rate of output, given current technology and resource prices.
   b. Another name for the long-run average cost curve is the *planning horizon*.

8. The long-run average cost curve is also U-shaped.
   a. Initially a firm experiences *economies of scale* due to specialization, a dimensional factor, or improved productive equipment.
   b. Eventually a firm might experience *diseconomies of scale* because a disproportionate increase in management and staff may be needed, and because the costs of information and communication also grow more than proportionally with output.

9. The minimum efficient scale is the lowest rate of output per unit time period at which average costs reach a minimum for a particular firm.

10. When increased deregulation of airlines led to increased competition, the number of airlines decreased rapidly, due to apparent economies of scale in that industry.

KEY TERMS

Marginal physical product
Total costs
Fixed costs
Variable costs
Average fixed costs
Average variable costs
Average total costs
Marginal costs
Long-run average cost curve
Planning curve
Economies of scale
Constant returns to scale
Production

KEY CONCEPTS

Explicit costs
Implicit costs
Accounting profit
Normal rate of return
Economic profits
Long run
Short run
Production function
Law of diminishing returns
Planning horizon
Minimum efficient scale
Firm

COMPLETION QUESTIONS

Fill in the blank or circle the correct term.

1. (Explicit, Implicit) costs are usually considered by accountants, but __________ costs typically are not.

2. Economists consider implicit costs because such costs (do, do not) include the opportunity costs of the resources used.

3. Accounting profits equal ________________ minus ________________; economic profits equal ________________ minus ________________; economic profits are less than accounting profits because economic profits subtract ________________ costs from total revenues.

4. Economists usually assume that the firm's goal is ______________.

5. Our definition of the short run will be the time during which ______________ is fixed, but ________________ is variable; in the long run (no, all) factors are variable.

6. Fixed costs (do, do not) vary with output; variable costs (do, do not) vary with output; ________________, ________________, and ________________ are examples of fixed costs; ________________ and ________________ are examples of variable costs.

7. Short-run average cost curves eventually are upward sloping due to ________________; at the minimum of the average total cost curve, marginal cost is (less than, greater than, equal to) average total cost; if marginal cost exceeds average total cost, then average total cost will (fall, rise, remain constant).

8. Because of diminishing returns, in the (short, long) run the marginal product of labor will eventually (fall, rise, remain constant).

9. The long-run cost curve may also be U-shaped, because initially as a firm expands its scale of operations, it realizes ________________ of scale; then it may realize ________________ returns to scale; eventually it realizes ________________ of scale.

10. Reasons for economies of scale include ________________, ________________, and ________________; a firm might experience diseconomies of scale due to ________________ and ________________.

TRUE-FALSE QUESTIONS

Circle the **T** if the statement is true, the **F** if it is false. Explain to yourself why a statement is false.

T F 1. Accountants typically do not consider implicit costs.

T F 2. Explicit costs include the opportunity costs of a resource.

T F 3. Accounting profits equal total revenues minus explicit costs.

T F 4. Accounting profits always exceed economic profits.

T F 5. Economists usually assume that the firm's goal is to maximize profits.

T F 6. Short-run cost curves that include variable costs eventually reflect the influence of the law of diminishing returns.

T F 7. Fixed costs vary with output.

T F 8. Eventually, as output expands, the short-run marginal cost curve must rise.

T F 9. When average costs exceed marginal cost, marginal cost must be rising.

T F 10. At the minimum average total cost output level, marginal cost equals average total cost.

T F 11. In the short run, the supply of labor to the firm is usually fixed.

T F 12. Because of the law of diminishing returns, the marginal product of labor will rise.

T F 13. Long-run cost curves are U-shaped due to the law of diminishing returns.

MULTIPLE CHOICE QUESTIONS

Circle the letter that corresponds to the best answer.

*1. Explicit costs
   a. are considered by accountants.
   b. are greater than implicit costs.
   c. are considered irrelevant by economists.
   d. are considered by accountants, but not by economists.

2. Implicit costs
   a. are considered important to accountants, but not to economists.
   b. are usually less than explicit costs.
   c. include the opportunity costs of resources.
   d. are considered irrelevant by businesses.

3. Accounting profits
   a. equal total revenues minus explicit costs.
   b. exceed economic profits.
   c. do not take implicit costs into account.
   d. All of the above

4. The opportunity cost of capital is
   a. an explicit cost of doing business.
   b. not an important cost of doing business.
   c. the normal rate of return on capital invested in a business.
   d. purely a technological concept.

5. Which of the following is unlike the others because it is not explicit?
   a. wages
   b. opportunity cost of capital
   c. taxes
   d. rent

*6. Analogy: Rent is to explicit costs as _____ are to implicit costs.
   a. labor services of a proprietor
   b. taxes
   c. wages
   d. accounting profits

7. Which of the following goals of the firm is most widely assumed by economists?
   a. staff maximization
   b. sales maximization
   c. growth maximization
   d. profit maximization

8. In the short run, for our purposes,
   a. all factors are variable.
   b. labor is variable.
   c. capital is variable
   d. both capital and labor are variable.

9. The long run
   a. permits the variation of all factors of production.
   b. is different for different firms.
   c. permits a firm to avoid the consequences of the law of diminishing returns.
   d. All of the above

10. Fixed costs
    a. vary with output.
    b. do not vary with output.
    c. reflect the effect of diminishing returns.
    d. include labor and raw material costs.

11. Which cost is most unlike the others because it is not fixed?
    a. rent
    b. wages
    c. opportunity cost of capital
    d. interest payments on borrowed money

12. If marginal cost is above average total cost, then average total cost
    a. will rise.
    b. will fall.
    c. will remain constant.
    d. cannot be calculated.

13. At that output where average total cost is at a minimum,
    a. marginal cost equals average total cost.
    b. marginal cost equals average variable cost.
    c. average total cost is rising.
    d. total cost is constant.

14. Which short-run curve is *not* U-shaped?
    a. average total cost
    b. marginal cost
    c. average variable cost
    d. average fixed cost

15. The production function
    a. is a technological relationship.
    b. is not an economic relationship.
    c. relates output to inputs.
    d. All of the above

16. Because of the law of diminishing returns,
    a. long-run average cost eventually rises.
    b. marginal cost falls.
    c. the marginal product of labor eventually falls.
    d. the average total cost curve falls.

17. Which is *not* due to the law of diminishing returns?
    a. rising short-run marginal cost
    b. rising long-run average total cost
    c. rising short-run average variable cost
    d. rising short-run average total cost

*18. Analogy: Diminishing returns is to rising short-run average total costs as _____ is to rising long-run average total costs.
    a. economies of scale
    b. diseconomies of scale
    c. law of diminishing returns
    d. constant returns to scale

19. Which of the following helps to account for a U-shaped short-run average total cost curve?
    a. economies of scale
    b. diseconomies of scale
    c. law of diminishing returns
    d. constant returns to scale

20. A firm might experience diseconomies of scale due to
    a. disproportionate rises in specialization.
    b. dimensional factors.
    c. information and communication costs that rise disproportionately.
    d. the ability to use larger-volume machinery that is efficient only at large outputs.

21. If the minimum efficient scale is relatively low, then
    a. there will likely be a relatively large number of firms in the industry.
    b. there will likely be a relatively small number of firms in the industry.
    c. economies of scale are very great.
    d. long-run average costs decline over broad ranges of output.

MATCHING

Choose the item in column (2) that best matches an item in column (1).

(1)	(2)
a. long run	i. falling long-run average cost
b. short run	j. rising long-run average cost
c. fixed cost	k. fixed plant size
d. variable cost	l. diminishing marginal product
e. opportunity cost of capital	m. overhead
f. economies of scale	n. wages of laborers
g. diseconomies of scale	o. implicit cost
h. law of diminishing returns	p. all factors variable

WORKING WITH GRAPHS

1. Assume that the High Rise Bakery produces a single product: loaves of bread. Further assume that the bread is produced using a fixed plant size, with ten ovens and varying quantities of labor. John Doe notices that as he hires additional workers, the total output of bread goes up for a while. Then he finds that after hiring several additional workers, the workers begin to get in one another's way and extra output begins to decline. John knows the principles of economics and something about diminishing marginal physical product. Given the information below, calculate the marginal physical product of John's bakers. Graph total and marginal products on the next page and tell John how many bakers he can employ before diminishing marginal returns set in. (Plot the marginal product at the midpoint between the number of bakers employed.)

Bakers	Output (loaves per day)	Marginal product
0	0	______
1	8	______
2	19	______
3	32	______
4	45	______
5	60	______
6	71	______
7	75	______
8	77	______
9	77	______
10	75	______
11	65	______

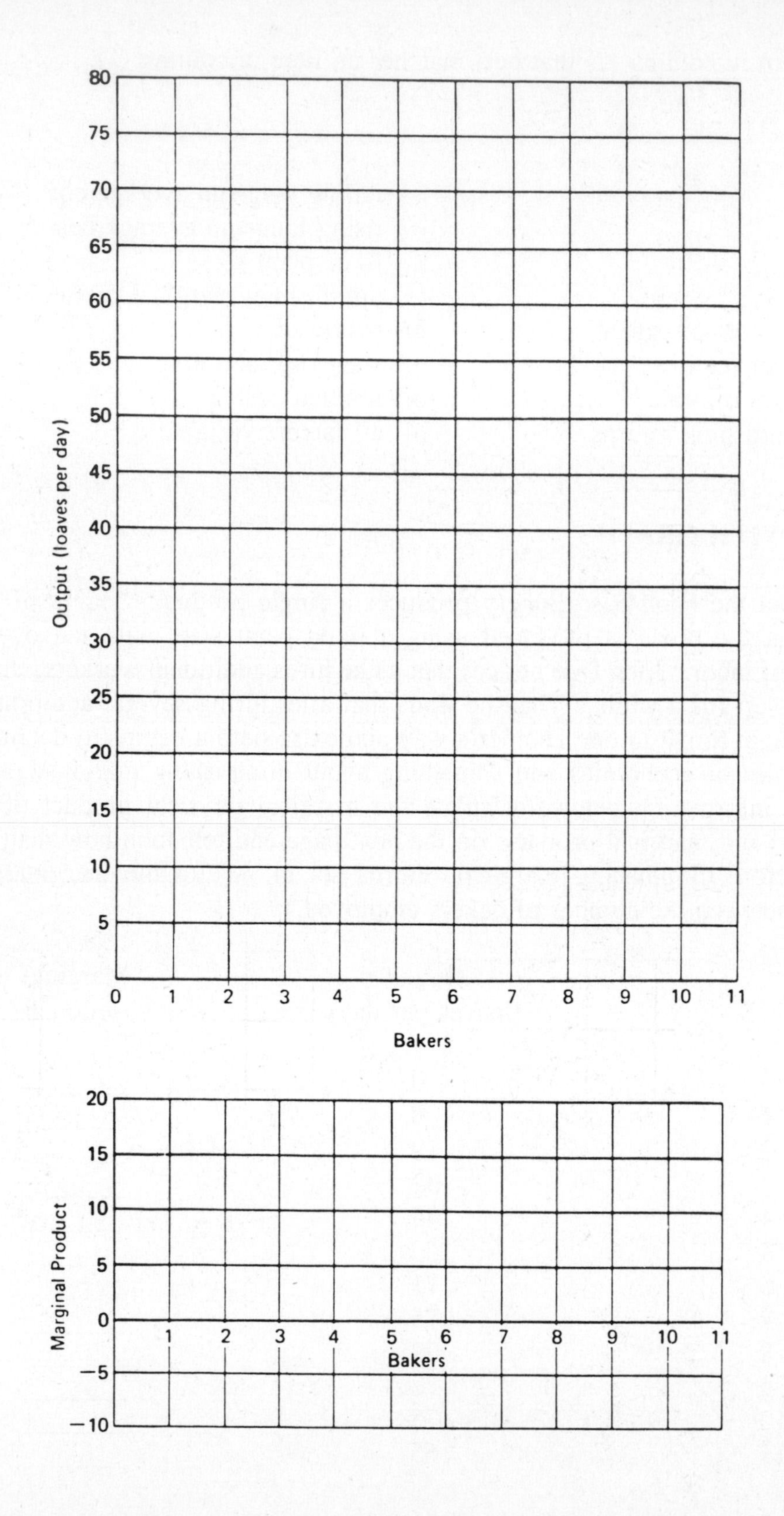

Output (loaves per day)
80
75
70
65
60
55
50
45
40
35
30
25
20
15
10
5
0
1
2
3
4
5
6
7
8
9
10
11
Bakers
Marginal Product
20
15
10
5
0
−5
−10
1
2
3
4
5
6
7
8
9
10
11
Bakers

2. Complete the following table of cost figures and then graph the information on the graphs provided below. Assume total fixed costs are $3.

Output	Total variable costs	Total costs	Average variable cost	Average total cost	Marginal cost
0	0.00	3.00	____	____	____
1	3.00	____	____	____	____
2	____	____	____	4.00	____
3	____	9.20	____	____	____
4	____	____	____	____	2.30
5	____	____	2.38	____	____
6	____	____	____	____	5.00
7	23.90	____	____	____	____
8	____	36.90	____	____	____

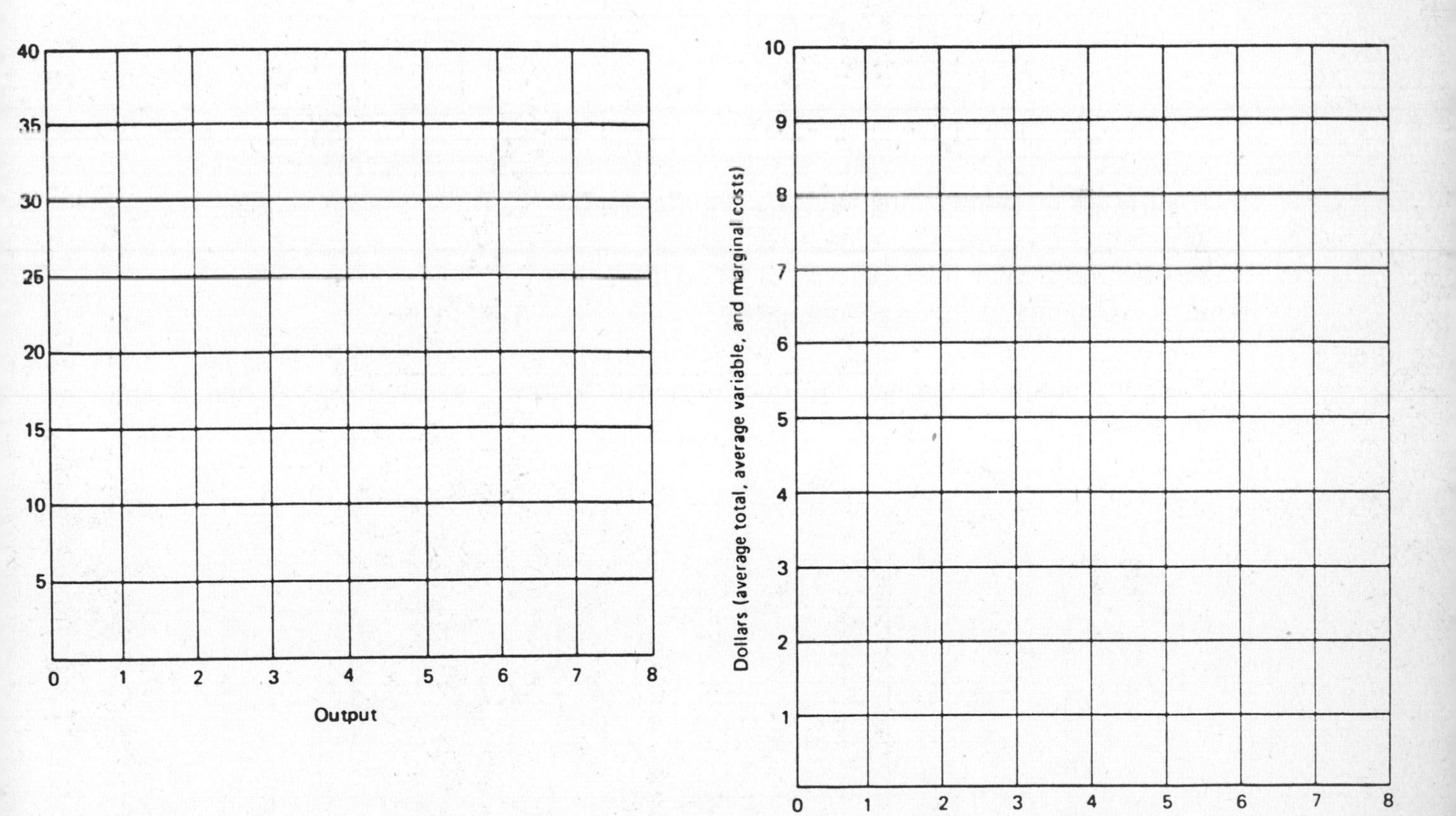

3. Use the graphs below to answer the questions that follow.

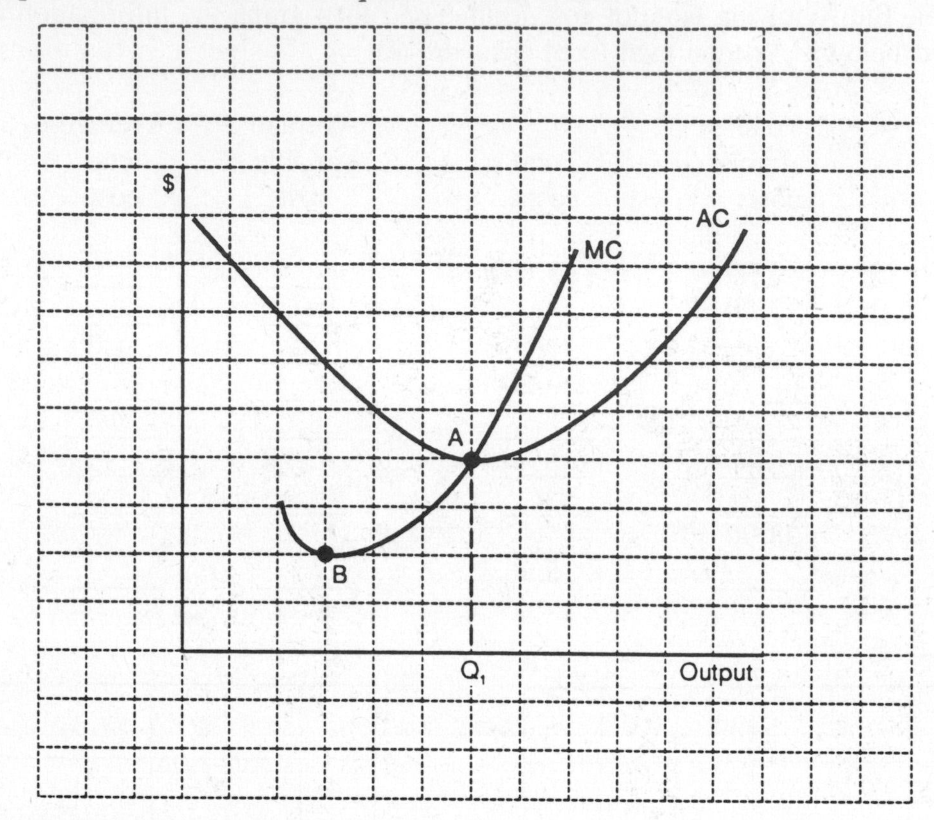

a. At what point do diminishing marginal returns begin?
b. At any output less than Q_1, why is AC falling?
c. At any output greater than Q_1, why is AC rising?
d. What is AC doing at the exact output Q_1?

4. Use the graphs below to answer the questions that follow. Assume that A and B are minimum points.

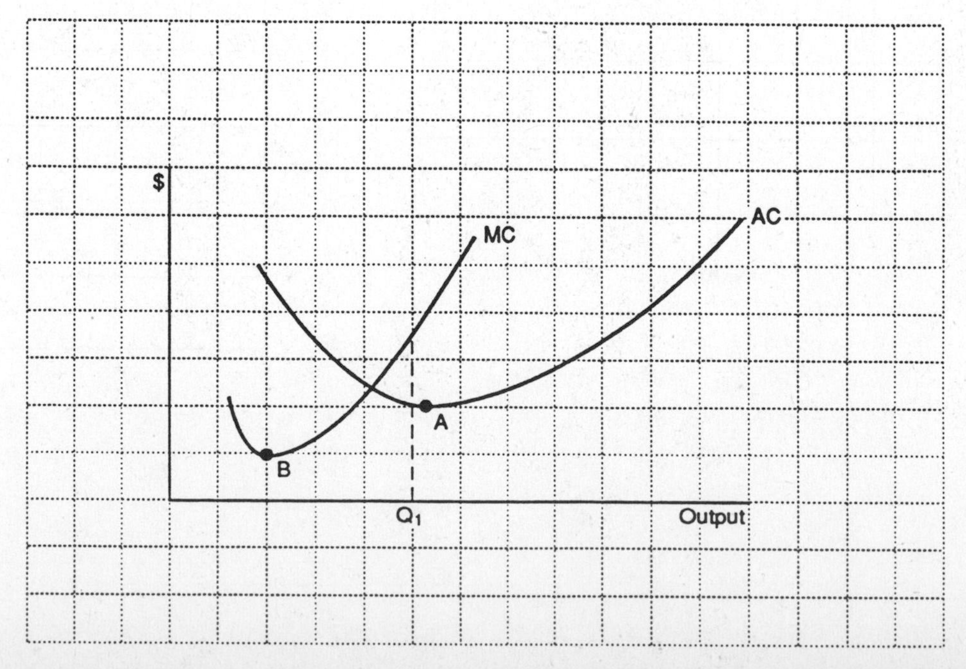

*a. Something is wrong with the graphs above. What is it?
b. According to the graphs above, what is happening at output Q_1, with respect to MC and AC? Is this possible?

PROBLEMS

1. Mr. DeMato owns his own car repair business. His annual total revenues are $200,000, and his total costs are $160,000. Upon further investigation it is discovered that Mr. DeMato did not include an estimate of the worth of his own wages in calculating his annual total profits of $40,000. Nor, it seems, did he estimate the annual rate of return that he could have earned on the $100,000 of his own savings that he used to enter his business. What advice would you give him?

2. Fill in the information in each blank below so that the equation is correct. (Note: Q is quantity of output.)

   a. TC = TFC + ____________
   b. AFC = ____________ - AVC
   c. ATC = (TVC/Q) + ____________
   d. TFC = Q x ____________
   e. AVC = (TC/Q) - ____________/Q
   f. TVC = (Q x ATC) - Q x ____________

CASE STUDY

Economists think that the distinction between marginal cost and sunk costs is crucial to decision-making. They define sunk costs as costs that do not change with the decision at hand. For example, assume that you own a restaurant that is open only at night, and you now want to decide whether you should open for lunch. The $1,000 per month rent and the $500 per month payment on a loan used to start your restaurant are sunk costs. *Moreover, such sunk cost should be ignored in making your decision.* Instead, you should compare the change in your total revenues (marginal revenues) to the change in your total costs (marginal costs) after you tried serving lunch for a reasonable period of time.

1. Suppose that your monthly revenues (due to your lunch trade) rise by $2,000 per month and your marginal costs (additional costs for labor, food and beverages, and so on) rise by $1,000 per month. Should you continue to open the restaurant for lunch? Why or why not?

2. Suppose your accountant tells you to allocate half your rent payment and half your loan payment as a "cost" of your lunch trade. Should you heed his advice? Why or why not?

ANSWERS TO CHAPTER 22

COMPLETION QUESTIONS

1. Explicit, implicit
2. do
3. total revenues, explicit costs; total revenues, implicit plus explicit costs; implicit
4. profit maximization
5. capital, labor; all
6. do not; do; rent, opportunity cost of capital, interest payments on mortgages; wages, raw material costs
7. diminishing returns; equal to; rise
8. short, fall
9. economies; constant; diseconomies
10. specialization, dimensional factors, improved productive equipment; disproportionate requirements for managers and staff, disproportionate costs of information and communication

TRUE-FALSE QUESTIONS

1. T
2. F Implicit costs do.
3. T
4. T
5. T
6. T
7. F By definition they do not.
8. T
9. F Not necessarily.
10. T
11. F Capital is fixed in the short run.
12. F It falls due to the law of diminishing returns.
13. F Diminishing returns occurs in the short run.

MULTIPLE CHOICE QUESTIONS

1.a; 2.c; 3.d; 4.c; 5.b; 6.a; 7.d; 8.b; 9.d; 10.b;
11.b; 12.a; 13.a; 14.d; 15.d; 16.c; 17.b; 18.b; 19.c; 20.c;
21.a

MATCHING

a and p; b and k; c and m; d and n; e and o; f and i; g and j; h and l

WORKING WITH GRAPHS

1. Marginal product: 8; 11; 13; 13; 15; 11; 4; 2; 0; -2; -10
   Diminishing returns set in when John hires the sixth baker.

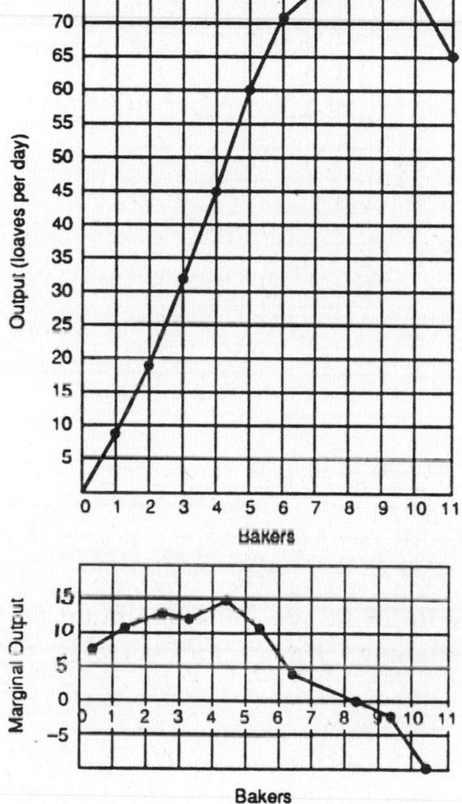

2.

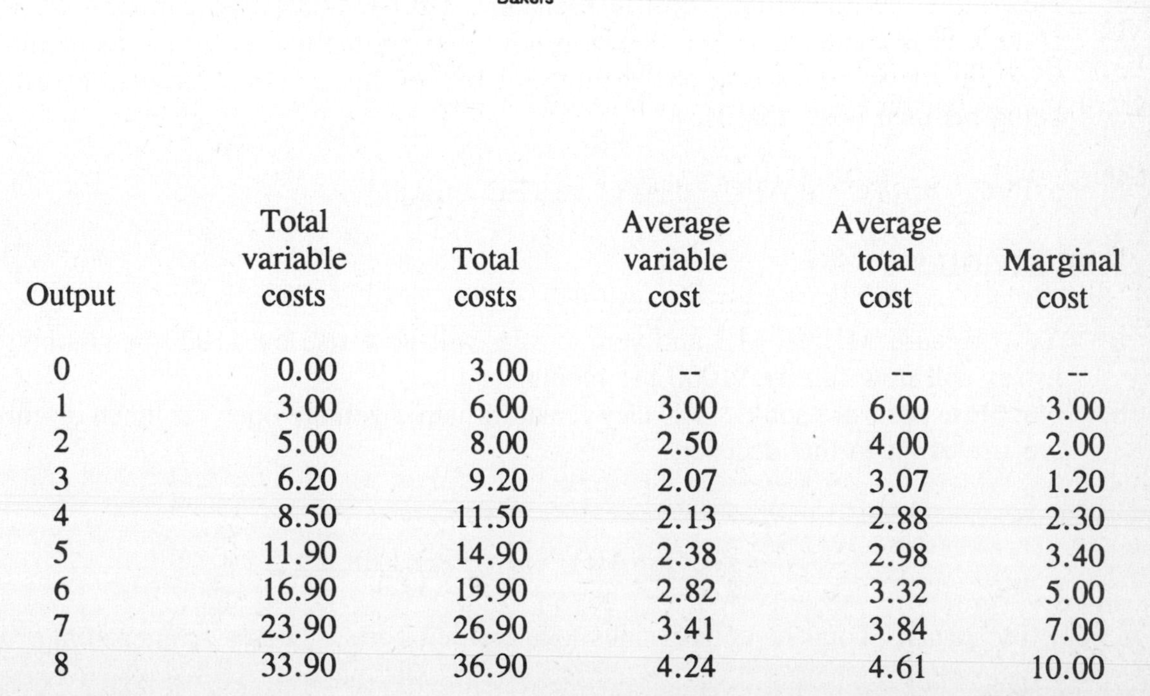

Output	Total variable costs	Total costs	Average variable cost	Average total cost	Marginal cost
0	0.00	3.00	--	--	--
1	3.00	6.00	3.00	6.00	3.00
2	5.00	8.00	2.50	4.00	2.00
3	6.20	9.20	2.07	3.07	1.20
4	8.50	11.50	2.13	2.88	2.30
5	11.90	14.90	2.38	2.98	3.40
6	16.90	19.90	2.82	3.32	5.00
7	23.90	26.90	3.41	3.84	7.00
8	33.90	36.90	4.24	4.61	10.00

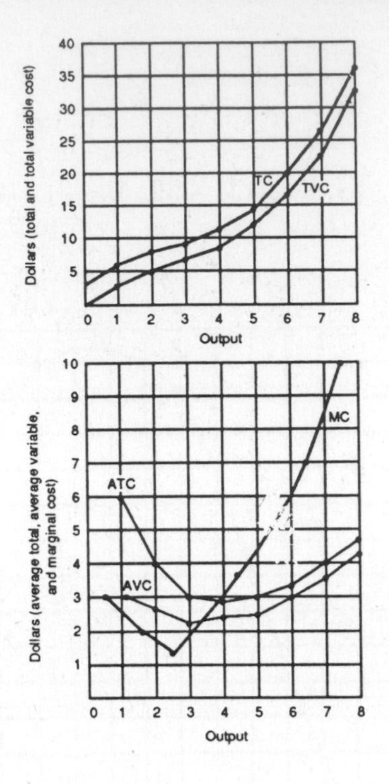

3. a. B
   b. MC is below AC, due to specialization
   c. MC is above AC
   d. AC is constant, because MC = AC.

4. a. MC cuts the AC curve to the left of AC's minimum point.
   b. MC > AC, yet AC is falling. No.

PROBLEMS

1. Determine the opportunity cost of his labor, and the interest he can earn on $100,000. If the sum is greater than $40,000 he is not covering implicit costs, and he might consider working for someone else and earning interest on his money. Unless he really enjoys being his own boss, that is.

2. a.TVC b.ATC c.AFC d.AFC e.TFC f.AFC

CASE STUDIES

a. Yes, because MR > MC and your profits will now rise by $1000 per month, or your losses will now fall by $1000 per month.

b. No; those costs are sunk costs--they remain whether you are open for lunch or not--so they are irrelevant to this decision.

GLOSSARY TO CHAPTER 22

Accounting profit Total revenues minus total explicit costs. Losses are negative profits.

Average fixed costs Total fixed costs divided by the number of units produced.

Average total costs Total costs divided by the number of units produced; sometimes called average per unit total costs.

Average variable costs Total variable costs divided by the number of units produced.

Constant returns to scale A situation in which the long-run average cost curve of a firm remains flat, or horizontal, as output increases.

Diseconomies of scale When output increases lead to increases in long- run average costs.

Economic profits Total revenues minus total opportunity cost of all inputs used, or total revenues minus the total of all implicit and explicit costs.

Economies of scale When output increases lead to decreases in long-run average costs.

Explicit costs Those costs that business managers must take account of because they must be paid; for example, wages, taxes, and rent.

Firm A business organization that employs resources to produce goods or services for a profit.

Fixed cost Those costs that do not vary with output. Fixed costs include such things as rent on a building and the cost of machinery. These costs are fixed for a certain period of time; in the long run they are variable.

Implicit cost Those costs that business managers do not necessarily have to take account of, such as the opportunity cost of factors of production that are owned; for example, owner-provided capital and owner-provided labor.

Law of diminishing (marginal) returns After some point, successive increases in a variable factor of production, such as labor, added to fixed factors of production, will result in smaller increases in output.

Long run That time period in which all factors of production can be varied.

Long-run average cost curve (LAC) The locus of points representing the minimum unit cost of producing any given rate of output, given current technology and resource prices.

Minimum efficient scale The lowest rate of output per unit time period at which average costs reach a minimum for a particular firm.

Marginal physical product The physical output that is due to the addition of one more unit of a variable factor of production; the change in total product occurring when a variable input is increased and all other inputs are held constant.

Normal rate of return (NROR) The normal rate of return to investment; otherwise known as the opportunity cost of capital.

Opportunity cost of capital The normal rate of return or the amount that must be paid to an investor to induce her or him to invest in a business. Economists consider this a cost of production and it is included in our cost examples.

Planning curve Another name for the long-run average cost curve.

Planning horizon Another name for the long-run. All inputs are variable during the planning horizon.

Production Any transformation of materials that makes them more valuable. The use of resources that transforms any good or service into a different good or service.

Production function The relationship between inputs and output. A production function is a technological, not an economic relationship.

Short run That time period in which a firm cannot alter its current size of plant.

Total costs All the costs of a firm combined, including rent, payments to workers, interest on borrowed money, and so on, including all implicit cost.

Variable costs Those costs that vary with the rate of production. They include wages paid to workers and the costs of materials.

CHAPTER 23

PERFECT COMPETITION

PUTTING THIS CHAPTER INTO PERSPECTIVE

Chapter 23 is the first of three chapters (the others are Chapters 24 and 25) that are concerned with how firms determine price and output under different market structures. The market structures studied are perfect competition (the subject of this chapter), monopoly (Chapter 24), monopolistic competition (Chapter 25), and oligopoly (also in Chapter 25).

Your understanding of the economic analysis of firms operating in various market structures will be facilitated if you see the "big picture." In effect, the same pattern of methodology can be found under each market structure analysis. First note well the specific characteristics of each particular market structure; memorize those characteristics and then try to see how each one helps to make the specific market structure unique.

Secondly, try to determine the firm's short-run (and then long-run) equilibrium output and price. You might find it helpful to know that regardless of the model we analyze, the firm's equilibrium output will occur where marginal benefit (MB) equals marginal cost (MC). Under different circumstances, the MB to an economic agent (firm, consumer, employer, laborer, etc.) will be called different things; so too will the specific economic agent's MC be called different things in different models and situations. Nevertheless, our assumption of the goal of maximization usually allows us to predict the optimal decision point. For example, in this chapter the competitive firm's MB is its selling price, or its marginal revenue; the marginal cost of a particular output is found on its marginal cost curve. The competitive firm maximizes at the point where MB = MC; that is, it produces up to the point where price = MC or where marginal revenue (MR) equals MC. Thus the profit maximizing output for the competitive firm is at that level for which MR = MC. (Note: you should always be able to show why the economic agent is not maximizing if MB > MC or if MB < MC.)

The final component of our "pattern" is to determine the extent to which the specific market structure is socially efficient or socially inefficient. That is, does price equal marginal cost? Is output at a level at which average total cost is minimized? Do economic profits persist in the long run?

If you try to see the pattern of analysis you may save yourself a lot of study time, and you can more easily *compare* the various market structures (a task which your instructor may well ask you to perform).

LEARNING OBJECTIVES

After you have studied this chapter, you should be able to

1. define market structure, price taker, total revenues, marginal revenue, short-run shutdown price, short-run break-even price, industry supply curve, long-run industry supply curve, constant-cost industry, increasing-cost industry, decreasing-cost industry, and marginal-cost pricing.

2. list four characteristics of the perfect competition market structure.

3. recognize the shape of a competitive firm's demand curve and recognize reasons for its shape.

4. determine a perfect competitor's optimal output rate, given sufficient information.

5. calculate the value of a perfect competitor's short-run profits, given sufficient information.

6. recognize and determine the perfectly competitive firm's short-run shutdown price and its short-run break-even price.

7. recognize a perfectly competitive firm's short-run supply curve and recognize how an *industry* short-run supply curve is derived.

8. predict the effect on price and output resulting from a change in demand in constant-cost, increasing-cost, and decreasing-cost industries.

9. recognize the long-run equilibrium position for a firm in a perfectly competitive industry.

10. indicate why a perfectly competitive market structure is socially efficient.

11. recognize how the asymmetry of information problem affects the perfect competition model.

CHAPTER OUTLINE

1. There are four major characteristics of the perfect competition market structure: a large number of buyers and sellers, homogeneous product, symmetric information, and unimpeded industry exit and entry.

2. Because in the perfect competition model many firms produce a homogeneous product, a single firm's demand curve is perfectly elastic; its demand curve is horizontal at the "going" market price.

3. In order to predict how much the perfect competitor will produce, we assume that it wants to maximize total profits.
   a. Total revenues equal quantity sold times price per unit.
   b. In the short run total costs are the sum of total fixed costs and total variable costs.
   c. Total revenues minus total costs equal total profits.
   d. Marginal revenue equals the change in total revenue divided by the change in output.
   e. Total profits are maximized at that rate of output where marginal revenue equals marginal cost.

4. Because a normal rate of return to investment is included in the average total cost curve, the "profits" we calculate are *economic profits*.

5. The firm's *short-run shutdown price* occurs at its minimum average variable cost value; at a higher price the firm should produce and contribute to payment of fixed costs; if the firm produced at a lower price, its losses would *exceed* total fixed costs.

6. The firm's *short-run break-even price* is found at the minimum point on its average total cost curve; at a higher price the firm will earn abnormal profits; at a lower price it suffers economic losses; at the minimum point economic profits equal zero.

7. The firm's *short-run supply curve* is its marginal cost curve above the short-run shutdown point.

8. The *short-run industry supply curve* is derived by summing horizontally all the firm supply curves; the industry supply curve shifts when nonprice determinants of supply change.

9. In a competitive market, the "going" price is set where the market demand curve intersects the industry supply curve.

10. In the long run, because abnormal industry profits induce entry and because negative industry profits induce exit, firms in a competitive industry will earn *zero economic profits*.
    a. Long-run supply curves relate price and quantity supplied after firms have time to enter or exit from an industry.
    b. A *constant-cost industry* is one whose long-run supply curve is horizontal, because input prices are unaffected by output.
    c. An *increasing-cost industry* is one whose long-run supply curve is positively sloped, because the price of specialized (or essential) inputs rises as industry output increases.
    d. A *decreasing-cost industry* is one whose long-run supply curve is negatively sloped, because specialized input prices fall as industry output expands.
    e. Assume an increase in the demand for Good A; output will rise but price will be unchanged in the long run in constant cost industries; output will rise and price will rise in increasing cost industries; output will rise and price will fall in decreasing cost industries.

11. In a perfectly competitive industry, a firm operates where price equals marginal revenue equals marginal cost equals short-run minimum average cost equals long-run minimum

average cost--in the long run.

a. Perfectly competitive industries are efficient from society's point of view because for such industries price equals marginal cost in long-run equilibrium.

b. They are also efficient because in long-run equilibrium the output rate is produced at minimum average cost.

c. The perfectly competitive model is not a realistic description of any real-world industry; nevertheless it helps economists explain and predict economic events.

12. If asymmetry of information exists--producers know the true quality of their good but buyers don't--the perfect competition condition is not met.
    a. This example of adverse selection can create the lemons problem.
        i. Firms producing low quality products may try to fool buyers into believing they are buying higher quality products and into paying a higher price.
        ii. Or, firms with a reputation for producing high quality products may "cheat" by cutting quality while still charging the relatively high price.
    b. Because customers cannot be fooled consistently, producers must choose between cheating or signaling to customers that their good is of high quality.
        i. Producers compare (a) the value of profits generated by cheating one time with (b) the value today of a stream of revenues generated by a price sufficiently high to cover the higher costs of a higher quality, i.e., the quality-assuring price.
        ii. If firms earn positive economic profits by charging a quality-assuring price this will lead to entrants into the high quality end of the market; in turn the price of higher quality goods would fall, which creates incentives to cheat by producing lemons.
        iii. Existing high-quality firms can signal that their goods are not lemons by making specific investments in such things as logos, trademarks, and advertising; such investments also act as barriers to entry to potential entrants.

KEY TERMS

Total revenue
Marginal revenue
Short-run shutdown price
Short-run breakeven price
Industry supply curve
Long-run industry supply curve
Perfectly competitive firm
Total costs
Exit and entry of firms

KEY CONCEPTS

Market structure
Perfect competition
Price taker
Signals
Quality-assuring price
Specific investments
Marginal cost pricing
Accounting vs. economic profits
Increasing cost industry
Decreasing cost industry
Constant cost industry

COMPLETION QUESTIONS

Fill in the blank or circle the correct term.

1. The four major characteristics of a perfect competition market structure are ______________, ______________, ______________, and ______________.

2. The demand curve facing a perfect competitor is ______________ elastic; such a demand curve is (horizontal, vertical) at the going market price.

3. We assume that the goal of the firm is to ____________________; if so, the perfect competitor should produce up to the point where MR equals __________; total profits are defined as ____________ minus ______________.

4. Marginal revenue equals ______________ divided by ________________.

*5. Because we include the opportunity cost of capital as a cost of production, the profits we define are (accounting, economic) profits.

6. If the firm's selling price cannot cover its short-run variable costs, then it should ________________________; if selling price equals minimum average total cost, the firm is just ________________________, and its economic profits are (negative, positive, zero).

7. The marginal cost curve eventually is upward sloping, due to the law of ____________________; the marginal cost curve intersects the average variable cost curve at ________________________, and it intersects the average total cost curve at ________________.

8. If marginal cost is below average cost, average cost will _______________; if marginal cost is above average cost, average cost will ________________.

9. If the firm is earning zero economic profits, it (would, would not) continue to operate.

10. The competitive firm's short-run supply curve is the portion of its ____________ curve lying above minimum AVC; the industry short-run supply curve is derived by ________________ all the firm supply curves.

11. In the long run a firm in a perfectly competitive industry will earn exactly zero economic profits. This is true because if economic profits are positive, some firms will ________________ the industry and price will fall; if economic profits are negative, some firms will ______________ the industry and price will rise.

12. If an industry expands and input prices do not change, such an industry is a(n) __________________-cost industry and the long-run supply curve is horizontal; if input prices rise, the industry is a(n) ________________-cost industry and the long-run industry supply curve is ____________________ sloping; if input prices fall, the industry is a(n) ______________________-cost industry and the industry's long-run supply curve is ______________ sloping.

13. In the long run a perfectly competitive firm will earn (negative, positive, zero) economic profits. Its price will be (greater than, less than, equal to) marginal cost, and output (will, will not) be produced at minimum average total cost. From society's point of view, all of this is (efficient, inefficient).

14. Prior to the sale of goods producers know better than buyers do concerning the quality of the good, hence this asymmetric information causes the (adverse selection, moral hazard) problem; producers therefore have an incentive to maintain price but reduce quality, causing the ________________ problem.

15. Because buyers cannot be fooled consistently, they must choose between ________________ and charging a ________________ price.

16. A quality-assuring price can generate positive economic profits, which will induce (entry, exit), which will then (reduce, raise) price, inducing high quality firms to cheat again.

17. By making specific investments in logos, trademarks, and advertising a firm can signal that its goods are of (low, high) quality and (encourage, prevent) entry by potential competitors.

TRUE-FALSE QUESTIONS

Circle the **T** if the statement is true, the **F** if it is false. Explain to yourself why a statement is false.

T F *1. A firm in a perfectly competitive industry is a price taker.

T F 2. Because firms in a perfectly competitive industry are all price takers, price cannot change in that industry.

T F 3. The demand curve facing a perfect competitor is perfectly elastic; it is horizontal at the going price.

T F 4. The perfectly competitive firm attempts to maximize marginal profits.

T F 5. The total profit maximization output occurs at the point where the firm's marginal cost equals its marginal revenue.

T F 6. Average revenue minus average cost equals total profits.

T F 7. If price is below minimum average variable costs in the short run, the firm will shut down, assuming output is where MR = MC.

T F 8. If price is below minimum average total cost, economic profits will be negative, assuming that output is where MR = MC.

T F 9. The firm's short-run supply curve is its average variable cost curve.

T F 10. The industry supply curve is derived by summing horizontally all the firm supply curves.

T F 11. Because of the law of diminishing returns, the firm's short-run supply curve will be upward sloping.

T F 12. Because of free exit and entry, long-run accounting profits for a perfect competitor must be zero.

T F 13. If demand increases in a constant cost industry, eventually price will return to its previous equilibrium level.

T F 14. If demand falls in a decreasing cost industry, in the long run both output and price will fall.

T F 15. In the long-run equilibrium situation, the perfectly competitive firm will earn zero economic profits and produce at minimum average cost.

T F 16. Because of excessive competition, the perfectly competitive industry is believed to be inefficient from society's point of view.

T F 17. The lemons problem is an example of moral hazard.

T F 18. Firms can signal that their product is of high quality by making specific investments in logos and advertising.

MULTIPLE CHOICE QUESTIONS

Circle the letter that corresponds to the best answer.

1. Which of the following is *not* a characteristic of the perfect competition market structure?
   a. symmetric information
   b. homogeneous product
   c. large number of buyers and sellers
   d. restricted entry and exit

2. The demand curve facing the perfect competitor is
   a. horizontal at the going price.
   b. vertical at the going price.
   c. perfectly inelastic.
   d. negatively sloped.

3. In the perfect competition model
   a. each seller is a price taker.
   b. all firms together can affect price.
   c. all firms produce a homogeneous product.
   d. All of the above

4. We assume the firm wants to maximize __________ profits.
   a. marginal
   b. average
   c. total
   d. fixed

5. The firm maximizes total profits at that output at which
   a. MC = MR.
   b. MC > MR.
   c. P = AC.
   d. AR = AC.

6. In which of these cases are economic profits negative?
   a. Total revenues exceed total costs.
   b. Average revenues exceed average costs.
   c. Price is below minimum average total cost.
   d. Average revenue is equal to price.

7. The perfect competitor
   a. can sell all it wants to sell at the going price.
   b. can sell nothing at a price higher than the going price.
   c. faces a perfectly elastic demand curve.
   d. All of the above

8. The competitive firm's short-run total profits equal
   a. average revenue minus average cost times quantity sold.
   b. average revenue minus average cost.
   c. price minus marginal cost.
   d. price minus average variable cost.

9. If selling price equals the firm's minimum average variable cost, then
   a. that is the firm's shutdown point.
   b. economic profits are negative.
   c. the firm is indifferent between producing and shutting down.
   d. All of the above

10. At the short-run break-even price,
    a. accounting profits equal economic profits.
    b. economic profits are negative.
    c. economic profits are zero.
    d. economic profits are positive.

11. The firm's short-run supply curve is its
    a. marginal cost curve above the shutdown point.
    b. average cost curve, above its minimum point.
    c. average variable cost curve, above the shutdown point.
    d. marginal revenue curve.

12. The industry supply curve is derived by summing horizontally all the firms'
    a. marginal cost curves above their shutdown points.
    b. average revenue curves.
    c. total revenue curves.
    d. marginal revenue curves.

13. Which of the following will *not* shift the industry supply curve?
    a. change in price
    b. change in the cost of raw materials
    c. change in number of firms in the industry
    d. change in wage rates

14. If economic profits are negative in an industry, then
    a. firms will enter that industry.
    b. some firms will exit from that industry.
    c. price is above minimum average total costs.
    d. accounting profits must also be negative.

15. In long-run equilibrium, a competitive firm
    a. earns zero economic profits.
    b. produces at minimum average cost.
    c. produces where price equals marginal cost.
    d. All of the above

16. If demand falls in an increasing cost industry, then in the long run
    a. price will fall.
    b. price will return to its previous level.
    c. output will rise.
    d. output will return to its previous level.

17. If demand rises in a decreasing cost industry, then in the long run
    a. price will fall.
    b. output will fall.
    c. price will return to its previous level.
    d. output will return to its previous level.

18. The marginal cost of producing good A
    a. includes fixed costs.
    b. represents the opportunity cost to society of producing one more unit of good A.
    c. is found by reading the average variable cost curve.
    d. includes only labor costs.

19. The lemons problem
    a. results from asymmetric information.
    b. is an example of adverse selection.
    c. can be reduced by firms charging a quality-assured price.
    d. All of the above

MATCHING

Choose the item in column (2) that best matches an item in colunn (1).

(1)	(2)
a. specific investment	h. horizontal long-run industry supply curve (given input prices)
b. constant returns to scale	i. perfectly competitive firm
c. price taker	j. advertising
d. decreasing cost-industry	k. marginal cost curve above shut-down point
e. short-run shutdown price	l. falling long-run industry supply curve
f. short-run supply curve	m. P = minimum AVC
g. profit maximizing output	n. MR = MC

WORKING WITH GRAPHS

1. Use the graphs below to answer the following questions. Assume that the firm is a profit maximizer operating in a competitive market.

   a. How many units of output will the firm produce and sell?
   b. What is TR at this level of output?
   c. What is the ATC at this level of output?
   d. What is the TFC at this level of output?
   e. What is the AVC at this level of output?
   f. What is TC at this level of output?
   g. What is the total profit or loss at this level of output?
   h. What is wrong with the ATC curve as it is drawn?

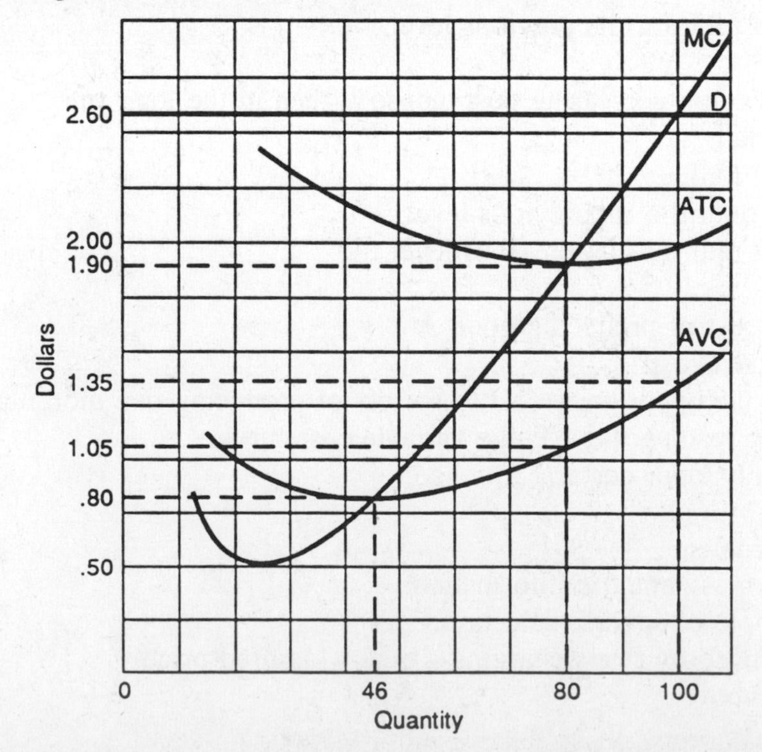

*2. Use the graphs below to answer the questions that follow.

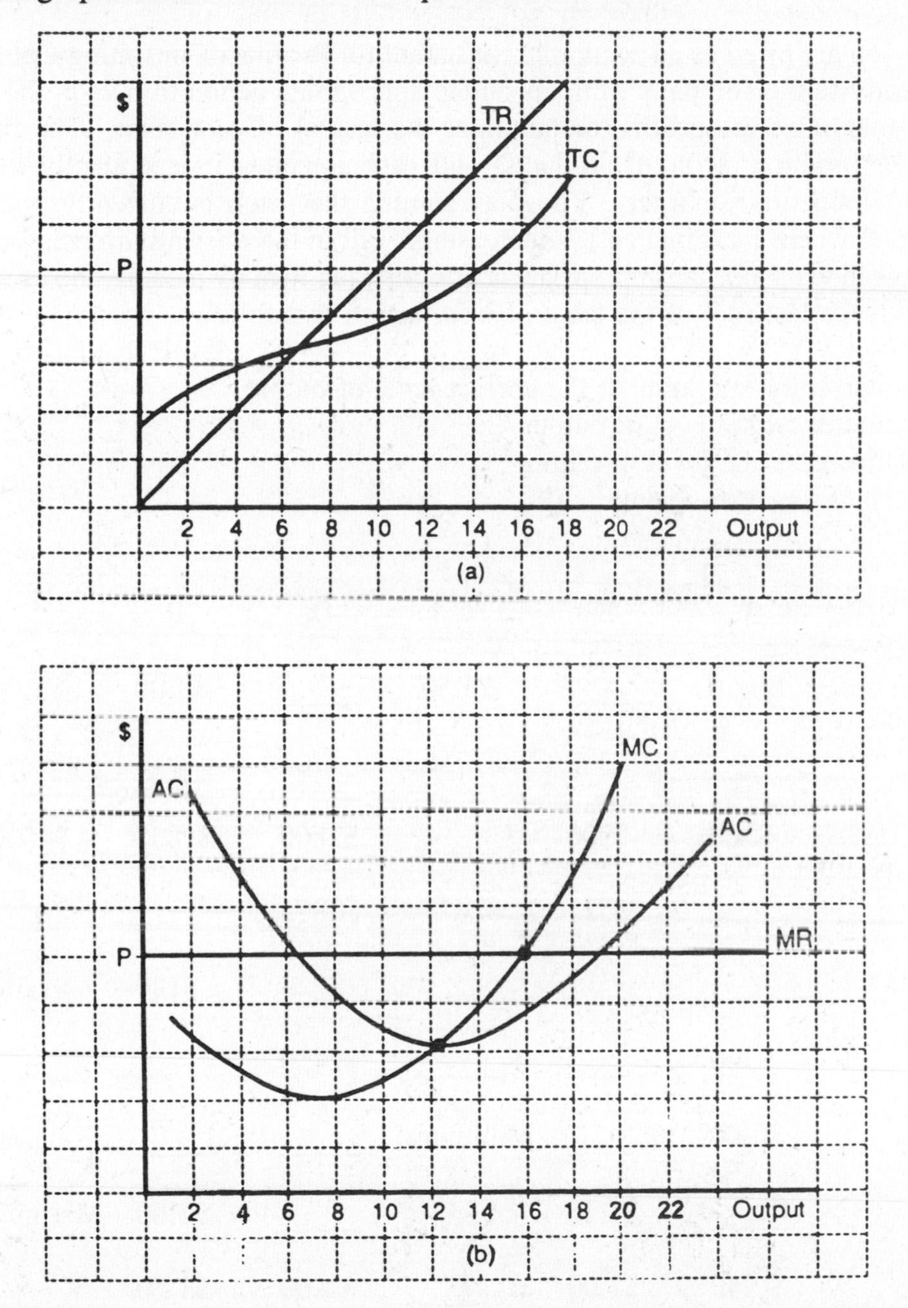

a. The total revenue curve is linear; therefore its slope is a ________; its slope equals what economic concept?

b. The slope of a tangent to a point on the TC curve is defined as what?

c. The firm tries to (minimize, maximize)______________ the positive difference between TR and TC. At what output level does that occur?

d. In panel (b), what is the firm's profit-maximizing output? Why?

e. How are your answers to parts c and d related?

PROBLEMS

1. Suppose you are hired as an economic consultant for Profmax Consulting Company. Your job is to advise the company's clients on the appropriate action to take in the short run in order to maximize the profits (or minimize the losses) of each firm. The firms you are to analyze produce different products, and each operates independently in a different perfectly competitive market. You may assume that each is currently operating at an output level where marginal cost is increasing. Fill in the missing information, and make your suggestions about the appropriate action for each firm by placing one of the following symbols in the last row of the table of information that follows.

   C = currently operating at the correct level of output
   I = increase the level of output
   D = decrease the level of output
   SD = shut down the plant

Firm	A	B	C	D	E	F	G
Price	$0.50	____	$3.50	____	$3.00	$5.00	____
Output	____	300	750	700	____	____	1000
TR	$500	$300	____	$2800	$1800	$4000	$5000
TC	____	$525	$2625	$2975	____	____	____
TFC	____	____	____	____	$180	$1200	____
TVC	$300	____	____	$2450	____	____	$3000
ATC	$0.40	____	Minimum	____	____	$5.50	$5.50
AVC	____	$1.20	$3.00	____	$2.00	Minimum	____
MC	$0.40	$1.00	____	$4.00	$3.50	____	$5.75
Suggestion	____	____	____	____	____	____	____

ANSWERS TO CHAPTER 23

COMPLETION QUESTIONS

1. large number of buyers and sellers, homogeneous product, symmetric information, unimpeded entry or exit
2. perfectly; horizontal
3. maximize total profits; MC; total revenues, total costs
4. change in total revenue, change in output
5. economic
6. shut down; breaking even, zero
7. diminishing returns; minimum AVC, minimum ATC
8. fall; rise
9. would
10. MC; summing horizontally
11. enter; exit
12. constant; increasing, upward; decreasing, downward
13. zero; equal to, will; efficient
14. adverse selection; lemons
15. cheating, quality-assuring
16. entry, reducc
17. high, prevent

TRUE-FALSE

1. T
2. F Price is a constant to an *individual* firm, but not to the group of firms.
3. T
4. F Firms attempt to maximize *total* profits.
5. T
6. F It equals average profits.
7. T
8. T
9. F The firm's marginal cost curve above minimum AVC is its short-run supply curve.
10. T
11. T
12. F Long-run *economic* profits must be zero.
13. T
14. F Price will rise.
15. T
16. F It is efficient because P = MC and economic profits = 0 in the long run.
17. F Examplc of adverse selection.
18. T

MULTIPLE CHOICE QUESTIONS

1.d;	2.a;	3.d;	4.c;	5.a;	6.c;	7.d;	8.a;	9.d;	10.c;
11.a;	12.a;	13.a;	14.b;	15.d;	16.a;	17.a;	18.b;	19.d	

MATCHING

a and j; b and h; c and i; d and l; e and m; f and k; g and n

WORKING WITH GRAPHS

1. a. 100
   b. $260
   c. $2
   d. $65
   e. $1.35
   f. $200
   g. $60 profit
   h. (ATC-AVC) x Quantity should be the same value at every output; here at Q = 80 that value is $68 and at Q = 100 that value is $65.

2. a. constant; MR (or P)
   b. MC
   c. maximize; 16 units of output
   d. 16 units of output; because MC = MR at that output level
   e. MC = MR at 16 units of output

PROBLEMS

Firm	A	B	C	D	E	F	G
Price	$0.50	$1.00	$3.50	$4.00	$3.00	$5.00	$5.00
Output	1000	300	750	700	600	800	1000
TR	$500	$300	$2625	$2800	$1800	$4000	$5000
TC	$400	$525	$2625	$2975	$1380	$4400	$5500
TFC	$100	$165	$375	$525	$180	$1200	$2500
TVC	$300	$360	$2250	$2450	$1200	$3200	$3000
ATC	$0.40	$1.75	Minimum	$4.25	$2.30	$5.50	$5.50
AVC	$0.30	$1.20	$3.00	$3.50	$2.00	Minimum	$3.00
MC	$0.40	$1.00	$3.50	$4.00	$3.50	$4.00	$5.75
Suggestion	I	SD	C	C	D	I	D

GLOSSARY TO CHAPTER 23

Constant-cost industry An industry whose total output can be increased without an increase in long-run per unit costs; an industry whose long-run supply curve is horizontal.

Decreasing-cost industry An industry in which an increase in industry output leads to a reduction in long-run per unit costs, such that the long-run industry supply curve is downward sloping.

Increasing-cost industry An industry in which an increase in industry output is accompanied by an increase in long-run per unit cost, such that the long-run industry supply curve is upward sloping.

Industry supply curve The locus of points showing the minimum prices at which given quantities will be forthcoming; also called the market supply curve.

Lemons problem The situation in which consumers, because they don't know about the quality of a product, are only willing to pay the price of a low-quality product, even if a higher-quality product at a higher price exists.

Long-run industry supply curve A market supply curve showing the relationship between price and quantities forthcoming after firms have been allowed the time to enter into or exit from an industry, depending on whether there have been positive or negative economic profits.

Marginal cost pricing A system of pricing in which the price charged is equal to the opportunity cost to society of producing one more unit of the good or service in question. The opportunity cost is the marginal cost to society.

Marginal revenue The change in total revenues resulting from a change in output (and sale) of one unit of the product in question.

Market failure A situation in which an unrestrained market operation leads to either too few or too many resources going to a specific economic activity.

Market structure Characteristics of a market, including the number of buyers and sellers, the degree to which products from different firms are in fact different, and the ease of entry into or exit from the market.

Perfect competition A market structure in which the decisions of individual buyers and sellers have no effect on market price.

Perfectly competitive firm A firm that is such a small part of the total industry that it cannot affect the price of the product it sells.

Price taker Another definition of a competitive firm. A price taker is a firm that must take the price of its product as given. The firm cannot influence its price.

Profit-maximizing rate of production That rate of production which maximizes total profits, or the difference between total revenues and total costs; also that rate of production at which marginal revenue equals marginal cost.

Quality-assuring price A price that is high enough to offer a stream of profits that is as great or greater than the very high profits that could be made by cheating customers in one period--offering them a low-quality product at a relatively high price.

Short-run break-even price The price where a firm's total revenues equal its total costs. In economics the break-even price is where the firm is just making a normal rate of return on its capital investment. (It is covering its explicit and implicit cost.)

Short-run shutdown price The price that just covers average variable costs. This occurs just below the intersection of the marginal cost curve and the average variable cost curve.

Signals Compact ways of indicating to economic decision makers information needed to make decisions. A "true signal" not only conveys information but also provides the incentive to "act appropriately" to the signal given. Economic profits and economic losses are such signals.

Specific investments Investments in a product that will lose their value rapidly if customers find out that a firm has cheated them; e.g. logos, trademarks, advertising.

Total costs The sum of total fixed costs and total variable costs.

CHAPTER 24

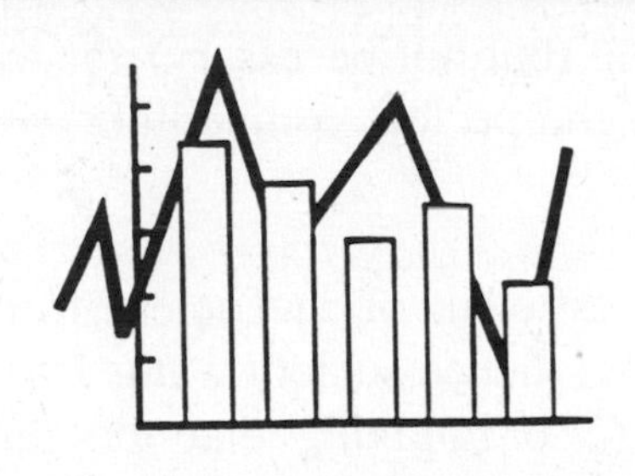

MONOPOLY

PUTTING THIS CHAPTER INTO PERSPECTIVE

Chapter 24 is the second chapter devoted to market structure analysis; the first was Chapter 23, which analyzed the perfect competition model. Chapter 24 introduces the monopoly market structure, and you should be able to compare the perfect competition model to the monopoly model. Here we follow the "pattern" of analysis suggested in Chapter 23 of this student learning guide.

First we consider the characteristics of the monopoly market structure. In the monopoly model one firm produces a homogeneous product and entry into the industry is impeded for one reason or another. Contrast this market structure with perfect competition, in which *many* firms produce a homogeneous product and entry into the industry is easy.

Because there is only one firm in the monopoly market structure, the firm's demand curve is the market demand curve; like all market demand curves, the monopolist's demand curve is negatively sloped. This, of course, is to be contrasted with the horizontal demand curve facing the perfect competitor. Stated differently, there are many close substitutes for the output of the perfect competitor (who is a price taker), but there are no close substitutes for the output of the monopolist (who is a price maker).

The second part of the pattern of analysis leads us to determine the equilibrium output-price combination. Because we assume that the monopolist desires to maximize profit, we (as usual) predict that the firm will produce output up to the point where the marginal benefit (MB) equals the marginal cost (MC) of doing so. In this chapter we assume that the cost of the monopolist is not unlike that of the perfect competitor; therefore its marginal cost is found by reading the marginal cost curve. The marginal benefit to the monopolist of producing one more unit of output is a bit more troublesome. As was true for the perfect competitor, for the monopolist the marginal benefit equals the marginal revenue. Unlike the situation under perfect competition, however, under monopoly marginal revenue falls, because the monopolist's demand curve is downward sloping. Marginal revenue is a constant to the perfect competitor because the demand curve is horizontal (and therefore average revenue is constant). Once the profit maximizing output is determined, the monopolist's price is already determined; the quantity produced can be sold only at one price, read from the monopolist's demand curve. Note that because average revenue equals price and because marginal revenue is less than average revenue, in equilibrium the monopolist must be producing where price exceeds marginal revenue (more about this later). Note that all of this assumes that the monopolist sells all of its output at the same price. If we relax that assumption, as we do near the end of Chapter 24, then we can analyze price discrimination.

Because entry into the monopoly industry is impeded, it is possible (but not necessary) for the monopolist to earn economic profits even in the long run--unlike the perfect competitor, who operates in an industry in which entry is easy.

Finally, we consider whether the monopoly market structure is efficient or inefficient from society's point of view. In equilibrium, price exceeds marginal cost (hence society wants *more* of this good) and long-run economic profits may be positive (also implying that too few resources are allocated to a monopoly industry)therefore, it is inefficient. In short, price is too high and output is too low in the monopoly market structure. Another monopoly cost to society includes a monopolist's rent-seeking behavior.

LEARNING OBJECTIVES

After you have studied this chapter, you should be able to

1. define monopolist, natural monopoly, barriers to entry, price discrimination, price differentiation, monopoly rent-seeking, tariff, and cartel.

2. list the characteristics of the monopoly market structure and distinguish them from the characteristics of the perfect competition market structure.

3. distinguish between the monopolist's demand curve and the perfect competitor's demand curve.

4. determine the profit maximizing output for the monopolist, given sufficient information; and determine the price that a monopolist would charge, given the profit-maximizing output.

5. list possible barriers to entry into an industry.

6. calculate a monopolist's total profits, given sufficient information.

7. recognize some misconceptions concerning monopoly.

8. distinguish between price discrimination and price differentiation, and list the conditions necessary for price discrimination.

9. list and recognize at least three costs to society of monopolies.

CHAPTER OUTLINE

1. A *monopolist* is a single supplier that constitutes an entire industry; the monopolist produces a good for which there are no close substitutes.
2. *Barriers to entry* are impediments that prevent new firms from entering an industry; there are numerous potential barriers to entry.

a. Some monopolists gain power through the exclusive ownership of a raw material that is essential to produce a good.
b. If an enormous capital investment is required to enter an industry, such a sum could be a barrier to entry.
c. Licenses, franchises, and certificates of convenience also constitute potential barriers to entry.
d. Patents issued to inventors constitute, for a time, effective barriers to entry.
e. If economies of scale are great relative to market demand, new entrants into an industry will be discouraged; persistent economies of scale could lead to a natural monopoly.
f. Governmental safety and quality regulation may raise fixed costs to firms in an industry significantly enough so as to deter new entrants.
g. If tariffs on imports are sufficiently high, then producers can gain some measure of monopoly power.

3. The monopolist faces the industry demand curve because the monopolist is the entire industry; examples of monopolies include local electric power companies and the post office.

4. It is instructive to compare the monopolist with the perfect competitor.
   a. The perfect competitor's demand curve is horizontal at the "going" price; price is the same as average revenue, and average revenue equals marginal revenue in this model.
   b. The monopolist's demand curve is negatively sloped; price (or average revenue) falls, and therefore marginal revenue is less than price because the monopolist must lower its price on all the units it sells, and not just on the marginal unit.

5. Where marginal revenue equals zero, total revenue is maximized; at the point on the demand curve corresponding to zero marginal revenue, the price elasticity of demand equals 1; at higher prices (lower outputs) demand is elastic, and at lower prices (higher outputs) demand is inelastic.

6. By assuming that the monopolist wants to maximize total profits and that the short-run cost curves are similar in shape to those of the perfect competitor, we can determine the monopolist's optimal output-price combination.
   a. The monopolist's total revenue curve is nonlinear (unlike the perfect competitor's); optimal output exists where the positive difference between total costs and total revenues is maximized.
   b. Stated differently, optimal output exists where $MR = MC$.
   c. If $MR > MC$, the firm can increase total profits by increasing output; if $MC > MR$, then the firm can increase total profits by reducing output.
   d. Once the profit-maximizing output is determined, the monopolist's price is already determined; it is read on the demand curve at that quantity.

7. Graphically, total profits are calculated by subtracting average costs from average revenues and multiplying that value by the quantity produced.

8. If the monopolist's average cost curve lies entirely above its demand curve, it will experience economic losses.

9. If the monopolist can prevent the resale of its homogeneous output and if it can separate its customers into different markets with different price elasticities, then it can price discriminate--and earn higher profits.

10. Monopolies are inefficient because they charge a price that is too high (P > MC) and because they produce an output that is too low.

11. Another cost of monopoly is using resources to obtain and maintain a monopoly position, referred to as monopoly rent seeking.

KEY TERMS

Monopolist
Barriers to entry
Price discrimination
Price differentiation
Tariff
Cartel

KEY CONCEPTS

Monopoly rent seeking
Barrier to entry
Natural monopoly

COMPLETION QUESTIONS

Fill in the blank or circle the correct term.

1. A monopolist is a ______________ supplier that constitutes the entire industry; its demand curve is ____________________ sloped.

2. Before a monopolist can earn long-run monopoly profits, there must be ___________ to entry.

3. Examples of barriers to entry include ____________________, ____________________, ____________________, ____________________, ____________________, and ____________________.

4. Because the perfect competitor's demand curve is horizontal, its selling price is constant; therefore its average revenue (falls, rises, remains constant) and its marginal revenue (falls, rises, remains constant).

5. Because the monopolist's demand curve is negatively sloped, its selling price falls with output; therefore its average revenue (falls, rises, remains constant) and its marginal revenue (falls, rises, remains constant).

6. If a monopolist must charge the same price to everyone, when it produces more, its marginal revenue will be (less than, greater than, equal to) its price.

7. When marginal revenue equals zero, total revenue is (minimized, maximized); at that point on the demand curve, the price elasticity of demand equals the number ________; at a higher price total revenues would fall, and therefore demand is price (elastic, inelastic); at a lower price total revenues would fall, and therefore demand is price ________________.

8. One misconception about monopoly is that the monopolist can sell any quantity that it chooses to at any ____________; instead the monopolist can sell any specific quantity at only one price. Another misconception is that a monopolist must earn economic profits; it won't, however, if the ____________ curve is above the monopolist's demand curve.

9. The monopolist maximizes total profits at that output for which __________ equals __________; given its profit-maximizing output, the monopolist (need not, must) charge a price consistent with that quantity.

10. If a monopolist need not charge the same price to everyone, then it can ______________, and its profits will rise; a monopolist can charge different prices to different groups if it can prevent the ____________________ of its product.

11. A monopolist charges a price that is too ____________, and it produces an output that is too ____________; therefore monopoly is (less, more) socially efficient than perfect competition.

12. A monopolist (need not, must) incur costs to protect its monopoly position; such behavior is referred to as ________________ and is considered wasteful from society's point of view.

TRUE-FALSE QUESTIONS

Circle the T if the statement is true, the F if it is false. Explain to yourself why a statement is false.

T F *1. The more broadly we define an industry, the less likely it is to be a monopoly.

T F 2. Because of barriers to entry, a monopolist must earn long-run profits.

T F 3. The monopolist's marginal revenue curve lies below its demand, or average revenue, curve.

T F 4. A monopolist must charge the same price to all buyers.

T F 5. The monopolist's total revenue curve is linear.

T F 6. At that output for which total revenue is maximized, price elasticity of demand equals 1.

T F 7. The profit maximizing monopolist will never produce on the inelastic portion of its demand curve.

T F 8. Total profits are maximized where total revenue equals total costs.

T F 9. If MR > MC, the firm can increase profits if it produces less.

T F 10. A monopolist can select only one profit-maximizing price, given the output it chooses to produce, assuming no price discrimination.

T F 11. If possible, a monopolist will charge a higher price to a price inelastic group than to a price elastic group.

T F 12. A monopolist tends to produce too little and to sell at a price that is too high.

T F 13. Rent-seeking behavior is considered socially efficient.

T F 14. Because there are no close substitutes for a monopolist's output, its demand curve is inelastic throughout.

MULTIPLE CHOICE QUESTIONS

Circle the letter that corresponds to the best answer.

1. Which of the following is *not* a characteristic of the monopoly market structure?
   a. one seller
   b. homogeneous product
   c. restricted entry
   d. price taker

2. Which of the following is a potential barrier to entry?
   a. government license requirement
   b. sole ownership of a key resource
   c. great economies of scale, relative to demand
   d. All of the above

3. Which is *not* true about monopolies?
   a. linear total revenue curve
   b. may earn long-run economic profits
   c. negatively sloped demand curve
   d. marginal revenue below price

4. The firm maximizes total profits at that output where
   a. total revenue equals total cost.
   b. marginal revenue equals marginal cost.
   c. the elasticity of demand equals 1.
   d. All of the above

5. Once a monopolist produces a profit-maximizing output,
   a. the price is determined for it, given its demand curve.
   b. it can select any price it wants.

c. its competitors select price.
d. price cannot be determined.

6. If MR < MC, then the firm
   a. is maximizing total profits.
   b. can increase total profits by producing more.
   c. can increase total profits by producing less.
   d. is maximizing total revenues.

7. Monopoly profit
   a. equals (AR - AC) times quantity sold.
   b. equals price times quantity sold.
   c. exists only in the short run.
   d. exists because no entry barriers exist.

8. A monopolist will price discriminate if
   a. price differentiation exists.
   b. it can separate markets by different price elasticities of demand and prevent resales.
   c. it chooses to maximize average revenues.
   d. all buyers have the same price elasticity of demand.

9. Which of the following is price differentiation?
   a. Students pay a higher rental price for apartments than do nonstudents because they cause more damage.
   b. Women pay higher prices for haircuts because it takes longer to cut their hair.
   c. People in ghetto areas pay higher prices for individual items because the theft rate is higher in such areas.
   d. All of the above

10. Assume that at a given output a monopolist's marginal revenue is $10 per unit and its marginal cost is $5. If the monopolist increases output, then
   a. price, marginal cost, and total profit will fall.
   b. price will fall, marginal cost will rise, and total profit will rise.
   c. price will rise, marginal cost will fall, and total profit will rise.
   d. price, marginal cost, and total profit will rise.

11. In order to maintain monopoly profits, a monopolist may enlist the protection of government and incur various costs to protect its favored position. Such behavior is called
   a. monopolizing.
   b. profit seeking.
   c. rent seeking.
   d. cartelization.

12. From society's point of view, monopoly rent-seeking
   a. creates wealth.
   b. transfers wealth from one group to another.
   c. is efficient.
   d. transfers wealth, but is otherwise costless.

MATCHING

Choose the item in column (2) that best matches an item in column (1).

(1)

a. perfect competition
b. monopolist
c. price differentiation
d. price discrimination
e. barrier to entry
f. monopoly rent seeking

(2)

g. nonlinear total revenue curve
h. payments to protect licenses and patents
i. great economies of scale
j. price taker
k. students pay higher rents for apartments than do non-students
l. students pay different tuition costs depending on need

WORKING WITH GRAPHS

1. Suppose you are given the demand schedule for a monopolist and the total cost figures below. Plot the monopolist's demand curve, marginal revenue curve, and marginal cost curve on the graph provided. Determine the optimal level of output for the monopolist. What do total profits equal? (Plot MC and MR on the mid-points.)

Output per unit of time	Price	Total Cost
0	$ 32	$ 12
1	28	20
2	24	25
3	20	31
4	16	41
5	12	56
6	8	79
7	4	117

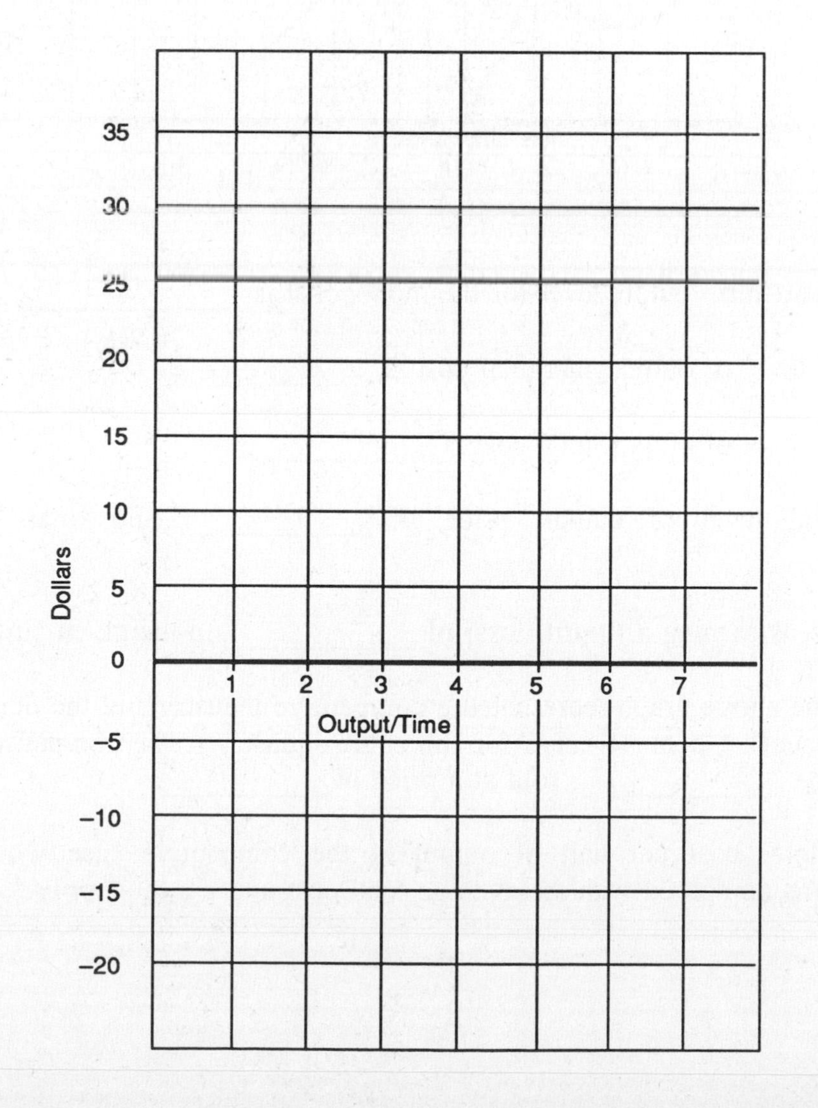

2. Suppose you are given the graphical summary of a monopolist below. Answer the following questions using this information.

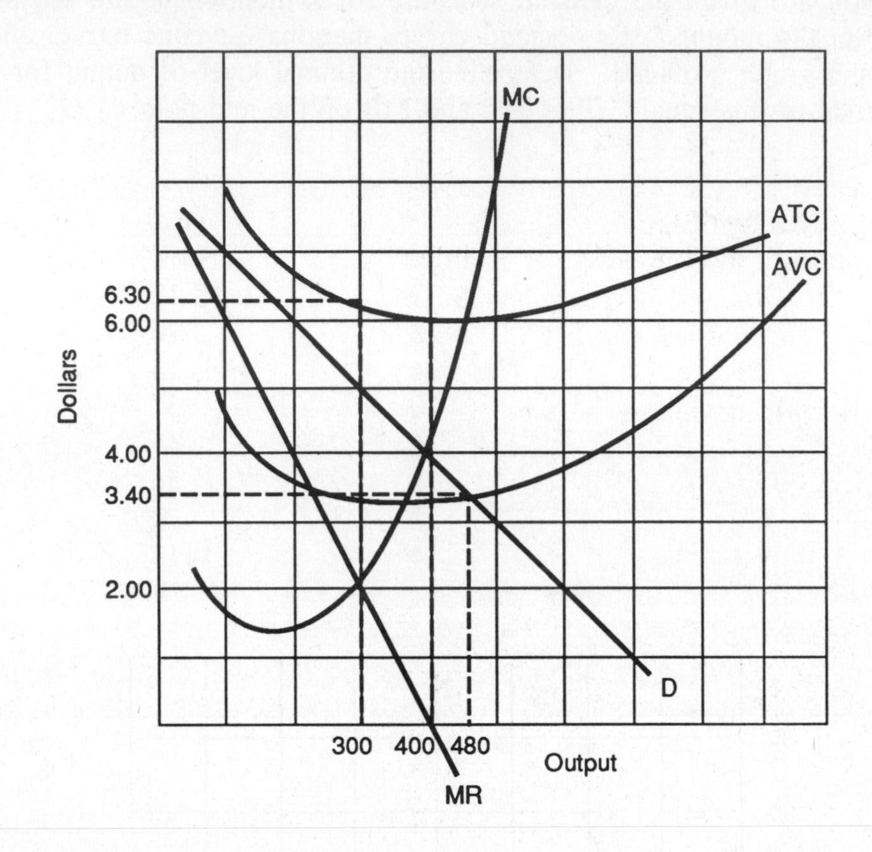

a. The optimal short-term output level for the monopolist is __________.

b. At the optimal level of output, marginal cost is __________.

c. At the optimal level of output, total cost is __________.

d. At the optimal level of output, price is __________ and total revenue is __________.

e. The monopolist is earning a (profit, loss) of __________ in the given situation.

f. Suppose that the above graph represented a competitive industry and the demand curve given was the market demand curve for the entire industry. The competitive level of output would be __________, sold at a price of __________.

g. The average total cost per unit of output in the competitive case would fall by __________, as compared with the average total cost under a monopoly.

PROBLEMS

1. Indicate whether the following may characterize the perfect competitor (PC), the monopolist (M), or both (B).

_____ a. horizontal demand curve

_____ b. increasing marginal cost curve

_____ c. downward sloping demand curve

_____ d. linear total revenue curve

_____ e. total profit maximizer

_____ f. possibility of earning long-run economic profits

_____ g. rent-seeking behavior

_____ h. homogeneous output

_____ i. price discriminator

_____ j. barriers to entry

_____ k. free exit and entry

_____ l. price maker

_____ m. price taker

_____ n. produces where MR = MC

_____ o. P = MC in equilibrium

_____ p. long-run equilibrium at minimum AC

_____ q. P = MR

_____ r. P = AR

CASE STUDY

In 1937 New York City issued 11,787 medallions (non-expiring, resaleable, licenses to operate a taxicab) for $10 each; that same number of medallions exists today. As the demand for taxicab services has increased over time, clearly the market price for a medallion has risen. In the mid 1990s the price was around $70,000 per medallion. In effect, this licensing arrangement is a barrier to entry, and it bestows monopolistic advantages to medallion owners.

1. What does the price of a medallion reflect?

2. Who benefits from such a licensing arrangement--new medallion buyers or original medallion recipients?

3. If New York City were to eliminate this system and permit anyone who has a driver's license to drive a cab, who would benefit, and who would be harmed?

ANSWERS TO CHAPTER 24

COMPLETION QUESTIONS

1. single; negatively
2. barriers
3. ownership of resources without close substitutes, large capital requirements to enter industry, legally required licenses, franchises, or certificates of convenience, patents, economies of scale, safety and quality regulation, high tariffs
4. remains constant, remains constant
5. falls, falls
6. less than
7. maximized; 1; elastic; inelastic
8. price; average total cost
9. MR, MC; must
10. price discriminate; resale
11. high, low; less
12. must; rent seeking

TRUE-FALSE QUESTIONS

1. T
2. F An inefficient monopolist need not earn economic profits.
3. T
4. F A monopolist can price discriminate under certain conditions.
5. F It is not linear because price falls as the monopolist produces more.
6. T
7. T
8. F Profit maximization occurs where MR = MC; if TR = TC, then economic profits are zero.
9. F If MR > MC, profits will rise if the firm produces more.
10. T
11. T
12. T
13. F It is socially inefficient because resources are spent wastefully--from society's point of view.
14. F A monopolist's demand curve has ranges of elasticity that exceed one.

MULTIPLE CHOICE QUESTIONS

1.d; 2.d; 3.a; 4.b; 5.a; 6.c; 7.a; 8.b; 9.d; 10.b; 11.c; 12.b

MATCHING

a and j; b and g; c and k; d and l; e and i; f and h

WORKING WITH GRAPHS

1.

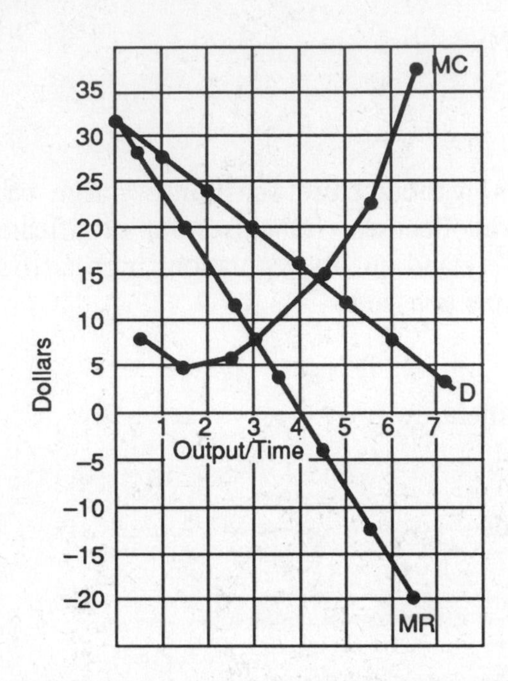

The profit-maximizing level of output is 3 units sold at a price of $20 each. This can be seen graphically. Total profits equal $29 at that output.

2. a. 300; b. $2; c. $1890; d. $5, $1500; e. loss, $390; f. 400, $4; g. $0.30

PROBLEMS

1. a. PC b. B c. M d. PC e. B f. M g. M h. B i. M
   j. M k. PC l. M m. PC n. B o. PC p. PC q. PC r. B

CASE STUDY

1. Demand conditions, because supply is fixed.
2. Original recipients, because the price to new buyers will reflect the monopolistic advantage.
3. New drivers would benefit, as well as customers; old owners, who paid a price for medallions that reflected the barrier to entry, would be harmed.

GLOSSARY TO CHAPTER 24

Cartel Any arrangement or agreement made by a number of independent entities to coordinate either buying or selling decisions, so that all of them will earn either monopsony or monopoly profits.

Monopolist The single supplier that comprises the entire industry.

Monopoly rent seeking The resources utilized in an attempt to create and maintain monopolies in order to earn monopoly profits.

Natural monopoly A monopoly that arises when there are large economies of scale relative to industry demand.

Price differentiation Price differences for similar products which reflect only differences in marginal cost in providing those commodities to different groups of buyers.

Price discrimination Selling a given product at more than one price with the price difference being unrelated to cost difference.

Tariff A tax on imported goods.

CHAPTER 25

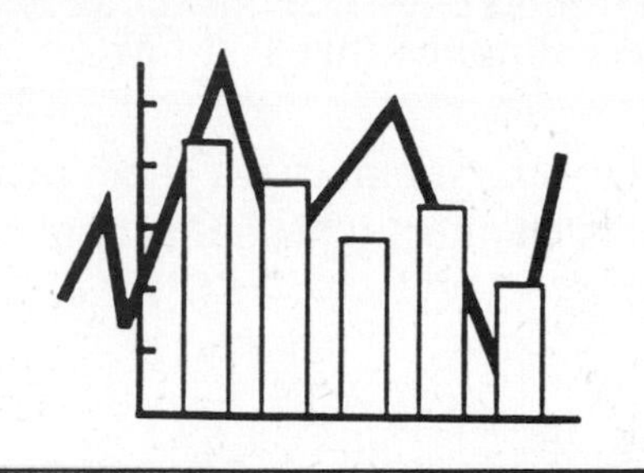

STRATEGIC COMPETITION AND OLIGOPOLY

PUTTING THIS CHAPTER INTO PERSPECTIVE

Chapter 25 is the third chapter that deals with market structures; Chapter 23 analyzed the perfect competition model and Chapter 24 analyzed the monopoly model. Chapter 25 examines two more market structures--monopolistic competition and oligopoly. Because this is a long chapter we suggest that you break it into several parts; let the first part cover the monopolistic competition model and the second part cover the oligopoly model (and the issues and applications).

In the monopolistic competition model the assumptions are (1) a significant number of sellers in a highly competitive (but not perfectly competitive) market, (2) differentiated products, (3) existence of advertising, and (4) easy entry into the industry.

Because of assumptions 1 through 3, the monopolistic competitor has some control over its selling price. This means that its demand curve is negatively sloped, which in turn means that its marginal revenue curve must be below its demand curve and that in equilibrium, price must exceed marginal cost. In short, assumptions 1 through 3 imply that monopolistic competition is less efficient than perfect competition because such assumptions necessitate that in equilibrium $P > MC$.

Because of assumption 4 we know that in the long run each monopolistic competitor must earn exactly zero economic profits. This means that the demand (average revenue) curve must be tangent to the monopolistic competitor's AC curve. Furthermore, because the demand curve is negatively sloped, the demand curve must be tangent to the AC curve somewhere to the left of AC's minimum point. (By definition, at AC's minimum point the slope must equal zero; therefore, as long as the demand curve is not horizontal, the demand curve cannot be tangent to AC at AC's minimum point.) This gives us another reason to believe that the monopolistic competition model leads to a less efficient solution than the perfect competition model: in equilibrium output will not be produced at minimum average cost.

Because there is independence among oligopolistic competitors, it is difficult to predict the price/output outcome resulting from their behavior. As a consequence economists have developed an approach, called game theory, that gives some insights into the oligopoly model. Your text introduces you to this fascinating topic.

If we assume that an oligopolist's rivals will find it in their own interest to match a price decrease but to ignore a price increase, then a kinked demand curve for each oligopolist is the result. The demand curve is negatively sloped, the marginal revenue curve is below it--and discontinuous. Ultimately this means social inefficiency because it implies that P > MC.

In order to help you sort out the different market structures, the text summarizes their main features in Table 13-3. After you have completed your study of this chapter, you should analyze that exhibit.

LEARNING OBJECTIVES

After you have studied this chapter you should be able to

1. define monopolistic competition, product differentiation, oligopoly, concentration ratio, horizontal and vertical mergers, reaction function, game theory, cooperative and noncooperative games, zero sum, positive sum, and negative sum games, strategy, dominant strategy, prisoner's dilemma, payoff matrix, price leadership, limit-pricing, price war, and entry-deterrence.

2. list the characteristics of the monopolistic competition market structure and of the oligopoly market structure.

3. distinguish between the monopolistic competitor's demand curve and the perfect competitor's demand curve

4. recognize reasons why the monopolistic competition market structure and the oligopoly market structure are socially inefficient.

5. compare the main features of perfect competition, monopoly, monopolistic competition, and oligopoly.

6. list at least three reasons for the existence of oligopolies.

7. calculate concentration ratios and recognize their limitations.

8. distinguish between a cooperative and a noncooperative game.

9. answer questions concerning the essence of the kinked demand curve and enumerate criticisms of the kinked demand curve model.

10. distinguish among zero sum, positive sum, and negative sum games.

11. recognize three ways that existing oligopolists deter entry into the industry.

CHAPTER OUTLINE

1. The theory of *monopolistic competition* was developed simultaneously by Edward Chamberlin and Joan Robinson in 1933; we analyze Chamberlin's model.

   a. There are four characteristics of monopolistic competition: a significant number of sellers in a highly competitive market, differentiated products, advertising, and easy entry.
   b. Although there are many sellers, there are not as many as there are in the perfect competition model; each monopolistic competitor has a little control over its price, but collusion is difficult and each firm acts independently of the others.
   c. Perhaps the most important feature of this model is *product differentiation*.
      i. Some economists distinguish between real and artificial differentiation; real differentiation refers to differences in physical characteristics.
      ii. Each separate differentiated product has close substitutes.
   d. Because the monopolistic competitor has at least some monopoly power, it may be profitable for it to advertise.
      i. The goal of advertising is to shift the demand curve to the right.
      ii. Advertising may also provide useful information to buyers.
   e. In the long run, entry into such a market structure is easy.

2. It is possible to predict the optimal price-output combination of the monopolistic competitor.
   a. The monopolistic competitor's demand curve is downward sloping; therefore its marginal revenue curve lies below its demand curve.
   b. Short-run equilibrium exists where MR = MC; economic profits or losses are possible in the short run.
   c. In the long run, because of free entry, the monopolistic competitor must earn exactly zero economic profits.

3. For the monopolistic competitor, social inefficiency exists because P > MC and because in the long run its rate of output lies to the left of the minimum point on the ATC curve.

4. *Oligopoly* is a market situation in which there are a very few sellers, each of which expects a reaction from its rivals to changes in its price and quantity; there are two major characteristics of oligopolies: a small number of firms and interdependence.

5. There are at least four reasons for the emergence of oligopolistic industries: economies of scale, barriers to entry, product differentiation and advertising, and merger (horizontal or vertical).
   a. Four- or eight-firm *concentration ratios* are often calculated to determine the extent to which an industry is "monopolized."
   b. Over time some industries experience drastic changes (up or down) in their concentration ratios; others show little change.

6. Before an oligopoly situation can be analyzed with respect to price and output, specific assumptions about rival *reactions* must be made; a different model arises with each assumption regarding the oligopolist's reaction function.

7. Because there is interdependence among oligopolistic competitors economists have developed an approach, called game theory, to describe how such firms interact rationally.
   a. If firms collude and form a cartel, the game is referred to as cooperative game.
   b. If cartels are too expensive to form or enforce, then a noncooperative game is played

among oligopolists.
   c. Games are classified as being zero sum, positive sum, or negative sum.

8. Oligopolistic decision makers derive a strategy, or rule used to make a choice; a dominant strategy is one that always yields the highest benefit, regardless of what the other oligopolists do.

9. The most famous example of game theory is called the prisoner's dilemma in which it can be shown that (under specified conditions) in situations in which there is more than one party to a crime, the dominant strategy for each prisoner is to confess.

10. A payoff matrix indicates the consequences of the strategies chosen by the players in the game.

11. Another oligopoly model results from assuming that rivals will match a price reduction, but ignore a price increase.
    a. In such a situation, for the oligopolist the price elasticity of demand above the current price will be very high, and the price elasticity of demand below the current price will be very low; the result is a kinked demand curve and a discontinuous marginal revenue curve.
    b. One implication of the kinked demand curve model is price rigidity; any change in marginal costs in the discontinuous gap of the marginal revenue curve will leave price unaltered.
    c. One criticism of this analysis is that it offers no explanation of how the current price was established; empirical evidence indicates that oligopolies tend to change price more frequently than do monopolies.

12. Sometimes even if no formal cartel arises among oligopolists, tacit collusion in the form of price leadership can occur; the largest firm announces its price and smaller competitors then follow this lead.

13. On occasion smaller rivals may set price too far below the price leader and a price war results.

14. Strategic decision making could lead to pricing or investing policies that deter entry by potential competitors; entry-deterrence strategies include threats of a price war, investment in excess capacity by existing firms, and inducing the U.S. government to set stringent environmental health or safety standards to raise the entry cost to potential foreign rivals.

15. The limit-pricing model suggests that existing oligopolists collude to set the highest price they can without encouraging entry into the industry.

KEY TERMS

Monopolistic competition
Oligopoly
Concentration ratio
Reaction function
Price war
Payoff matrix
Game theory
Cooperative game
Noncooperative game

KEY CONCEPTS

Zero sum game
Positive sum game
Negative sum game
Entry-deterrence strategies
Price leadership
Limit pricing
Dominant strategy
Prisoner's dilemma

COMPLETION QUESTIONS

Fill in the blank or circle the correct term.

1. The four characteristics of monopolistic competition are ______________________, ______________________, ______________________, and ______________________.

2. Under monopolistic competition, collusion is (easy, difficult); each firm (must, need not) take into account the reactions of rivals, and each firm has (a little, much, no) control over its selling price.

3. The goal of advertising is to ______________________. The perfect competitor (does, does not) advertise; the monopolistic competitor (does, does not) advertise because it has a ______________________ product.

4. Advertising is useful to the extent that it provides______________ to buyers.

5. The demand curve for the monopolistic competitor is ____________ sloped; therefore its marginal revenue curve is (below, above) its demand, or AR curve; therefore in equilibrium price must be (less than, greater than, equal to) marginal cost; therefore social (inefficiency, efficiency) exists in the monopolistic competition market structure.

6. In the long run, ease of entry causes the monopolistic competitor to earn ______________ economic profits; therefore its negatively sloped demand curve must be (above, below, tangent to) its ATC curve. As a consequence, in long-run equilibrium, output must be produced at a cost (below, above, at) minimum average total cost.

7. Two key characteristics of oligopoly are ______________________, and ______________________; oligopolies may emerge because of ______________________, ______________________, ______________________, and ______________________.

8. Concentration ratios (fall, rise) as the definition of "industry" is narrowed, and they ____________ as the definition is broadened.

9. Economists have developed an approach to analyze the interdependence among oligopolists called ________________ theory; if oligopolists collude and form a cartel this is a ________________ game; if cartels are too expensive to form or enforce then oligopolists will play a ________________ game.

10. Games are referred to as ________________ sum if one player benefits at the expense of the other, ________________ sum if both players benefit, and ________________ sum if neither player benefits.

11. The most famous example of game theory is ________________________ in which the dominant strategy of prisoners (usually) is to (confess, not confess).

12. Assume that firm B is an oligopolist. If its rivals match its price reductions but ignore its price increases, firm B will have a ________________ demand curve; its marginal revenue curve will be ________________; firm B probably (will, will not) change its price very often. Because its demand curve is negatively sloped, in equilibrium firm B's (P = MC, P > MC, P < MC) and from society's point of view it will produce (too little, too much, just enough) and its price will be (too low, too high, just right).

13. Even if no formal cartel arises in an oligopolistic industry, tacit collusion in the form of ________________ leadership may result; occasionally such a system breaks down and a price ____________ results.

14. Existing oligopolists can use the following strategies to deter entry: ______________________, ______________________, and ______________________; the ________________ model suggests that existing firms set the highest price they can without encouraging entry.

TRUE-FALSE QUESTIONS

Circle the **T** if the statement is true, the **F** if it is false. Explain to yourself why a statement is false.

T F 1. The monopolistic competitor has a negatively sloped demand curve.

T F 2. The monopolistic competitor must take into account the reactions of its competitors.

T F 3. The most important feature of the monopolistic competitive market is product differentiation.

T F 4. Product differentiation exists in the wheat industry.

T F 5. The goal of advertising is to shift the demand curve to the right.

T F 6. The monopolistic competition model leads to social efficiency because in the long run P = MC.

T F 7. The main characteristic of the oligopoly market structure is that an oligopolist must consider the reaction of its rivals.

T F 8. Perhaps the strongest reason for the existence of oligopolies is economies of scale relative to market demand.

T F 9. Concentration ratios provide an accurate measure of the degree of monopoly power in an industry.

T F *10. If an oligopolist's rivals match all of its price changes, its demand curve will be kinked.

T F 11. Cartels are usually expensive to set up and enforce.

T F 12. A dominant strategy is one that is always preferred by a player, regardless of what other players do.

T F 13. Price wars result because all players are in a positive sum game.

T F 14. The limit-pricing model suggests that oligopolists set price at the highest price they can.

T F 15. Collusion may be found in both formal and tacit arrangements.

MULTIPLE CHOICE QUESTIONS

Circle the letter that corresponds to the best answer.

1. Which is *not* a characteristic of monopolistic competition?
   a. significant number of sellers
   b. differentiated products
   c. advertising
   d. must take into account rival's reaction to price changes

2. Under monopolistic competition, collusion is
   a. easy.
   b. difficult.
   c. impossible.
   d. nonexistent.

3. Which firm has the *least* control over price?
   a. perfect competitor
   b. monopolistic competitor
   c. oligopolist
   d. monopolist

4. Product differentiation is the *central* feature of the _____ model.
   a. monopoly
   b. oligopoly
   c. monopolistic competition
   d. perfect competition

*5. Which market structure is most *unlike* the others?
   a. perfect competition
   b. oligopoly
   c. monopolistic competition
   d. monopoly

*6. Analogy: Product differentiation is to monopolistic competition as _______ is to oligopoly.
   a. competition
   b. interdependence
   c. advertising
   d. economies of scale

7. Advertising
   a. attempts to increase demand for one's product.
   b. helps to differentiate one's product.
   c. can lead to more information for buyers.
   d. All of the above

8. Which firm's demand curve is *not* negatively sloped?
   a. oligopolist
   b. perfect competition
   c. monopolist
   d. monopolistic competition

9. Only when a firm's demand curve is negatively sloped will
   a. its MR curve lie below its demand curve.
   b. in equilibrium, MR = MC.
   c. economic profits equal zero in the long run.
   d. All of the above

10. For the monopolistic competitor, in the long run
   a. the demand curve must be tangent to the ATC curve.
   b. output is too high, from society's point of view.
   c. output is produced to the right of the minimum ATC point.
   d. economic profits can be positive.

11. In which of the following will *all* players benefit?
   a. negative sum game
   b. zero sum game
   c. positive sum game
   d. prisoner's dilemma

12. If oligopoly B's rivals ignore its price increases but match its price decreases, then B's demand curve will be
    a. discontinuous.
    b. kinked at the going price.
    c. below its marginal revenue curve.
    d. proportionate to the industry demand curve.

13. In long-run equilibrium for the oligopolist,
    a. MR = MC.
    b. P > MR.
    c. economic profits are possible.
    d. All of the above

14. Which firms must have zero economic profits in the long run?
    a. monopolist, perfect competitor
    b. oligopolist, monopolistic competitor
    c. perfect competitor, monopolistic competitor
    d. perfect competitor, oligopolist

15. The *best* explanation for the existence of oligopolies is
    a. no economies of scale exist.
    b. large economies of scale relative to market demand.
    c. advertising.
    d. one firm has exclusive ownership of an important raw material.

16. In an oligopolistic industry, entry will result if
    a. normal profits exist.
    b. the industry LAC curve is below the market demand curve.
    c. the industry LAC curve is above the market demand curve.
    d. advertising is permitted.

17. The kinked demand curve theory
    a. is supported by empirical evidence.
    b. requires that an oligopolist's rivals exactly match its price changes.
    c. predicts price rigidity.
    d. requires collusion.

18. Which of the following is a strategy to deter entry by potential competitors?
    a. threats of a price war
    b. investment in excess capacity by existing firms
    c. limit-pricing strategy
    d. All of the above

MATCHING

(1)		(2)	
a.	monopolistic competition	g.	horizontal demand curve
b.	positive sum game	h.	all players benefit
c.	oligopoly	i.	one seller
d.	concentration ratio	j.	product differentiation
e.	price taker	k.	kinked demand curve
f.	monopoly	l.	measure of concentration

WORKING WITH GRAPHS

1. Use the graphs of a monopolistic competitor below to answer each of the following questions.

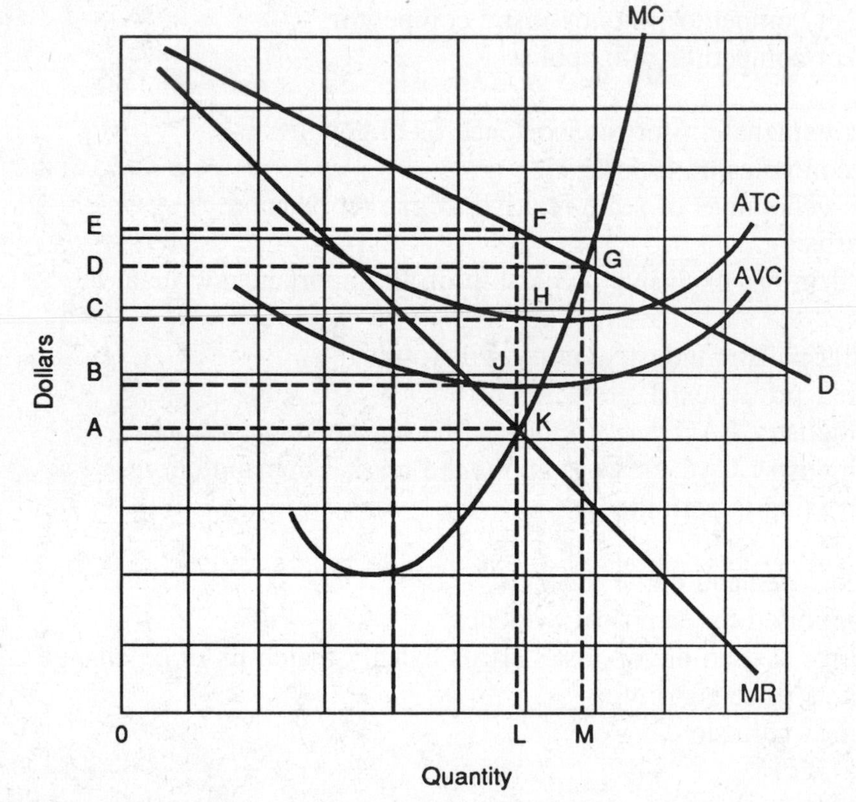

a. At what level of output will this firm operate? __________
b. What is marginal revenue at this level of output? __________
c. What price will this firm charge for its product? __________
d. The area of what rectangle is equal to total revenue? __________
e. What is the firm's average cost in equilibrium? __________
f. The area of what rectangle is equal to the firm's total cost? __________
g. Is the firm making profits or incurring losses? __________
h. The area of what rectangle is equal to profits or losses? __________

2. Use the graphs below to answer the questions that follow.

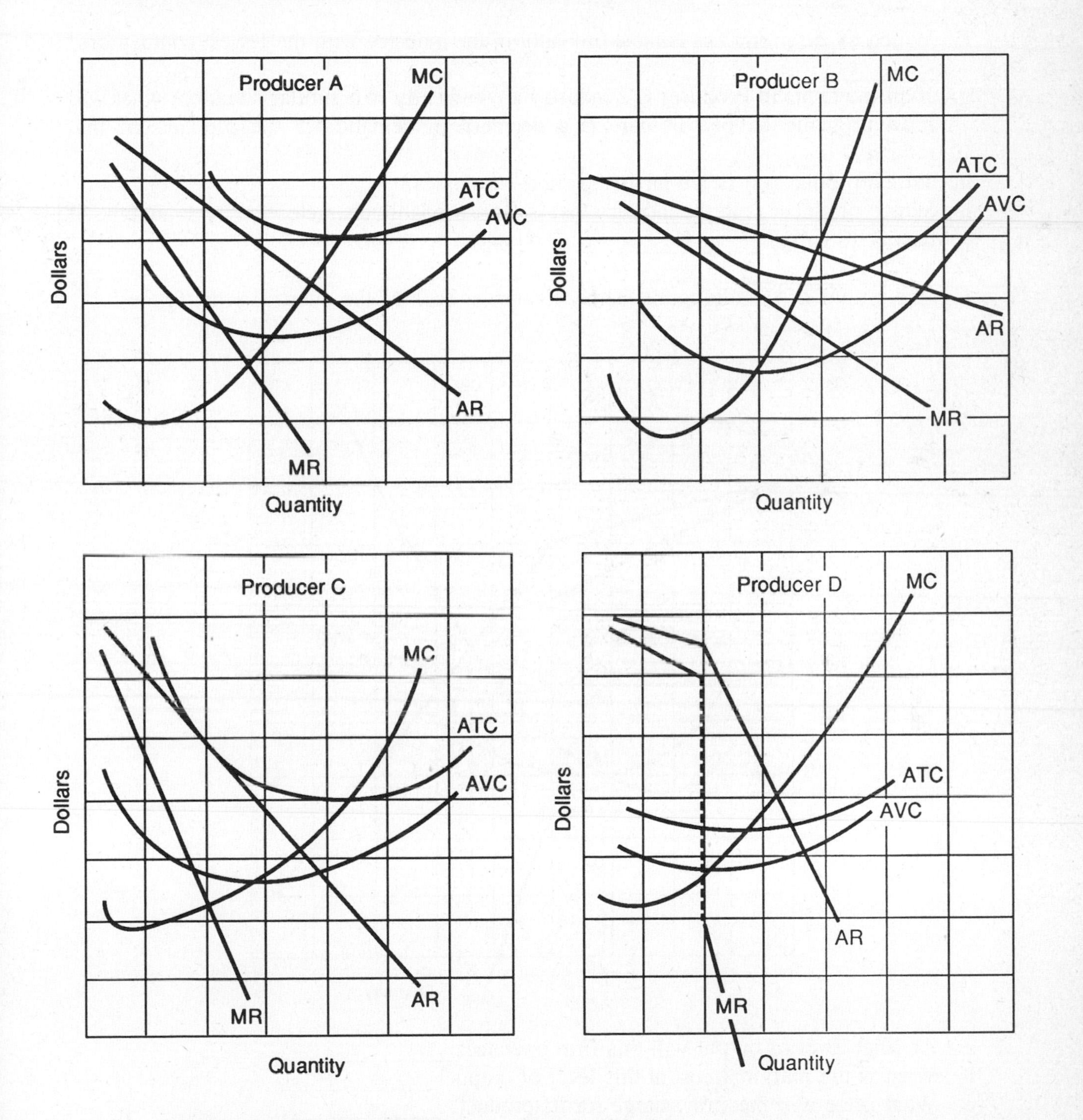

a. Which of the producers is a monopolistic competitor making positive economic profits? __________
b. Which of the producers appears to be in an industry that may have reached a long-run equilibrium? __________
c. Which of the producers is most likely to leave the industry in which it is currently operating? __________
d. If costs increase by a small amount, which producer is most likely to maintain its present price-quantity combination? __________

e. Which of the producers is in an industry that is most likely to attract additional firms? __________

f. Which of the producers is most probably in the industry with the fewest competitors? __________

g. If all the firms in Producer C's industry are currently in a similar situation, what will most probably happen if there is a decrease in demand for the products of that industry? __________

h. Which producer(s) is/are incurring short-run losses? __________

i. Which producer is in the industry that is most probably characterized by some type of barrier to entry? __________

3. Use the graphs of the oligopolist below to answer each of the questions that follow.

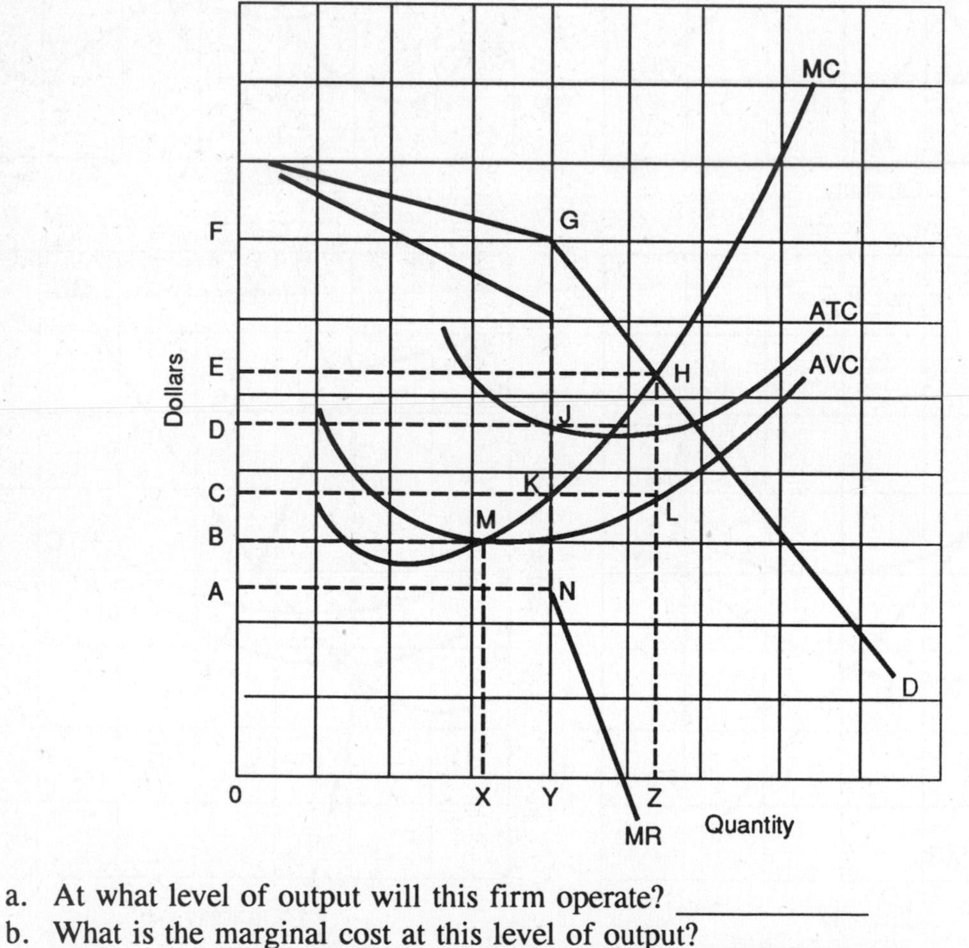

a. At what level of output will this firm operate? __________
b. What is the marginal cost at this level of output? __________
c. What price will the firm charge for its product? __________
d. The area of what rectangle equals total revenue? __________
e. What is the firm's average cost? __________
f. The area of what rectangle is equal to the firm's total cost? __________
g. The area of what rectangle is equal to the firm's profit? __________
h. Suppose the firm is operating at an output level of Y units. How low would marginal costs at Y units of output have to drop before the firm would lower its price? __________

PROBLEMS

1. Let PC = perfect competition, M = monopoly, MC = monopolistic competition, and O = oligopoly. Indicate which of the following may be consistent with one, several, or all of those markets.

_____ a. profit maximizer
_____ b. advertising
_____ c. long-run economic profits
_____ d. social inefficiency
_____ e. P > MC in equilibrium
_____ f. product differentiation
_____ g. large economies of scale relative to market demand
_____ h. long-run equilibrium at minimum ATC
_____ i. short-run economic profits
_____ j. easy entry
_____ k. few firms
_____ l. interdependence of firms
_____ m. ability to set price

2. Consider the table below, then answer the questions that follow. All information is for domestic firms.

Domestic Firms in Industry A	Annual Sales
1	$2,000,000
2	1,500,000
3	1,400,000
4	1,100,000
5	1,000,000
6	700,000
7	200,000
8	100,000
9-20 (remaining firms)	1,000,000

a. What is the 4-firm concentration ratio?
b. What is the 8-firm concentration ratio?
c. What would happen to the concentration ratios if industry B's product is a substitute for Industry A's product?
d. What would happen to the concentration ratios if the sales of imported goods in Industries A and B that are sold in domestic markets were included?

CASE STUDY

Many noneconomists believe that they can cite exceptions to the law of demand. They point to instances in which some company changed the "image" of its good through advertising, raised the price of the good, and sold more. Their interpretation is that an increase in price led to an increase in quantity demand; hence the law of demand is wrong.

Actually, if advertising convinces people that Good A is of higher quality, or if people can now receive more "prestige" by purchasing Good A, this is an increase in the demand for Good A; that is, the demand curve for Good A shifts rightward.

1. If the demand for Good A shifts rightward (due to advertising) given the supply of Good A, what happens to the equilibrium price? The equilibrium quantity?

2. What mistake have noneconomists made in interpreting the law of demand?

3. Does the law of demand hold along *each* demand curve--the old and the new?

ANSWERS TO CHAPTER 25

COMPLETION QUESTIONS

1. significant number of sellers, differentiated product, advertising, easy entry.
2. difficult; need not, a little
3. increase demand; does not; does, differentiated
4. information
5. negatively; below; greater than; inefficiency
6. zero; tangent to; above
7. small number of firms, interdependence; economies of scale, barriers to entry, product differentiation and advertising, merger
8. rise, fall
9. game; cooperative; noncooperative
10. zero, positive, negative
11. the prisoner's dilemma, confess
12. kinked; below its demand curve and discontinuous; will not; $P > MC$, too little, too high
13. price; war
14. threats of pricc wars, investment in excess capacity, get government to set stringent health and safety regulations, limit-pricing

TRUE-FALSE

1. T
2. F There are so many rivals, they can be ignored.
3. T
4. F Wheat is largely homogeneous.
5. T
6. F Social inefficiency exists because the monopolistic competitor's demand curve is negatively sloped; therefore, $P > MC$ in equilibrium.
7. T
8. T
9. F They are very inaccurate, if only because inter-industry competition exists; foreign competition exists too.
10. F Its demand curve will be proportionate to the industry demand curve.
11. T
12. T
13. F They result when price leadership strategies break down.
14. F They set price at the highest level that *will still discourage entry*.
15. T

MULTIPLE CHOICE QUESTIONS

1.d; 2.b; 3.a; 4.c; 5.a; 6.b; 7.d; 8.b; 9.a; 10.a;
11.c; 12.b; 13.d; 14.c; 15.b; 16.b; 17.c; 18.d

MATCHING

a and j; b and h; c and k; d and l; e and g; f and i

WORKING WITH GRAPHS

1. a. 0L; b. 0A; c. 0E; d. 0EFL; e. 0C; f. 0CHL; g. profits; h. CEFH
2. a. B; b. C; c. A; d. D; e. B; f. D; g. some firms will exit the industry; h. A; i. D;
3. a. 0Y; b. 0C; c. 0F; d. 0FGY; e. 0D; f. 0DJY; g. DFGJ; h. below 0A

PROBLEMS

1. a. PC, M, MC, O; b. M, MC, O; c. M, O; d. M, MC, O; e. M, MC, O; f. MC, O; g. M, O; h. PC; i. PC, M, MC, O; j. PC, MC; k. O; l. O;

   m. M, MC, O
2. a. 6/9 (or .67) b. 8/9 (or .89) c. They would fall. d. They would fall.

CASE STUDY

1. The equilibrium price and equilibrium quantity both rise.
2. The law of demand is derived holding other things constant; in the example, price would increase *and* perceived quality and/or taste changed along with price.
3. Yes.

GLOSSARY TO CHAPTER 25

Concentration ratio The percentage of all sales contributed by the leading four or leading eight firms in an industry; sometimes called the industry concentration ratio.

Cooperative game A game in which the players explicitly collude to make themselves better off. As applied to firms, it involves companies colluding in order to make higher than competitive rates of return.

Dominant strategies Strategies that always yield the highest benefit, i.e., regardless of what other players do, a dominant strategy will yield the most benefit for the player using it.

Entry-deterrence strategy Any strategy undertaken by firms in an industry, either individually or together, with the design or effect of raising the cost of entry into the industry by a new firm.

Horizontal merger The joining of firms that are producing or selling a similar product.

Limit-pricing model A model that hypothesizes a group of colluding sellers will together set the highest common price that they believe they can charge without new firms seeking to enter that industry in search of relatively high profits.

Monopolistic competition A market situation where a large number of firms produce similar but not identical products. There is relatively easy entry into the industry.

Negative-sum game A game in which both players are worse off at the end of the game.

Non-cooperative game A game in which the players neither negotiate nor collude in any way. As applied to firms in an industry, the common situation in which there are relatively few firms, and when each firm has some ability to change price.

Oligopoly A market situation in which there are very few sellers. Each seller knows that the other sellers will react to its changes in prices and quantities.

Payoff matrix A matrix of outcomes, or consequences, of the strategies chosen by players in a game.

Positive-sum game A game in which both players are better off at the end of the game.

Price leadership A purported pricing practice in many oligopolistic industries in which the largest firm publishes its price list ahead of its competitors, who then follow those prices already announced. Also called parallel pricing.

Price war A pricing campaign designed to drive competing firms out of a market by repeatedly cutting prices.

Prisoner's dilemma The most famous of strategic games in which two prisoners have a choice between confessing and not confessing to a crime. If neither confesses, they serve a minimum sentence. If both confess, they serve a maximum sentence. If one confesses and the other doesn't, the one who confesses goes free. The dominant strategy is always to confess.

Product differentiation The distinguishing of products by brand name, color, minor attributes, and the like. Product differentiation occurs in other than perfectly competitive markets where products are, in theory, homogeneous, such as wheat or corn.

Reaction function The manner in which one oligopolist reacts to a change in price (or output or quality) of another oligopolist.

Strategic dependence A situation in which one firm's actions with respect to, for example, price changes, may be strategically countered by one or more other firms in the industry. Such dependence can only exist when there are a few major firms in an industry.

Strategy Any rule that is used to make a choice, e.g., always pick "heads". An alternative definition of strategy is any potential choice that can be made by players in a game.

Zero-sum game A game in which one player's losses are exactly offset by the other player's gains.

CHAPTER 26

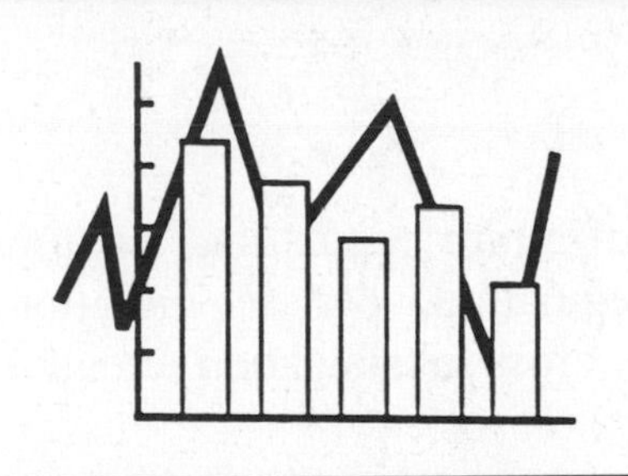

REGULATION AND ANTITRUST POLICY

PUTTING THIS CHAPTER INTO PERSPECTIVE

Chapter 26 is the second-to last chapter in Part Six, which deals with market structure, and it returns to analyze again the monopoly model. You should not have much trouble with this chapter because it presents no new theory; much of what you have learned in previous chapters of Part Six is discussed again in Chapter 26.

Natural monopoly describes a situation in which enormous economies of scale (relative to industry demand) lead to persisting declines in average cost and marginal cost. Therefore the firm that gets larger and larger before other firms will reap tremendous cost advantages and will price its output so as to drive out all competitors. Presumably, after it has attained monopoly status, it will maximize profits by charging a higher price and producing a lower output than social efficiency requires. (Interestingly enough, because of the advantages of economies of scale, it is possible that it would produce more, at a lower price, than would the perfect competition market structure.)

There are two basic approaches for coming to grips with a natural monopoly: antitrust policy and regulation. Antitrust, in essence, attempts to prevent the monopoly from arising in the first place; it makes "monopolizing" actions illegal. The regulation approach is to permit the monopoly to emerge (indeed, to *help* it to do so) and then to force it to behave in socially desirable ways.

One form of regulation forces the monopolist to price at the firm's marginal cost of output. Unfortunately (as your text points out), in such a situation marginal cost is below average cost; hence the monopolist would suffer economic losses. In order to deal with that problem, natural monopolists are regulated via rate regulation, which takes two forms. First, there is "cost of service" regulation, which requires the natural monopolist to charge according to the *average* cost of production (rather than the marginal cost, and therefore is socially inefficient). Second is the "rate of return" regulation which permits the natural monopolist to earn only a "normal" or competitive rate of return on the investment in the business.

This chapter also analyzes the behavior of regulators. The model maintains that regulators are just like the rest of us: they usually, but not always, do things that are in their own self-interest--and not society's. Two hypotheses are presented: the capture hypothesis and the share the gains/share the pains theory.

Then Chapter 26 explores the phenomenona of deregulation and reregulation.

LEARNING OBJECTIVES

After you have studied this chapter you should be able to

1. define natural monopoly, cost-of-service regulation, rate-of-return regulation, capture hypothesis, share the gains/share the pains theory, deregulation, per se violation, Herfindahl index, contestable markets, hub-and-spoke system, cross subsidization, creative response, and reregulation.

2. recognize how a natural monopoly can emerge.

3. indicate the problem with requiring a monopolist to engage in marginal cost pricing and list two ways to counter this problem.

4. distinguish between cost-of-service regulation and rate-of-return regulation, and answer questions that indicate an understanding of the difficulties involved with such regulation.

5. apply the regulator behavior model to predict the behavior of regulators.

6. list the main features of deregulation in the trucking and airline industries.

7. enumerate the essential features of the major antitrust laws.

8. calculate a Herfindahl index, and distinguish it from a concentration index.

9. list four exemptions to the antitrust laws.

CHAPTER OUTLINE

1. A natural monopoly arises when there are large economies of scale relative to industry demand and one firm can produce at a lower cost than can be achieved by multiple firms.

2. When long-run average costs are falling, the long-run marginal cost curve is below the long-run average cost curve; the first firm to take advantage of decreasing costs can drive out all competitors by underpricing them.
   a. If regulators force the natural monopolist to engage in marginal cost pricing, the firm will suffer economic losses and will shut down.
   b. In such a situation, regulators might subsidize the natural monopolist to engage in marginal cost pricing.

3. There are three types of government regulation: regulation of natural monopolies, regulation of inherently competitive industries, and social regulation.
   a. Economic regulation typically concerns controlling prices that regulated enterprises are allowed to charge.

   i. Cost-of-service regulation allows regulated companies to charge in accordance with actual average costs.
   ii. Rate-of-return regulation allows regulated firms to earn a normal rate of return on their investment in the business.

  b. Regulators can control prices, but because quality is difficult to measure and control, regulated firms can change their price per constant-quality unit when forced to underprice services.
  c. Regulated firms engage in creative response, which is a response to a regulation that conforms to the letter of the law while undermining its spirit.

4. The regulator behavior model suggests that regulation benefits firms already in a regulated industry--not potential entrants or consumers.
   a. The capture hypothesis predicts that regulators will eventually be controlled by the special interests of the industry that is being regulated.
   b. The share the gains/share the pains theory maintains that regulators must take into account the demands of three groups: legislators, firms in the industry, and consumers of the regulated industry.

5. By the end of the 1970s a substantial deregulation movement was set in motion in the United States.
   a. The 1980 Motor Carrier Act removed many of the entry restrictions in the trucking industry and greatly expanded the business activities for each class of carrier.
   b. The Airline Deregulation Act of 1978 permitted airlines to set fares and choose the routes they wanted to serve; predictably, some airlines were forced into bankruptcy once they lost the protection of regulators.
   c. Deregulation benefits most consumers, but not all; cross subsidization benefits to some consumers are eliminated because of the competition that accompanies deregulation.
   d. In the short run, a regulated industry that becomes deregulated may experience numerous temporary adjustments; in the long run, prices will be closer to marginal cost and fewer monopoly profits will be earned.

6. Antitrust policy attempts to prevent the emergence of monopoly and monopolistic behavior.
   a. In 1890 the Sherman Act was passed; it made illegal every contract and combination, in the form of a trust, that restrained trade.
   b. In 1914 the Clayton Act was passed; it made price discrimination and interlocking directorates illegal.
   c. The Federal Trade Commission Act of 1914 established that commission to prevent "unfair competition"; the 1938 Wheeler-Lea Act amended the 1914 act to allow the FTC to battle against false or misleading advertising.
   d. The Robinson-Patman Act of 1936 was aimed at preventing large producers from driving out small competitors by means of selective discriminatory price cuts.
   e. Numerous antitrust acts serve to exempt certain business (and union) practices from antitrust action.

7. Positive economics is of little help in deciding when and whom to prosecute in antitrust cases.
   a. In 1982 the Justice Department indicated it would no longer prevent the following

mergers: conglomerate, customer-supplier, and those that do not significantly affect competition.

b. The contestable market theory suggests that antitrust should be concerned with ease of entry into an industry--and not with the current structure of an industry.

8. Recently prestigious private universities have been charged with price fixing, artificially inflating tuition and financial aid costs, and with exchanging information that eliminates price choices for students; most agreed to stop such practices, but MIT fought and lost.

KEY TERMS

Cost of service regulation
Rate of return regulation
Deregulation
Herfindahl index
Hub-and-spoke system
Reregulation

KEY CONCEPTS

Natural monopoly
Capture hypothesis
Share the gains/share the pains theory
Cross subsidization
Per se violation
Contestable markets hypothesis
Creative response

COMPLETION QUESTIONS

Fill in the blank or circle the correct term.

1. A natural monopoly arises when there are large ______________ of scale relative to __________________; in such a case the firm's average total costs persistently ____________ and its marginal cost curve lies (below, above) its average cost curve; the first firm to expand will be able to offer a price that is _______________ than those of its rivals and drive them out of business.

2. If a natural monopolist were forced to engage in marginal cost pricing for social efficiency, that firm would experience _______________ economic profits; in order to counter that, regulators might __________________ the natural monopolist.

3. There are three types of government regulation: regulation of __________________ and _____________________, and _____________________.

4. Cost of service regulation requires firms to charge customers based on actual (marginal, average) costs; rate-of-return regulation permits regulated firms to earn ____________________ profits. Because price is easier to measure and regulate than quality, regulated firms can (lower, raise) the price per constant-quality unit even if price is constant.

5. Regulated firms often try to avoid the effects of regulation, so they react to regulation by making a _________ response; that is they follow the letter, but not the spirit, of a

regulation.

6. The regulator behavior model suggests that much regulation is for the benefit of (consumers, firms already in the industry); two such theories are ______________________ and ______________________.

7. In the 1980s (regulation, deregulation) of industry had become fashionable; two industries that were deregulated during those years are ____________________ and ____________________.

8. One predictable short-run result of deregulation is ___________; long-run results include __________________ and _______________.

9. The Sherman Act makes illegal those contracts or trusts that act to ____________ trade; the provisions of this act are (vague, clear); the Clayton Act makes price _____________ illegal if it substantially lessens competition, and it makes ___________________ per se illegal.

10. The Federal Trade Commission (FTC) Act attempts to prevent ______________ competition; the Wheeler-Lea Act amended the FTC Act and permits the FTC to battle against false or misleading _____________. The FTC Act was formed to protect __________________, while the Wheeler-Lea Act attempts to protect __________________.

11. The ______________________ Act is aimed at preventing producers from driving out competitors by means of selected discriminatory price cuts; it is commonly referred to as the ______________ act.

12. Four exemptions to antitrust laws are ____________________________, ______________________________, ______________________________ and ___________________________.

13. Concentration ratios equal total sales attributed to the top four or eight firms divided by total _______________; the Herfindahl index _______________ the market share of each supplier of the industry and adds them. If the sum, or index, is ___________ or less, the Justice Department will allow a merger.

14. The contestable markets theory suggests that antitrust should be more concerned with the ______________ into an industry and not the current _________________ of the industry.

15. Elite private universities (have, have not) engaged in price discrimination and in monopolistic behavior.

TRUE-FALSE QUESTIONS

Circle the **T** if the statement is true, the **F** if it is false. Explain to yourself why a statement is false.

T F 1. Natural monopolies arise mainly due to large economies of scale.

T F 2. If a natural monopolist is required to engage in marginal cost pricing, it will earn abnormal profits.

T F 3. All consumers benefit from deregulation, even if all producers don't.

T F 4. Traditionally in the United States inherently competitive industries have not been regulated.

T F 5. Regulated firms often follow the letter of a rule, but violate its spirit.

T F 6. Regulators can easily regulate the price per constant-quality unit of regulated firms.

T F 7. According to the regulator behavior theory, regulators are mostly concerned with the well-being of consumers.

T F 8. In recent years, deregulation has permitted airlines to set their own fares and choose their own routes.

T F 9. One predictable result of deregulation is bankruptcy for the less efficient firms.

T F 10. The Wheeler-Lea Act attempts to protect small competitors, while the FTC Act attempts to protect consumers.

T F 11. The Robinson-Patman Act was aimed at preventing producers from driving out smaller competitors by means of selected discriminatory price cuts.

T F 12. Labor unions are exempted from antitrust laws, even if their actions restrain trade.

T F 13. Since 1982 the Justice Department permits conglomerate mergers and those mergers that do not significantly affect competition.

T F 14. Some elite private universities in the U.S. have engaged in behavior that may violate antitrust laws.

MULTIPLE CHOICE QUESTIONS

Circle the letter that corresponds to the best answer.

1. A natural monopoly results because
   a. of large economies of scale.
   b. of persisting declining average and marginal costs.
   c. the largest firm can underprice its competitors.
   d. All of the above

2. If the natural monopolist were forced to price at marginal cost, it would earn
   a. abnormal profits.
   b. economic profits.
   c. economic losses.
   d. zero economic profit.

3. If an industry is deregulated,
   a. some buyers would lose the benefits of cross subsidization.
   b. all producers would be hurt.
   c. all consumers would be helped.
   d. All of the above

4. Which of the following is *not* a recognized type of government regulation?
   a. regulation of natural monopolies
   b. regulation for the benefit of Congress
   c. regulation of inherently competitive industries
   d. regulation for public welfare across all industries

5. Which of the following is probably the most difficult to regulate?
   a. price
   b. output
   c. quality
   d. profit

6. Which of the following is *not* consistent with the regulator behavior model?
   a. Regulators are concerned with benefiting themselves.
   b. Regulators are concerned with benefiting vocal customers.
   c. Regulators are concerned with benefiting firms already in the industry.
   d. Regulators are concerned with benefiting potential entrants into an industry.

7. Which of the following is a predictable consequence of deregulation?
   a. increased bankruptcies in the short run
   b. long-run abnormal profits
   c. Long-run price is even greater than MC.
   d. short-run misallocation of resources

8. Which action is a per se violation of antitrust legislation?
   a. interlocking directorates
   b. price discrimination
   c. discount pricing
   d. mergers

9. Which of the following are *not* exempt from antitrust laws?
   a. labor unions
   b. professional sports
   c. suppliers of military equipment
   d. all unincorporated businesses

10. The Herfindahl index is a measure of
    a. GDP concentration.
    b. market concentration.
    c. monopoly.
    d. merger activity.

11. The contestable market theory maintains that antitrust enforcers should be primarily concerned with
    a. the degree to which entry into an industry is possible.
    b. concentration ratios.
    c. Herfindahl indexes.
    d. interlocking directorates.

12. Elite private U.S. universities allegedly
    a. cross subsidize lower income minority students.
    b. charge higher prices to lower price elastic students.
    c. share pricing information.
    d. All of the above

MATCHING

Choose the item in column (2) that best matches an item in column (1).

(1)	(2)
a. contestable markets	f. price discrimination
b. cross subsidization	g. persistent fall in long run AC
c. natural monopoly	h. behavior of regulated firms
d. creative response	i. behavior of regulators
e. capture hypothesis	j. ease of entry into industry

WORKING WITH GRAPHS

1. Suppose you are an analyst for a regulatory board that is in charge of the regulation of local monopolies. Given the information in the graph that follows, answer the list of questions submitted by your supervisor.

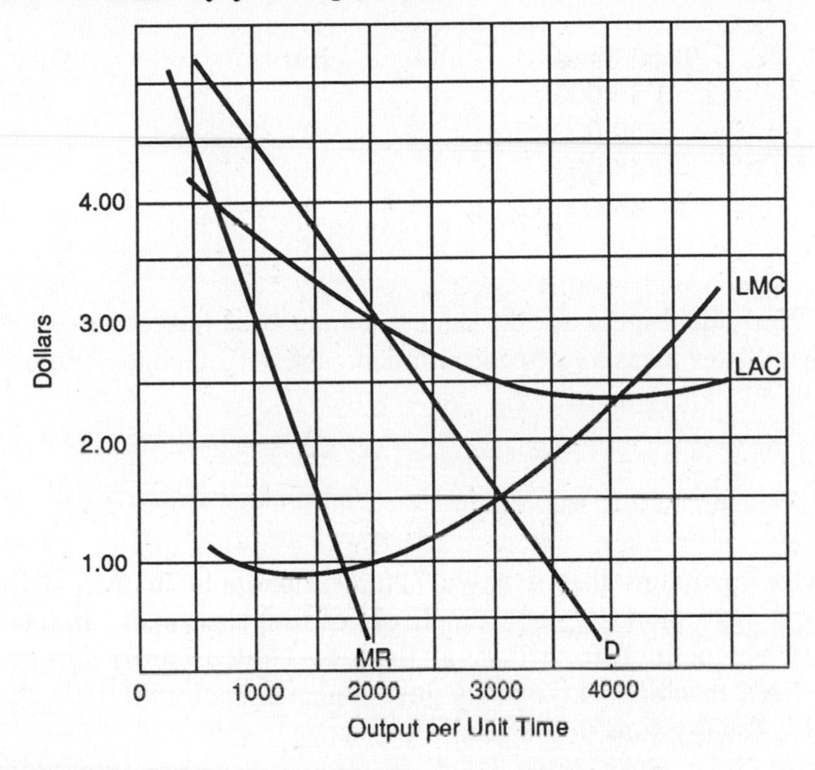

a. If this monopolist is not regulated, what will be the level of
   output? __________
   price? __________
   total revenue? __________
   total costs? __________
   profit or loss? __________

b. If this monopolist is regulated by marginal cost pricing, what will be the level of
   output? __________
   price? __________
   total revenue? __________
   total costs? __________
   profits or loss? __________
   Will the monopoly need a subsidy? __________
   If so, how much? __________

c. If cost-of-service regulation is imposed on this monopolist, what will be the level of
   output? __________
   price? __________
   total revenue? __________
   total costs? __________
   profit or loss? __________

PROBLEMS

1. Calculate 4-firm concentration indexes for the following two industries.

Industry A		Industry B	
Firm	Total Sales	Firm	Total Sales
1	$ 50,000	1	$150,000
2	50,000	2	15,000
3	45,000	3	15,000
4	45,000	4	10,000

2. Now calculate a Herfindahl index for the same two industries in problem 1. Which index seems to provide a better measure of concentration: the 4-firm concentration ratio or the Herfindahl index?

CASE STUDY

The U.S. Postal Service maintains that it has a natural monopoly in mail delivery. It is regulated, and, by law, it has a monopoly on the delivery of first class mail. In recent years the post office has met stiff competition from Federal Express, United Parcel Service, and other sources--including the FAX machine. Like many government agencies the U.S. Postal Service is unprofitable; indeed it usually runs in the red.

1. If the U.S. Postal Service really is a natural monopoly, does it need to be granted a legal monopoly in the delivery of first class mail?

2. If the U.S. Postal Service loses its legal monopoly on the delivery of first class mail, what cross-subsidized customers will be hurt?

ANSWERS TO CHAPTER 26

COMPLETIONS QUESTIONS

1. economies, industry demand; fall, below; lower
2. negative; subsidize
3. natural monopoly, inherently competitive industries, social regulation
4. average; normal; raise
5. creative
6. firms already in the industry; capture theory, share the gains/share the pains
7. deregulation; airlines, trucking
8. increased bankruptcy; prices closer to marginal cost, smaller abnormal profits
9. restrain; vague; discrimination, interlocking directorates
10. unfair; advertising; small competitors, consumers
11. Robinson-Patman; chain store
12. labor unions, public utilities, professional sports, cooperative acts among American exporters, schools and hospitals, public transit and water systems, suppliers of military equipment, joint publishing arrangements by two or more newspapers in a single city
13. industry sales; squares; 1000
14. degree to which entry is permitted, market structure
15. have

TRUE-FALSE QUESTIONS

1. T
2. F It will realize losses.
3. F Some consumers lose the benefits of cross subsidization.
4. F Inherently competitive industries such as trucking and airlines have been regulated.
5. T
6. F It is difficult to regulate quality.
7. F They, like the rest of us, are usually concerned with their own well-being.
8. T
9. T
10. F Just the opposite.
11. T
12. T
13. T
14. T

MULTIPLE CHOICE QUESTIONS

1.d; 2.c; 3.a; 4.b; 5.c; 6.d; 7.a; 8.a; 9.d; 10.b;
11.a; 12.d

MATCHING

a and j; b and f; c and g; d and h; e and i

WORKING WITH GRAPHS

1. a. 1700 units, $3.50, $5950, $5440, profit of $510 (**note:** dollar figures are approximations.)
   b. 3000 units, $1.50, $4500, $7500, loss of $3000, yes, $3000
   c. 2000, $3, $6000, $6000, $0

PROBLEMS

1. Both industries have a concentration ratio of 100%.
2. The Herfindahl index for industry A is 2506.9, and for industry B it is 6322.7; note that the 4-firm concentration ratio yields the same measure of concentration even though the market structures are different. The Herfindahl measure indicates that industry A is more competitive, which seems to be the case; the 4-firm concentration ratio implies that they are equally competitive.

CASE STUDY

1. If it *really* is a natural monopoly, it will easily drive rivals out of business.
2. Businesses that pay artificially low rates for third class (or "junk") mail and rural customers would have to pay higher rates if private firms entered the business.

GLOSSARY TO CHAPTER 26

Capture hypothesis A theory of regulatory behavior that predicts that the regulators will eventually be captured by the special interests of the industry that is being regulated.

Cost-of-service regulation A type of regulation based on allowing prices that reflect only the actual cost of production and do not include monopoly profits.

Creative response A firm's behavioral modification that allows it to comply with the letter of the law without complying with the spirit of the law so that the law's effects are lessened significantly.

Cross subsidization The selling of a product or service in one market below cost, with the losses being made up for by selling the same product or service in another market at above marginal cost.

Deregulation The elimination or phasing out of past regulations of economic activity.

Herfindahl index An index of market concentration obtained by squaring the market share of each supplier and adding up these squared values.

Hub-and-spoke system A system of physical airline organization in which a major airport, called the hub, becomes the place from which all originating flights come. Passengers then change planes to reach their final destination flights.

Natural monopoly A monopoly that arises from the peculiar production characteristics in the industry. Usually a natural monopoly arises when production of the service or product requires extremely large capital investments such that only one firm can profitably be supported by consumers. A natural monopoly arises when there are large economies of scale relative to the industry demand, and one firm can produce at a lower cost than can be achieved by multiple firms.

Per se violation An activity that is specifically spelled out as a violation of the law. In antitrust law, whether or not competition is lessened does not have to be proven. A violation based on the facts only and not on the effects, which are taken as given.

Rate-of-return regulation Regulation that seeks to keep the rate of return in the industry at a competitive level by not allowing excessive prices to be charged.

Reregulation The political process by which formerly heavily regulated industries that have been deregulated will once again have increased restrictions put on their behavior with respect to entry, pricing, and quality and types of services offered.

Share the gains/share the pains theory A theory of regulatory behavior in which the regulators must take account of the demands of three groups: legislators, who established and who oversee the regulatory agency; those in the regulated industry; and consumers of the regulated industry.

Theory of contestable markets The hypothesis concerning the pricing behavior of firms in which even though there are only a few in the industry, they are forced to price their products more or less competitively because of the ease of entry by outsiders. The key aspect of a contestable market is relatively costless entry into and exit from the industry.

CHAPTER 27

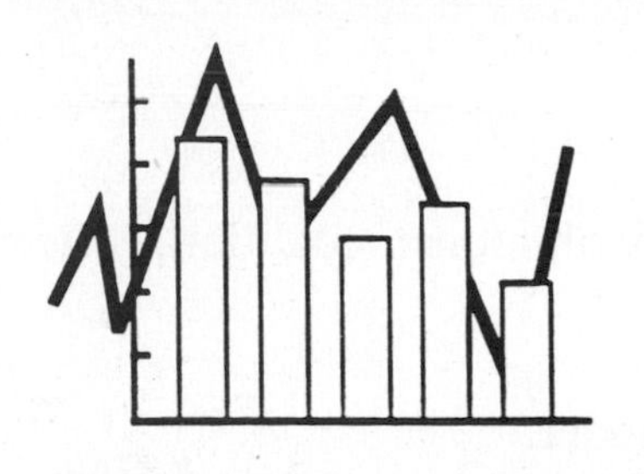

PUBLIC CHOICE

PUTTING THIS CHAPTER INTO PERSPECTIVE

Chapter 27 deals with the public choice model and the appendix is concerned with the United States' farm sector. Professor Miller ties these two seemingly disparate topics together by showing how our farm policy can best be understood by viewing it as a specific application of the public choice theory. You should be able to apply the principles of the public choice model to the farm sector after you have studied this chapter.

The public choice model, in effect, applies some of the principles developed in the chapters concerned with the private marketplace. The most important application is the assumption that voters, politicians, and bureaucrats behave just like businesses and consumers: they usually (but not always) pursue their own, not society's, self-interest. Starting with this premise and drawing on general economic principles, it is possible to gain some very interesting insights into how resources are allocated in the public sector, and into the workings of the U.S. government's farm policy.

One important insight is that voters have only one "all or nothing" vote to cast (unlike consumers, who have dollar votes that enable them to indicate the intensity of wants), and hence cannot indicate the intensity of their wants in the public sector. As a result, logrolling, or vote trading, has evolved. Logrolling permits voters, through their elected representatives, to indicate the intensity of their wants; in that sense logrolling is economically efficient and permits the political process to move more closely to the ideal democracy. On the other hand, logrolling permits special interest groups to work efficiently--at the expense of the rest of us. Thus, politicians (and bureaucrats) representing the interest of farmers can, in effect, trade votes with politicians representing other special interest groups; the net effect is that national efficiency suffers.

Another insight yielded by the public choice model is that in many instances it is rational for voters to remain ignorant of political issues because information is costly to obtain and most issues will affect them only slightly. Stated in a more familiar way, the marginal benefit to obtaining political information is often quite low relative to the marginal cost of obtaining such information.

The public choice model also yields insights concerning distributional coalitions. Distributional coalitions form when it is possible for a small group to benefit relatively hugely at the expense of a large group that pays, *individually*, relatively small amounts. How else can we account for our incredibly expensive agricultural policy that helps so few people?

LEARNING OBJECTIVES

After you have studied this chapter, you should be able to

1. define theory of public choice, median voter theorem, distributional coalition, price supports, logrolling and bureaucrats.

2. recognize the fundamental assumptions of the public choice model.

3. predict the conditions under which a voter will choose to remain ignorant about a specific political issue.

4. recognize differences and similarities between market and collective decision-making.

5. predict the conditions under which a distributional coalition will emerge.

6. predict some consequences of the median voter theorem.

7. recognize why a private economy would generate a different composition of goods and services than would a representative of government.

CHAPTER OUTLINE

1. In order to understand how resources are allocated by governments, economists have developed the public choice model.

2. There are similarities and dissimilarities in how resources are allocated in the private sector vs. the public (government) sector.
   a. As is true for private economy decision-makers, all participants in the political marketplace follow the dictates of rational self-interest; additionally, the principle of minimum differentiation exists in both areas.
   b. In the private marketplace firms specialize in the production of specific goods, while political candidates must appear to know something about every problem; in the private sector buyers can reveal the intensity of their wants via a proportional rule (dollar votes), whereas in the political sector an all or nothing majority rule is followed, hence the composition of output would be different under each system.
   c. Logrolling permits elected officials to indicate the intensity of their constituents' wants.

3. The median voter theorem is that political decisions will be made in accord with the self-interest of the median voter.
   a. Each political party will promote programs that appeal to the median voter, hence each will produce nearly identical platforms.
   b. Candidates will take more extreme positions during the primaries because they are appealing to the median voter *within* a party; during the national election, however, appealing to the median voter will lead to a similarity of platforms between the opponents.
   c. People who disagree with political outcomes that appeal to the median voter can vote

with their feet and move to a jurisdiction that better suits them.

d. The problem with the median voter theorem is that it cannot explain why small groups gain disproportionate shares of government benefits.

4. The theory of distributional coalitions is that small groups can use the government to redistribute disproportionate benefits to themselves if small amounts can be taken from each of many people.

5. Bureaucrats are nonelected governmental officials who organize special interest groups and defend the rights of such "clients."
   a. Because performance in government is often measured by the number of clients served, bureaucrats have an incentive to expand the size of their clientele.
      i. Bureaucratic rewards do not depend on profits (as would be the case in the private sector); therefore their rewards appear not so much in high salaries but in job perks which provide further incentives for bureaucrats to protect their jobs.

6. For most issues it is not worth the time and effort for citizens to incur the costs of gathering information regarding political issues; hence it is usually rational for citizens in democracies to remain ignorant.

KEY TERMS

Collective decision making
Public choice theory
Price supports
Bureaucrats
Proportional rule
Majority rule

KEY CONCEPTS

Median voter theorem
Distributional coalition
Rational ignorance
Logrolling
Principal of minimum differentiation

COMPLETION QUESTIONS

Fill in the blank or circle the correct term.

*1. The public choice model assumes that even though regulators and bureaucrats are (like, unlike) the rest of us, they face a (similar, different) incentive system.

2. The public choice model assumes that politicians, bureaucrats, and regulators pursue (society's, their own) self-interest.

3. Consumer special interest groups to fight (say) milk price supports are not forthcoming because individual milk buyers endure (low, high) costs as a result of such price supports.

4. For both private and public decision-makers the principal of minimum ________________ exists.

5. Private sector buyers can reveal the intensity of their wants via a ________________ through ________________ votes; in the political sector the all or nothing ________________ rule is followed; we can conclude that the composition of output will (differ, be the same) under those two rules of supplying goods to customer/clients.

6. The median voter theorem predicts that during primaries opposing candidates will present (more, less) radical platforms than will opposing candidates in a national election.

7. A ________________ will be formed if small groups can use the government to redistribute disproportionate benefits to themselves from small amounts extracted from each of many people.

8. Bureaucrats are (elected, nonelected) governmental officials whose clients are ______________ groups; bureaucrats' rewards take the form of ________________.

9. Each member of congress has an incentive to (favor, oppose) spending that benefits other Congress members' constituents, but to ________________ spending that benefits his or her own constituents; an exception to this rule occurs when politicians find it beneficial to trade votes, in a process called ________________.

10. Because information to voters is not ________________ and because voters will not be concerned with expenditure programs that affect them only slightly, voters often choose to be ________________.

11. In the private marketplace, individuals "vote" with their ________________; in the political marketplace, ________________ are consumers and ________________ are political entrepreneurs.

12. Fundamental to the theory of public choice is the idea that voters, bureaucrats, and politicians follow the dictates of rational ________________, just as do private decision makers.

13. Distributional coalitions form when a (small, large) number of people can gain relatively large amounts at the expense of a (small, large) number of people, each of whom pays a relatively (small, large) amount.

TRUE-FALSE QUESTIONS

Circle the **T** if the statement is true, the **F** if it is false. Explain to yourself why a statement is false.

T F 1. The public choice model assumes that regulators and bureaucrats are mostly concerned with their own--not the public's--self-interest.

T F 2. The public choice model indicates that households will be provided the same goods by elected representatives as they would by the private sector.

T F 3. The various programs to benefit farmers cost more in dollars than farmers receive in dollar payments.

T F 4. Distributional coalitions benefit everyone in the economy.

T F 5. It is often rational for voters to remain ignorant of political issues and of candidates.

T F 6. Bureaucrats can often exert great influence on matters that concern themselves.

T F 7. The principal of minimum differentiation exists in both political and private market decision-making.

T F 8. In the private marketplace dollar votes indicate majority, not proportional rule.

T F 9. Logrolling helps politicians to indicate the intensity of wants of their clients.

T F 10. The median voter theorem helps to explain how small groups can gain a disproportionate share of governmental benefits.

MULTIPLE CHOICE QUESTIONS

Circle the letter that corresponds to the best answer.

1. Which of the following characterizes collective, but not market, decision making?
   a. the legal use of force
   b. a positive price usually is charged to users
   c. intensity of wants is easily revealed
   d. proportional rule

2. People who work in the public sector
   a. are more competent than other workers.
   b. are less competent than other workers.
   c. face a different incentive structure than many workers in the private sector.
   d. would behave in the same way if they worked for a small private business.

3. If Mr. Ayers loves good A, he can convey the intensity of his wants if good A is
   a. a private good.
   b. a public good.
   c. not subject to the exclusion principle.
   d. expensive.

*4. The theory of public choice assumes that
   a. politicians are political entrepreneurs who supply services.
   b. voters demand political services.
   c. a market exists for political services.
   d. All of the above

5. The public-choice theory assumes that voters, bureaucrats, and politicians usually
   a. attempt to pursue their self-interest.
   b. are concerned with society's interests.
   c. exhibit behavior not subject to economic analysis.
   d. are indifferent to what voters want.

*6. Distributional collectives are more likely to form if
   a. costs are concentrated in a small number of individuals.
   b. benefits are dispersed among a large number of individuals.
   c. the group is small and homogeneous.
   d. political instability exists.

7. Distributional collectives are seldom countered because it is not usually worthwhile for ______________ to fight them.
   a. those that receive the benefits
   b. those that pay the costs
   c. taxpayers
   d. unions

8. An individual Congress member has an incentive to
   a. vote against expenditures that do not directly benefit his own constituents.
   b. vote for expenditures that benefit only his constituents.
   c. vote for expenditures that benefit everyone.
   d. All of the above.

9. Voters often find it rational to remain ignorant of issues and candidates because
   a. ignorance is bliss.
   b. politicians don't care what voters want anyway.
   c. information is costly to obtain.
   d. they don't have to pay for expenditures anyway.

10. Voters tend to be
   a. very knowledgeable about the issues.
   b. ignorant of many political issues.
   c. very knowledgeable about a candidate's political platform.
   d. willing to spend much time and effort to become knowledgeable.

11. Bureaucrats
    a. often can exert great influence on matters concerning themselves.
    b. seldom can exert great influence on matters concerning themselves.
    c. cannot influence public demand; they only have political influence.
    d. refrain from exerting political influence because they are concerned with society's interests.

*12. According to the public choice model, people enter politics mostly to
    a. maximize their income and wealth.
    b. do good for society.
    c. help the poor.
    d. eliminate economic rents.

MATCHING

Choose the item in column (2) that best matches an item in column (1).

(1)	(2)
a. price support	i. union
b. public choice theory	j. different parties have similar platforms
c. distributional coalition	k. trade votes
d. median voter theorem	l. proportional rule
e. logrolling	m. firms produce similar-quality goods
f. minimum differentiation	n. information is costly to obtain
g. intensity of wants revealed	o. nonrecourse loan
h. rational ignorance	p. self-interested politicians

CASE STUDY

Nobel prize winner George Stigler named "Director's Law" after Aaron Director, formerly of the University of Chicago. Director's Law states that public expenditures are made for the primary benefit of the middle class and are financed with taxes borne largely by the rich and the poor.

One example of Director's Law is government expenditures on college education. Upper income people, in the main, send their children to private schools, while lower income people tend not to go to college (at least when Director's Law was developed) because the main cost of going to college is the opportunity cost of foregone wage earnings. As a rule, middle income people send their children to state-subsidized colleges, while the rich and the poor pay disproportionate amounts. As you observed in this chapter of the text, the farm program largely benefits middle income farmers.

1. Does Director's Law hold for the welfare system?

2. Does Director's Law hold for defense spending?

ANSWERS TO CHAPTER 27

COMPLETION QUESTIONS

1. like, different
2. their own
3. low
4. differentiation
5. proportional rule, dollar; majority; differ
6. more
7. distributional coalition
8. nonelected; special interest; perks such as large staffs, pensions, etc.
9. oppose; favor; logrolling
10. costless, rationally ignorant
11. dollars; voters or special interest groups, politicians
12. self-interest
13. small, large, small

TRUE-FALSE QUESTIONS

1. T
2. F The goods will differ because proportional rule in the private sector can reveal intensity of wants, while majority rule cannot.
3. T
4. F Only relatively small interest groups benefit.
5. T
6. T
7. T
8. F Dollar votes indicate a proportional rule system.
9. T
10. F The theory of distributional coalitions does this.

MULTIPLE CHOICE QUESTIONS

1.a; 2.c; 3.a; 4.d; 5.a; 6.c; 7.b; 8.d; 9.c; 10.b;
11.a; 12.a

MATCHING

a and o; b and p; c and i; d and j; e and k; f and m; g and l; h and n

CASE STUDY

1. Perhaps, especially if we note that most (around 80 per cent) of welfare dollars go to administration of the program; and that middle income people often qualify for benefits.
2. Maybe. Rich people can diversify assets in such a way as to avoid the consequences of foreign nations that take over their country; and they can buy influence with hostile governments. Low income people have few assets to protect--and they tend to be the people drafted.

GLOSSARY TO CHAPTER 27

Bureaucrats Non-elected government officials who are responsible for the day-to-day operation of government regulations and laws.

Collective decision making How voters, politicians, and other interested parties act, and how these actions influence nonmarket decisions.

Distributional coalitions Associations such as cartels, unions, and cooperatives that are formed to gain special government privileges in order to redistribute wealth by taking small amounts from each of many people and giving large amounts to each of only a few.

Logrolling The practice of exchanging political favors by elected representatives. Typically, one elected official agrees to vote for the policy of another official in exchange for the vote of the latter in favor of the former's desired policy.

Majority rule A collective decision-making system in which group decisions are made on the basis of 50.1 percent of the vote. In other words, whatever more than 50 percent of the population votes for, the entire population has to take.

Median voter A voter who lies exactly in the middle of the political spectrum on a particular issue or group of issues.

Price supports Minimum prices set by the government. To be effective, price supports must be coupled with a mechanism to rid the market of surplus goods that arise whenever the support price is greater than the market clearing price.

Proportional rule A decision-making system in which actions are based on the proportion of the "votes" cast and are in proportion to those votes cast. In a market system, if 10 percent of the dollar votes are cast for blue cars, 10 percent of the people get to buy blue cars.

Theory of public choice Hypotheses concerning political structures, the motives behind political actions, and their effect on economic policy.

APPENDIX F

PUBLIC CHOICE IN ACTION: FARM POLICY

Farmers really do have problems. In the long run the agricultural sector is fated to decrease in importance because the real price of food and other agricultural goods falls secularly. Low price elasticity of demand and a variable supply curve (due to the many uncertainties and hazards of farming) also creates a short-run problem for farmers: high income variability.

Because the prices of agricultural goods are closely related to incomes of farmers--and because the prices of farm goods are volatile--much effort and money has been allocated to stabilizing farm prices. This has created numerous problems, to which the appendix attests.

Because of rapid technological advances on the farm, the supply of agricultural goods has increased relative to their demand; the result would normally be a rapid decline in the relative price of farm outputs. Various price support programs, however, have prevented prices of farm goods from falling to a new (lower) equilibrium level.

You learned in Chapter 3 that if price is above equilibrium , a surplus exists. You learn in Chapter 27 that the only way a *prolonged* (long period) surplus can exist is if price is set above equilibrium and government buys the resulting surplus--thereby preventing price from falling.

Rising physical food surpluses that coincide with world hunger obviously present a political problem. Governments, therefore, have tried to tackle the problem of what to do with the surpluses. School lunches and foreign aid to poor countries absorb some of the surpluses--but not much. Other measures, such as the soil bank program and target prices, try to reduce surpluses while still offering aid to farmers. None of these measures, however, seems to lead to the long-run solution--a reduction in the amount of resources (including farm labor) allocated to the farm sector. The public choice model, however, leads us to expect that the U.S. farm problem is not likely to go away in the near future, despite the fact that the globalization of our economy and GATT treaties tend to call for reduced subsidies for farmers.

LEARNING OBJECTIVES

After you have studied this chapter, you should be able to

1. define price supports, parity, nonrecourse loan, target price, deficiency payment, and quota system.

2. predict the consequences of a low income elasticity of demand, a low price elasticity of demand, and a volatile supply schedule for the income of farmers.

3. predict the consequences of a price support system that keeps price above the market clearing price.

4. enumerate the two necessary conditions for a *prolonged* surplus to exist.

5. distinguish between the main elements of a price support system and a target price program.

6. identify who benefits from and who pays for agricultural price supports.

APPENDIX OUTLINE

1. The U.S. government agriculture policy provides fertile ground for analyzing the public choice model.

2. The U.S. farm sector approaches the perfectly competitive market structure analyzed in Chapter 3 and 23.

3. The income elasticity of demand for food is quite low; this means that in the long run the farm sector must become decreasingly important as an absorber of resources--labor and nonlabor.
   a. The price elasticity of demand for food is also very low.
   b. The price elasticity of supply of food is also very low.

4. The golden age of American farming occurred during the 20 years prior to World War I; since then the farm sector has been in decline; nevertheless, on average farmers are at least as well off financially as are nonfarmers.

5. In an attempt to stabilize farm incomes, the government attempts to stabilize farm prices; it establishes *price supports* by setting market price above equilibrium.
   a. In order to maintain market price above the equilibrium level, the government must purchase the resulting surplus and store it--or sell it abroad.
   b. Through the Commodity Credit Corporation the government granted farmers *nonrecourse loans*--loans that never have to be repaid--in exchange for the surplus goods it purchased.
   c. Because a price support subsidizes farmers per unit of output, those with large farms typically receive higher payments; also much of the benefits of a price support system are capitalized in the value of farmland, most of which is owned by such farmers.

6. In order to reduce the amount of surplus accumulation, such programs as the *soil bank* and the PIK program were introduced.
   a. Such programs were designed to reduce farm output, but they were not successful.
   b. To the extent that acreage restrictions programs worked, they induced farmers to substitute fertilizer, capital, and labor for land--a substitution that is efficient from the farmer's point of view, but inefficient from society's perspective.

7. Another scheme to reduce farm surpluses, while still helping farmers, is the *target price* system.
   a. The government sets a target price and pays the farmer the difference between the target price and the market price per unit, multiplied by the quantity sold on the market.
   b. While a target price system reduces the size of the agricultural surplus and permits consumers to pay a lower price for farm goods than a price support system does, taxpayers must still pay for the farm aid; also, such a program does not reduce the allocation of resources absorbed by the farm sector.

8. Agricultural programs are enormously expensive.
   a. During the early 1990s, the combined cost of the various programs produced *direct* cash benefits to farmers worth over $25 billion per year.
   b. During that period, the cost to taxpayers and consumers averaged about $35 billion per year.
   c. The *direct* efficiency loss (or waste), therefore, was about $10 billion per year.

9. The farm program can best be understood via the public choice model.

KEY TERMS

Public choice model
Price supports
Nonrecourse loans
Soil bank
Deficiency payment
Acreage allotment

KEY CONCEPTS

Price parity
Target price
Import quota system

COMPLETION QUESTIONS

Fill in the blank or circle the correct term.

1. If price is above equilibrium, a _______________ exists; normally price will ____________ and quantity demanded will ____________ while quantity supplied ____________; eventually the _______________ disappears.

2. Prolonged or long period of surpluses in agricultural goods have existed because the government has set price (below, above) equilibrium and has _______________ the surpluses; these actions prevent price from _______________ to the equilibrium level.

3. The income elasticity of demand for food is quite (low, high); this means that in the (short, long) run the agricultural sector must diminish in importance.

*4. The price elasticity of demand for food is (low, high); the price elasticity of supply of food is ___________. The supply of food is volatile because of weather and other farming hazards; these facts mean that farm prices are (stable, volatile) and therefore farm incomes are (low, high, highly variable).

5. A target price system sets a target price for food; if the target price is set above the market price, then farmers will produce based on the (target, market) price; farmers will receive deficiency payments equal to _______________ times the quantity they sell; under such a system surpluses will tend to be (less, greater) than surpluses existing under a price support system.

6. Price supports are based on an individual farm's output; as a consequence the larger subsidies will go to owners of (small, large) farms. The benefits of a price support system will be reflected in the price of land; hence owners of (small, large) farms will receive most of such capitalized benefits.

7. The soil bank program, the PIK program, and various acreage allotment programs are attempts to (decrease, increase) farm surpluses by encouraging farmers to produce (less, more).

*8. In the near future we can expect (smaller, larger) farm sizes, (more, fewer) farms, and (fewer, more) farmers in the United States.

9. In order to keep domestic food prices high, the U.S. government imposes _______________ quotas on foreign produced goods.

TRUE-FALSE QUESTIONS

Circle the **T** if the statement is true, the **F** if it is false. Explain to yourself why a statement is false.

T F 1. The U.S. agricultural sector could resemble the perfectly competitive market structure, were it not for government intervention.

T F 2. The income elasticity of demand for food is quite high.

T F 3. The price elasticity of demand for food is quite low.

T F 4. Although farm prices are volatile, farm incomes are quite stable.

T F 5. For a given increase in supply, the more inelastic is the demand, the greater the decline in price.

T F 6. The combination of price supports and government purchases of surpluses creates long periods of food surpluses.

T F 7. The price parity ratio relates the prices that farmers actually receive for their goods to the prices they should receive.

T F 8. Price supports tend to benefit landowners, because the value of supports is reflected in the price of farmland.

T F 9. In an effort to reduce surpluses, the government institutes various schemes to limit farm output.

T F 10. To the extent that acreage restrictions work, they are efficient from society's perspective because they induce farmers to subsidize capital and fertilizer for land.

T F 11. In theory, target prices reduce surpluses.

T F 12. Deficiency payments equal target price minus market price, multiplied times quantity sold.

MULTIPLE CHOICE QUESTIONS

Circle the letter that corresponds to the best answer.

1. The U.S. farm industry is characterized by
   a. production of homogeneous goods
   b. many buyers and sellers
   c. fairly easy entry
   d. All of the above

2. Which of the following is *not* true concerning food?
   a. low income elasticity of demand
   b. stable supply curve
   c. low price elasticity of demand
   d. low price elasticity of supply

3. For a given increase in supply, the more inelastic is demand, the
   a. more price will fall.
   b. more price will rise.
   c. less price will fall.
   d. less price will rise.

4. Because farm prices are highly variable,
   a. farm incomes are highly stable.
   b. farm incomes are highly variable.
   c. farm surpluses emerge.
   d. farmers never earn profits.

5. Which of the following is necessary for prolonged surpluses?
   a. price supports above equilibrium
   b. price supports above equilibrium and government purchases of the surplus
   c. price supports below equilibrium
   d. target prices

6. The price parity ratio
   a. relates prices of goods that farmers sell to prices that they pay.
   b. sets a relatively high or relatively low support price depending on the base year chosen.
   c. if used to justify price supports, is an exercise in normative, not positive, economics.
   d. All of the above

7. Price supports benefit
   a. farmers at the expense of nonfarmers.
   b. farmland owners.
   c. individual farmers based on their total output.
   d. All of the above

8. In order to reduce surpluses, the U.S. government has instituted such programs as
   a. price supports.
   b. pricc parity.
   c. acreage restrictions.
   d. All of the above

9. To the extent that acreage restriction is effective,
   a. surpluses will rise in quantity.
   b. farmers will substitute capital and fertilizer for land.
   c. farm goods will be produced efficiently from society's point of view.
   d. farmers will substitute land for other factors of production.

*10. Which of the following is *unlike* the others?
   a. soil bank
   b. PIK program
   c. price supports
   d. acreage restriction

11. Analogy: Nonrecourse loan is to price supports as deficiency payment is to
   a. target price.
   b. price support.
   c. soil bank.
   d. acreage restriction.

12. The soil bank and acreage allotment programs induce farmers to substitute other factors of production for land; this is efficient for
   a. farmers, but not for society.
   b. society, but not for farmers.
   c. neither farmers nor society.
   d. everyone.

MATCHING

Choose the item in column (2) that best matches an item in column (1).

(1)	(2)
a. price support	e. nonrecourse loan
b. volatile price	f. inelastic supply and demand
c. target price	g. deficiency payment
d. acreage restriction	h. soil bank

WORKING WITH GRAPHS

1. Study the following graphs, then answer the questions that follow.

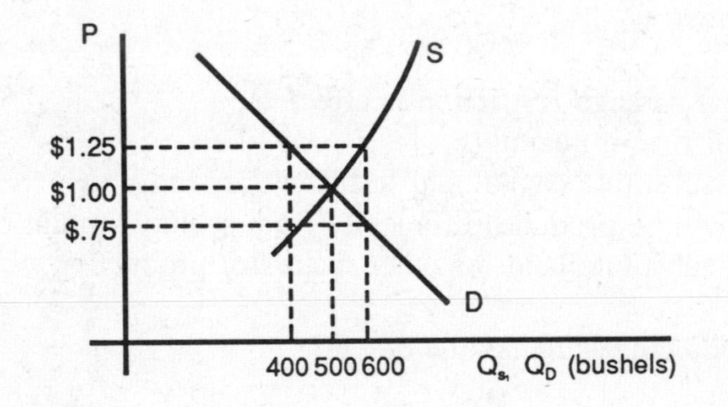

a. The equilibrium price is ________________.

b. If the government price support is $1.25 per bushel, quantity supplied by farmers is __________ bushels; quantity demanded by the private sector is __________ bushels; the government must purchase the resulting surplus of __________ bushels, at a total cost of $____________.

c. If instead the government decides to use a target price system and it targets price at $1.25 per bushel, farmers will produce __________ bushels; the market price then will be $__________, and at that price quantity demanded equals __________ bushels; the surplus now equals __________ bushels. The per bushel deficiency payment is $__________, and the target program costs $____________ to taxpayers.

d. The price that food consumers pay is lower under the ______________ program.

2. Use the following graphs to answer these questions.

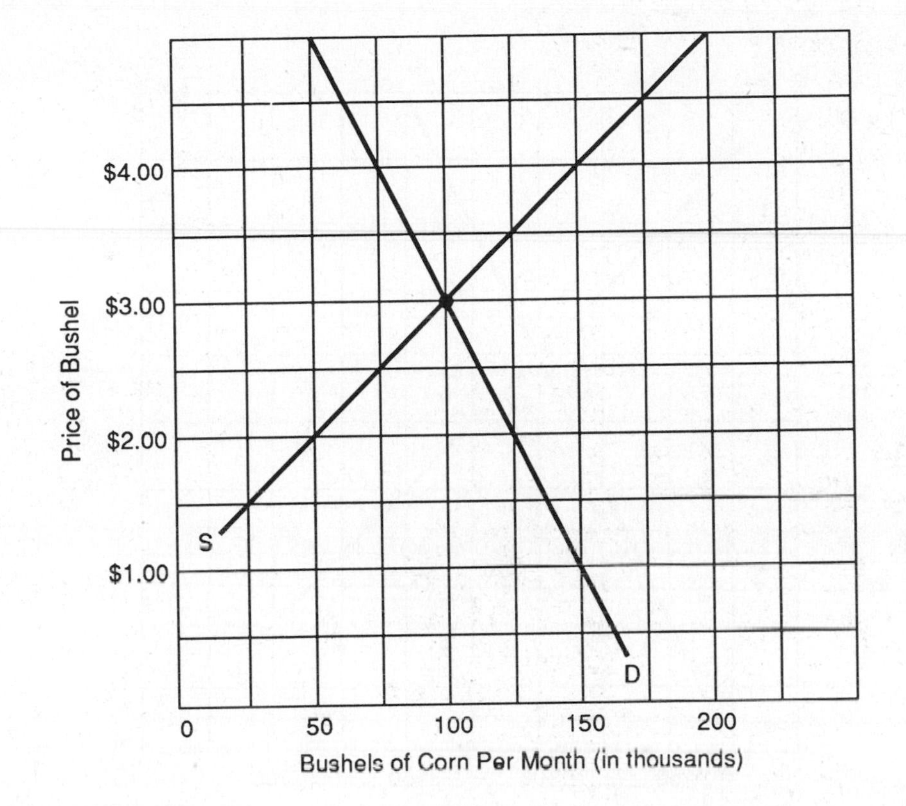

a. In the market for corn, in the absence of any government intervention, the market clearing price per bushel will be ____________, with a quantity of ____________ bushels per month being sold.

b. The total income of corn farmers in this market will be ______________ per month.

c. Suppose that the government has established the need for price supports in the corn market and begins to support the price of corn at $4 per bushel. As a result, farmers will produce ____________ bushels per month.

d. Farmers will sell ____________ bushels per month to consumers and ____________ bushels per month to the government.

e. Total income of farmers will rise to ____________ per month, with the government paying out ____________ per month of the farmers' incomes.

f. In this case, the government is purchasing the (shortage/surplus) created by the price support for corn.

3. Use the graphs that follow to answer the following questions.

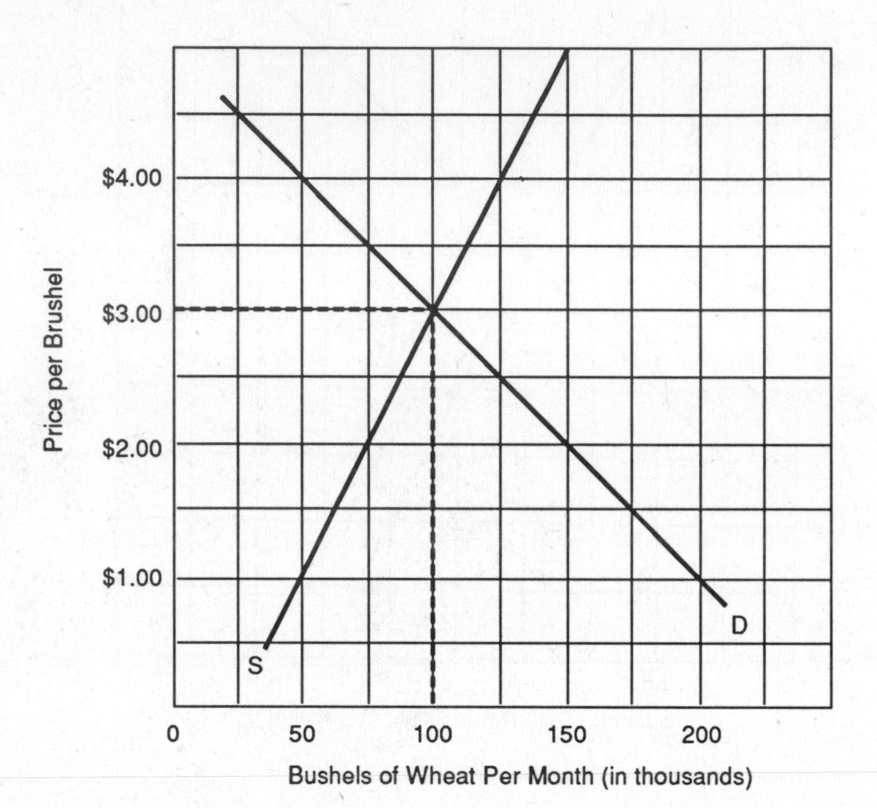

a. In the market for wheat, in the absence of any government intervention, the market clearing price per bushel will be ___________, with a quantity of ___________ bushels per month being sold.

b. The total income of farmers in this market will be ___________ per month.

c. Suppose that the government establishes a target price for wheat of $4 per bushel. As a result, farmers will produce ___________ bushels per month.

d. Farmers will now sell ___________ bushels per month to consumers at a price of ___________ per bushel.

e. The government will pay a subsidy of ___________ per bushel to farmers, which will make their total incomes ___________ per month.

f. Suppose that the market demand for wheat increases, because of an increase in the foreign demand for U.S. wheat, so that the new market clearing price is $4.50 per bushel. Farmers will now receive a subsidy of ___________ per bushel.

ANSWERS TO APPENDIX F

COMPLETION QUESTIONS

1. surplus; fall, rise, falls; surplus
2. above, purchased; falling
3. low; long
4. low; low; volatile, highly variable
5. target; the target price minus the market price; less
6. large; large
7. decrease, less
8. larger, fewer, fewer
9. import

TRUE-FALSE QUESTIONS

1. T
2. F It is very low; as income rises, smaller percentages of income are spent on food.
3. T
4. F Because farm prices multiplied times output equals farm income, volatile prices lead to volatile incomes.
5. T
6. T
7. F It is the ratio of prices received to prices paid.
8. T
9. T
10. F Such substitutions are inefficient, because they result *only* due to acreage restrictions.
11. T
12. T

MULTIPLE CHOICE QUESTIONS

1.d; 2.b; 3.a; 4.b; 5.b; 6.d; 7.d; 8.c; 9.b; 10.c;
11.a; 12.a

MATCHING

a and e; b and f; c and g; d and h

WORKING WITH GRAPHS

1. a. $1.00; b. 600; 400; 200, $250 = (200)($1.25); c. 600; $0.75, 600; 0, $0.50, $300; d. target price.
2. a. $3, 100,000; b. $300,000; c. 150,000; d. 75,000, 75,000; e. $600,000, $300,000; f. surplus
3. a. $3, 100,000; b. $300,000; c. 125,000; d. 125,000, $2.50; e. $1.50, $500,000; f. $0

GLOSSARY TO APPENDIX F

Commodity Credit Corporation (CCC) A government agency that lends farmers an amount of money equal to the support price of crops, multiplied by the amount of the crop offered as collateral.

Deficiency payment A direct subsidy paid to farmers equal to the amount of a crop they produce, multiplied by the difference between the target price for that good and its market price.

Nonrecourse loan A loan that never has to be repaid. The Commodity Credit Corporation gives nonrecourse to farmers in return for collateral in the form of the farmers' crops.

Parity A measure of the relative price of agricultural products. The federal government determines parity by using a formula in which the price of agricultural goods is compared with the price of manufactured goods for the period 1910-1914. A parity price ratio of 100 means farmers receive the same relative price for their products (compared to what they buy) that they received during the period 1910-1914.

Quota The maximum amount of a commodity that the U.S. government permits a particular country to export to the United States.

Subsidy Negative tax; payment to producers or consumers of a good or service. For example, farmers often get subsidies for producing wheat, corn, or peanuts.

Target price A price set by the government for specific agricultural products. If the market-clearing price is below the target price a **deficiency payment**, equal to the difference between the market price and the target price, is given to farmers for each unit of the good they produce.

CHAPTER 28

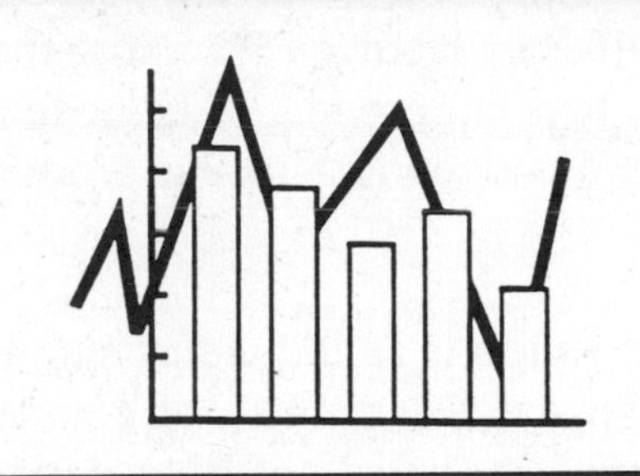

RESOURCE DEMAND AND SUPPLY

PUTTING THIS CHAPTER INTO PERSPECTIVE

Chapter 28 is the first chapter in Part Four, five chapters that deal with the factor markets. This chapter and the next deal with labor.

Fortunately, much of what you learned in Part Three can be applied to Part Four. Most fundamentally, you can apply the maximization or rational behavior model that you learned earlier. Recall that a rational person--supplier, buyer, owner, or manager of a firm--will do any activity up to the point where the marginal benefit (MB) of doing so equals the marginal cost (MC) of doing so. For this model to work, eventually marginal cost must rise relative to marginal benefit. If MC rises and MB falls, this condition is obviously met; it is also met if MB is constant and MC rises, or if MC is constant and MB falls. If MB > MC, then maximizing behavior requires that the person (or firm) do more; if MC > MB, then maximizing behavior requires that less be done. If MB = MC (and MC is rising relative to MB), then the person or firm is maximizing.

The trick is to identify the MB and the MC of any activity. (It is almost always the case in economic applications that MC rises relative to MB, so that is usually no problem.) If you keep this in mind, and if you remember the rules in the previous paragraph, then Part Four (and Part Three) will be much easier for you to understand as you analyze the various market structures.

The first market structure analyzed in Chapter 28 is perfect competition in both the product market and the labor market. The activity in question is hiring labor; as usual we assume that the firm wants to maximize profits. The firm's marginal benefit from hiring labor is the marginal physical product of labor multiplied by the price of the good sold (MRP); thus MB = MRP. The MRP falls because the marginal physical product of labor falls (due to the law of diminishing returns) and price, P, is constant because the firm is a price taker. The marginal cost of hiring labor is the wage rate, which is constant because the firm is a price taker in the labor market, too. Predictably, the firm hires labor up to the point where MB = MC, as in this model where the MRP of labor equals the wage rate.

The second major model analyzed in Chapter 28 assumes perfect competition in the labor market, but imperfect competition (monopoly, actually, but the conclusions are the same for monopolistic competition and oligopoly) in the product market. Because an imperfect competitor must reduce price in order to sell more, in this model marginal benefit is more complicated. The MB for hiring labor is marginal revenue (MR) multiplied by the marginal physical product, or MRP, of labor. Recall that if demand is negatively sloped, then price, P, must exceed MR. Because we assume perfect competition in the labor market, the firm is there a price taker;

hence the MC of hiring labor is again the wage rate, W. Thus the profit maximizing quantity of labor to hire occurs where MB equals MC, or in this model MRP of labor = W. Note that in this model, MR, or MRP, falls for two reasons: the marginal physical product of labor falls due to diminishing returns, and price falls because the firm is a monopolist in the product market.

In Chapter 28 the industry demand for labor curve is also derived; so too is an individual supply of labor curve and an industry supply of labor curve. Wage rates are determined, of course, at the intersection of the industry demand for labor curve and the industry supply of labor curve. Minimum wage analysis deals with a situation in which wage rates are not set by supply and demand.

LEARNING OBJECTIVES

After you have studied this chapter you should be able to

1. define marginal factor cost, marginal physical product, derived demand, marginal revenue product, minimum wage, and signaling.

2. determine the profit-maximizing quantity of labor to hire for a firm that is a perfect competitor in both the product and the labor market.

3. determine the profit-maximizing quantity of labor to hire for a firm that is a perfect competitor in the labor market and a monopolist in the product market.

4. distinguish between the MRP of labor curve for a perfect competitor and the MRP of labor curve for a monopolist.

5. determine the equilibrium wage rate, given the supply of labor and the demand for labor.

6. list five determinants of the price elasticity of demand for an input.

7. apply the substitution effect and the income effect to account for a positively sloped supply of labor curve for an individual worker.

8. list three factors that cause the total demand curve for labor to shift.

9. list two factors that cause the total supply of labor curve to shift.

10. recognize the minimum total cost condition for producing a given rate of output.

11. list the pros and cons of minimum wage legislation.

CHAPTER OUTLINE

1. What is the profit-maximizing quantity of labor to hire for a firm that is a perfect competitor in both the labor market and the product market?
   a. The marginal physical product of labor is the change in total output accounted for by hiring one worker, holding all other factors of production constant.
   b. Because of the law of diminishing returns, the marginal physical product of labor eventually declines.
   c. Because this firm is in a competitive labor market, it is a price taker; it can hire as much labor as it wants to hire at the going wage rate.
   d. The marginal benefit from hiring one more unit of labor is that laborer's marginal physical product multiplied by the firm's constant selling price, or the marginal revenue product (MRP).
   e. The profit maximizing rule for hiring is to hire laborers up to the point where the wage rate equals the MRP of labor.

2. The demand for labor is a derived demand; labor (or other inputs) are desired only because they can be used to produce products that are expected to be sold at a profit.

3. The entire market demand for labor curve is negatively sloped.

4. There are five principal determinants of the price elasticity of demand for an input. The price elasticity of demand for a variable input will be greater
   a. the greater the price elasticity of demand for the final product.
   b. the easier it is to substitute for that variable input.
   c. the greater the price elasticity of supply of all other inputs.
   d. the larger the proportion of total costs accounted for by a particular variable input.
   e. the longer the time period being considered.

5. The entire industry supply of labor curve is upward sloping; the perfectly competitive firm, however, faces a horizontal supply curve at the going wage rate.
   a. Individual workers face a trade-off between leisure and the income derived from working.
      i. As the wage rate rises, other things being constant, a worker will substitute income for leisure and work longer hours.
      ii. But as the wage rate rises, other things being constant, the worker also experiences a real income effect; he may also choose to buy more leisure, or work less.
      iii. Typically the substitution effect outweighs the income effect; at relatively high income levels the reverse may be true and a backward bending supply of labor curve then results.
   b. The equilibrium market wage rate is determined where the industry demand for labor curve intersects the industry supply of labor curve.

6. When nonwage determinants of the supply of and the demand for labor change, those curves shift.
   a. The labor demand curve shifts if there is a change in (1) the demand for the final product, (2) labor productivity, or (3) the price of related factors of production.

b. The labor supply curve shifts if there is a change in the (1) alternative wage rate offered in other industries, or (2) nonmonetary aspects of the occupation under study.
c. A shortage of a particular skill can persist for many years if the demand for that skill rises faster than the wage rate adjusts upward.

7. What is the profit-maximizing quantity of labor to hire for a firm that is a perfect competitor in the labor market but a monopolist in the product market?
   a. Such a firm's demand for labor (or any other input) is negatively sloped because (1) the marginal physical product falls and (2) the price (and, therefore, MR) falls as output increases.
   b. Such a firm's MB curve, or demand curve, is its MRP curve, which equals labor's marginal physical product multiplied by the firm's MR; thus MRP = MR x MPP.
   c. Given the going market wage rate, this firm hires up to the point where MRP equals the wage rate.
   d. The monopolist hires fewer workers than a perfectly competitive producer would, other things being constant.

8. How much of *each* variable factor should the firm use when combining those factors to produce a given output?
   a. The firm will hire all variable inputs up to the point where each input's MRP equals its price.
   b. In order to minimize the total cost of producing a given output, the firm should equate the ratios of each factor's marginal physical product to its respective price; this condition is referred to as the *least-cost combination of resources.*

9. Under *minimum wage* legislation, wage rates that firms must pay are set above market equilibrium; if strictly enforced, minimum wage rates will increase overall unemployment and benefit some low-income workers at the expense of other low-income workers.

KEY TERMS

Marginal physical product
Marginal factor cost
Marginal revenue product
Minimum wages

KEY CONCEPTS

Derived demand
Labor-leisure choice
Least-cost combination of resources
Labor market signaling

COMPLETION QUESTIONS

Fill in the blank or circle the correct term.

1. To a firm that is a perfect competitor in both the labor and the product market, the marginal benefit from hiring labor equals labor's ______________ times ______________, or MRP.

2. A competitive firm's MRP curve is negatively sloped because labor's ______________ falls, due to the law of ______________.

3. To such a competitive firm, the marginal cost of hiring labor is the ______________, which (falls, rises, remains constant) as the firm hires more laborers; in the labor market, such a firm is a price (taker, maker).

4. The competitive firm hires labor up to the point where __________ equals ______________; at that point it is maximizing __________.

5. The demand for labor is a ______________ demand; therefore if selling price increases, the competitive firm's demand for labor curve will shift to the ______________; the entire market demand curve for labor will be __________ sloped.

6. Determinants of the price elasticity of demand for an input include ______________________________, ______________________________, ______________________________, ______________________________, and ______________________________.

7. The supply of labor to a competitive firm is ______________ elastic, therefore its labor supply curve is (vertical, horizontal); the supply of labor curve for the industry, however, is ______________ sloped.

8. An individual worker's supply of labor curve is ______________ sloped, due to the net result of the ______________ effect and the ______________ effect; the ______________ effect induces a worker to work more hours as the wage rate rises; the __________ effect induces a worker to work fewer hours as the wage rate rises.

9. The industry demand for labor curve shifts if there is a change in the ______________, ______________, or ______________; the industry supply curve shifts if there is a change in ______________ or ______________.

10. Assume a firm is a perfect competitor in the labor market but a monopolist in the product market. Its marginal benefit from hiring labor equals ______________ times ______________, or MRP of labor. This firm's MRP curve is negatively sloped because ______________ falls due to the law of ______________ and because ______________ falls due to the fact that this firm must reduce its ______________ as it produces more. This firm will hire labor up to the point where ______________ equals ______________.

11. If a competitive firm hires more than one variable input, its equilibrium condition is that ____________________; stated alternatively, it can minimize the total cost of producing a given output by equating ________________________.

TRUE-FALSE QUESTIONS

Circle the **T** if the statement is true, the **F** if it is false. Explain to yourself why a statement is false.

T F 1. A firm that is a competitor in all markets will discover that its demand for labor curve is horizontal at the going wage rate.

T F 2. A competitive firm will hire labor up to the point where MRP equals the going wage rate.

T F 3. The marginal physical product of labor declines due to diseconomies of scale.

T F 4. Because the demand for labor is a derived demand, it shifts when wage rates change.

T F 5. The price elasticity of demand for labor will be higher the lower is the price elasticity of demand for the final good.

T F 6. A competitive firm's supply of labor curve is horizontal, but the entire industry supply of labor curve is upward sloping.

T F 7. The income effect implies that an individual worker's supply of labor curve is upward sloping.

T F 8. If labor productivity rises, the demand for labor rises.

T F 9. A firm that is a competitor in the labor market but a monopolist in the product market hires labor up to the point where the MRP of labor equals the going wage rate.

T F 10. If a firm suddenly monopolizes a perfectly competitive industry, more workers will be hired.

T F 11. If a competitive firm hires two factors of production it will hire up to the point where the MRP of one factor divided by that factor's price equals the MRP of the other factor divided by that factor's price.

T F 12. Advocates of minimum wages favor letting wage rates be determined by supply and demand.

T F 13. Because labor market signaling occurs, the rate of return to college education may not be as high as it seems.

MULTIPLE CHOICE QUESTIONS

Circle the letter that corresponds to the best answer.

1. Which of the following is *not* true about a firm that is a perfect competitor in all markets?
   a. Its supply of labor curve is horizontal.
   b. Its demand for labor curve is downward sloping.
   c. Its price falls as it produces more output.
   d. Its marginal physical product of labor falls as it hires more labor.

2. For a firm that is a perfect competitor in all markets, the profit maximizing quantity of labor to hire occurs where
   a. a falling MRP equals a rising wage rate.
   b. a rising MRP equals a rising wage rate.
   c. a falling MRP equals a falling wage rate.
   d. a falling MRP equals a constant wage rate.

3. A firm that is a perfect competitor in all markets finds that its MRP for labor falls because as it hires more labor
   a. the marginal physical product of labor falls.
   b. the price of output falls as output increases.
   c. Both of the above

4. The marginal factor cost of labor
   a. equals the going wage rate to a competitive firm.
   b. equals the change in wage rates divided by the change in labor.
   c. rises for the competitive firm.
   d. equals the change in total cost divided by the change in wage rates.

5. The demand for labor
   a. is a derived demand.
   b. shifts as selling price of the good produced changes.
   c. shifts to the right if labor productivity increases.
   d. All of the above

6. Which of the following will *not* lead to a high price elasticity of demand for labor?
   a. high price elasticity of demand for the final product
   b. no good substitutes for the labor skill in question
   c. high price elasticity of supply of nonlabor inputs
   d. a very long period of time after the price change

7. The supply of labor
   a. to a perfect competitor is positively sloped.
   b. for the entire industry is perfectly elastic.
   c. for an individual worker is positively sloped, due to the substitution effect.
   d. depends on labor's marginal physical product.

8. As the wage rate rises, other things being constant, an individual laborer will probably
   a. substitute more income for less leisure.
   b. want to purchase some more leisure due to an increase in real income.
   c. on balance, want to work more hours per unit of time.
   d. All of the above

9. If an individual worker's supply of labor curve is backward bending, at relatively high wage rates the
   a. income effect is outweighed by the substitution effect.
   b. substitution effect is outweighed by the income effect.
   c. substitution effect and the income effect reinforce each other.
   d. supply of labor decreases.

10. Which of the following will *not* lead to an increase in the demand for labor?
   a. price of labor falls
   b. increase in the productivity of labor
   c. increase in the price of a labor substitute input
   d. increase in the demand for the final product

11. If firm B is a competitor in the labor market and a monopolist in the product market, then
   a. its demand for labor is negatively sloped.
   b. its supply of labor is positively sloped.
   c. its selling price is a constant.
   d. its wage rates rise as it hires more labor.

12. If firm B is a competitor in the labor market and a monopolist in the product market, then
   a. its supply of labor curve is horizontal at the going wage rate.
   b. it hires labor up to the point where MRP of labor equals the going wage rate.
   c. its MRP curve falls because the marginal product of labor falls and its selling price falls.
   d. All of the above

13. The monopolist in the product market finds that its MRP for labor falls as it hires labor because
   a. the MPP of labor falls and output price is constant.
   b. the MPP of labor falls and output price falls.
   c. the MPP of labor is constant and output price falls.
   d. the MPP of labor rises but output price falls faster.

14. If a perfectly competitive market is suddenly monopolized, the amount of labor hired will
   a. remain constant.
   b. fall.
   c. rise.
   d. fall in the short run, rise in the long run.

15. If a monopolist firm hires two variable inputs, A and B, it is maximizing total profits when
   a. MPP of A/price of A = MPP of B/price of B.

b. MPP of A/price of B = MPP of B/price of A.
c. MRP of A/price of A = MRP of B/price of B.
d. MRP of A/price of B = MRP of B/price of A.

16. If a perfect competitor hires two variable inputs, A and B, it can produce a given output at a minimum total cost when
a. MPP of A/price of A > MPP of B/price of B.
b. MPP of A/price of A < MPP of B/price of B.
c. MPP of A/price of A = MPP of B/price of B.
d. MPP of A = MPP of B.

17. Legal minimum wage rates, if set above equilibrium and strictly enforced
a. lead to an increase in overall unemployment.
b. decrease teenage employment.
c. benefit workers who keep their jobs.
d. All of the above

MATCHING

Choose the item in column (2) that best matches an item in column (1).

(1)	(2)
a. MPP	h. backward bending curve
b. MPP x MR	i. MRP of competitive firm
c. MPP x price	j. MRP of monopolistic firm
d. least cost combination	k. labor demand curve
e. profit maximization	l. change in output for a unit input change
f. derived demand	m. equate MPP/price of input
g. individual's labor supply curve	n. equate MRP with price of input

WORKING WITH GRAPHS

1. Analyze the graphs below, then answer the questions that follow. Assume that the minimum wage rate is $4.50 per hour.

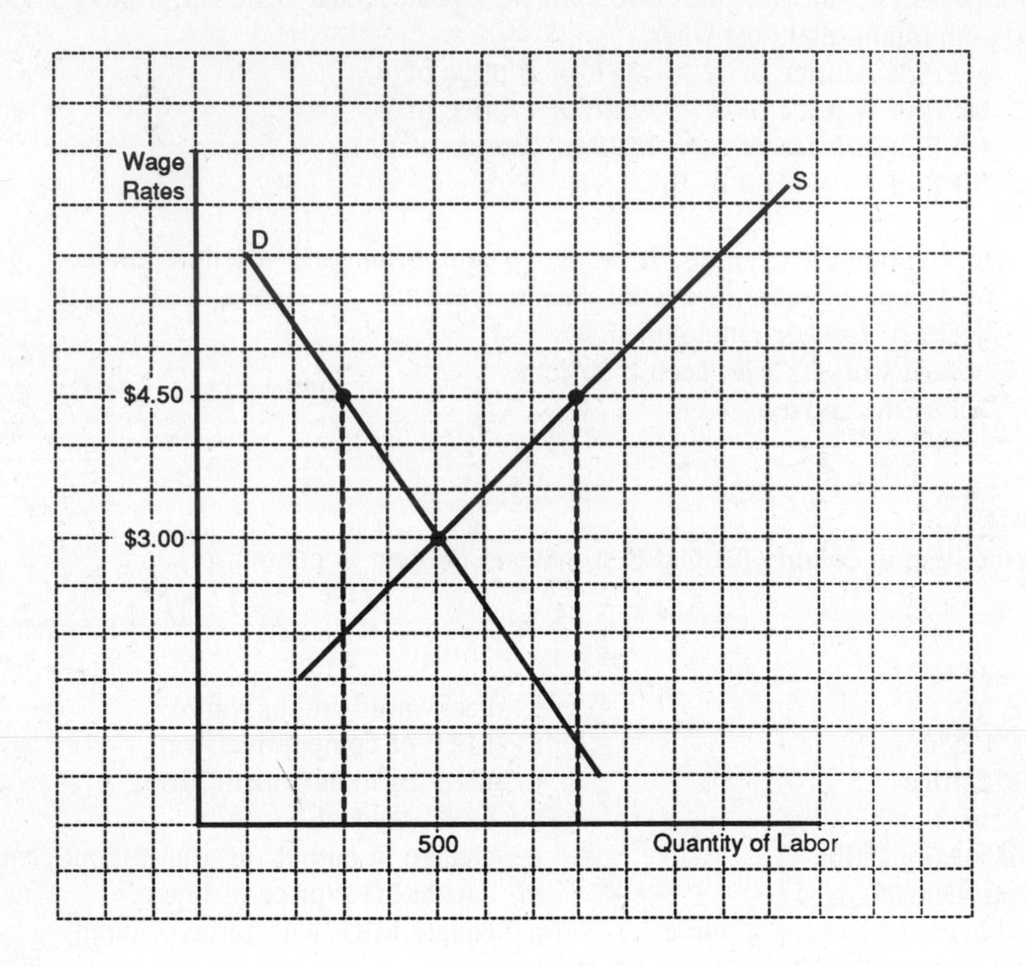

a. What is the equilibrium wage rate in this market?

b. What is the quantity supplied of labor at the minimum wage rate?

c. What is the quantity demanded for labor at the minimum wage rate?

d. What market situation exists at the minimum wage rate?

e. How many workers were laid-off, due to the minimum wage rate?

f. How many workers entered the labor force, seeking a job, due to the minimum wage rate?

g. Are workers in this industry better off or worse off as a result of this minimum wage?

PROBLEMS

1. In the following table you are given information about a firm operating in a competitive market. Consider all factors of production fixed at the moment, with the exception of labor services. The other factors of production cost the firm $50 per day, which may be thought of as a fixed cost. Assume the firm is a profit maximizer.

Labor input (workers per day)	Total physical product (units per day)	Marginal physical product (units per day)	Marginal revenue product ($ per worker)
0	0		
1	22	________	________
2	40	________	________
3	56	________	________
4	70	________	________
5	82	________	________
6	92	________	________
7	100	________	________
8	106	________	________

a. Assume that the firm sells its output at $3 per unit. Complete the last two columns in the table above.

b. If the going market wage is $36 per day, the firm will hire ________ workers per day and produce ________ units of output.

c. Given your answer to part b, the firm will have total revenues of ________ per day and total costs of ________ per day.

d. The above will result in a (profit, loss) of ________ per day.

*2. Suppose you work for a firm that sells its output in a monopoly market. Answer the following questions.

a. If you hire an additional worker, output goes up by 50 units to 125 units per day. If you wish to sell the additional 50 units, you must lower your price from $3 per unit to $2 per unit. What is the maximum wage you would be willing to pay the additional worker?

b. Assume you hired the worker from part a and output now stands at 125 units per day. If another worker is hired, output rises to 165 units per day. Given the demand curve for your product, you know that in order to sell the additional output, price will have to be dropped from $2 per unit to $1 per unit. What is the maximum wage you would be willing to pay this additional worker?

CASE STUDY

Many studies indicate that when students "invest" in a college education, the rate of return to such an investment is quite high. An abundance of evidence exists to indicate that college graduates earn much more, over their lifetimes, than high school graduates. But this notion has been challenged by (among others) Harvard's Michael Spence, who has developed the theory of labor market signaling.

Spence notes that employers find it too expensive to gather detailed information about the marginal revenue product of each worker. Consequently, employers look for clues, or signals. One such signal is how much a worker has invested in education. In general, people of higher ability find education less difficult than do people of lower ability, and the former are more likely to invest in a college education. Thus employers prefer to hire college graduates due to the higher probability of their success; in turn such employer behavior provides a signal to high ability workers to obtain more education.

1. Does Spence's theory imply that college educated people would probably earn higher-than-average incomes, even if they didn't go to college? Why or Why not?

2. What does Spence's theory suggest about the measured rate of return to a college education?

ANSWERS TO CHAPTER 28

COMPLETION QUESTIONS

1. marginal physical product, price for the perfect competitor, but always marginal revenue
2. marginal physical product, diminishing returns
3. wage rate, remains constant; taker
4. MRP of labor, wage rate; total profits
5. derived; right; negatively
6. price elasticity of demand for final good, ease with which other inputs can substitute for this input, price elasticity of supply of other inputs, proportion of total costs accounted for by the input in question, length of time period being considered
7. perfectly, horizontal; positively
8. positively, substitution, income; substitution; income
9. demand for final good, labor productivity, price of related factors; wage rate in other industries, nonmoney job aspects
10. marginal physical product of labor, MR; marginal physical product, diminishing returns, MR, price; MRP, the wage rate
11. the ratio of MRP to price of factor is equated for all factors; the ratio of marginal physical product to factor price for all factors

TRUE-FALSE QUESTIONS

1. F It's demand for labor curve is negatively sloped.
2. T
3. F It declines due to the law of diminishing returns.
4. F If wage rates change, we move along a given labor demand curve.
5. F It will be lower.
6. T
7. F The substitution effect implies that.
8. T
9. T
10. F Fewer workers will be hired, because output falls.
11. T
12. F They want wage rates to be above the equilibrium rate.
13. T

MULTIPLE CHOICE QUESTIONS

1.c; 2.d; 3.a; 4.a; 5.d; 6.b; 7.c; 8.d; 9.b; 10.a;
11.a; 12.d; 13.b; 14.b; 15.c; 16.c; 17.d

MATCHING

a and l; b and j; c and i; d and m; e and n; f and k; g and h

WORKING WITH GRAPHS

1. a. $3.00
   b. 800
   c. 300
   d. surplus, or excess quantity supplied of labor
   e. 200
   f. 300
   g. Those who kept their jobs are better off; those who became unemployed are worse off. Group income fell from $1500 to $1350 because demand was (here) price elastic.

PROBLEMS

1. a. MPP: 22, 18, 16, 14, 12, 10, 8, 6
   MRP: 66, 54, 48, 42, 36, 30, 24, 18
   b. 5, 82
   c. $246, (5 x $36) + $50 = $230
   d. profit, $16

2. a. $25 per day since MRP = $25
   b. A negative wage, because the price decrease necessary to sell the additional output causes total revenues to decline (MR < 0), MRP for this worker is negative, and the firm must be paid to hire another unit of labor.

CASE STUDY

1. Yes, because they tend to be the more productive workers.
2. It implies that the measured rate of return to college education overstates the true rate of return; many graduates would have had relatively higher incomes anyway.

GLOSSARY TO CHAPTER 28

Derived demand Input factor demand derived from demand for the final product being produced.

Labor market signaling The process by which potential worker's acquisition of credentials, such as B.A. or an M.S., is utilized by the employer to predicate future productivity.

Marginal factor cost (MFC) The cost of using an additional unit of an input. For example, if a firm can hire all the workers it wants at the going wage rate, the marginal factor cost of labor is the wage rate.

Marginal physical product (MPP) of labor The change in output resulting from the addition of one more worker. The MPP of the worker equals the change in total output accounted for by hiring the worker, holding all other factors of production constant.

Marginal Revenue Product (MRP) The marginal physical product (MPP) times marginal revenue. The MRP gives the additional revenue obtained from a one-unit change in labor input.

CHAPTER 29

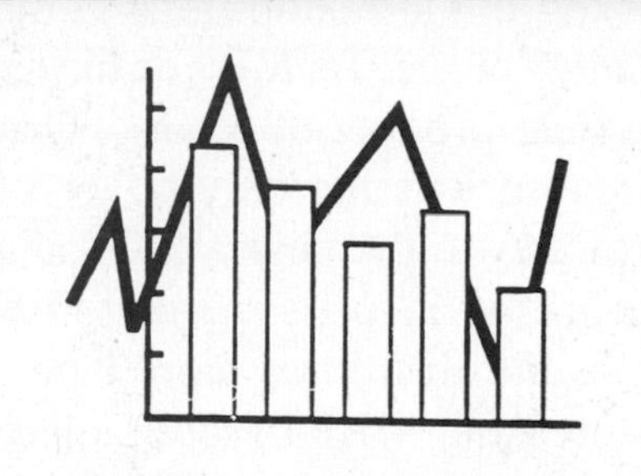

UNIONS AND LABOR MARKET MONOPOLY POWER

PUTTING THIS CHAPTER INTO PERSPECTIVE

Chapter 29 is the second chapter devoted to an analysis of the labor market; the next chapter is devoted to the other factors of production. It is important for you to keep a proper perspective about the labor market. Even though this chapter considers noncompetitive labor markets--monopoly supply and monopoly demand--the U.S. labor market is inherently very competitive. There are millions of employers and over a hundred million people in the labor force. It is not likely that monopoly demand or monopoly supply could arise under such conditions. To be sure, in our past there have been "company towns," but by and large they are the exceptions; and it is true that some major employers have dominated at the local level. Still, our laborers traditionally have had both the freedom and the willingness to relocate; labor mobility, then, has certainly limited the economic power that any particular employer could exert on workers.

What does a competitive market imply? Because employers compete for workers, wage rates will be driven up to labor's true productivity value. Similarly, because workers compete for jobs, wage rates will be driven down toward labor's true productivity value. In short, competitive supply and demand set wage rates at market-clearing values and workers get paid (approximately) the value of their marginal product.

One major source of monopolistic power in the labor market is the government. Because employers know that their competition for labor will drive wage rates up toward the value of labor's marginal product, they have exerted time and effort to obtain special privilege from the government--usually in the form of exemption from antitrust action. Examples can be taken from professional sports. Also, witness the intercollegiate athletics monopsony considered in this chapter.

Monopoly power on the seller side of the labor market also is derived from government sources. As mentioned in Chapter 28, unions are exempted from antitrust action even though they act in restraint of trade. Similarly, the American Medical Association and scores of other professional associations attempt to restrict the supply of labor into specific occupations through licensing; note how government sanction is necessary for such monopsonistic power to arise. Laborers know only too well that if they compete, their wage rates will be driven down to competitive levels. Without becoming involved in the weighty debate over whether licensing is a good idea or whether the government should be involved in granting monopsonist power to specific groups, we merely point out here that without the help of government, such monopsonistic power would largely disappear.

Consider first a firm that is a perfect competitor in the product market, but a monopsonist in the labor market. Such a firm faces a downward sloping demand for labor curve; its MB for hiring labor is labor's MRP, which falls due to a declining marginal physical product of labor. That firm faces an upward sloping supply of labor curve, however, because it is the only buyer of labor. In order to obtain another worker it must pay a higher wage rate--to the new worker and to all the previously employed workers. Hence that firm's MC of hiring labor is the marginal factor cost (MFC) of labor, which exceeds the wage rate and rises as the firm hires more labor. The profit-maximizing quantity of labor to hire occurs where the decreasing MRP of labor curve intersects the rising marginal factor cost curve. That firm then sets the wage rate at a level consistent with obtaining that quantity of labor--as given by the industry supply of labor curve.

In the second model, consider a labor-hiring firm that is a monopolist in the product market and a monopsonist in the labor market. Its MB curve is labor's MRP curve, which falls due to decreasing marginal product of labor *and* a falling output price. Its MC curve is its MFC curve, which rises because it must pay higher wages (to new and old workers) as it hires more labor. The profit maximizing quantity of labor to hire occurs where the rising MFC of labor equals the declining MRP of labor; that is, at the point where the MC = MB of hiring labor, the firm maximizes total profits. You will do well to study Table 17-1.

Also theoretically noteworthy in this chapter is the treatment of unions as a monopolistic seller of labor. The issue becomes: what do unions maximize? It is not clear what unions maximize; once this is decided, then it becomes easier to predict their behavior. You should be aware that unions can set wage rates, or they can choose the quantity of labor employed; they cannot do both. In general, unions redistribute income to high-seniority workers (who keep their jobs when unions set wage rates above equilibrium) from low-seniority workers (who lose their jobs when unions so behave). Because low seniority job losers find work elsewhere--thereby increasing the supply of labor in other areas--unions don't raise *overall* wage rates. Union action causes wage rates to rise in some areas and to fall in other areas.

LEARNING OBJECTIVES

After you have studied this chapter you should be able to

1. define unions, craft unions, collective bargaining, industrial unions, right-to-work laws, closed shop, union shop, jurisdictional dispute, sympathy strike, secondary boycott, featherbedding, monopsonist, monopsonistic exploitation, strikebreaker, and bilateral monopoly.

2. identify the key provisions of major legislation dealing with unions.

3. distinguish between craft unions and industrial unions.

4. list three possible union goals and predict the quantity of labor that will be employed under each union strategy.

5. show how unions can redistribute income from low seniority to high seniority workers.

6. predict the quantity of labor hired and the wage rate that will result, given a market structure in which a firm is a perfect competitor in the product market and a monopsonist in the labor market.

7. predict the quantity of labor hired and the wage rate that will result, given a firm that is a monopolist in the product market and a monopsonist in the labor market.

8. list reasons why the NCAA qualifies as a cartel with monopsony power.

CHAPTER OUTLINE

1. Unions are workers' organizations that usually seek to secure economic improvements for their members.
   a. The American labor movement started with *craft unions*, which are composed of workers who engage in a particular skill or trade.
   b. The American Federation of Labor (AFL), a craft union, was formed by Samuel Gompers in 1886; its membership growth flourished until World War I, when government withdrew its support.
   c. The Great Depression brought the National Recovery Act in 1933, which attempted to raise wages to predepression levels; its key provision was to guarantee the right of labor to bargain collectively.
   d. The Wagner Act, labor's "Magna Carta," also guaranteed *collective bargaining*; it guaranteed workers the right to form unions.
   e. In 1938 John L. Lewis formed the Congress of Industrial Organizations (CIO), which was composed of *industrial unions*, that is, unions with membership from an entire industry.
   f. The Taft-Hartley Act was enacted to stem union power; it allows individual states to pass *right-to-work* laws, which make illegal the requirement of union membership for continued employment. It also bans the closed shop everywhere and the union shop in states with right-to-work laws, and makes illegal jurisdictional disputes, sympathy strikes, and secondary boycotts.
   g. In 1955 the AFL-CIO merged under the leadership of George Meany; in 1969 Walter Reuther withdrew his UAW union and merged it with the Teamsters union.
   h. International union business procedures became more regulated with the passage of the Landrum-Griffin Act.
   i. While the degree of unionization in the private sector has declined, it has increased for public employees since 1968.
   j. The percentage of the labor force that is unionized has fallen because of the following: higher percentages of women are in the labor force, persistent illegal immigration, and the number of white collar workers in the service sector has increased relative to the number of blue collar manufacturing workers.

2. Unions can be analyzed as setters of minimum wages; the strike is the ultimate bargaining tool for unions.

3. It is not clear what unions wish to maximize. Unions can either set wage rates or select the quantity of its membership that will be employed; they can't do both.

a. To the extent that unions set wage rates above equilibrium, they create a surplus of labor, or a shortage of jobs that they ration.
b. If unions wish to employ all members, they must accept a relatively low wage rate.
c. If unions wish to maximize total wages, they set wage rates where the price elasticity of demand equals 1; some members will be unemployed.
d. If unions maximize wage rates for a given number of workers--presumably high-seniority workers--low-seniority workers will become unemployed because wage rates probably will be set above equilibrium.
e. If unions behave so as to maximize members' wealth, they maximize the difference between the *total wage bill* and the wage bill necessary to bid workers away from alternative employment.
f. One union strategy is to limit total union membership to the original quantity; over time, if demand increases, wage rates will rise.
g. Unions can raise wage rates for members by (a) limiting membership, and (b) increasing the demand for union labor by increasing labor productivity and increasing the demand for union labor relative to nonunion labor.

4. It is not apparent that unions have raised *overall* wage rates; on average, unions redistribute income within unions from low- to high-seniority workers.

5. Recent studies indicate that unions can both (a) act as monopolies that redistribute income from low-seniority to high-seniority members and (b) increase labor productivity.

6. Consider a firm that is a perfect competitor in the product market and a *monopsonist* in the labor market.
   a. That firm faces an upward sloping supply of labor curve; before it can hire more labor it must raise wage rates for *all* of its employees.
   b. As a consequence, the marginal factor cost of hiring labor to that firm exceeds the wage rate; the MFC curve is that firm's MC to hiring labor, and it rises as the firm hires more labor.
   c. The marginal benefit to hiring labor to such a firm is its MRP curve, which falls (due to declining marginal product of labor) as it hires more labor.
   d. The profit-maximizing employment level occurs where the decreasing MRP curve intersects the rising MFC curve; the wage rate is set on the supply curve, consistent with that quantity of labor.
   e. In such a situation monopsonistic exploitation of labor results, because the wage rate is below the MRP of labor.

7. A summary of monopoly, monopsony, and perfectly competitive situations is presented in Table 17-1.

8. The NCAA qualifies as a cartel and therefore behaves in an economically predictable way; it sets "wage rates" to college athletes below the value of their marginal product.

9. The Davis-Bacon Act, which (in effect) requires that construction projects using federal money pay union wages, tends to harm unskilled, minority laborers.

KEY TERMS

Craft unions vs. industrial unions
Collective bargaining
Right-to-work laws
Jurisdictional dispute
Monopsonist
Davis-Bacon Act

KEY CONCEPTS

Featherbedding
Closed-shop
Monopsonistic exploitation
Union shop
Sympathy strike
Secondary boycott
Bilateral monopoly

COMPLETION QUESTIONS

Fill in the blank or circle the correct term.

1. The American labor movement started with local __________ unions, which are comprised of workers in a particular ____________; the other major type of union is the ________________ union, which consists of workers from a particular ____________________.

2. The Great Depression generated legislation that (helped, hurt) the union movement.

3. The Taft-Hartley Act of 1947 (is, is not) considered pro-labor union; it allows states to pass ________________________ laws. The act makes illegal the following union practices: ____________________________, ______________________________, a ________________________ strike, and a ________________________ boycott.

4. The ________________________ Act of 1959 was concerned with regulating internal union business procedures. In recent years, private-sector union membership has (decreased, increased), while public-sector union membership has ________________.

5. The ultimate bargaining tool for the union is the ______________.

6. If a union sets wage rates above market-clearing levels, it creates a ________________ of labor; viewed alternatively, it creates a ______________ of jobs, which it must then ration to workers.

7. If a union chooses to employ all of its members, it (must, need not) accept a relatively lower wage rate; if the union wants to maximize the value of total wages, it sets wage rates where the price elasticity of demand for labor equals the number ______; if the union wants to set relatively high wages for its high-seniority members, its ________________ members will be laid off.

8. Assume that a firm is a perfect competitor in the product market and a monopsonist in the labor market. The marginal benefit to hiring labor for such a firm is its ____________________ curve, which is (horizontal, negatively sloped, positively sloped), due to the law of ________________; the marginal cost to hiring labor for such a firm is its ____________________ curve, which is (horizontal, positively sloped, negatively sloped). The firm's MFC curve rises because as it hires more labor, wage rates (fall, rise, remain constant) because the industry supply of labor curve is _______________ sloping; the firm's MFC is (equal to, greater than, less than) the wage rate.

9. Assume a firm is a monopolist in the product market and a monopsonist in the labor market. The marginal benefit to hiring labor for that firm is its ________________ curve, which falls due to ______________ and ________________ as output increases. The marginal cost to hiring labor is that firm's ________________ curve, which rises because in order to hire more labor, that firm must __________ wage rates of ___________ employees; this is because the firm's supply of labor curve is ___________ sloping.

10. A firm maximizes total profits by hiring labor up to the point where the (MB > MC, MB < MC, MB = MC) of doing so. Suppose Firm A is a perfect competitor in the product market and a monopsonist in the labor market. Firm A will hire labor up to the point where a downward sloping ________________ curve intersects an upward sloping ________________ curve; given that quantity of labor, the wage rate will be set at that level consistent with the (supply, demand) curve of labor.

11. Firm B is a monopolist in the product market and a monopsonist in the labor market. If it wants to maximize total profits, it will hire labor up to the point where a downward sloping ___________ curve intersects an upward sloping _______________ curve.

12. The NCAA qualifies as a cartel because it __________________________, __________________________, __________________________, and __________________________.

13. When a resource is paid less than its ______________, monopsonistic exploitation exists.

TRUE-FALSE QUESTIONS

Circle the T if the statement is true, the F if it is false. Explain to yourself why a statement is false.

T F 1. The growth rate of unions and the extent to which unions are effective depend largely on government support.

T F 2. The Wagner Act increases union power, but the Taft-Hartley Act reduces it.

T F 3. The Landrum-Griffin Act makes the closed shop illegal.

T F 4. In recent years, public employee union membership has increased significantly.

T F *5. Unions tend to create a shortage of labor and a surplus of jobs.

T F 6. In the United States, unions can set wage rates or determine the quantity of labor hired, but they can't do both.

T F 7. If a union wants to maximize the value of total wages, it sets wage rates as high as it possibly can.

T F 8. If a union can restrict the total quantity of laborers to a fixed number, its members must earn higher wages in the future.

T F 9. Recent studies indicate that unions do not increase labor's productivity.

T F 10. A profit-maximizing firm that is a perfect competitor in the product market but a monopsonist in the labor market will hire labor up to the point where MRP of labor equals the going wage rate.

T F 11. A firm that is a monopolist in the product market and a monopsonist in the labor market maximizes total profit by hiring labor up to the point where the MRP of labor equals the MFC of labor.

T F 12. The NCAA qualifies as a cartel with monopsony power.

T F 13. Monopsonistic exploitation exists when workers receive a wage below their MRP.

T F 14. The Davis-Bacon Act tends to harm minority workers.

MULTIPLE CHOICE QUESTIONS

Circle the letter that corresponds to the best answer.

1. Which of the following is *not* associated with a craft union?
   a. United Auto Workers
   b. AFL
   c. Knights of Labor
   d. Pipefitters Union

2. Which of the following acts is *not* pro labor union?
   a. National Industrial Recovery Act
   b. Wagner Act
   c. Taft-Hartley Act
   d. National Labor Relations Act

3. Which of the following is legal in *non* right-to-work states?
   a. closed shop
   b. union shop
   c. sympathy strike
   d. secondary boycott

4. Which of the following is true about the union movement?
   a. The growth and effectiveness of unions depends largely on the extent of government help.
   b. Since 1968 private-employee union membership has risen.
   c. Since 1968 public-employee union membership has fallen dramatically.
   d. All of the above

5. Unions tend to
   a. set minimum wages for members above the market clearing level.
   b. create unemployment for low-seniority members.
   c. create surpluses of labor and shortages of union jobs.
   d. All of the above

6. If a union sets wage rates above market clearing levels, then
   a. jobs must be rationed among union members.
   b. a surplus of jobs is created.
   c. a shortage of labor is created.
   d. high-seniority members will complain.

*7. Which of the following is inconsistent with the others?
   a. surplus of labor
   b. shortage of jobs
   c. wage rate above market-clearing level
   d. wage rate below market-clearing level

8. If unions want to maximize the value of total wages, they set wage rates
   a. as high as they can.
   b. as low as they can.
   c. where the price elasticity of demand for labor equals 1.
   d. in the inelastic range of the product demand curve.

9. If unions maximize the wage rate of high-seniority workers, then
   a. low-seniority workers will become laid off.
   b. all union members will remain employed.
   c. they violate the Davis-Bacon Act.
   d. they violate the Taft-Hartley Act.

10. Which of the following statements probably best describes the impact of unions on wage rates?
    a. Unions have increased all wage rates in the economy.
    b. Unions have increased all union worker wage rates.
    c. Unions increase the wage rates of some workers at the expense of other workers.
    d. Unions cannot raise wage rates for their members.

11. Unions
    a. can set wage rates, but not employment levels.
    b. can set wage rates and employment levels.
    c. can set neither wage rates nor employment levels.
    d. can set either wage rates or employment levels, but not both.

12. Unions, according to the Freeman-Medoff analysis,
    a. on net, probably raise social efficiency.
    b. reduce wage inequality.
    c. create workplace practices valuable to workers and costless to management.
    d. All of the above

13. If Firm B is a monopsonist in the labor market and a perfect competitor in the product market, then
    a. it faces a horizontal supply of labor curve.
    b. it faces a horizontal demand for labor curve.
    c. its wage rate equals its MFC.
    d. its MB to hiring labor equals the MRP of labor.

14. Firm B, in the previous question, can maximize total profits by hiring labor up to the point where
    a. a decreasing MRP of labor curve intersects a decreasing MFC of labor curve.
    b. a decreasing MRP of labor curve intersects a rising MFC of labor curve.
    c. a decreasing MRP of labor curve intersects a horizontal supply of labor curve, at the going wage rate.
    d. a horizontal MRP of labor curve is intersected by a rising MFC of labor curve.

*15. Firm B, in questions 13 and 14, faces a(n)
    a. rising MFC of labor.
    b. declining labor MRP
    c. upward sloping supply of labor curve.
    d. All of the above

16. If Firm A is a monopolist in the product market and a monopsonist in the labor market, then
    a. it faces a horizontal labor supply and a horizontal labor demand curve.
    b. it faces a downward sloping supply of labor curve.
    c. its MB of hiring labor falls and its marginal cost to hiring labor rises.
    d. its MB to hiring labor is constant and its marginal cost to hiring labor rises.

17. Firm A, in the previous question, can maximize total profits by hiring labor up to the point where
    a. a downward sloping MRP of labor curve intersects an upward sloping MFC of labor curve.
    b. an upward sloping MRP of labor equals a constant wage rate.
    c. a constant MRP of labor curve equals a falling MFC of labor.
    d. a horizontal MRP of labor curve is intersected by a rising supply of labor curve.

*18. Firm A in question 16
    a. observes a MFC that exceeds the wage rate.
    b. observes a selling price that exceeds the marginal revenue of an extra unit of output.
    c. maximizes profits by hiring where MRP of labor = MFC of labor.
    d. All of the above

19. The NCAA
    a. cannot regulate the number of athletes a university can "hire."
    b. cannot enforce its regulations and rules.
    c. sets the prices, wages, and conditions under which universities can "hire" student athletes.
    d. sets the "wage rates" for student athletes at levels above their market value.

20. Which of the following is probably an example of exploitation, as defined in this text?
    a. A low-skilled laborer is paid $1 per hour in a competitive labor market.
    b. A professional athlete gets paid $1 million per year but his MRP is $1.5 million per year.
    c. Mr. Smith can earn $35,000 per year as a plumber but chooses to work as a high school teacher for $20,000 per year.
    d. Mrs. Calvo has a Ph.D. in English, but only earns $10,000 per semester teaching university English because there are so many qualified teachers in that area.

21. Monopsonistic exploitation equals
    a. marginal physical product of labor minus the wage rate.
    b. marginal revenue product of labor minus the wage rate.
    c. marginal physical product of labor minus marginal revenue product of labor.
    d. marginal factor cost of labor minus marginal physical product.

WORKING WITH GRAPHS

1. Suppose you are given the following graphical representation for a monopsonist selling its output in a competitive market. Answer the following questions.

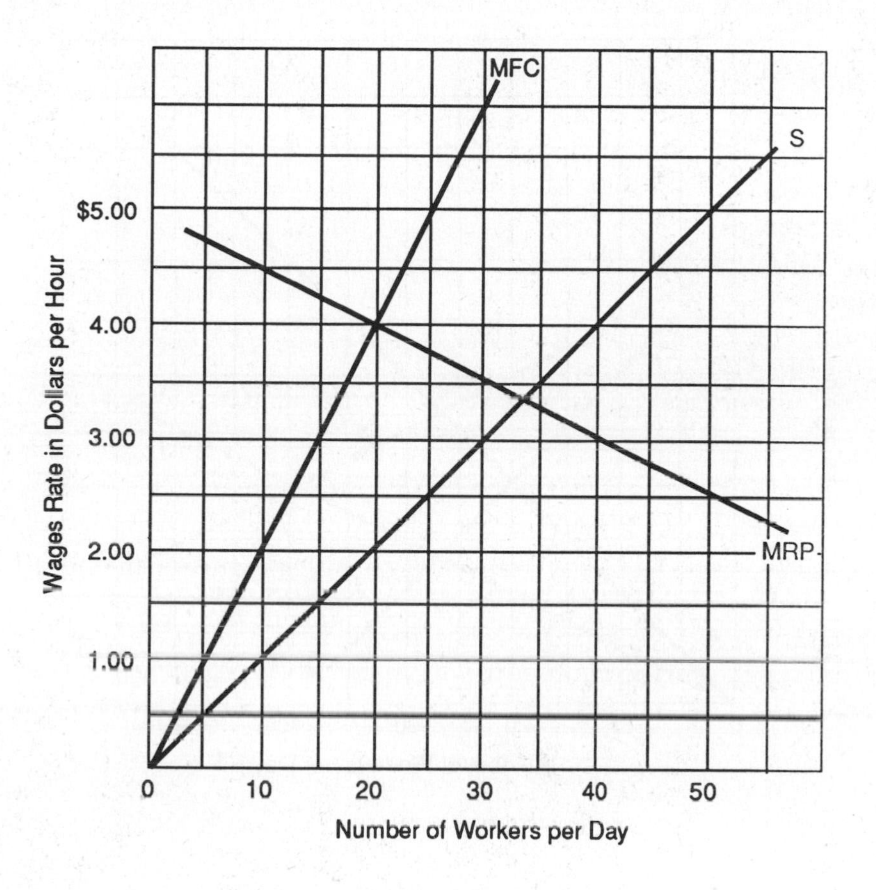

   a. Given the market conditions that exist in the above graph, the monopsonist will hire __________ workers per day at a wage of __________ per hour.

   b. Suppose that the government (or a labor union) initiates a minimum wage of $2.50 per hour in this particular market. As a result, the monopsonist will (increase, decrease) its employment rate to __________ workers per day at a wage of __________ per hour.

*2. Use the graph below to answer the following questions. Note: define monopolistic exploitation as being equal to the difference between VMP (or price times the marginal product of labor) and MRP--as defined in the text. (Note: VMP is not defined in your text, therefore this is a difficult question. It is purely optional.)

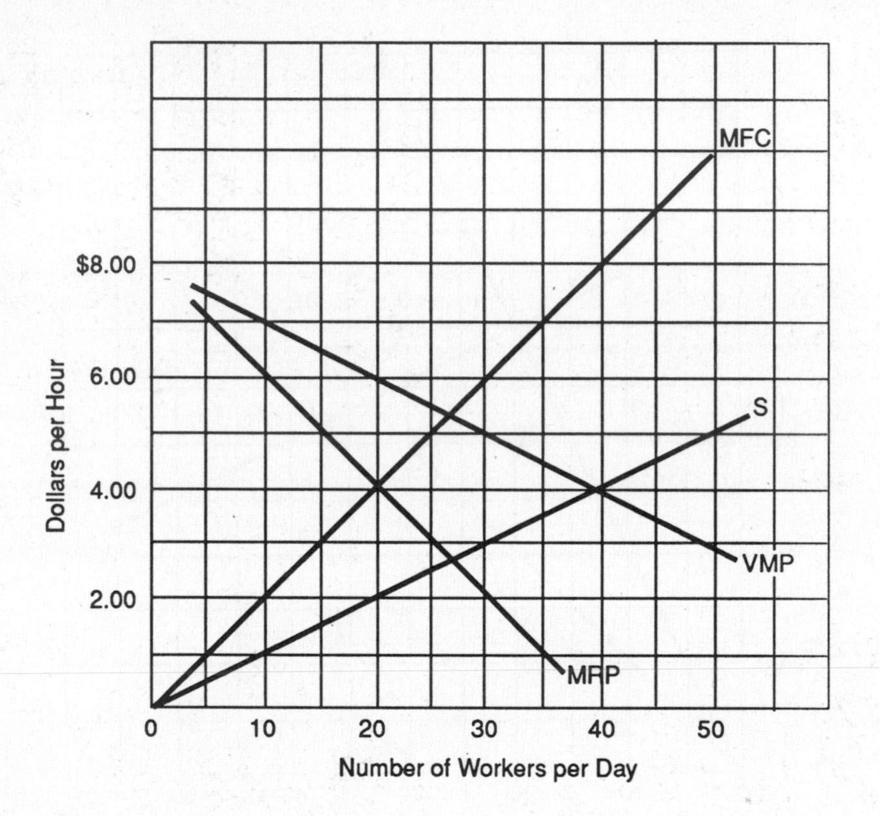

a. This monopolist-monopsonist will hire __________ workers per day and pay a wage of __________ per hour.

b. At this rate of employment, the value of marginal product of labor (VMP) is __________ per hour.

c. With no outside intervention in this market, we will observe (monopsonistic, monopolistic, both monopsonistic and monopolistic) exploitation.

d. The level of monopsonistic exploitation is __________ per hour, and the level of monopolistic exploitation is __________ per hour.

e. The total level of exploitation is __________ per hour, represented by the difference between the ______________ and ______________.

CASE STUDY

When unions set wage rates above the equilibrium wage rate, they create a surplus of labor at that wage rate. That is, at the union-set wage rate the quantity supplied of labor exceeds the quantity demanded for labor. Another way to view this situation is that at such an above-equilibrium wage rate, a *shortage of jobs exists*. In other words, such (relatively high paying) jobs are now scarcer and, like any scarce resource, they have to be rationed.

Economist Walter Williams has pointed out that historically unions have rationed blacks out of such jobs; union leaders in union crafts have allocated these artificially scarce jobs to the families of members already in the union. Williams cites as evidence that after the Civil War much higher percentages of blacks held jobs in the skilled crafts than was the case after World War II. The labor union movement flourished between those two periods.

1. How would blacks have been able to avoid being rationed out of craft jobs had there been no unions?

2. Can there be a shortage of some jobs, but a surplus of others? Can there be a shortage of all jobs?

ANSWERS TO CHAPTER 29

COMPLETION QUESTIONS

1. craft, skill or trade; industrial, industry
2. helped
3. is not; right-to-work; closed shop (union shop in right-to-work states), jurisdictional disputes, sympathy, secondary
4. Landrum-Griffin; decreased, increased
5. strike
6. surplus; shortage
7. must; 1; low-seniority
8. MRP of labor, negatively sloped, diminishing returns; MFC of labor, positively sloped; rise, upward; greater than
9. MRP of labor, diminishing marginal physical product of labor, decreasing product price; MFC of labor, raise, all; upward
10. MB = MC; MRP of labor, MFC of labor; supply
11. MRP of labor; MFC of labor
12. regulates number of student athletes per school, fixes the price of university games, sets prices, wages, and conditions for university hiring of athletes, enforces its rules with sanctions and penalties
13. contribution to marginal revenues

TRUE-FALSE QUESTIONS

1. T
2. T
3. F That act is concerned with regulating internal union business procedures.
4. T
5. F They create a surplus of labor and a shortage of jobs.
6. T
7. F It sets wage rates where the price elasticity of demand equals 1.
8. F Not necessarily; demand may fall dramatically.
9. F They may increase productivity by creating a safe and secure environment.
10. F It hires up to where MRP = MRC = MFC of labor
11. T
12. T
13. T
14. T

MULTIPLE CHOICE QUESTIONS

1.a; 2.c; 3.b; 4.a; 5.d; 6.a; 7.d; 8.c; 9.a; 10.c;
11.d; 12.d; 13.d; 14.b; 15.d; 16.c; 17.a; 18.d; 19.c; 20.b;
21.b

WORKING WITH GRAPHS

1. a. 20, $2; b. increase, 25, $2.50
2. a. 20, $2; b. $6; c. both monopsonistic and monopolistic; d. $2,$2; e. $4, VMP of $6 per hour, wage of $2 per hour

CASE STUDY

1. They could have offered to work for lower wages (in effect, they could have bid "higher" for jobs).
2. Yes, a shortage of jobs arises when wage rates are set above equilibrium, and a surplus when wage rates are set below equilibrium; when the equilibrium wage rate exists, there is neither a shortage nor a surplus of jobs. A shortage of all jobs cannot exist--unless wage rates are set above equilibrium in all labor markets.

GLOSSARY FOR CHAPTER 29

Closed shop A business enterprise in which an employee must belong to the union before he or she can be employed. The employee must remain in the union after he or she becomes employed.

Collective bargaining Bargaining between management of a company or of a group of companies and management of a union or a group of unions for the purpose of setting a mutually agreeable contract on wages, fringe benefits, and working conditions for all employees in the union(s). Different from individual bargaining, where each employee strikes a bargain with his or her employer individually.

Craft unions Labor unions composed of workers who engage in a particular trade or skill, such as baking, carpentry, or plumbing.

Featherbedding Any practice that forces employers to use more labor than they would otherwise or to use existing labor in an inefficient manner.

Industrial unions Labor unions that consist of workers from a particular industry, such as automobile manufacturing or steel manufacturing.

Jurisdictional dispute A dispute by two or more unions over which should have control of a particular jurisdiction, such as over a particular craft or skill or over a particular firm or industry.

Labor unions Workers' organizations that usually seek to secure economic improvements for their members.

Marginal factor cost (MFC) The change in total costs due to a one-unit increase in the variable input. The cost of using more of a factor of production.

Monopsonist A single buyer.

Monopsonistic exploitation Paying a worker a wage below that worker's marginal revenue product.

Right-to-work laws Laws that make it illegal to require union membership as a condition of continuing employment in a particular firm.

Secondary boycott A boycott of companies or products sold by companies that are dealing with a company that has already been struck.

Sympathy strike A strike by a union in response to, or in sympathy with, another union's already existing strike.

Union shop A business enterprise that allows nonunion members to become employed, conditional upon their joining the union by some specified date after employment begins.

CHAPTER 30

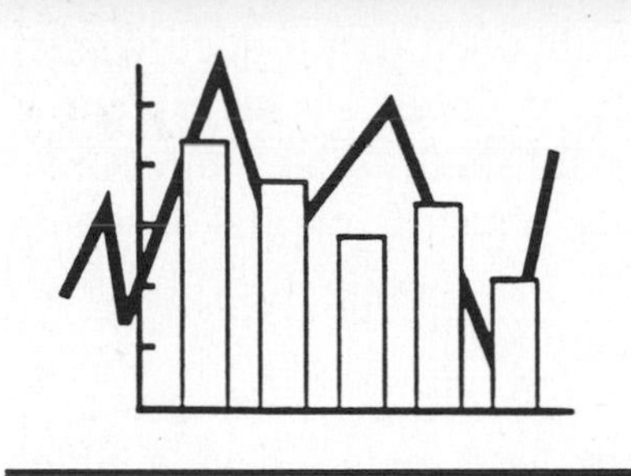

RENT, INTEREST, AND PROFITS

PUTTING THIS CHAPTER INTO PERSPECTIVE

Chapter 30 is the third chapter that deals with the analysis of the four factors of production. Chapters 28 and 29 dealt with labor and its payment: wage rates. Chapter 30 analyzes land, capital, and entrepreneurship, and the (roughly) corresponding payments to those factors: rent, interest, and profits.

Probably the most important thing you can learn from this chapter is that rent, interest, and profits (and wage rates too) are *prices*. As such they perform an allocative function; in a market economy, land, capital, and labor flow to the highest (business) bidder. (Profits are a little more difficult to analyze; we deal with them later in this section.) In general, the highest bidders will be those firms that are the most profitable or have the best profit record in the past. Consequently, through the price system, resources flow from less profitable firms to more profitable firms; this means that resources (factors of production) flow from lower-valued to higher-valued uses, and economic efficiency prevails. To the extent that such governmental price controls as usury laws, minimum wage laws and comparable worth laws, and excess profits taxes exist, then economic efficiency suffers. Inefficiency results also when governments subsidize firms that are going bankrupt. Note, however, that just because government economic policies are inefficient does not mean that we *should not* permit such interferences; remember that questions of "should" are normative in nature. Economists can only present the results of their positive economic analysis to society; society can then determine whether or not other matters outweigh efficiency considerations.

Rent is typically regarded as a payment for land. Economists have extended the term *rent* to include the payment to any resource that is fixed in supply. More specifically, we define rent as the payment to any resource over and above what is necessary to keep the resource in supply at its current level. This extended concept of rent permits us to analyze economic rents involved with professional athletes and entertainers. Note again the point about price as an allocating, or rationing, device. Suppose Prince would be *willing* to perform for $500 a night. At such a price he would be in great demand and a shortage of his services would exist. If a law were passed that limited his income to $500 a performance, his economic rents would disappear, but how would we ration his performances? That is, where would he entertain? In a market system, his shows might be bid up to $10,000 a night. Prince sells his services to the highest bidder and earns economic rents, and economic efficiency obtains. Society maximizes the value of his services, because the highest bidders value his services most highly.

Interest is the cost of obtaining credit; it arises because most people prefer to consume in the present rather than in the future--due to the uncertainty of life. In order to induce people to save now, they are offered interest, which permits them to consume more in the future. Borrowers can reward lenders in the future if they use the funds (saving) so obtained to produce capital goods that increase output in the future. Hence we have a supply of credit by savers and a demand for credit by businesses, and the interest rate is thereby established. The interest rate is a price, and it allocates credit to the highest bidder; ultimately physical capital is being allocated because business-borrowers purchase capital goods with the money they borrow. Capital is allocated to its most profitable use and economic efficiency results.

Profits are less easy to analyze. The economic function of profit is to help society decide which industries, and which firms within an industry, are to expand and which are to contract. In the process, resources move from lower-valued to higher-valued uses.

You should note well that the economic concepts of rent, interest, and profits are not easily measured; consequently it is misleading to associate the values associated with our measurements of those variables with our theoretical concepts.

LEARNING OBJECTIVES

After you have studied this chapter you should be able to

1. define economic rent, pure economic rent, transfer earnings, interest, nominal rate of interest, real rate of interest, labor theory of value, present value, discount rate, and discounting.

2. distinguish between pure economic rent and a transfer earning.

3. distinguish between the nominal interest rate and the real interest rate.

4. calculate the (approximate) nominal interest rate, given the real interest rate and the anticipated rate of inflation.

5. list three things that account for variations in interest rates.

6. answer questions that require an understanding of the rationing function of rent, interest, and profits.

7. calculate the present value of an amount of money to be received at a future date.

8. identify Karl Marx's relationship between the labor theory of value and capitalist profits.

CHAPTER OUTLINE

1. *Economic rent* is a payment for the use of any resource that is in fixed supply.
   a. Land is often believed to be in fixed supply.
   b. Even if land is absolutely in fixed supply, rent payments help society to decide how land is to be used.

c. Economic rents also accrue to factors of production other than land.
d. Assume that a professional athlete earns $1,000,000 per year, and that he or she could earn, at best, $50,000 per year doing something else. That person's transfer earnings equal $50,000 and his or her economic rents equal $950,000 per year.
    i. If a factor's supply curve is horizontal, all of its income equals transfer earnings.
    ii. If a factor's supply curve is positively sloped, the area under the supply curve equals transfer earnings and the area above the supply curve (and under the equilibrium wage rate line) equals economic rent.

2. The term *interest* is used to mean two things: (1) the price paid by debtors to creditors for the use of loanable funds, and (2) the market return earned by capital as a factor of production.
    a. Interest is the payment for obtaining credit.
    b. Interest rates vary with the length of loan, risk, and handling charges.
    c. The equilibrium rate of interest is found at the intersection of the downward sloping demand for loanable funds curve and the upward sloping supply of loanable funds curve.
    d. The *nominal interest* rate is (approximately) equal to the sum of the real interest rate and the expected rate of inflation.
    e. The interest rate, ultimately, allocates physical capital to various firms for investment projects.

3. Interest rates link the present with the future.
    a. A money value in the future can be expressed in today's value by a process referred to as *discounting* to present worth.
    b. Discounting is the method by which the present value of a future sum, or a stream of future sums, is obtained.
    c. The *discount rate* is the interest rate used in the discounting to present worth equation.

4. Profit is the reward to the entrepreneurial factor of production.
    a. Accounting profits are the difference between total revenues and total explicit costs; economic profits equal the difference between total revenues and the opportunity cost of all factors of production.
    b. Various explanations for profit exist.
        i. According to Karl Marx, profits exist due to labor exploitation, as indicated by his application of the classical labor *theory of value*.
        ii. Economic profits can be the result of barriers to entry.
        iii. Some economists, notably Joseph Schumpeter, maintain that economic profits result from innovation.
        iv. Frank Knight believed that profit is the reward for assuming uninsurable risk.
    c. The function of economic profit is to (a) spur innovation and investment and (b) allocate resources from lower-valued to higher-valued uses.

5. It is not easy to measure wages, interest, rents, and profits; in general, the share of national income allocated to wages and salaries plus proprietors' income has remained relatively constant in the United States over the last 85 years.

6. Credit card interest rates have remained relatively high because people use them as unsecured loans and because of adverse selection; interest rate caps on credit cards would tend to hurt low income minority high-risk groups and benefit upper-income groups.

KEY TERMS

Interest
Nominal interest rate
Real interest rate
Economic vs. accounting profits
Labor theory of value
Usury
Credit card caps
Discount rate

KEY CONCEPTS

Transfer earnings
Economic rent
Pure economic rent
Discounting
Labor theory of value
Allocative function of profits
Unisurable risk

COMPLETION QUESTIONS

Fill in the blank or circle the correct term.

1. A payment for the use of any resource that is ________________ in supply is an economic rent.

2. Frank Knight believed that profit was the reward for assuming __________________ risk.

3. Interest is the cost of obtaining __________________. Interest is used to mean two different things: (1) ________________________, and (2) ________________________.

4. Interest rates vary due to ______________________, ______________________, and ______________________.

5. Interest rates are determined at the intersection of the demand for ________________ curve and the supply of __________________ curve. The supply curve is positively sloped because as people save more, the marginal utility of *present* consumption (falls, rises, remains constant); therefore before people will save more, the interest rate must ____________.

6. The three major sources of demand for loanable funds are ____________________, ______________________, and ______________________.

7. The consumer demand for loanable funds exists because people, typically, prefer to consume (earlier than later, later than earlier); businesses demand loanable funds for investments that increase ___________________.

8. The nominal interest rate equals the real interest rate plus the ______________________; ultimately the interest rate allocates _________________ to various firms for investment projects.

9. Transfer earnings equal the ______________cost of a resource; if a resource is perfectly elastic in supply, transfer earnings (equal, are less than, exceed) total earnings.

10. Karl Marx argued that the source of profits was ________________; this conclusion was based on his ______________ theory of value, which maintained that workers (do, do not) earn the full market value of the service they provide.

11. The process of finding the value today of a sum of money in the future is called ______________; the interest rate used in that process is called the ___________ rate.

12. The concept of adverse selection helps to explain why interest rates are so high on ___________________.

TRUE-FALSE QUESTIONS

Circle the T if the statement is true, the F if it is false. Explain to yourself why a statement is false.

T F 1. Economic rent accrues only to the factor land.

T F 2. Economic rent is the price paid to a factor that is perfectly elastic in supply.

T F 3. Transfer earnings reflect the opportunity cost of a factor of production.

T F 4. For a factor fixed in supply, economic rent has no economic function.

T F 5. People who use credit cards receive a secured loan.

T F 6. If a rock star prices tickets at a price way below equilibrium, that is an efficient way to help poor people.

T F 7. Other things being constant, the greater the risk of nonrepayment, the higher the interest rate.

T F 8. At higher interest rates, businesses will find fewer investments in capital goods profitable, other things being constant.

T F 9. The nominal interest rate (approximately) equals the real rate of interest plus the expected interest rate.

T F 10. Ultimately, the interest rate allocates physical capital to *specific firms* and households.

T F 11. Discounting is the process of converting future money values to present worth.

T F 12. According to Karl Marx, laborers are paid less than their fair market value.

T F 13. Profits serve no economic function.

T F 14. The largest share of national income goes to owners of nonlabor factors of production.

T F *15. State lotteries understate the true value of their awards.

T F 16. If an inefficient firm goes bankrupt, that is socially efficient.

MULTIPLE CHOICE QUESTIONS

Circle the letter that corresponds to the best answer.

1. For a factor that earns pure economic rent,
   a. its quantity varies only in the long run.
   b. its supply is perfectly elastic.
   c. its supply curve is vertical.
   d. no taxation is possible because no surplus exists.

2. In David Ricardo's economic model,
   a. land was fixed in supply.
   b. wages and salaries were set at subsistence level.
   c. land rent rises as industrialization occurs.
   d. All of the above

3. Who believed that wage rates were set at workers' subsistence levels?
   a. Marx and Ricardo
   b. Marx and Keynes
   c. Ricardo and Miller
   d. Schumpeter and Marx

4. Economic rents
   a. have no allocative function.
   b. have no economic function.
   c. do not bring forth a greater quantity of the resource.
   d. exist only for land.

5. Mr. Pulsinelli earns $800,000 per year as a tennis pro; he could earn, at best, $100,000 per year as an economist. Which statement is the most accurate?
   a. He should be a tennis pro.
   b. His transfer earnings are $100,000 per year.
   c. His economic rent equals $800,00 per year.
   d. His comparative advantage is as an economist.

6. Credit card interest rates are high because
   a. such loans are unsecured.
   b. of adverse selection.
   c. risks are high to the issuers of credit cards.
   d. All of the above

7. Economic rents
   a. accrue only to land.
   b. accrue only to labor.
   c. accrue only to entrepreneurs.
   d. can accrue to any factor, in principle.

8. Other things being constant, the interest rate varies with the
   a. length of a loan.
   b. risk of nonrepayment.
   c. handling charges.
   d. All of the above

9. Which of the following statements is *not* true?
   a. As people save more, their marginal utility for present consumption falls.
   b. In order to induce households to save more, the interest rate must rise.
   c. The supply of loanable funds curve is positively sloped.
   d. At higher interest rates people substitute future consumption for present consumption.

10. Which of the following statements is *not* true?
    a. Households demand loanable funds to purchase durable goods.
    b. Governments demand loanable funds to finance surpluses.
    c. Businesses demand loanable funds to purchase investment capital.
    d. Households demand loanable funds to maintain consumption when income falls temporarily.

11. The nominal interest rate approximately equals the real interest rate
    a. minus the expected interest rate.
    b. plus the expected interest rate.
    c. plus the expected rate of inflation.
    d. minus the expected inflation rate.

12. Interest rates
    a. have no economic function.
    b. allocate money capital to less efficient firms.
    c. allocate physical capital to firms in a random manner.
    d. allocate physical capital to specific firms for investment projects.

13. Discounting
    a. converts future dollar values into present values.
    b. connects the future with the present.
    c. uses the interest rate.
    d. All of the above

14. If the interest rate is 5 per cent, the present value of $100 that is to be received one year from now is about
    a. $90
    b. $950
    c. $95
    d. $105

15. According to Karl Marx,
    a. exploitation is the source of profits.
    b. the value of goods, including labor's services, is determined by the amount of labor required to produce them.
    c. laborers are paid fair market wages, given the rules of capitalism.
    d. All of the above

16. Profits
    a. perform no economic function.
    b. move resources from lower-valued to higher-valued uses.
    c. provide useful information, but losses do not.
    d. lead to a misallocation of resources because producers produce for profit, not for consumer needs.

17. When Professor Miller won the $1,000,000 lottery in Florida, he found out that the money would be paid to him at the rate of $50,000 per year for the next twenty years. Which of the following is probably true?
    a. Miller will refuse the money, after he finds out what the lottery is really worth.
    b. The lottery winnings are worth considerably less than $1 million.
    c. Miller would *prefer* to receive his lottery winnings over twenty years, instead of all at once.
    d. Miller would have preferred to receive $25,000 per year for 40 years.

MATCHING

Choose the item in column (2) that best matches an item in column (1).

(1)	(2)
a. transfer earnings	e. inflationary expectation
b. nominal interest rate	f. discount rate
c. economic rent	g. opportunity cost of resource
d. present value calculation	h. payment to resource fixed in supply

WORKING WITH GRAPHS

1. Use the information given below to answer the questions that follow. The figures other than the rate of interest are given in thousands of dollars per month.

Rate of interest	Quantity demanded of: Consumption loans	Investment loans	Total loans	Supply of loanable funds
16	10	30	____	300
14	20	40	____	250
12	30	60	____	200
10	40	100	____	140
8	50	140	____	90
6	60	180	____	50
4	70	210	____	30

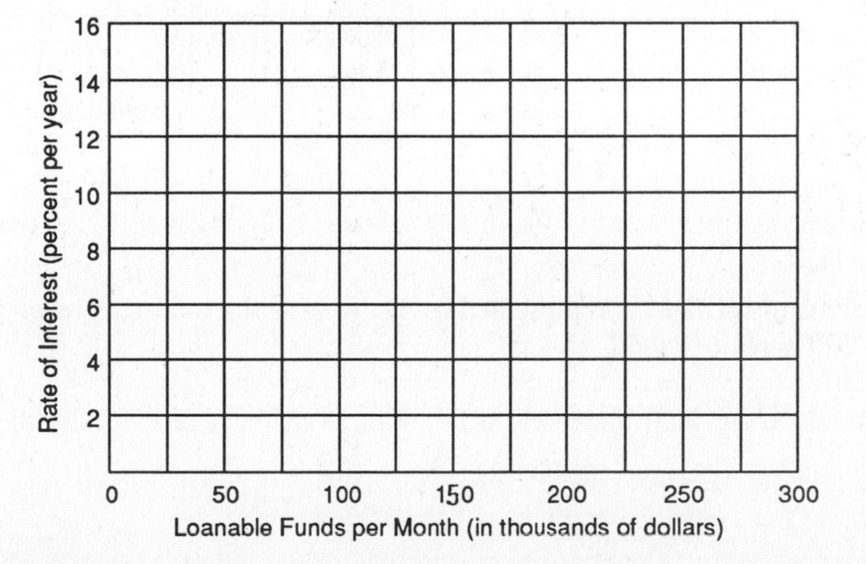

a. On the grid provided above, plot the demand curve for consumption loans and label it D (consumption), and plot the demand curve for investment loans and label it D (investment).

b. Complete the column for the total loans demanded in the above table.

c. On the above grid, plot the total demand curve for loanable funds and the supply curve for loanable funds.

d. The equilibrium rate of interest is ____________, and the equilibrium quantity of loanable funds is ____________ per month.

e. ____________ per month will be lent for the purpose of consumption loans at equilibrium, and ____________ will be lent for investment.

2. Use the following graphs to answer the questions that follow.

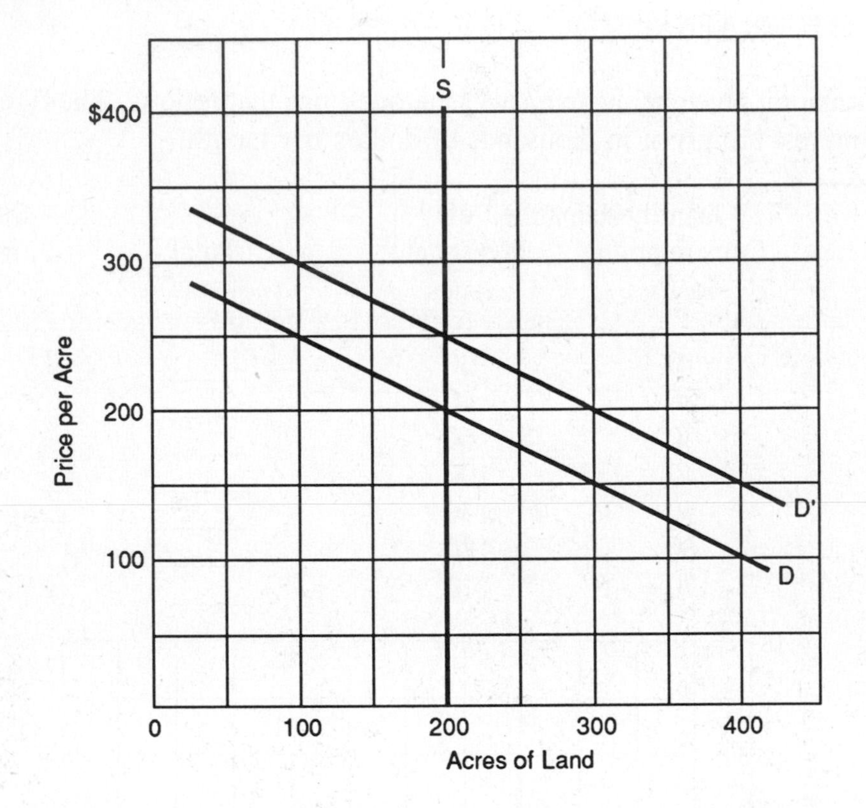

a. If the demand for land is represented by D, what is the total rent received by the owner of the 200 acres of land?

b. If the demand for land increases to D', what is the rent received by the landowner?

PROBLEMS

1. Suppose you win a lottery that offers the following payoff. At the end of each year for the next 3 years you are to receive $1000. At the end of each of the following 3 years you will receive $500, for a total of $4500 over the six-year period. If the current going rate of interest is 8%, what is the present value of your winnings? If someone offered you $3700 today for your lottery ticket, should you take it?

2. Gladstone Gander just learned that a long-lost aunt has set up a trust for him, whereby he will receive $1 million exactly ten years from now. Assume that the relevant interest rate is 10 per cent.

   a. Can Gladstone sell his inheritance, right now, for $1 million? Why or why not?

   b. What is the present value of Gladstone's inheritance?

3. Suppose that you had used a discount rate of 20 per cent in question (2) above. How would you answer (a) and (b) now?

   c. How are present value and the interest rate related?

CASE STUDY

Rock stars and athletes sometimes want to help low income people by allowing them to view their performances and so, on occasion, they insist that a relatively low price be set per seat--or that a certain section be sold at relatively low prices. What often happens, however, is that large blocks are purchased by scalpers and radio stations. Scalpers resell the tickets at a higher price and radio stations have promotions.

1. Do the stars actually achieve their goal?

2. Can the stars help low income people in a more efficient way?

ANSWERS TO CHAPTER 30

COMPLETION QUESTIONS

1. fixed
2. uninsurable
3. credit; price paid by creditors to debtors, return to capital
4. length of loan, risk of nonrepayment, handling charges
5. loanable funds, loanable funds; rises; rise
6. households, businesses, governments
7. earlier than later; profits or productivity
8. expected inflation rate; physical capital
9. opportunity; equal
10. exploitation of labor; labor, do
11. discounting; discount
12. credit cards

TRUE-FALSE QUESTIONS

1. F It accrues to any factor fixed in supply.
2. F It is the price paid to a perfectly *in*elastic resource supply.
3. T
4. F It allocates the fixed factor to its highest-valued use.
5. F Such loans are unsecured.
6. F Giving them money directly would be more efficient.
7. T
8. T
9. F Plus the expected *inflation* rate.
10. T
11. T
12. F His theory assumes they get paid their fair market value.
13. F They help to allocate capital, and they help to decide which firms should grow and which should contract.
14. F It goes to laborers.
15. F They overstate, because they don't tell the discounted value.
16. T

MULTIPLE CHOICE QUESTIONS

1.c; 2.d; 3.a; 4.c; 5.b; 6.d; 7.d; 8.d; 9.a; 10.b;
11.c; 12.d; 13.d; 14.c; 15.d; 16.b; 17.b

MATCHING

a and g; b and e; c and h; d and f

WORKING WITH GRAPHS

1. a. See the graph below.

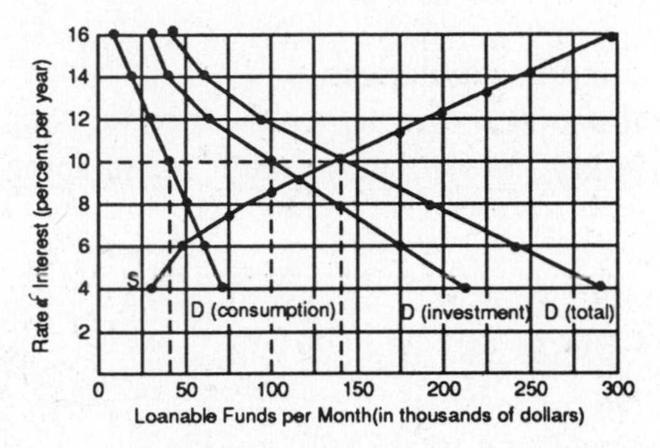

b. 40, 60, 90, 140, 190, 240, 280;
c. See the graph above;
d. 10 percent, $140,000;
e. $40,000, $100,000

2. a. $40,000; b. $50,000

PROBLEMS

1. From Table 18-1 we can see:

Year	Present Value	(Found by)
1	$ 926.00	(.926 x 1000)
2	857.00	(.857 x 1000)
3	794.00	(.794 x 1000)
4	367.50	(.735 x 500)
5	340.50	(.681 x 500)
6	315.00	(.630 x 500)
Total	$3600.00	

Yes, you would be $100 better off, as is seen by the present value calculation.

2. a. No, no one would give him $1 million right now because such a sum could be invested and earn interest for ten years, and at the end of that period it would be worth $1 million plus the accumulated interest.

b. $\frac{\$1,000,000}{(1.1)^{10}} = \frac{\$1,000,000}{2.5937425} = \$385,543$

3. a. See (2) above
   b. $161,506.
   c. They are inversely related.

CASE STUDY

1. Scalpers and radio station owners seem to be the main beneficiaries.
2. Perhaps the stars could charge full price and give the money directly to low income people, who would spend it so as to maximize their total utility. *Maybe* they would spend some of that money to purchase tickets to see the stars.

GLOSSARY TO CHAPTER 30

Accounting profit The difference between total revenues and total explicit costs.

Discounting The method by which the present value of a future sum or a future stream of sums is obtained.

Discount rate That rate of interest used to discount future sums back to present value.

Economic profit The difference between total revenues and the opportunity cost of all factors of production.

Economic rent A payment for the use of any resource that is in fixed supply.

Interest The payment for current rather than future command over resources; the cost of obtaining credit. Also the return paid to owners of capital.

Labor theory of value A theory that the value of all commodities is equal to the value of the labor used in producing them.

Nominal rate of interest The market rate of interest that's expressed in terms of current dollars.

Present value The value of a future amount expressed in today's dollars; the most that someone would pay today to receive a certain sum at some point in the future.

Pure economic rent The payment to any resource that is in completely inelastic supply. The payment to any resource over and above what is necessary to keep the resource in supply at its current level.

Real rate of interest The rate of interest obtained by subtracting the anticipated rate of inflation from the nominal rate of interest.

Transfer earnings That part of total earnings which represent what the factor of production could earn in its next best alternative use; a measure of the opportunity cost of a resource.

CHAPTER 31

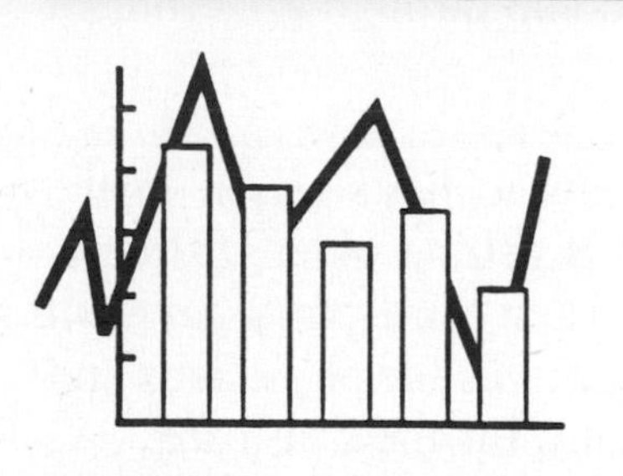

INCOME, POVERTY, AND HEALTH CARE

PUTTING THIS CHAPTER INTO PERSPECTIVE

To this point we have analyzed factor markets and learned how factors of production are evaluated and priced in competitive and noncompetitive markets. Ultimately, payments to factors of production represent income to the people who own those factors. Chapter 19 explores how those incomes are distributed across the population.

It might be helpful for you to think of a "natural" distribution of income that would result from a perfectly competitive economic system. Each person would be paid (approximately, subject to imperfect information limitations) the value of his or her marginal product--for labor and nonlabor resources. Such a distribution of income would doubtless be very uneven because we each have different talents and skills, and we each start out with different degrees of family connections, inherited property, and other variables that potentially affect income. Depending on the tastes of society, a good deal of inequality of income results from the amount of luck (or ill fortune) in the matchup between inherent physical and mental traits and consumer tastes. Then, of course, there are traits that we can acquire by training and/or hard work.

Although such an unequal distribution might be "natural" in some sense, it hardly follows that such a distribution is *desirable*. A "natural" distribution of income can theoretically be consistent with a very small number having extremely high incomes and a large number living at near-subsistence.

This brings us to a potential problem. A "natural" distribution does have some benefits: it is consistent with economic freedom and provides economic incentives for people to improve their marginal productivity through training, education, risk-taking, and old-fashioned hard work. On the other hand, a natural distribution of income also reflects mere luck. One's income may be relatively low due to a failure to inherit traits and characteristics that the marketplace (which reflects society's tastes for goods and services) values, or to a failure to inherit wealth from one's ancestors.

Unfortunately, when we tax some to give to others we affect economic incentives and economic freedom. In short, there is a trade-off between income equality and economic efficiency. There is, therefore, an optimal amount of inequality, but such an optimum depends on one's particular value system. The optimal distribution of income cannot be derived through positive economics; once again economic analysis can provide only limited aid in solving a crucial societal problem. Nevertheless, economic analysis can serve to remind us that there are costs, as well as benefits, to redistributing income through government tax and transfer programs.

This chapter is also concerned with the health care "crisis" that seems to have arisen in the United States in recent years. A combination of (a) a population that is getting older, (b) new, expensive, technological advances in medical equipment (and drugs), (c) a third-party payment system, much of which is government subsidized, and (d) a lack of incentives for physicians and hospitals to contain costs, have led to a dramatic increase in the demand for medical care. As a consequence the costs of such care has skyrocketed and so too (predictably) has the cost of health insurance.

LEARNING OBJECTIVES

After you have studied this chapter you should be able to

1. define distribution of income, Lorenz curve, income-in-kind, Gini coefficient, comparable worth doctrine, age-earnings cycle, and third parties.

2. list criticisms of using the Lorenz curve and the Gini coefficient as indicators of the degree of income inequality in a country.

3. distinguish between income and wealth.

4. recognize facts concerning income distribution and poverty in the United States.

5. list three determinants of income differences.

6. list three normative standards of income distribution and distinguish among them.

7. distinguish between absolute poverty and relative poverty.

8. enumerate costs associated with forcing more income equality in a nation.

9. enumerate three reasons that explain why medical costs have risen rapidly in the U.S.

CHAPTER OUTLINE

1. This chapter attempts to define distribution of income and present theories of why income is unevenly distributed across the population.

2. The Lorenz curve is a geometric representation of the distribution of income.
   a. There are some criticisms of using the Lorenz curve to measure the degree of income inequality in a nation.
      i. The curve does not take into account income-in-kind.
      ii. It does not account for differences in family size and effort.
      iii. It does not account for age differences.

   iv. It measures pretax money income.
   v. It does not measure underground economy earnings.

b. The *Gini coefficient of inequality* is a numerical representation of income inequality in a nation.
   i. Specifically, it is defined as the ratio of the area between the diagonal line and the actual Lorenz curve to the triangular area under the diagonal line.
   ii. Because it is derived from the Lorenz curve, it suffers from the same inadequacies.

c. Since World War II the distribution of money income in the United States has not changed very much.

d. The distribution of total income, which includes in-kind transfers, has become more equal in the U.S. since 1962.

3. Wealth and income are not synonymous.
   a. Wealth is a stock concept, and income is a flow concept.
   b. A stock is evaluated at a given moment in time; a flow is evaluated during a period of time.
   c. Each of us inherits a different endowment, including human attributes and nonhuman wealth, which strongly affects our ability to earn income in the marketplace.

4. There are numerous determinants of income differences.
   a. The *wage-earnings cycle* typically shows that at a young age income is low; it builds gradually to a peak at around age 45 to 50, and then gradually curves down until it approaches zero at retirement age.
   b. In competitive markets, workers can expect to earn, approximately, their marginal revenue product (MRP).
   c. Determinants of an individual's marginal productivity include innate abilities and attributes, education, experience, and training.

5. Inheritance is also a determinant of income differences.

6. Discrimination also contributes somewhat to income differences.
   a. White males, on average, hold jobs in the highest-paying occupations; the lowest paying jobs are held by nonwhite males, and by white and nonwhite females.
   b. Minorities are often denied equal access to higher education.

7. The comparable worth doctrine contends that females (or minorities) should receive the same wages as males if the levels of skills and responsibility in their different jobs are equal. Skill and responsibility levels, in practice, are difficult to define and arbitrariness inevitably results in setting such wage rates.

8. Investment in human capital, on average, earns a rate of return on a par with the rate of return to investment in other areas.

9. There are three normative standards of income distribution: need, equality, and productivity.

10. Western nations have sustained enough economic growth over the last several hundred

years so that mass poverty has disappeared.

11. If poverty is measured in absolute terms, it will be eliminated by economic growth. If poverty is defined in relative terms, it will be mathematically impossible to eliminate it, unless everyone has the same income, an improbable event.
    a. If we correct poverty levels for in-kind transfers, they fall dramatically in the United States.
    b. Traditionally the poor have usually fallen into one of the following classifications: minority groups, elderly, young, rural, or households headed by women; in recent years, however, the "new poor" are single parent families, minority youths, and single elderly people.

12. There are a variety of income-maintenance programs designed to help the poor; they include social insurance, Supplemental Security Income, Aid to Families with Dependent Children, and food stamps.

13. In spite of the numerous programs designed to reduce poverty, officially defined poverty rates have shown no long run tendency to drop since their relatively dramatic decline through 1973.

14. More income equality reduces economic incentives to both the people who are taxed and the people who receive transfers, and economic freedoms are reduced if more income equality is enforced; hence a trade-off exists between efficiency and equality of income.

15. In recent years the price of health care services and health care insurance have increased dramatically in the U.S.; American citizens have been spending higher and higher percentages of their income on health care; some refer to this situation as a "crisis."

16. There are several explanations as to why health care costs have risen rapidly in the United States.
    a. Our population is, on average, getting older and the elderly are the main users of health care.
    b. Technological advances in medicine have spawned expensive machinery that everyone wants to use (both suppliers and demanders).
    c. The state and federal governments account for about 40 percent of total spending on health care; private insurance accounts for about 30 percent of the spending.
        i. Because health care is subsidized by government, people want more than they would otherwise.
        ii. Both government and private-provided health care insurance create a situation in which third parties (insurers) pay most of the costs of medical services; hence people want more health care than if they were paying for it themselves.
    d. The third-party payment system has created a situation in which physicians and hospitals have no incentive to keep health care costs down.

17. Some have suggested a national health care plan to replace the private insurance system that the U.S. has; an essential ingredient of such a system is price ceilings on physician's fees and hospital costs.

18. Others have suggested a national health insurance plan which, presumably, would be offered only to lower income groups.

KEY TERMS

Lorenz curve
Gini coefficient of inequality
Income-maintenance programs
Official measure of poverty

KEY CONCEPTS

Distribution of income
Age-earnings cycle
Comparable worth doctrine
Income-in-kind
Poverty
Third parties

COMPLETION QUESTIONS

Fill in the blank or circle the correct term.

1. A Lorenz curve shows what portion of total money income is accounted for by different ________________ of a nation's households; if it is a 45 degree line, then ______________ income inequality exists. Another measure of a nation's degree of income inequality is the ______________ coefficient of inequality.

2. The Lorenz curve as a representation of income inequality has been criticized because it does not ________________, or account for ________________, ________________, ________________, and ________________.

3. Since World War II, the lowest 20 percent of the income distribution in the United States had a combined money income of _________ percent of the total money income of the entire population; however, if income-in-kind is taken into account, income inequality has (decreased, increased) since then.

4. (Wealth, Income) is a stock concept, while ______________ is a flow concept.

5. One determinant of income inequality is age; the age-earnings cycle indicates that teenagers' incomes are relatively (low, high), then incomes rise gradually to a peak at around age ___________, and then gradually fall toward zero as people approach ___________. People earn different amounts over their lifetime because age is related to a worker's ________________.

*6. If a worker's MRP exceeds her wage rate, chances are that she will (change jobs, be laid off); if a worker's wage rate is greater than her MRP, then chances are she will be ________________. As long as it is costly to obtain information about a specific worker's MRP, there (will, will not) be some difference between a worker's wage and his or her MRP.

7. Four determinants of an individual's marginal productivity are ________________, ________________, ________________, and ________________; other than differences in marginal productivity, income differences are also due to ________________ and ________________.

8. Three theories of normative standards of income distribution are ________________, ________________, and ________________.

9. (Absolute, Relative) poverty will automatically be eliminated by economic growth, but ________________ poverty can never be eliminated, in practice.

10. The poor are usually classified in one of the following groups: ________________, ________________, ________________, or ________________.

11. In the United States there are several income-maintenance programs aimed at eliminating poverty. The best known is ______________ Security, which in effect is an intergenerational income transfer; another is SSI, which establishes a nationwide ________________ income for the aged, the blind, and the disabled; the AFDC provides aid to families in which ________________ do not have financial support.

12. In the United States since 1973 there (has, has not) been a long-run trend toward reduced officially defined poverty.

13. Many economists believe that the major cost to increased income equality is ________________; hence a trade-off exists.

14. In recent years the percent of total income spent on medical care has (decreased, increased) dramatically because our population, on average, is getting (younger, older), technological advances in medical equipment have caused a(n) (decrease, increase) in the demand for medical services, third-party billing has (decreased, increased) due to health insurance, and because physicians and hospitals have (little, strong) incentives to keep costs down.

*15. Most national health care plans incorporate a system to put a (floor, ceiling) on medical fees and services; this will create (surpluses, shortages) eventually.

TRUE-FALSE QUESTIONS

Circle the T if the statement is true, the F if it false. Explain to yourself why a statement is false.

T F 1. In the real world, no country has a linear Lorenz curve.

T F 2. The Gini coefficient of income inequality avoids most problems associated with the Lorenz curve.

T F 3. When in-kind transfers are considered, income inequality in the U.S. rises and poverty levels fall.

T F 4. Not considering income-in-kind, the bottom 20 percent of United States income earners earn about 5% of total U.S. income.

T F 5. Income and wealth are unrelated.

T F 6. The comparable worth doctrine accepts the notion that workers should be paid their MRP.

T F 7. In the United States, over time, income inequality has increased dramatically.

T F 8. An age-earnings cycle exists because age and marginal productivity are related.

T F 9. In a competitive economy, workers tend to get paid the value of their marginal productivity.

T F 10. In the United States inheritance and discrimination are more important determinants of income differences than are marginal productivity differences.

T F 11. In the United States, there has been discrimination against blacks and other minorities regarding access to quality education.

T F 12. In the United States the return to investment in human capital is significantly higher than it is for other investments.

T F 13. Mass poverty is still a problem for even the advanced Western economies.

T F 14. Economic growth will eventually eliminate relative poverty.

T F 15. Despite massive sums of money devoted to income redistribution programs in the United States, officially measured poverty has remained roughly unchanged since 1973.

T F 16. All economists agree that more income equality in the United States is desirable.

T F 17. Because health care is usually paid for by third parties, buyers are largely insensitive to price increases.

T F 18. Physicians and hospitals, like other service providers, have an incentive to keep costs down.

MULTIPLE CHOICE QUESTIONS

Circle the letter that corresponds to the best answer.

1. The Lorenz curve
   a. gives a numerical measure of a nation's degree of income inequality.
   b. is a straight line in modern, industrial societies.
   c. is a straight line in socialist countries.
   d. overstates the true degree of income inequality, as it is currently measured.

2. Which of the following is *not* a correct statement about the Lorenz curve?
   a. It does not adjust for age.
   b. It does not consider income-in-kind transfers.
   c. It considers income earned in the underground economy.
   d. It considers pretax income.

3. In 1985, in the United States, the lowest 20 percent of income earning families had a combined income of about ______ percent of the total money income of the entire population.
   a. 5
   b. 10
   c. 15
   d. 20

4. Which of the following statements is *false*?
   a. The U.S. population, on average, is getting older.
   b. Technological advances in medicine have reduced health care costs.
   c. Much of health care is subsidized by governments.
   d. Most health care is paid by third parties.

*5. Analogy: Income is to flow as ________ is to stock.
   a. wealth
   b. poverty
   c. consumption
   d. investment

*6. Economic wealth
   a. is a flow concept.
   b. includes human attributes.
   c. excludes nonhuman wealth.
   d. is zero for most people in the United States.

7. In the United States the long-run trend shows
   a. increased poverty.
   b. increased income inequality.
   c. little change in measured poverty.
   d. increased poverty once income-in-kind adjustments are made.

8. In the United States, over the age-earnings cycle,
   a. productivity changes.
   b. income peaks at about age 65.
   c. income rises with age, throughout.
   d. income first falls with age, then rises with age.

9. In the United States an age-earnings cycle exists because
   a. age is unrelated to income.
   b. age and income are related by law.
   c. productivity and age are related.
   d. of minimum wage laws.

10. Which of the following is probably the *most* important determinant of income differences in the United States?
    a. differences in marginal productivity
    b. inheritance of nonhuman wealth
    c. discrimination
    d. welfare programs

11. Which is *least* like the others, with respect to productivity?
    a. innate abilities and attributes
    b. experience
    c. education and training
    d. inheritance of nonhuman wealth

12. Which of the following is *not* a normative theory of income distribution analyzed in the text?
    a. need
    b. survival of the fittest
    c. equality
    d. productivity

13. Which of the following does *not* occur with economic growth?
    a. elimination of absolute poverty
    b. elimination of relative poverty
    c. increasing living standards
    d. increasing life expectancy

14. In recent years, in the United States,
    a. health care costs have increased as a percentage of national income.
    b. the population, on average, is getting younger.
    c. technological discoveries have reduced the cost of medical care.
    d. health care costs have risen, but national income has risen more rapidly.

15. The welfare system creates
    a. incentives for those taxed to work.
    b. disincentives to welfare recipients to work.
    c. incentives for welfare recipients to increase MRP.
    d. neither incentives nor disincentives for anyone to work.

16. Which of the following could explain increased official poverty levels?
    a. effect of increased welfare programs
    b. downturn in overall business activity
    c. increase in the number of households headed by nonwhite women
    d. All of the above

17. The optimal amount of income inequality
    a. is zero.
    b. is a positive economics concept.
    c. is a normative economics concept.
    d. is agreed to by all economists.

*18. In a nation in which perfect income equality has been achieved,
    a. economic incentives would be reduced dramatically.
    b. economic freedom would be curtailed dramatically.
    c. national output and national income would fall dramatically.
    d. All of the above

MATCHING

Choose the item in column (2) that best matches an item in column (1).

(1)	(2)
a. Lorenz curve	g. equal pay for equal work
b. Gini coefficient	h. inherited traits or MRP
c. comparable worth doctrine	i. stock
d. determinant of income inequality	j. numerical representation of income inequality
e. wealth	k. flow
f. income	l. geometric measure of income distribution

WORKING WITH GRAPHS

1. Use the table below and the grid provided to construct a Lorenz curve.

Cumulative percent of population	Cumulative percent of income
20	5
40	10
60	30
80	70
100	100

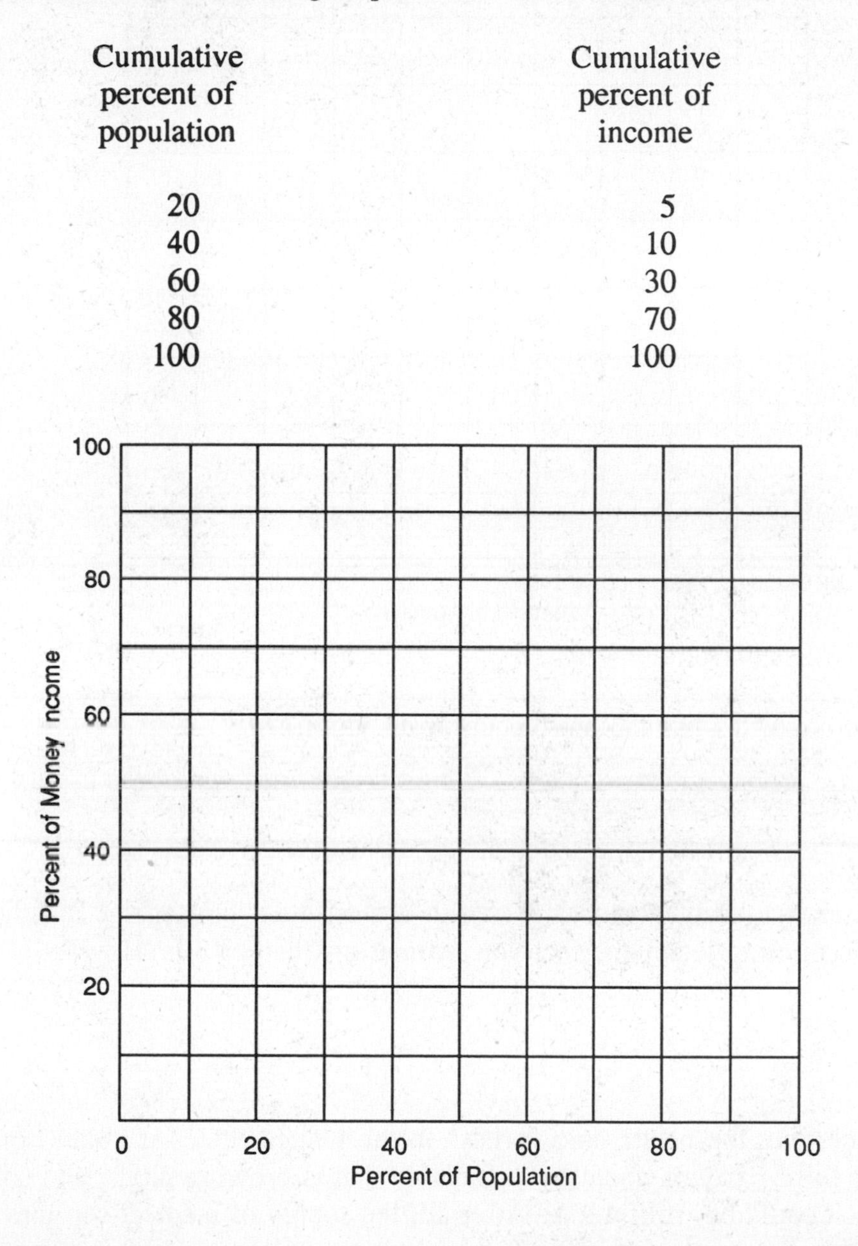

2. Below are income figures for two countries. Plot the Lorenz curve for both countries on the grid provided.

Percent of population	Percent of Income Country A	Percent of Income Country B
20	5	10
40	20	20
60	40	30
80	60	50
100	100	100

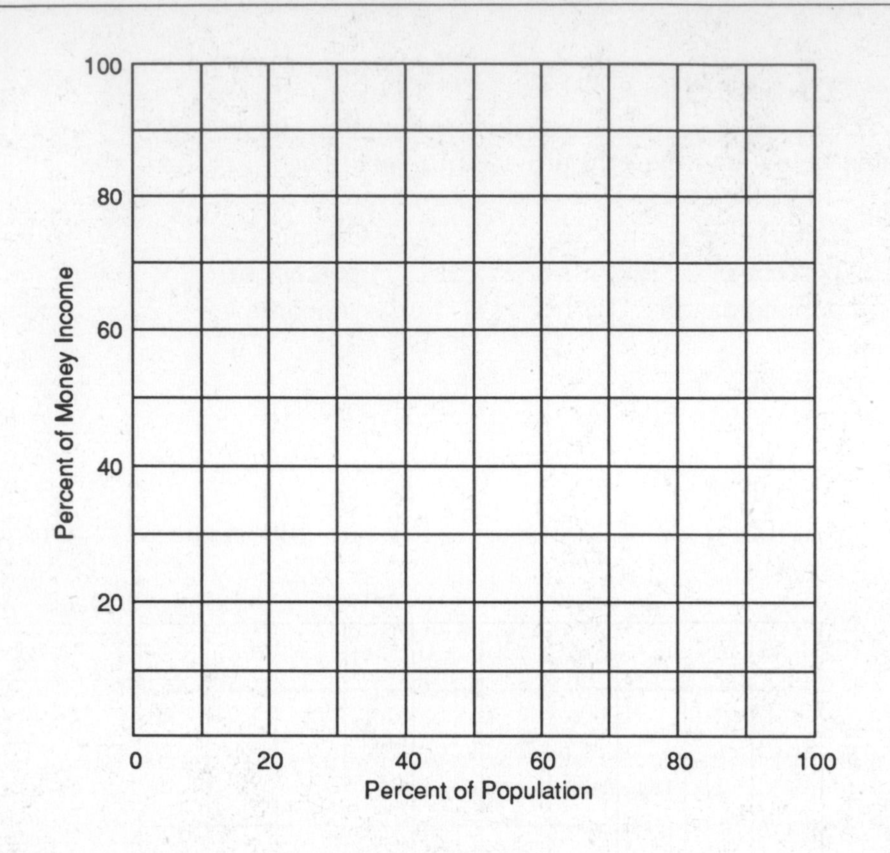

Which of the two countries has the more equal distribution?

PROBLEM

1. In your text you learned that income and wealth are different concepts. But they can be related via the discounting technique that you learned in Chapter 30. How?

CASE STUDY

Most discussion concerning the health care "crisis" in the United States is about how demand has increased--due to third-party payments, a population that is growing older, and so on. Yet, a supply-side approach could be fruitful too. After all, the supply of medical services is largely restricted. For example the number of medical schools is severely restricted and the number of students admitted to medical schools is vastly below the number of competent students who would like to attend. Additionally, a "certificate of need" is required before existing hospitals can engage in new construction--or even to add more beds to existing structures.

1. If our medical schools expanded and turned out many more physicians, what effect would this increased competition have on the costs of health care?
2. If non-physicians were allowed to perform less demanding tasks such as delivering babies and setting broken bones, what effect would this have on health care costs?
3. What would be the impact of permitting more foreign-trained physicians to immigrate to the United States?

ANSWERS TO CHAPTER 31

COMPLETION QUESTIONS

1. proportions; zero; Gini
2. include income-in-kind, differences in family size and effort, age, taxes, underground economy earnings
3. about 5; decreased
4. Wealth; income
5. low, 40-45, retirement; productivity
6. change jobs; laid off; will
7. age, innate abilities and attributes, education, experience or training; inheritance, discrimination
8. need, equality, productivity
9. Absolute, relative
10. elderly, young, rural population, households headed by women, youthful minorities, single family, senior citizens
11. Social; minimum; dependent children
12. has not
13. less economic efficiency
14. increased, older, increase, increased, little
15. ceiling; shortages

TRUE-FALSE QUESTIONS

1. T
2. F It is based on the Lorenz curve; hence it is subject to the same criticisms.
3. F Income inequality falls.
4. T
5. F The present value of income equals "human" wealth; see the problem section.
6. F It rejects MRP and substitutes an entirely different approach.
7. F It has remained constant, or fallen somewhat.
8. T
9. T
10. F Marginal productivity differences are the most important.
11. T
12. F The rate of return is about the same.
13. F Economic growth has eliminated it.
14. F Relative poverty can never be eliminated.
15. T
16. F Many believe it undesirable; almost all recognize its costs.
17. T
18. F No, such a lack of incentive is one reason costs have risen.

MULTIPLE CHOICE QUESTIONS

1.d; 2.c; 3.a; 4.b; 5.a; 6.b; 7.c; 8.a; 9.c; 10.a;
11.d; 12.b; 13.b; 14.a; 15.b; 16.d; 17.c; 18.d

MATCHING

a and l; b and j; c and g; d and h; e and i; f and k

WORKING WITH GRAPHS

1. See graph below.

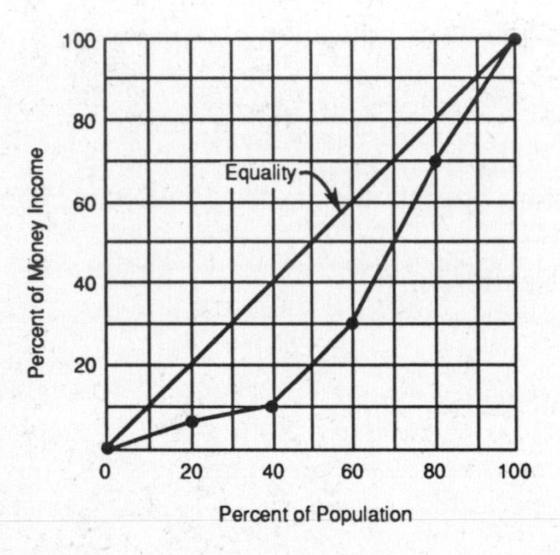

2. See graph below. Country A has a more equal distribution of income.

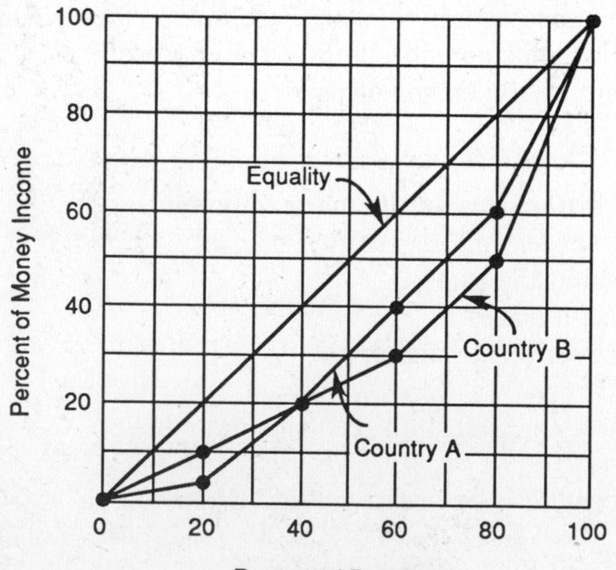

PROBLEMS

1. The value of "human" wealth can be considered as being the present value of the (net) income stream that a person earns over his or her worklife.

CASE STUDY

1. A significant increase in the number of licensed physicians will, at the very least, reduce the rate at which health care costs are rising.
2. This, too, would help to curtail the growth of medical care costs. But, physicians may not like the idea.
3. See (2) above.

GLOSSARY TO CHAPTER 31

Age-earnings cycle The regular earnings profile of an individual throughout his or her lifetime. The age-earnings cycle usually starts with a low income, builds gradually to a peak at around age 45 to 50, and then gradually curves down until it approaches zero.

Comparable worth doctrine A doctrine which contends that females should receive the same wages as males if the levels of skill and responsibility in their different jobs are equal.

Distribution of income The way income is allocated among the population. For example, a perfectly equal distribution of income would result in the lowest 20 percent of income earners receiving 20 percent of national income and the top 20 percent also receiving 20 percent of national income. The middle 60 percent of income earners would receive 60 percent of national income.

Gini coefficient of inequality A numerical representation of the degree of income inequality in a nation; defined as the ratio of the area between the diagonal line and the actual Lorenz curve to the triangular area under that diagonal line.

Income-in-kind Income that is received in the form of actual goods and services, such as housing or medical care. To be contrasted with money income, which is simply income in dollars or general purchasing power that can be used to buy any goods and services.

Lorenz curve A geometric representation of the distribution of income. A Lorenz curve that is perfectly straight represents perfect income equality. The more bowed a Lorenz curve, the more unequally income is distributed.

Third parties The buyer and seller are the first two parties; others who are a party to the transaction are called third parties.

CHAPTER 32

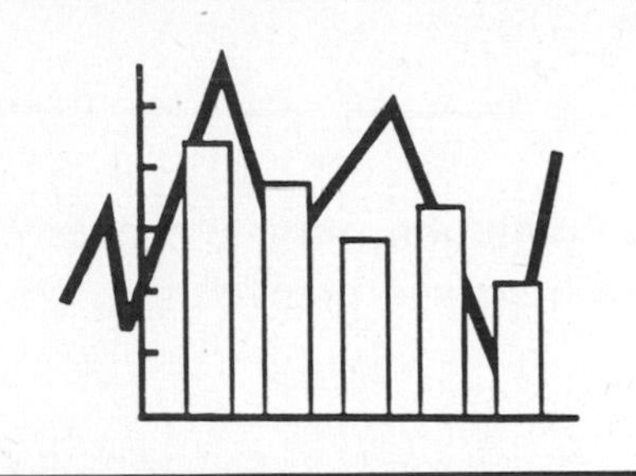

ENVIRONMENTAL ECONOMICS

PUTTING THIS CHAPTER INTO PERSPECTIVE

Chapter 32 is the last chapter in Part Four, and it provides a good opportunity to put all of Part Three and Part Four in perspective.

One of the most important concepts brought out in Chapter 32 is the notion of the socially optimum quantity of a good or service to produce. The optimum quantity, from society's point of view, occurs where the MB to society equals the MC to society; at that quantity the opportunity cost to society of the last unit produced just equals the marginal benefit society derives from it. By now you know that if the MB to society exceeds the MC to society, then society wants more; and if the MB to society is less than the MC to society, then society wants less. In short, from society's point of view, if MB does not equal MC, then a misallocation of resources (or social inefficiency) exists.

In Part Three you learned that economic agents are rational when they attempt to maximize: businesses maximize total profits and households maximize total utility. In each case the economic agent pursues an activity--either buying or selling in a product or a factor market up to the point where its private MB equals its private MC. That is, an economic agent pursues its own self-interest and is not concerned (usually) with society's well-being. A major lesson learned in Part Three is that if firms attempt to maximize total profits in perfectly competitive markets, then social efficiency results. Stated differently, when economic agents pursue their private self-interest, social efficiency results--usually.

As Part Four indicates, however, if imperfect competition exists in either the product market or the factor market, then if economic agents pursue their own self-interest, social inefficiency results. If a firm is not a perfect competitor, too little will be produced from society's--not the firm's--point of view.

In Chapter 32 you discover yet another instance in which social inefficiency results when individuals pursue their own self-interest: negative externalities. If society's MC exceeds private MC, then a negative externality (such as pollution) exists, and social inefficiency results because too much will be produced. Individuals pursue their own self-interest, but in equilibrium the MC to society exceeds the MB to society.

In this chapter you also learn about the "tragedy of the commons," alternatives to pollution-causing resource use, tradeable pollution permits for sulfer dioxide, recycling and precycling, and trade-offs among species.

LEARNING OBJECTIVES

After you have studied this chapter you should be able to

1. define private costs, social costs, externality, optimal quantity of pollution, private property rights, common property, offset policy, transactions costs, recycling, and precycling.

2. distinguish between private costs and social costs.

3. identify positive and negative externalities.

4. list three choices that businesses must make if they are charged to pollute.

5. determine the optimal quantity of pollution, when given sufficient information.

6. distinguish between private property rights and common property rights, and predict how rational economic agents behave under each.

7. list various ways to reduce pollution toward the optimal quantity.

8. recognize how to test whether or not a resource is becoming scarcer.

9. recognize the costs of saving a specific species.

CHAPTER OUTLINE

1. It is important to distinguish between private costs and social costs.
   a. *Private costs* are those incurred by individuals when they use scarce resources.
   b. *Social costs* include private costs plus the cost of actions borne by people other than those who commit the actions; social costs embody the full opportunity cost of a resource-using action.
   c. When people use resources in production or consumption, pollution may be an unwanted by-product; if so, the social costs of consuming and producing will exceed the private costs of doing so.

2. An *externality* exists when a private cost or benefit diverges from a social cost or benefit; if an externality exists, the costs or benefits of an action are not fully borne by the two parties engaged in an exchange, or by an individual using resources.

3. In theory, it is possible to change the signals in an economy so that individuals can be forced to take into account all the costs of their actions.
   a. If polluters are charged to pollute, they will (i) install abatement equipment, (ii) reduce pollution-causing activities, or (iii) pay the price to pollute.
   b. In general, charging a uniform price to pollute is inefficient because a given physical quantity of pollution has different social costs in different places.

4. Ultimately, the *optimal quantity of pollution* is a normative, not a positive, economics

concept.

a. The waste-disposing capacity of our ecosystem is a scarce resource that can be analyzed like any other resource; the marginal benefit curve for a cleaner environment declines, and the marginal cost curve for a cleaner environment rises.

b. The optimal quantity of pollution occurs where the declining marginal benefit curve intersects the rising marginal cost curve; in general the optimal quantity of pollution will exceed zero.

5. *Common property* is owned by everyone; hence private property rights, which allow the use, transfer, and exchange of property, do not exist for common property.

   a. If a resource is scarce and it is common property, it will be wasted.

   b. A resource that is scarce, but is not common property, can be used efficiently under certain conditions.

   c. Externalities can be internalized via voluntary contracting even when property rights do not exist:

      i. if the transactions costs associated with making, reaching, and enforcing agreements are low relative to the expected benefits of reaching an agreement.

      ii. if the number of individuals involved is small.

   d. Private property rights can be assigned (through governments), so that an externality can be internalized.

   e. In summary there are three ways to fill the private/social costs gap: taxation, subsidization, and regulation.

   f. If the rights to pollute are bought and sold on markets, it is possible to move toward the optimal quantity of pollution; the EPA has approved such an offset policy.

   g. An alternative to an offset policy is a system of pollution credits; companies that pollute below set standards earn credits which can be sold to other companies or to environmentalists who want an even cleaner environment.

6. It is not likely that producers and consumers voluntarily will reduce pollution-creating activities, because those individuals that do so are placed at a competitive disadvantage.

7. Recycling and precycling have the potential to save scarce resources and reduce pollution; unfortunately the existing state of the art is such that these processes are costly, and themselves create pollution.

8. The fact that the price of landfills is falling implies that the U.S. is not "running out" of landfills; in fact, the prices of *most* resources have been falling, which means that, in general, the resource base is getting larger!

9. Unfortunately, every attempt to protect one species endangers that species that is the main food supply of the protected species; a trade-off exists in species protection.

KEY TERMS

Private costs
Social costs
Transactions costs
Private property rights
Common property
Offset policy

KEY CONCEPTS

Externalities
Negative externality
Species tradeoff
Optimal quantity of pollution
Pollution credits

COMPLETION QUESTIONS

Fill in the blank or circle the correct term.

1. Costs incurred by individuals when they use scarce resources are called ________________ costs; ________________ costs include private costs and represent the full cost that society bears when a resource-using action occurs.

2. When we add external costs to internal costs, we get ____________ costs; an externality exists if there is a divergence between ________________________ and ________________________.

3. In theory, decision makers can be made to take into account all of the costs of their actions if people who impose costs on others are (taxed, subsidized).

4. If polluters are charged to pollute, they have the following three options: ________________________, ________________________, and ________________________.

5. A uniform tax on polluters will not be economically efficient if a given physical quantity of pollution imposes different ______________________ costs in different places.

6. As more and more pollution is reduced, then the marginal benefit (falls, rises) and the marginal cost ______________; the optimal quantity of pollution occurs where ______________.

7. If at a zero price the quantity demanded of a resource ___________ its quantity supplied, that resource is scarce; if a scarce resource is common property, it probably (will, will not) be wasted.

8. If there is a gap between private costs and social costs, that gap can be filled if polluters are __________________, if those damaged by pollution are __________________, and/or if the government __________________ industry pollution.

9. If a businessperson/environmentalist treats pollution voluntarily, he or she will be at a competitive (advantage, disadvantage) in the marketplace.

10. Externalities can be internalized if ___________ costs are low and if the number of parties involved is (small, large).

11. Recycling and precycling, in theory, can save scarce resources; however they are very ________________ and themselves create ________________.

12. Many people feel that the world is running out of resources; the evidence is that the inflation-adjusted price of most resources has (fallen, increased) historically.

13. Attempts to protect a specific species usually involve a ________________.

TRUE-FALSE QUESTIONS

Circle the **T** if the statement is true, the **F** if it is false. Explain to yourself why a statement is false.

T F 1. Social costs do not include private costs.

T F 2. Private costs do not include external costs.

T F 3. If social costs exceed private costs, too much of the good will be produced.

T F 4. Pollution is an example of a negative externality.

T F 5. The optimal quantity of pollution is zero.

T F 6. Air pollution is a problem because air is common property.

T F 7. A given quantity of physical pollution causes the same amount of economic damage everywhere.

T F 8. If polluters are charged to pollute, we may end up with less pollution.

T F 9. If a specific firm pays to reduce its output of pollution, it may be at a competitive disadvantage.

T F 10. If private property rights don't exist, the private sector cannot internalize negative externalities.

T F 11. Externalities can be internalized if the government assigns private property rights.

T F 12. Pollution credits, in effect, allow some companies to sell pollution rights to other companies.

T F 13. Attempts to protect one species may well endanger another species.

T F 14. Recycling is always a good idea.

T F 15. The inflation-adjusted price of most resources has fallen, historically.

MULTIPLE CHOICE QUESTIONS

Circle the letter that corresponds to the best answer.

1. Social costs
   a. exclude internal costs.
   b. exclude external costs.
   c. exclude both internal and external costs.
   d. include both internal and external costs.

2. Air pollution
   a. is an internal cost to firms.
   b. is an external cost to firms.
   c. exists because air is a privately owned resource.
   d. has the same costs to society everywhere.

*3. A misallocation of resources may result if
   a. social costs exceed private costs.
   b. social benefits exceed private benefits.
   c. a scarce resource is communally owned.
   d. All of the above

4. If polluters are charged to pollute, then
   a. pollution will disappear.
   b. the environment will be damaged severely.
   c. less pollution is a probable result.
   d. less voluntary pollution abatement will result.

5. Which of the following will *not* help to reduce the problem that exists if social costs exceed social benefits?
   a. subsidize polluters
   b. subsidize parties damaged by pollution
   c. charge polluters to pollute
   d. internalize external costs

6. If polluters are charged to pollute, efficiency requires that
   a. they be charged according to the economic damages they create.
   b. they be charged the same amount.
   c. they be charged according to the physical quantity of pollution they generate.
   d. nonpolluters be charged also.

7. The optimal quantity of pollution exists at that level of pollution at which, for pollution abatement, a
   a. rising marginal benefit equals a falling marginal cost.
   b. rising marginal cost equals a falling marginal benefit.
   c. constant marginal cost equals a falling marginal benefit.
   d. constant marginal benefit equals a rising marginal cost.

8. Externalities can be internalized by the private sector if
   a. transactions costs of doing so are low.
   b. benefits of doing so are high.
   c. the number of people involved is small.
   d. All of the above

9. Which statement is *not* true?
   a. Recycling can be costly and can add to pollution.
   b. Attempts to protect one species often harm another.
   c. The evidence is that most natural resources are becoming scarcer.
   d. The inflation-adjusted price of landfills has been falling in the U.S.

10. Recycling and precycling
    a. may save resources.
    b. are very costly.
    c. can create their own pollution problems.
    d. All of the above

WORKING WITH GRAPHS

1. Use the graphs below to answer the questions that follow. Note that D represents the private demand curve, and that DS represents the demand curve that incorporates the benefits received by third parties as well as the buyers in the original transactions. Assume that no negative externalities exist.

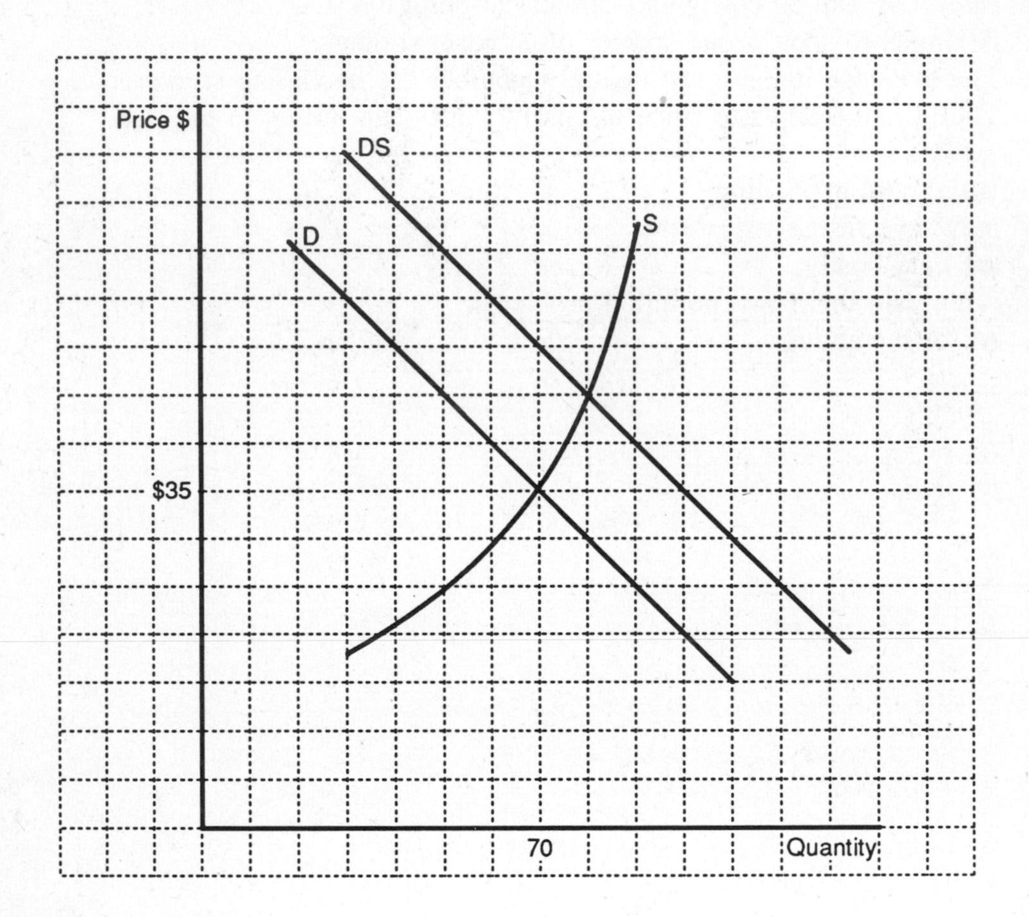

   a. Which curve reflects the marginal benefits to private buyers?

   b. Which curve reflects the marginal benefits to society (which includes third parties)?

   c. Which curve reflects the marginal private costs and the marginal social costs of producing the good in question?

   d. How many units of this good will be provided by the private sector? At that quantity, what is the marginal benefit to society? the marginal cost to society?

   e. What is the optimal quantity of this good, from society's point of view? Why?

2. Use the graphs below to answer the questions that follow. Note that S represents the industry supply curve and SS represents the marginal costs to society--which include marginal private costs and negative externalities. Assume that no positive externalities exist.

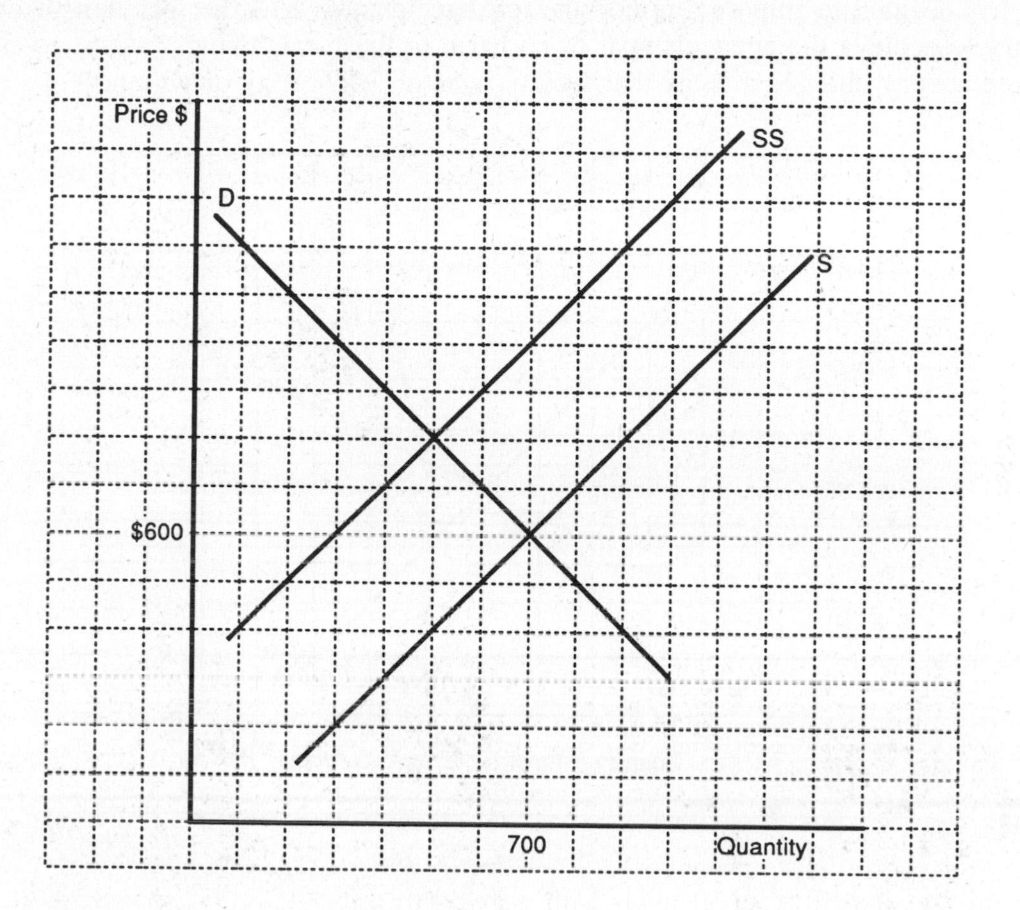

a. Which curve represents the marginal private costs of producing the good in question?

b. Which curve reflects the marginal social costs of producing this good?

c. Which curve represents both the marginal private benefits and the marginal social benefits of this good?

d. How many units of this good will be produced by the private sector? What is the value of the marginal social cost of that quantity? the value of the marginal social benefits?

e. What is the optimal quantity of this good, from society's point of view? Why?

3. Suppose you are given the following graph for the demand and supply of fertilizer per week. As a by-product of fertilizer production, the fertilizer plant dumps harmful chemicals into local streams. A local agency has determined that if fertilizer production were limited to 2 tons per week, the local streams would be able to handle the by-products without harm. The agency has decided to impose a tax on the fertilizer plant. What tax per unit of output is necessary to achieve the agency's goal of no harm to the local streams? Can we conclude that if the agency charges this tax that society is better off? Why or why not?

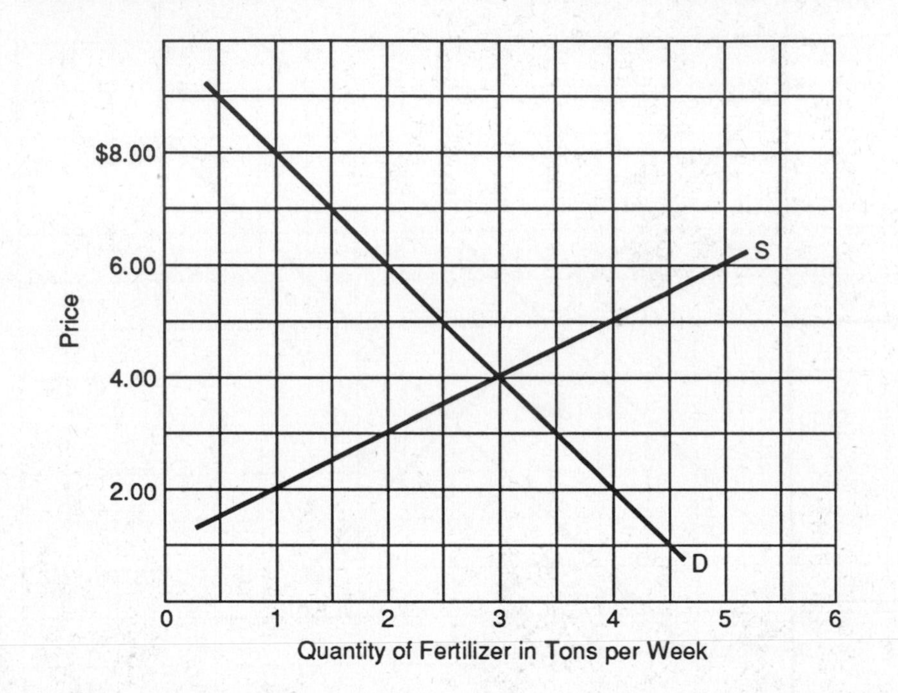

PROBLEMS

*1. Suppose you live in a small town with a privately owned solid-waste disposal facility (garbage dump) just west of town that services a larger city about 30 miles away. Because of the prevailing westerly wind, your town suffers from an unpleasant odor generated at the dump. The more garbage that arrives at the dump in a given week, the more unpleasant the odor. A study is undertaken, and the results are partially summarized in the table that follows.

(1) Garbage processed in tons per week	(2) Dump's marginal cost	(3) Consumers' valuation of disposal services	(4) External costs due to odor	(5) Marginal social cost
5	$4.00	$8.00	$0.00	$4.00
10	4.25	7.60	0.20	4.45
15	4.50	6.60	0.50	5.00
20	4.80	5.80	1.00	______
25	5.20	5.20	1.75	______
30	5.80	4.80	2.75	______

Column 1 represents the quantity of garbage disposed of at the dump in tons per week.

Column 2 is the private marginal cost of disposing of various quantities of garbage--the supply of disposal services.

Column 3 represents the demand (willingness to pay) for various quantities of garbage disposal by the consumers of the service in the city to the west.

Column 4 is the external costs that are imposed on residents in your town by the dumping of various quantities of garbage.

Column 5 is the marginal social cost of the dumping services, which includes both private and external costs.

a. Under present conditions, with the disposal plant ignoring external cost, what is the equilibrium price and quantity of disposal services in the market?

b. Complete column 5.

c. Using your answers from a and b, can you tell what is happening in this market at the present?

d. If the disposal plant were forced to internalize all the relevant costs of operation, what would be the equilibrium price and quantity in this market?

CASE STUDY

Dan Dudek, an economist who works for the Environmental Defense Fund, has suggested extending the domestic pollution credits idea to the global economy. As you are probably aware by now, many (but certainly not all) scientists believe that the world will soon experience ill-effects from the "Greenhouse effect"; carbon gases (and other sources) buildup is believed to be causing the world to become warmer.

Fossil fuel burning and land use conversion distribute carbon into the atmosphere, and oceans and plant life absorb carbon; some believe that the first two now outweigh the last two, hence the net effect is carbon buildup.

Some agency can be empowered to issue pollution credits to nations, and credits can be *given* to nations that preserve their forest lands. Thus, tropical rain forest countries in Central and South America can be given credits, which they can then sell. A lively market will develop and the total number of credits issued can change as the Greenhouse effect becomes more or less serious.

1. What will determine the price of such carbon polluting credits?

2. How does this scheme eliminate, at once, both positive and negative externalities?

ANSWERS TO CHAPTER 32

COMPLETION QUESTIONS

1. private; social
2. social; social costs and private costs or social benefits and private benefits.
3. taxed
4. install pollution abatement equipment, reduce pollution-causing activity, pay the price to pollute
5. social
6. falls, rises; MB = MC of pollution reduction
7. exceeds; will
8. taxed, subsidized, regulates
9. disadvantage
10. transactions, small
11. expensive, pollution
12. fallen
13. tradeoff

TRUE-FALSE QUESTIONS

1. F They are the sum of private costs and negative externalities (if any).
2. T
3. T
4. T
5. F It is a positive amount, because it costs society resources to have a cleaner environment.
6. T
7. F The next unit of air pollution causes more economic damage in New York City than it does in a small town in Arizona.
8. T
9. T
10. F The private sector, throughout history, has sometimes been able to do so, when transactions costs are low.
11. T
12. T
13. T
14. F Sometimes recycling is too costly, or it creates pollution itself.
15. T

MULTIPLE CHOICE QUESTIONS

1.d; 2.b; 3.d; 4.c; 5.a; 6.a; 7.b; 8.d; 9.c; 10.d

WORKING WITH GRAPHS

1. a. curve D
   b. curve DS

c. curve S
d. 70; $50; $35
e. 80; that is where the MB to society equals the MC to society

2. a. curve S
b. curve SS
c. curve D
d. 700; $1000; $600
e. 500; that is where the MB to society equals the MC to society

3. $3 per ton of fertilizer; No. We are given no information about how much society values unharmed streams in the area, so we are not justified in concluding that the tax has made society better off.

PROBLEMS

1. a. $5.20, 25 tons per week
b. Marginal social cost: $5.80, $6.95, $8.55
c. With the external costs being ignored, the disposal plants' marginal cost at the equilibrium level is below the true marginal social cost
d. 5.80, 20 tons per week

CASE STUDY

1. Supply and demand conditions; for example, if the Greenhouse effect worsens fewer credits will be issued, such credits will be scarcer, and their price will rise.

2. Positive externalities are eliminated when countries that preserve their rain forests are given saleable pollution credits; negative externalities are eliminated when polluting countries are forced to buy credits.

GLOSSARY TO CHAPTER 32

Common property Property that is owned by everyone and therefore owned by no one. Examples of common property resources which have historically been owned in common are air and water.

External benefit A benefit received by a third party for which no specific payment was made. You receive an external benefit from well-manicured lawns when you drive by them. Your pleasure or benefit may have been external to the decision-making process of the person who mowed the lawn or had it mowed.

Offset policy A policy requiring one company wishing to build a plant that would pollute to work out an offsetting reduction in pollution at some other plant in a specific geographical area.

Optimal quantity of pollution That level of pollution for which the marginal benefit of one additional unit of clean air just equals the marginal cost of that one additional unit of clean air.

Private costs Those costs incurred by individuals when they use scarce resources. For example, the private cost of running an automobile is equal to the gas, oil, insurance, maintenance, and depreciation costs. Also called internal costs.

Private property rights Exclusive rights of ownership which allow the use, transfer, and exchange of property.

Recycling The reuse of raw materials from used manufactured products.

Social costs The full cost that society bears when a resource-using action occurs. For example, the social cost of driving a car is equal to all of the private costs plus any additional cost that society bears, including air pollution and traffic congestion.

Transactions costs All costs associated with making, reaching, and enforcing agreements.

CHAPTER 33

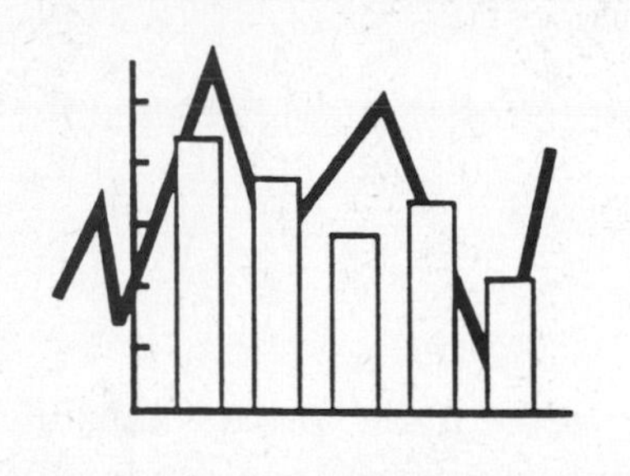

COMPARATIVE ADVANTAGE AND THE OPEN ECONOMY

PUTTING THIS CHAPTER INTO PERSPECTIVE

Chapter 33 is the first chapter in Part Five, and the first of two chapters dealing with international trade. International trade and finance have always been important topics in economics, and they have become increasingly important over the past ten years. The percentage of GDP due to exports has increased, our international trade deficit has been an increasing "problem," our nation and many of our trading partners seem to be moving toward "protection from foreign competition," and monetary policy and fiscal policy have become increasingly difficult as recent technological innovations in communications and computers have made the countries of the world more interdependent. For these and other reasons analyzed in Part Five, it is important for you to understand the principles that underlie international trade and finance.

The most important goal of Chapter 33 is to demonstrate how voluntary trade between nations is based on comparative advantage. Each nation specializes in the production of those goods for which it has a comparative advantage, which means that it produces those goods with the lowest opportunity costs. As a result, world economic growth is fostered and world living standards, with minor short-run exceptions, rise.

You are encouraged to master the derivation of a nation's export supply curve and its import demand curve. The crucial thing that section indicates is that a nation, potentially, can produce *any* good--at sufficiently high prices. What a nation does, however, is specialize in the production, for domestic consumption and export, of those goods that it can produce relatively cheaply. And it imports those goods that can be produced more cheaply elsewhere. In short, each nation specializes in the production of those goods for which it has a comparative advantage. It might help you to understand this point if you realize that this is just what people *within* a nation also do. This is, specialization and trade among nations arise for precisely the same reason that specialization and trade occur among individuals.

Another objective of Chapter 33 is to expose some myths concerning international trade. Many people are induced to favor import restrictions because they believe that imports take jobs away from domestic workers. The truth is that import restrictions merely help save some workers' jobs at the expense of others, and as a by-product consumers must pay higher prices.

Chapter 33 also analyzes several methods by which nations restrict foreign trade. It is a source of wonderment that the one issue on which nearly all economists agree--that free trade is advantageous--is the same issue on which nearly all non-economists seem to disagree. We don't insist that others agree with us; we merely ask that you try to understand our reasoning. We hope that your text and this Student Guide will help you do so.

LEARNING OBJECTIVES

After you have studied this chapter you should be able to

1. define excess demand schedule, excess supply schedule, zero trade price, absolute advantage, comparative advantage, quota, dumping, intra-industry international trade, and bilateral trade.

2. list three ways in which a nation pays for its imports.

3. distinguish between absolute advantage and comparative advantage and determine each for nations, giving sufficient information.

4. answer questions that indicate knowledge of how an excess demand schedule and an excess supply schedule are derived.

5. recognize the international equilibrium price and quantity for a two-nation economy in which trade takes place, given sufficient information.

6. relate comparative advantage to opportunity cost.

7. list two reasons why trade arises between nations.

8. list two potential costs of international trade.

9. identify the pros and cons of arguments against free trade among nations.

10. contrast and compare the results of import quotas and tariffs.

11. enumerate and recognize arguments against the notion that restricting imports saves domestic jobs.

CHAPTER OUTLINE

1. The proportion of GDP accounted for by trade for individual nations varies greatly, but if trade were curtailed, even such nations as the United States (which have relatively low proportions) would be affected significantly.
   a. A nation pays for its imports by exports, by sales of real or financial assets, or through an extension of credit from other nations; thus restrictions on imports ultimately reduce exports.
   b. If trade is voluntary, then both nations participating in an exchange benefit.

2. A nation has an *absolute advantage* in the production of good A if it can produce more units of good A than other nations can, from a given quantity of inputs; a nation has a *comparative advantage* in producing good A if, out of all the goods it can produce, good

A has the lowest opportunity cost.

3. Opportunity costs, and hence comparative advantages, differ among nations.
   a. Because different nations have different resource bases, they have a comparative advantage in producing different goods.
   b. Because people in different nations have different collective tastes, they will have different comparative advantages if production economies exist.
   c. If nations engage in trade, they also incur costs, because over time a nation's comparative advantage changes and short-run dislocations arise; another cost is that each nation becomes more dependent on its trading partners.

4. Economies of scale and differentiated products help to solve the puzzle of intra-industry international trade.

5. We develop a single two-nation world economy to indicate international equilibrium price and equilibrium quantity for a traded good.
   a. A nation's excess *demand schedule* for a good is derived by calculating all the excess demand quantities (below that nation's equilibrium price) that exist.
   b. This excess demand schedule can be thought of as an import demand schedule for that nation; what domestic buyers can't purchase at such prices can potentially be bought from foreign countries.

6. In a two country model, international trade equilibrium for a good occurs where one nation's excess demand for imports curve intersects the other nation's excess supply for exports curve; at the world price at which such an intersection occurs, the quantity of exports supplied equals the quantity of imports demanded.

7. There are numerous arguments that have been presented as being anti-free trade. Such arguments include the *infant industry argument*, protecting a way of life, stability, protecting domestic jobs, and countering foreign subsidies and dumping. Some of these arguments are simply wrong, and others emphasize costs to the neglect of benefits. In recent years the economic security argument has replaced the national security rationalization for protection.

8. There are numerous methods that nations have used to restrict foreign trade.
   a. Some nations place *import quotas* on foreign goods.
   b. Some nations place taxes or *tariffs* on foreign goods.
   c. Both quotas and tariffs raise prices to domestic consumers and reduce the quantity of goods traded; a tariff, however, generates revenues to the government, while a quota does not.

9. Regional trade agreements have generated bilateral trade, which also interferes with free trade; such agreements distort trade patterns and are therefore inefficient.

KEY TERMS

Excess demand schedule
Excess supply schedule
Zero trade price
Infant industry argument
Tariff
Quota system
Intra-industry trade
Bilateral trade

KEY CONCEPTS

Comparative advantage
Absolute advantage
Dumping
Free trade

COMPLETION QUESTIONS

Fill in the blank or circle the correct term.

1. A nation pays for imports by ________________, or by selling ________________, or through an extension of ________________ from other countries.

*2. If world trade ceased to exist, all trade-related jobs (would, would not) be lost in the long run; instead nations would simply ________________. Nevertheless, worldwide living standards would (fall, rise) significantly.

3. In the domestic market, at all prices above equilibrium, an excess ______________ exists; the quantities offered for sale by domestic producers at prices above the domestic equilibrium price represent an (export, import) supply curve for the domestic industry above those quantities purchased by domestic residents.

4. In the domestic market, at all prices below equilibrium, an excess ______________ exists; the quantities demanded by domestic residents at prices below the domestic equilibrium price represent an (export, import) demand schedule for domestic residents above those quantities offered for sale by domestic producers.

5. In a two country world with international trade for good A, equilibrium exists where one nation's excess supply schedule for (imports, exports) intersects the other country's excess demand schedule for ________________. At that equilibrium price, the quantity of world ________________ of A equals the quantity of world ________________ of A.

6. International trade permits each nation to specialize in the production of those goods for which it has a(n) ________________ advantage; each nation specializes in the production of goods for which its opportunity costs are the (lowest, highest).

*7. Nations have an incentive to specialize and trade because they have different collective tastes and because different nations will always have different ________________ costs to producing goods.

8. Traditional comparative advantage (does, does not) explain intra-industry international

trade; such trade, if tastes vary widely and economies of scale exist, permit different nations to specialize and trade (differentiated, identical) products.

9. There are numerous arguments against free trade; they include the ______________ industry argument, the argument that trade leads to (increased, decreased) stability as comparative advantage changes with technological changes and changes in taste, and the argument that restrictions on imports ______________ domestic trade; a recent argument is to protect (national, economic) security.

10. Two ways to restrict foreign trade analyzed in the text are ______________ on imports and ______________ on imported goods.

11. Most restrictions on international trade have one major element in common: they interfere with nations' specializing in the production of goods for which they have a ______________ advantage. Therefore they are economically (inefficient, efficient).

12. Because a nation mostly pays for imports with its ______________, restricting imports to save jobs destroys jobs in the ______________ sector of the economy; hence, on net, import restrictions (do, do not) save jobs.

TRUE-FALSE QUESTIONS

Circle the **T** if the statement is true, the **F** if it is false. Explain to yourself why a statement is false.

T F 1. If all world trade ceased, import sector jobs and export sector jobs would be permanently destroyed.

T F *2. Because international trade is voluntary in the private sector, both nations benefit from trade that is continued.

T F 3. Imports are paid for by exports, or by domestic sales of real or financial assets, or by an extension of credit by other countries.

T F 4. Output quantities produced by domestic producers at prices below the domestic equilibrium price are used for exports.

T F 5. Some of the output quantities produced by domestic producers at prices above equilibrium are available for exports.

T F 6. International equilibrium in a two-world economy exists at that price where one nation's import demand schedule intersects the other nation's export supply schedule.

T F 7. If the world price for a good is below country A's domestic equilibrium price, then country A will import that good.

T F 8. If the world price for a good is above country A's domestic equilibrium price, then country A will export that good.

T F *9. In a two-country world, it is possible for both countries to have a comparative advantage in the production of a specific (undifferentiated) good.

T F 10. If the United States has a comparative advantage in producing wheat, it must be true that the opportunity cost for producing wheat in the United States is below the opportunity cost of the other goods it produces.

T F *11. Because in the real world nations have different resource endowments and different collective tastes, trade will always be advantageous.

T F 12. It is easy to determine the industries to which the infant industry argument applies.

T F 13. If a nation imposes anti-dumping laws, its consumers will pay lower prices for goods.

T F *14. Free trade increases a nation's instability in the short run, because over time a nation's comparative advantage can change.

T F *15. When a nation restricts imports to protect jobs it, in effect, preserves less productive employment at the expense of more productive employment.

T F 16. One difference between the economic effects of quotas vs. tariffs is that tariffs lead to a higher price to consumers but quotas do not.

T F 17. Tariffs increase government revenues, but import quotas do not.

T F 18. Bilateral trade is a form of protectionism.

MULTIPLE CHOICE QUESTIONS

Circle the letter that corresponds to the best answer.

1. A nation pays for its imports by
   a. exporting.
   b. buying real and financial assets from the exporting nation.
   c. extending credit to the exporting nation.
   d. All of the above

2. The U.S. ratio of imports to GDP is about _______ percent.
   a. 7
   b. 9
   c. 13
   d. 15

*3. If trade between two nations is voluntary and continued, then

a. both nations benefit.
b. one nation could benefit more than the other.
c. living standards are higher in both nations than if trade were not permitted.
d. All of the above

4. At a price above the domestic equilibrium price for good A
   a. a nation will want to import goods from another country.
   b a nation will have an excess quantity demanded.
   c. a nation will be willing to export some of the output of good A.
   d. a shortage exists for good A in that country.

5. If the world price is below country B's equilibrium price for oranges, then
   a. country B will have oranges to export.
   b. country B will want to import oranges.
   c. country B has a comparative advantage in producing oranges.
   d. orange producers in country B won't be able to sell any oranges in country B.

6. Country B's excess supply curve for wheat
   a. lies above its domestic equilibrium price for wheat.
   b. indicates quantities it is prepared to import at various prices.
   c. is found at international equilibrium.
   d. can be thought of as an import demand curve.

7. Country A's excess demand curve for oranges
   a. can be thought of as its import demand curve.
   b. lies below its domestic equilibrium price for oranges.
   c. indicates quantities it is prepared to import at various prices.
   d. All of the above

8. In a two-country world in which only wheat and oranges are traded, in international equilibrium,
   a. the quantity of oranges traded equals the quantity of wheat traded.
   b. the quantity of wheat exported equals the quantity of wheat imported.
   c. both countries have a comparative advantage in wheat and orange production.
   d. each country produces that good which maximizes its opportunity cost of production.

9. In a two-country world, if good A is traded, then in international equilibrium,
   a. the quantity of good A exported equals the quantity of good A imported.
   b. one country's excess demand schedule for imports intersects the other's excess supply schedule for exports.
   c. one world price for good A is established.
   d. All of the above

10. Country A can produce both wheat and oranges using fewer resources than country B. Which of the following statements if true?
    a. Country A has a comparative advantage in producing both goods.
    b. Country A has an absolute advantage in producing both goods.
    c. Country B has no comparative advantage.
    d. Country B must have an absolute advantage in producing one of the goods.

11. If Country C has a comparative advantage in producing wheat, then its opportunity cost of producing wheat
    a. is maximized.
    b. equals the opportunity cost of producing other goods.
    c. cannot be determined.
    d. is lowest among its trading partners.

*12. Nations find it advantageous to trade because they
    a. have different resource endowments.
    b. have different collective tastes.
    c. have different comparative advantages.
    d. All of the above

*13. Which of the following is *not* an argument used against free trade?
    a. Free trade makes nations more interdependent.
    b. Free trade causes instability in a nation because a nation's comparative advantage changes over time.
    c. Free trade increases average and total worldwide incomes.
    d. Imports destroy domestic jobs.

14. Which of the following is most *unlike* the others?
    a. import quota
    b. tariff
    c. free trade
    d. anti-dumping laws

15. Concerning import quotas and tariffs, which of the following statements is true?
    a. Both lead to lower prices for consumers.
    b. Both lead to more imports.
    c. Tariffs lead to higher prices, but quotas do not.
    d. Tariffs generate government revenues, but import quotas do not.

*16. Which statement is *not* true, concerning the use of import restrictions to save jobs?
    a. The cost to consumers often exceeds the value of the jobs saved.
    b. Some jobs are destroyed in the export sector.
    c. In the long run they do not save jobs in those industries in which a nation has lost its comparative advantage.
    d. They are the most efficient way to help domestic workers threatened by foreign competition.

MATCHING

Choose the item in column (2) that best matches an item in column (1).

(1)	(2)
a. anti-dumping law	i. domestic equilibrium price
b. tariff	j. minimum opportunity cost of production
c. comparative advantage	k. trade restriction
d. absolute advantage	l. trade distortion
e. bilateral trade	m. tax on foreign-produced goods
f. zero trade price	n. producing at a lower cost
g. excess demand schedule	o. potential export schedule
h. excess supply schedule	p. potential import schedule

WORKING WITH GRAPHS

1. Suppose that you are given the following information on the markets for fertilizer in the United States and Canada. The price of fertilizer in each country is in dollars per 100 pounds. The quantities are given in hundreds of tons per year.

U.S. Fertilizer Market

Price	Quantity demanded	Quantity supplied	Excess demand	Excess supply
$ 5.00	20.0	7.5	____	____
6.00	18.0	8.0	____	____
7.00	16.0	8.5	____	____
8.00	14.0	9.0	____	____
9.00	12.0	9.5	____	____
10.00	10.0	10.0	____	____
11.00	8.0	10.5	____	____
12.00	6.0	11.0	____	____
13.00	4.0	11.5	____	____
14.00	2.0	12.0	____	____
15.00	0.0	12.5	____	____

Canadian Fertilizer Market

Price	Quantity demanded	Quantity supplied	Excess demand	Excess supply
$ 9.00	31.5	19.0	_____	_____
10.00	30.0	20.0	_____	_____
11.00	28.5	21.0	_____	_____
12.00	27.0	22.0	_____	_____
13.00	25.5	23.0	_____	_____
14.00	24.0	24.0	_____	_____
15.00	22.5	25.0	_____	_____
16.00	21.0	26.0	_____	_____
17.00	19.5	27.0	_____	_____
18.00	18.0	28.0	_____	_____
19.00	16.5	29.0	_____	_____

a. Fill in the columns labeled Excess demand and Excess supply for each country. Whenever excess demand is present leave the excess supply column blank. Use the same procedure for excess supply.

b. What is the zero trade price for each country?

c. Graph the demand and supply curves for fertilizer in each country in the grids provided.

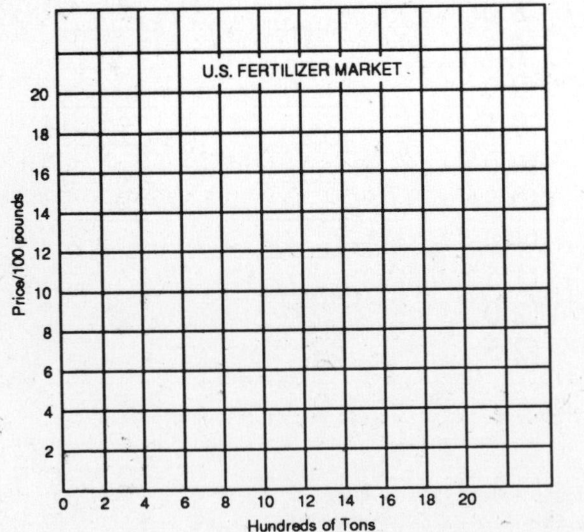

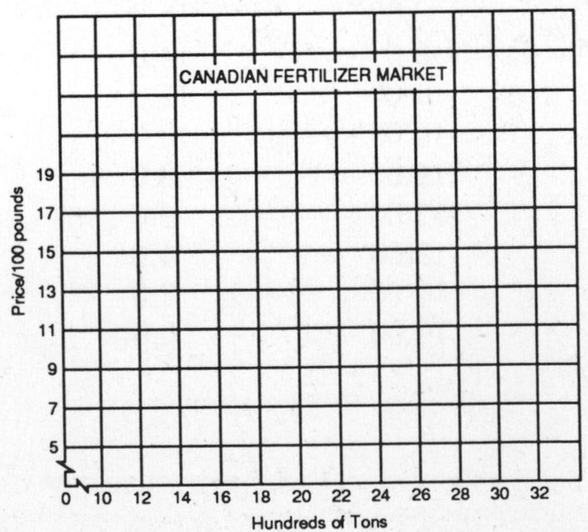

d. Graph the excess demand and supply curves for each country in the grid provided below.

EXCESS DEMAND AND EXCESS SUPPLY

Price/100 pounds: 2, 4, 6, 8, 10, 12, 14, 16, 18, 20

Hundreds of Tons: 2, 4, 6, 8, 10, 12, 14, 16

e. From your answer in part d, we see that the world equilibrium price of fertilizer will be $________ per 100 pounds. The United States will (import, export) ________ hundred tons per year and Canada will (import, export) ________ hundred tons per year.

PROBLEMS

1. Suppose that Germany and the United States are both fully employed and can produce the following amounts of wine and beer per week. Use this information to answer the following questions.

	Wine (gallons)	Beer (gallons)
Germany	600	1200
United States	400	1600

a. Germany has a comparative advantage in the production of ______________, whereas the United States has a comparative advantage in the production of ______________.

b. What is the cost of wine in terms of beer in Germany? What is the cost of wine in terms of beer in the United States?

*2. Let us assume we are again in a two-country world, with the countries being Germany and the United States. Again, to simplify, let us assume that there are only two goods produced, coal and steel. In the table that follows, you will find the production possibilities of both countries. Assume that each country is currently operating at combination B on its production possibilities schedule. Use this information to answer the following questions. (Hint: Remember that movements along production possibilities curves involve opportunity costs and that comparative advantage and trade depend on opportunity costs.) Entries are in thousands of tons per week.

		A	B	C	D
Germany:	Coal	0	24	48	72
	Steel	18	12	6	0
United States:	Coal	0	36	72	108
	Steel	36	24	12	0

a. Which country has an absolute advantage in the production of coal? ________________ steel? ________________

b. Which country has a comparative advantage in the production of coal? ________________ steel? ________________

c. What is the cost of coal in terms of steel in Germany? ______________ What is the cost of coal in terms of steel in the United States? ______________

(Remember that these are opportunity costs as determined by production possibilities.)

d. What is the current world production of coal and steel? ________________

e. If both countries specialize in the production of goods in which they have a comparative advantage, Germany will produce ________ thousand tons of ______________, the United States will produce ________ thousand tons of ______________, and the world output of coal will increase by ________ thousand tons.

CASE STUDY

As the mid 1990's get under way more and more people are calling for restrictions on free trade. Perhaps they have forgotten the studies conducted in the late 1980's concerning the costs to consumers of protectionism. Robert W. Crandall of the Brookings Institution investigated the cost of "saving" U.S. jobs in the automobile industry. He estimated that import restrictions raised the price of U.S.-produced cars by about $400 per car, and of Japanese-produced cars by about $1000 per car; the total cost to the U.S. consumer was about $4.3 billion. He then estimates that about 26,000 jobs were saved (ignoring the jobs lost in the U.S. export sector). In effect, U.S. consumers could have *given* $80,000 to each unemployed worker to not work and still have been able to save over $2 billion in lower-priced autos.

1. In light of Crandall's findings, why haven't import restrictions been removed?

2. Does it follow from Crandall's findings that import quotas *should* be removed?

ANSWERS TO CHAPTER 33

COMPLETION QUESTIONS

1. exporting, real and financial assets, credit
2. would not; produce the goods themselves; fall
3. supply; export
4. demand; import
5. exports, imports; imports, exports
6. comparative; lowest
7. opportunity
8. does not; differentiated
9. infant, decreased, protect; economic
10. quotas, tariffs
11. comparative; inefficient
12. exports, export; do not

TRUE-FALSE QUESTIONS

1. F Eventually each nation will produce its own goods--but at a higher cost and (perhaps) lower quality.
2. T
3. T
4. F Output produced at prices *above* equilibrium price are potentially exportable goods.
5. T
6. T
7. T
8. T
9. F Not for a *specific* good; they might each trade *differentiated* goods.
10. T
11. T
12. F In practice it is difficult to predict which industries will eventually be successful without aid.
13. F Consumers will pay higher prices.
14. T
15. T
16. F Both lead to higher prices for consumers.
17. T
18. T

MULTIPLE CHOICE QUESTIONS

1.a; 2.b; 3.d; 4.c; 5.b; 6.a; 7.d; 8.b; 9.d; 10.b;
11.d; 12.d; 13.c; 14.c; 15.d; 16.d

MATCHING

a and k; b and m; c and j; d and n; e and l; f and i; g and p; h and o

WORKING WITH GRAPHS

1. a.

U.S. Fertilizer Market

Price	Quantity demanded	Quantity supplied	Excess demand	Excess supply
$ 5.00	20.0	7.5	12.5	
6.00	18.0	8.0	10.0	
7.00	16.0	8.5	7.5	
8.00	14.0	9.0	5.0	
9.00	12.0	9.5	2.5	
10.00	10.0	10.0	0.0	0.0
11.00	8.0	10.5		2.5
12.00	6.0	11.0		5.0
13.00	4.0	11.5		7.5
14.00	2.0	12.0		10.0
15.00	0.0	12.5		12.5

Canadian Fertilizer Market

Price	Quantity demanded	Quantity supplied	Excess demand	Excess supply
$ 9.00	31.5	19.0	12.5	
10.00	30.0	20.0	10.0	
11.00	28.5	21.0	7.5	
12.00	27.0	22.0	5.0	
13.00	25.5	23.0	2.5	
14.00	24.0	24.0	0.0	0.0
15.00	22.5	25.0		2.5
16.00	21.0	26.0		5.0
17.00	19.5	27.0		7.5
18.00	18.0	28.0		10.0
19.00	16.5	29.0		12.5

b. United States, $10.00 per 100 lbs.; Canada, $14.00 per 100 lbs.
c. see graphs i and ii (next page)
d. see graph iii (next page)
e. $12.00, export 5, import 5

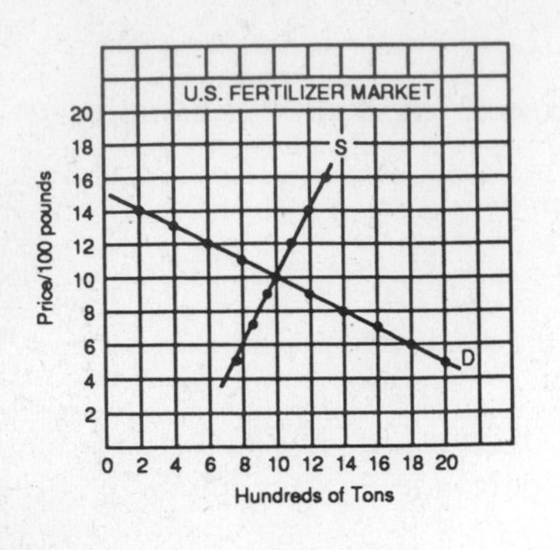

(i)

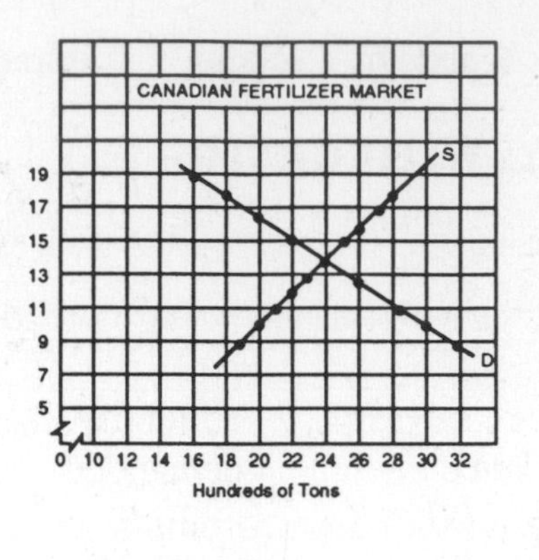

(ii)

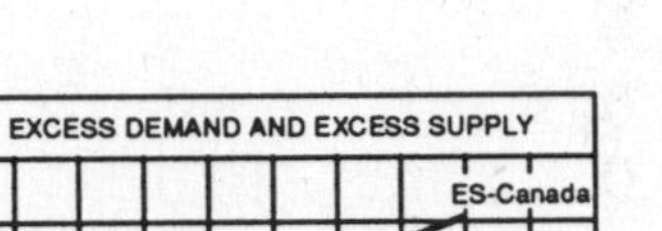

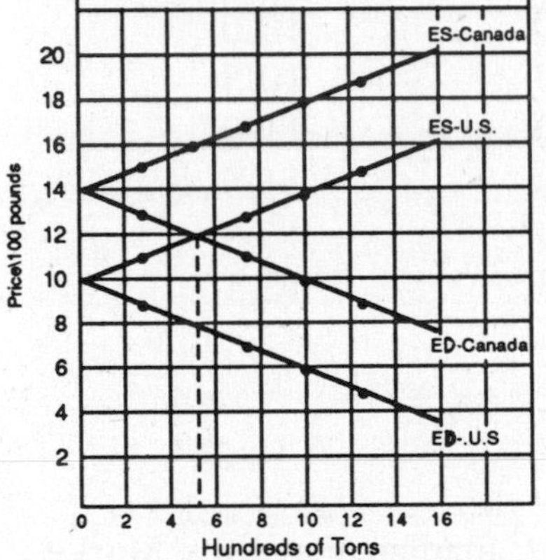

(iii)

PROBLEMS

1. a. wine, beer
   b. 1 gallon wine = 2 gallons beer; 1 gallon wine = 4 gallons beer
2. a. United States, United States
   b. Germany, United States
   c. 4000 tons coal = 1000 tons steel; 3000 tons coal = 1000 tons steel
   d. 60,000 tons coal; 36,000 tons steel
   e. 72, coal, 36, steel, 12

CASE STUDY

1. It is politic to save jobs by imposing import restrictions. Automobile producers and unions have enormous power and they can influence Congress; auto consumers are not united.
2. Crandall's study merely shows that import quotas are an inefficient method of saving jobs; whether we *should* continue to impose import quotas is a normative issue that cannot be solved through positive reasoning alone.

GLOSSARY TO CHAPTER 33

Absolute advantage The ability to produce more output from given inputs of resources than others can. For example, America may have an absolute advantage in the production of agricultural goods in the sense that, per unit of labor, we can produce more bushels of wheat than any other country.

Bilateral trade Trade between two countries only.

Comparative advantage It is better for individuals and nations to specialize in those activities in which their advantages over other people or nations are greatest (or in which their disadvantages compared to others are the smallest). Comparative advantage always exists as long as the opportunity cost of doing the same job differs for different individuals or different countries.

Dumping Selling a good or service abroad at a price below its cost of production or below the price charged in the home market.

Excess demand schedule When applied to imports, a demand schedule derived from the difference between the quantities of a product supplied domestically and the quantities demanded at prices below the domestic equilibrium price.

Excess supply schedule When applied to exports, a supply schedule derived from the difference between the quantities of a product supplied domestically and the quantities demanded at prices above domestic equilibrium prices.

Infant industry argument An argument in support of tariffs: Tariffs should be imposed to protect (from import competition) an industry that is trying to get started. Presumably, after the industry becomes technologically efficient, the tariff can be lifted.

Intra-industry trade International trade that involves goods made within the same industry, e.g. Germany buys Chevies while America buys Mercedes.

Quota system A government imposed restriction on the quantity of a specific good that another country is allowed to sell in the United States. In other words, quotas are restrictions on imports. These restrictions are usually applied to a specific country or countries.

Tariff A tax on imported goods.

Zero trade price The price on an excess demand and supply diagram at which there is no foreign trade. At this price, the domestic demand and supply schedules intersect.

CHAPTER 34

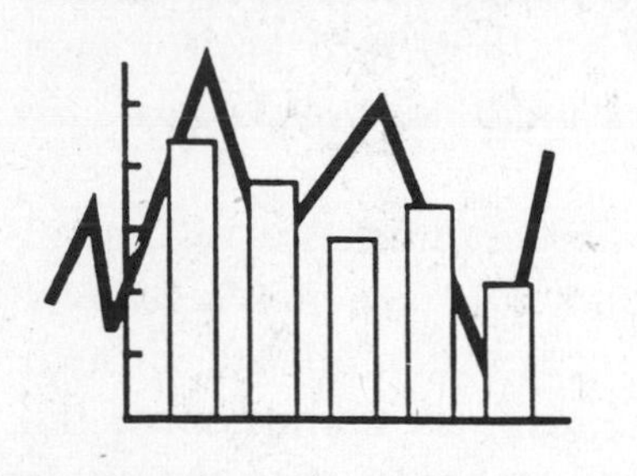

EXCHANGE RATES AND THE BALANCE OF PAYMENTS

PUTTING THIS CHAPTER INTO PERSPECTIVE

Chapter 34 is the second of two chapters on international economics. Chapter 33 discussed why trade arises between nations, the various arguments against free international trade, and the various restrictions on such trade. Chapter 34 is concerned with how trade between nations is financed. The summary that follows below is rather complex, but well worth the effort to learn if your teacher emphasizes this chapter. It is, we hope, a rigorous and thorough perspective on this chapter.

For simplicity let's assume a two-country world in which residents of one nation transact with residents of the other nation in three ways. First, they sell (export) to and buy (import) from each other; second, they lend to or borrow from each other; and third, they give gifts to or receive gifts from each other. When a nation exports goods and services to, borrows from, and receives gifts from another country, it (in effect) receives the other country's currency. On the other hand, when a nation imports from, lends to, or gives gifts to another country, it (in effect) surrenders its own currency to the other country.

If the value of country A's exports exceeds the value of its imports, then A's balance of trade is a positive number. (Most people would refer to this as a trade surplus.) If the value of its exports is less than the value of its imports, then A's balance of trade is a negative number (also referred to as a trade deficit). In a two-country world, by definition, the other country, B, has a positive balance of trade if A has a negative balance of trade. (B has a trade surplus if A has a trade deficit.)

If the value of the goods and services that A exports plus the value of private and government gifts it receives from B exceed the value of the goods and services that it imports plus the value of private and government gifts it gives to B, then B will have a negative balance on current account and A will have a positive balance on current account.

Countries A and B also transact by direct investments (purchases) of each other's financial assets and by lending to and borrowing from each other. If the value of A's direct investments in B's financial assets plus the value of its loans to B exceed the value of B's investments in A and B's loans to A (A's borrowings from B), then A's balance on capital account will be a negative number and B's balance on capital account, by definition, will be a positive number.

If governments did not enter the picture, then, if A's current account were negative, its capital account would be positive and exactly offsetting. And, by definition, B's current account would be positive and its capital account would be negative and exactly offsetting. In other words, if the residents in A buy more from and give more to B than B buys from and gives to A, then B must "finance" this activity by acquiring A's assets or by lending to A. In the process for each nation the sum of its balance on current account and its balance on capital account is zero.

Once government gets into the act, however, all bets are off. Governments, by mutual agreement, can permit country A to have a negative current account *and* a negative capital account. (A can be a big spender, a big donor, and a big lender!) This is accomplished through *official* (government) transactions that, in effect, finance such activities. By definition, if the sum of A's current account balance plus its capital account balance is nonzero, then the value of official transactions will be that number that makes that sum equal to zero.

Note that all of the above is definitional. That does not mean that negative or positive numbers for the current account plus capital account sum can persist indefinitely; eventually an *equilibrium* in the balance of payments must prevail. If governments do not intervene, forces will be set in motion that see to it that eventually the value of what residents of one nation buy from, give to, and lend to other nations (the other nation in our simple two-country model) will roughly be equal to the value of what those same residents sell to, receive from, and borrow from other nations. Exactly what those forces are depends on what the particular international financial structure is, which is the subject of the second major section of Chapter 22.

Assume, for simplicity, that no government transactions exist. When residents of country A sell (export) goods and services to, receive gifts from, and borrow from residents in country B, then country A receives B's currency, which it supplies on the foreign exchange market because residents of country A ultimately demand their own currency. Thus such activities lead, simultaneously, to a supply of B's currency and a demand for A's currency.

When residents of country A buy (import) goods and services, give gifts to, and lend to residents in country B, then B's residents take A's currency and supply it to foreign exchange markets, because B's residents demand their own currency. Thus, when A's residents import, give gifts, and lend to foreigners (in B), these actions lead, simultaneously, to a demand for B's currency and a supply of A's currency.

In short, when residents of A and B interact economically, a supply of and a demand for each country's currency automatically arises. And foreign exchange markets reflect such supply and demand conditions.

Assume that the sum of A's current account plus its capital account is a negative number and that, therefore, the sum of B's current account plus its capital account is a positive number. This means that there will be an excess demand for (shortage of) B's currency and (by definition) a surplus of A's currency. Under a freely floating or flexible exchange rate international payments system, B's currency will appreciate and A's currency will depreciate. In other words, it will take more units of A's currency to equal one unit of B's currency. This change in the exchange rate will induce residents in country A to import less from, give less to, and lend less to residents in B; and it will induce residents in country B to import more from, give more to, and lend more to residents in A. Thus, a change in the exchange rate will occur until residents of each nation *voluntarily* behave so as to generate a current account plus capital account sum that is roughly equal to zero. Thus exchange rates will adjust until a payments equilibrium exists.

What if the world is on a *fixed* exchange rate system and the sum of A's current account plus its capital account is negative? As residents in A rush to supply their own currency to buy B's currency, they (ultimately) pay for such actions by reducing their deposits in domestic banks. This causes A's total money supply to fall, which leads to a lower price level and perhaps a recession in country A. In country B just the opposite occurs. Residents of B convert A's currency into their own, so B's money supply rises and with it so does B's price level; therefore B experiences a boom. In short, A's price level falls relative to B's. This induces residents in A to import less and export more, and it induces residents in B to import more and export less, and to give more and lend more to A. Thus, relative price levels will adjust until a balance of payments equilibrium prevails.

If the world is on a gold standard, then A will pay for its "excess spending" with gold; gold flows from A to B. A's price level (and national income level) falls relative to B's, because gold and currencies are exchangeable under such a system. The results are the same as under the other fixed exchange rate system analyzed in the previous paragraph; under a gold standard gold flows occur (if disequilibrium exists) until relative price levels change sufficiently to create a balance of payments equilibrium.

LEARNING OBJECTIVES

After you have studied this chapter you should be able to

1. define foreign exchange rate, freely floating (or flexible) exchange rates, appreciation, depreciation, fixed exchange rates, devaluation, revaluation, gold standard, balance of trade, balance of payments, special drawing rights, purchasing power parity, dirty float, par value, and J-curve phenomenon.

2. list transactions that lead to an increase in the supply of a domestic country's currency and an increase in the demand for foreign currency, and distinguish such transactions from transactions that lead to a demand for a domestic country's currency and a supply of a foreign country's currency.

3. recognize the equilibrium exchange rate from graphs, and predict how specific events will change the exchange rate.

4. distinguish between a fixed exchange rate international payments system and a floating, or flexible, exchange rate international payments system.

5. answer questions that require a knowledge of how a gold standard eliminates balance of payments deficits and surpluses between one nation and the rest of the world.

6. distinguish among the balance of trade, the balance on current account, the balance on capital account, and the balance of payments.

7. list three factors that affect a nation's balance of payments.

8. enumerate official reserve account transactions.

9. explain why a nation's trade deficit might worsen, temporarily, after the currency depreciates because of the J-curve effect.

CHAPTER OUTLINE

1. A *balance of trade* reflects the difference between the value of a nation's merchandise exports and its merchandise imports; the balance of payments reflects all economic transactions between a nation and the rest of the world.
   a. The *current account balance* equals the sum of (1) the balance of trade, (2) the balance of services, and (3) net unilateral transfers (private gifts and government grants). If the current account balance is negative, a current account deficit exists; if it is positive, a current account surplus exists.
   b. *Capital account* transactions consist of direct investment purchases in financial assets among countries and loans to and from foreigners. If the capital account is a negative number, a capital account deficit exists; if it is positive, a capital account surplus exists.
   c. If the sum of a nation's current account and its capital account is negative, that nation has an international *payments disequilibrium (deficit)* which must be financed by official (government) reserve account transactions; of course, another nation must have an international *payments surplus*.
      i. Official reserve account transactions include sales or purchases of foreign currencies, gold, *special drawing rights*, the reserve position in the International Monetary Fund, and financial assets held by official government agencies.
      ii. Official transactions must exactly equal (but be of opposite sign to) the *balance of payments*.

2. A nation's balance of payments is affected by its relative (a) inflation rate, and (b) political stability.

3. Under a *floating*, or *flexible*, *exchange rate system* of international payments, exchange rates between nations are determined by the forces of supply and demand.
   a. When U.S. residents import a foreign good or service, this leads to a supply of dollars and a demand for foreign currency on foreign exchange markets.
   b. When U.S. residents export goods and services to a foreign country, this leads to a supply of foreign currency and a demand for dollars.
   c. The equilibrium exchange rate is determined in the same way that the equilibrium price for anything is established.
      i. The U.S. demand curve for (say) French francs is negatively sloped; as the dollar price of the franc falls--it takes fewer dollars to purchase a given quantity of francs--the quantity demanded for francs, by U.S. residents, rises.

ii. The U.S. demand for francs is a derived demand; we demand French francs because we demand French goods and services.

iii. The French supply francs because they want (say) U.S. goods and services; as the dollar price of francs rises--it takes fewer francs to purchase one dollar--the French will increase their quantity supplied of francs in order to purchase more U.S. goods.

iv. The equilibrium dollar price per franc is established at the intersection of the U.S. demand for francs curve and the French supply of francs curve; the equilibrium franc price per dollar is automatically determined thereby.

d. If U.S. residents experience a change in tastes in favor of French goods, the demand for francs will increase. The dollar price of francs rises and the franc price of dollars falls; the dollar *depreciates* and the franc *appreciates*.

e. If the inflation rate in France rises relative to the inflation rate in the United States, the relative price of U.S. goods falls. This induces the French to increase their supply of francs in order to purchase more U.S. goods; the dollar appreciates and the franc depreciates.

f. Other determinants of exchange rates include (relative) changes in real interest rates, changes in productivity, changes in tastes, and perceptions of economic stability.

4. Under a *fixed exchange rate* international payments system, each government intervenes in the foreign exchange market to fix the value of its currency in terms of the other countries' currencies.
   a. Under such a system, if the U.S. price level rises relative to the French price level, then there will be an excess supply of dollars (an excess demand for francs).
   b. In order to prevent the dollar's exchange rate from depreciating, the Fed buys U.S. dollars with French francs on the international exchange market.
   c. This Fed action causes the U.S. money supply to fall, because Americans buy their francs with dollars and the Fed, ultimately, reduces reserves of U.S. banks.
   d. If the Fed pursues an expansionary monetary policy to offset the reduced U.S. money supply, the international disequilibrium can persist for a while; eventually the Fed must be concerned about losing French francs reserves or gold, and a currency crisis arises.
   e. In order to end the currency crisis, the United States might devalue the dollar or France might revalue the franc.

5. Between a floating exchange rate system and a fixed exchange rate is a "dirty float," or a managed exchange rate system, in which governments (through their central banks) intervene in foreign exchange markets in order to affect the price of currencies; such is the current world monetary system.

6. Under a *gold standard*, each nation fixes its exchange rate in terms of gold; therefore all exchange rates are fixed.
   a. If the French inflation rate exceeds the American inflation rate, under the gold standard, this causes a surplus of francs and a shortage of dollars.
   b. With their surplus of francs, Americans can purchase gold from France; this causes an increase in the U.S. money supply and a decrease in the French money supply, which causes the U.S. price level to rise relative to the French price level.

c. Gold flows from France to the United States and their relative price levels adjust until, at the fixed exchange rate, the quantity supplied of francs equals the quantity demanded for francs and the quantity demanded for dollars equals the quantity supplied of dollars.
d. If unemployment had existed in the United States, then gold flows from France to the United States would have increased real U.S. incomes; this would have led to an increase in the U.S. demand for francs as Americans desired to import more goods. This action would have caused the market exchange rate to approach the fixed exchange rate.
e. Under the pure gold standard, each nation would have to abandon an independent monetary policy; each nation's money supply would automatically change whenever a balance of payments disequilibrium occurred.

7. In 1944 representatives of the world's capitalist nations met in Bretton Woods to create a new international payments system to replace the gold standard that had collapsed in the 1930.
   a. The *International Monetary Fund (IMF)* was established in 1944; the IMF established a system of fixed exchange rates and a means to lend foreign exchange to deficit nations.
   b. Member governments were obligated to intervene in foreign exchange markets, to maintain the values of their currencies within 1 percent of the declared par value.
   c. In 1967 the IMF created Special Drawing Rights (SDRs), a new type of international money exchange (only) between monetary authorities.

8. When a nation's currency depreciates, its trade deficit will *increase* in the short run if the price elasticity of demand for its imports is relatively low; this is called the J-curve phenomenon.

KEY TERMS

Floating or flexible exchange rates
Foreign exchange market
Foreign exchange rate
Currency appreciation
Currency depreciation
Fixed exchange rate system
Devaluation
Revaluation
Gold standard
Balance of trade
Balance on current account
Balance on capital account
Balance of payments
Special drawing rights
Payments surplus, payments deficit
Official reserve transactions

KEY CONCEPTS

Currency crisis
Payments equilibrium
Payments disequilibrium
Purchasing power parity
J-curve phenomenon
Dirty float
Par value

COMPLETION QUESTIONS

Fill in the blank or circle the correct term.

1. When Americans wish to import French-made goods, they supply ______________ to the foreign exchange market and demand ______________ on that market; when the French wish to import American-made goods, they supply ______________ and demand ______________ on the foreign exchange market.

2. In a freely floating exchange rate system, exchange rates are determined by (governments, supply and demand); if the exchange rate goes from 25 cents per franc to 50 cents per franc, the dollar has (appreciated, depreciated) and the franc has ________________.

3. If the franc depreciates, it takes (fewer, more) francs to purchase a dollar; this leads to a(n) (increase, decrease) in the quantity demanded of francs by Americans and a(n) (increase, decrease) in the quantity supplied of francs by the French.

4. If American tastes move in favor of French goods, there will be a(n) ____________ in the demand for francs; other things being constant, the franc will (appreciate, depreciate) on the foreign exchange market. This eventually will induce Americans to export (less, more) to the French and import ___________ from the French.

5. Under a system of fixed exchange rates, exchange rates are determined by (governments, supply and demand); under that system, if the French inflation rate rises relative to the U.S. inflation rate, Americans will import (less, more) from the French and export ___________ to them. This means there will be an excess quantity (demanded for, supplied of) French francs and the French monetary authorities must (buy, sell) francs to maintain the fixed exchange rate; this causes the French money supply to (fall, rise) and that causes France's GDP to (fall, rise).

6. A country devalues and revalues its currency under a (floating, fixed) exchange rate system; when a nation devalues its currency, it then requires (fewer, more) units of its own currency to purchase a given quantity of another currency.

7. Under a pure gold standard, exchange rates (float, are fixed); under such a system, if there is an excess quantity supplied of U.S. dollars, then the Fed must (sell, buy) dollars. When it does so, gold flows (from, into) the United States, causing the U.S. money supply and the U.S. price level to ______________; eventually this gold flow will cause the quantity supplied of dollars to (equal, exceed) the quantity demanded for dollars.

8. If the value of U.S. imports exceeds the value of its exports, the U.S. balance of trade will be a (negative, positive) number, and another country's balance of trade must be a ___________________ number; then the United States is said to have a trade (deficit, surplus), while the other nation has a trade ________________.

9. If governments do not intervene, by definition the sum of a nation's balance on current account plus its balance on capital account will equal ______________; if governments intervene in the balance of payments process, then the sum of a nation's balance on current account plus its balance on capital account must exactly ________________, but be of opposite sign to, its official transactions.

10. Official reserve account transactions involve the following assets of individual countries: ________________, ________________, ________________, ________________, and ________________.

11. A nation's balance of payments is affected by, among other things, relative changes in that nation's ____________________, and ____________________.

12. If the value of a nation's exports is less than the value of its imports, it is running a trade________; its currency will (depreciate, appreciate) under a floating exchange rate system. If the price elasticity of demand for its imports is low, that nation will experience a (smaller, larger) trade deficit in the short run, and a ______________ trade deficit in the long run; this is referred to as the ______________ phenomenon.

13. When nations intervene in foreign exchange markets in order to affect exchange rates, a freely floating exchange rate system becomes a ______________ float.

TRUE-FALSE QUESTIONS

Circle the **T** if the statement is true, the **F** if it is false. Explain to yourself why a statement is false.

T F 1. If you wish to buy German goods, you ultimately offer dollars and demand German currency.

T F 2. If you wish to send money to your relatives in England, you ultimately offer dollars and demand English currency.

T F 3. In a freely floating exchange rate system, gold flows lead to international payments equilibrium.

T F 4. If French tastes move in favor of American goods, the supply of dollars on the foreign exchange market rises relative to the demand for dollars.

T F 5. The U.S. demand for French francs rises if the French inflation rate exceeds the U.S. inflation rate.

T F 6. In a freely floating exchange rate system, if French tastes move away from American goods (other things being constant), both the dollar and the franc will depreciate.

T F 7. Technically, devaluation and revaluation occur only in a fixed exchange rate system.

T F 8. The gold standard is one form of fixed exchange rate system.

T F 9. Under the gold standard, if disequilibrium exists in the world's balance of payments, gold will flow from one nation to another until payments equilibrium is restored.

T F 10. Under a floating exchange rate system, if disequilibrium exists in the world's balance of payments, exchange rates will change until payments equilibrium is restored.

T F 11. Under a (nongold) fixed exchange rate system, balance of payments equilibrium is brought about by automatic changes in each nation's price level.

T F 12. Under a floating exchange rate system, each nation must give up control over its own monetary policy.

T F 13. In today's world, the sum of a nation's current account balance plus its capital account balance must be zero.

T F 14. If one nation has a current account deficit, another nation must have a current account surplus.

T F 15. A nation can finance a current account deficit with a capital account surplus.

T F *16. In recent years a dirty float has resulted because nations have not wanted to pay the price of adjusting to a balance of payments disequilibrium.

T F *17. Under a floating exchange rate system, payments equilibrium is brought about by a change in the exchange rate; under a fixed rate system, national price levels change to restore payments equilibrium.

T F 18. The J-curve phenomenon will occur if the price elasticity of demand for imports is very low.

MULTIPLE CHOICE QUESTIONS

Circle the letter that corresponds to the best answer.

1. If the foreign exchange rate is that $1 is equivalent to 5 francs, then 1 franc is worth
   a. $5.
   b. 50 cents.
   c. 20 cents.
   d. 5 cents.

2. Which of the following is most *unlike* the others?
   a. flexible exchange rate system
   b. fixed exchange rate system
   c. gold standard

3. The demand schedule for francs on the foreign exchange market
   a. is derived partially from foreign demand for French goods.
   b. reflects the fact that the French want to import goods and services.
   c. shows the quantity demanded for francs at different income levels.
   d. is unimportant if France is on a fixed exchange rate system.

*4. Which of the following does *not* lead to an increase in the demand for French francs?
   a. A worldwide change in tastes in favor of French goods occurs.
   b. The French inflation rate exceeds the world inflation rate.
   c. France's interest rate rises relative to world rates.
   d. World real income rises.

5. Which of the following leads to an increase in the demand for the U.S. dollar on the foreign exchange market?
   a. an increase in U.S. exports
   b. an increase in foreign investment in the United States
   c. an increase in gifts from foreigners to U.S. residents
   d. All of the above

*6. Analogy: currency depreciation is to flexible exchange rates as ______ is to fixed exchange rates.
   a. appreciation
   b. revaluation
   c. devaluation
   d. gold flows

7. If a nation has an international payments surplus in a freely floating exchange rate system, then
   a. its currency will appreciate.
   b. its price level will rise.
   c. gold will flow from it to nations with a payments surplus.
   d. All of the above

*8. If a nation has an international payments surplus in a fixed (nongold standard) exchange rate system, then its
   a. currency will appreciate.
   b. currency will depreciate.
   c. central bank will sell its currency on the foreign exchange market.
   d. trading partner must also have a payments surplus.

*9. If a nation has an international payments deficit on a pure gold standard, then
   a. its exchange rate will appreciate.
   b. its exchange rate will depreciate.
   c. its central bank will sell its currency for gold.
   d. its central bank will buy its currency with gold.

*10. Which of the following statements is *not* true?
   a. Under floating exchange rates, international payments equilibrium is restored through changes in exchange rates.
   b. Under a fixed exchange rate system, international payments equilibrium is restored through changes in national price levels.
   c. Under a freely floating exchange rate system, a nation cannot pursue a monetary policy that is independent of its trading partners.
   d. Under the gold standard, international payments disequilibrium leads to gold flows, which restore equilibrium.

11. When a nation experiences a payments deficit under a fixed exchange rate system,
   a. there is a surplus of its currency on the foreign exchange market.
   b. its central bank will purchase its currency with foreign reserves or gold.
   c. its money supply will fall.
   d. All of the above

12. Currency crises
   a. are common under freely floating exchange rate systems.
   b. arise because changes in the supply and demand for a currency cause the market equilibrium exchange rate to differ from the fixed exchange rate.
   c. arise because nations wish to pursue a common monetary policy.
   d. are unlikely under a fixed exchange rate system.

*13. If France has a payments deficit, payments equilibrium can be restored if France's
   a. price level rises relative to the world's.
   b. interest rate rises relative to the world's.
   c. real national income rises relative to the world's.
   d. money supply rises relative to the world's.

14. A nation can finance a deficit on its current account with
   a. a surplus on its capital account.
   b. a deficit on its capital account.
   c. official purchases of foreign currencies with its own currency.
   d. purchases of gold from foreign countries with its own currency.

15. If a nation has a deficit on both its current account and its capital account, then
   a. it is in a balance of payments equilibrium.
   b. the world must be on a freely floating exchange rate system.
   c. it must have official transactions that are identical to (but opposite in sign to) the sum of those two deficits.
   d. it will experience gold inflows.

*16. A nation's balance of payments is affected by its relative
   a. interest rate.
   b. political stability.
   c. inflation rate.
   d. All of the above

*17. The dirty float
   a. has emerged in recent years because nations want less flexible exchange rates.
   b. makes fixed exchange rates more flexible.
   c. is common under a gold standard.
   d. is favored over a pure float by people who want their nation to have a monetary policy independent of its trading partners.

MATCHING

Choose the item in column (2) that best matches an item in column (1).

(1)	(2)
a. appreciation	i. rise in one currency's value relative to another's
b. depreciation	j. rise in a currency's value relative to gold
c. devaluation	k. fall in a currency's value relative to gold
d. revaluation	l. fall in one currency's value relative to another's
e. fixed exchange rate system	m. inelastic demand for imports
f. special drawing right	n. balance of payments settlements
g. purchasing power parity	o. gold standard
h. J-curve	p. inflation's effects on exchange rates

WORKING WITH GRAPHS

*1. Consider a situation in which exchange rates are free to fluctuate. Consumers in the United States wish to import a good from Germany.
   a. Calculate the U.S. price of this good, given the German price of the good and the different exchange rates that might prevail as listed in the table below, and place these calculations in the appropriate column. Calculate the quantity of German marks demanded by U.S. consumers in order to purchase the import good at different exchange rates. Enter these numbers in the last column.

Exchange rate ($/DM)	German price of the good	U.S. price of the good	Quantity demanded	Total U.S. DM expenditures
2.20/1	1 DM	_______	90	_______
2.40/1	1 DM	_______	80	_______
2.60/1	1 DM	_______	70	_______
2.80/1	1 DM	_______	60	_______
3.00/1	1 DM	_______	50	_______

By looking at the table above, one can conclude that as it takes more dollars to purchase one German mark (DM), the dollar price of the import good will _______________.

b. In the table above, you are given the quantity of the import good at different prices. Graph the demand for German marks on the grid provided below.

c. Let us now assume that people in Germany wish to import from the United States some good that costs $1 per unit. Calculate the German price of the good given the U.S. price and the different exchange rates that might prevail, as listed in the table below, and place these numbers in the appropriate column.

Exchange rate ($/DM)	U.S. price of the good	German price of the good	Quantity demanded	Total German $ expenditures
2.20/1	$ 1	_______	66.7	_______
2.40/1	$ 1	_______	119.0	_______
2.60/1	$ 1	_______	184.2	_______
2.80/1	$ 1	_______	250.0	_______
3.00/1	$ 1	_______	333.0	_______

By looking at the above table, one can conclude that as it takes more dollars to purchase 1 German mark, the mark price of the good will _______________.

d. In the last table, you are given the quantity of the import good that German consumers wish to purchase at different German prices. Use this information to calculate the quantity of German marks that German consumers will be willing to supply at different exchange rates in order to import the U.S. good. (Note: Round off to the nearest whole number.) Enter these numbers in the last column. Graph the supply of German marks on the same grid as your graph of part b.

e. Assume for simplicity that the only trade between the United States and Germany involves the two goods discussed above. Under this assumption, the equilibrium exchange rate will be approximately __________ dollars per German mark or __________ German marks per dollar.

f. Suppose that now U.S. consumers undergo a change in tastes and preferences for the German import good. As a result, the U.S. demand for the import good increases as shown in the table below.

Exchange rate ($/DM)	German price of the good	U.S. price of the good	Quantity demanded	Total U.S. DM expenditures
2.20/1	1 DM	_______	120	_______
2.40/1	1 DM	_______	110	_______
2.60/1	1 DM	_______	100	_______
2.80/1	1 DM	_______	90	_______
3.00/1	1 DM	_______	80	_______

Enter in the last column the quantity of German marks now demanded by U.S. consumers for use in purchasing the German import good. Graph the new demand for German marks on the same grid provided for part b.

The new equilibrium exchange rate will be approximately __________ dollars per German mark, or __________ German marks per dollar. As a result of the increase in the U.S. demand for German imports, with all else constant, the dollar will __________ and the mark will __________.

g. Now consider the above problem assuming that the exchange rate was fixed at $2.60/mark. When the U.S. demand for German goods increased, the United States would have purchased __________ units and paid a total of $_____________ for German imports. The Germans would have bought __________ units from the United States and paid a total of $_____________ for U.S. exports. As a result, the United States would have lost $_____________, or approximately __________ marks, in foreign exchange.

2. The figure below shows the supply of, and the demand for, British ponds, as a function of the exchange rate--expressed in U.S. dollars per pound. Assume that Britain and the United States are the only two countries in the world.

a. How might the shift from D to D' be accounted for?

b. Given the shift from D to D', what exists at $2.60?

c. Will the pound now appreciate or depreciate?

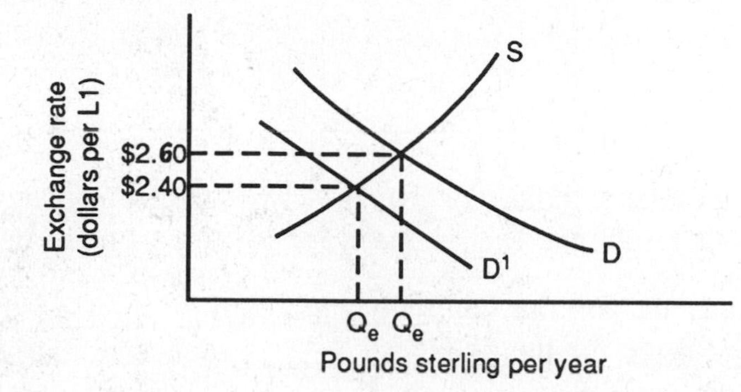

PROBLEMS

*1. Below are balance-of-payments figures for Pleasureland during 1992. (All figures are in billions of dollars.

Allocations of special drawing rights	$ 710
Balance on the capital account	-3507
Foreign official assets	10475
Errors and omissions	-1879
Balance on the current account	-5795
Pleasureland official assets	-4

a. The official settlement balance was (+/-) _____ $____________________.

b. The official reserve transactions were

(1) the sum of $__________, __________, and __________

(2) totaled (+/-) _____ $__________

*2. Suppose both France and the United States had been on a pure gold standard; and the French government had been willing to buy and sell gold at a price of 140 French francs for an ounce of gold, and the American government had been willing to buy and sell gold at a price of $35 an ounce. In the foreign exchange markets the price of a French franc would have been $________________ and the price of a dollar would have been ____________ French francs.

*3. Below are hypothetical demand and supply schedules for the German deutsche mark during a week. (The quantities of deutsche marks demanded and supplied are measured in millions and the exchange rate for the deutsche mark is measured in dollars.)

Quantity Demanded	Exchanged Rate	Quantity Supplied
100	$0.28	570
200	0.27	520
300	0.26	460
400	0.25	400
500	0.24	330
600	0.23	260
700	0.22	180

a. The equilibrium exchange rate for the deutsche mark is $________; and at this equilibrium the rate of exchange for the dollar is ________ deutsche marks.

b. At the equilibrium exchange rate:

(1) ____________ million deutsche marks are demanded and supplied each week.

(2) ____________ million dollars are bought and sold each week.

c. If the German central bank wished to peg the exchange rate for the deutsche mark at:

(1) $0.26 it would have to (buy/sell) (how many) ____________ million deutsche marks for dollars each week.

(2) $0.24 it would have to (buy/sell) (how many) ____________ million deutsche marks for dollars each week.

4. Which of the following will cause the yen to appreciate?

a. U.S. real incomes increase relative to Japanese real incomes.

b. It is expected that in the future the yen will depreciate relative to the dollar.

c. The U.S. inflation rate rises relative to the Japanese inflation rate.

d. The after-tax, risk-adjusted real interest rate in the United States rises relative to that in Japan.

e. U.S. tastes change in favor of Japanese-made goods.

CASE STUDY

It is widely accepted that the United States is the world's largest debtor nation. This view has been challenged by Charles Wolf, Jr., director of the Rand Corporations's research on international economic policy, and Sarah Hooker, a Rand consultant. They note that the U.S. international balance sheet has three specific sources of error.

1. Direct investments abroad by U.S. corporations are generally of earlier vintage than corresponding investments in the United States by foreign corporations. If one converts historical, or book, values into current market values, the U.S. balance sheet deficit falls.

2. U.S. gold reserves are valued at the official price of $42 per ounce, which is considerably below market value. (The price of gold was around $350 per ounce in July 1990.)

3. The book value of loans owed to U.S. banks and nonbanking institutions by the less developed countries (LDCs) is substantially greater than the current market value of those loans.

Note that a correction of points 1 and 2 above reduces the net debtor position of the United States, while correcting point 3 increases it. Wolf and Hooker estimated that the *net* effect of correcting all these errors is to change the U.S. foreign balance sheet from -$264 billion to +$50 billion in 1986.

1. If Wolf and Hooker are correct, how should that fact affect the protectionist debate?

2. What lesson can be learned from this?

ANSWERS TO CHAPTER 34

COMPLETION QUESTIONS

1. dollars, francs; francs, dollars
2. supply and demand; depreciated, appreciated
3. more; increase, decrease
4. increase; appreciate; more, less
5. governments; less, more; supplied of, buy; fall, fall
6. fixed; more
7. are fixed; buy; from, fall; equal
8. negative, positive; deficit, surplus
9. zero; equal
10. foreign currencies, gold, SDRs, reserve position in the IMF, any financial asset held by an official government agency
11. inflation rate, political stability
12. deficit; depreciate; larger, smaller; J-curve
13. dirty

TRUE-FALSE QUESTIONS

1. T
2. T
3. F Changes in exchange rates lead to payments equilibrium.
4. F The demand for dollars rises relative to the supply of dollars, because the French want to buy relatively more U.S. goods.
5. F Americans will demand fewer francs because French goods are now relatively higher priced.
6. F The dollar will depreciate relative to the franc; the franc therefore must appreciate relative to the dollar.
7. T
8. T
9. T
10. T
11. T
12. F Floating exchange rate systems permit an independent monetary policy.
13. F In today's world, nations intervene in exchange markets; hence international settlements among governments are necessary.
14. T
15. T
16. T
17. T
18. T

MULTIPLE CHOICE QUESTIONS

1.c; 2.a; 3.a; 4.b; 5.d; 6.c; 7.a; 8.c; 9.d; 10.c;
11.d; 12.b; 13.b; 14.a; 15.c; 16.d; 17.a

MATCHING

a and i; b and l; c and k; d and j; e and o; f and n; g and p; h and m

WORKING WITH GRAPHS

1. a. U.S. prices of the good: 2.20, 2.40, 2.60, 2.80, 3.00. Total U.S. DM expenditures: 90, 80, 70, 60, 50; rise
   b. See graph
   c. German prices of the good: 0.45, 0.42, 0.38, 0.36, 0.33; fall
   d. Total German expenditures in DM: 30, 50, 70, 90, 110. See graph below
   e. 2.60, 0.38
   f. Total U.S. DM expenditures: 120, 110, 100, 90, 80. See graph. 2.80, 0.36; depreciate, appreciate
   g. 100, 260; 184.2, 184.2; 75.8, 29.

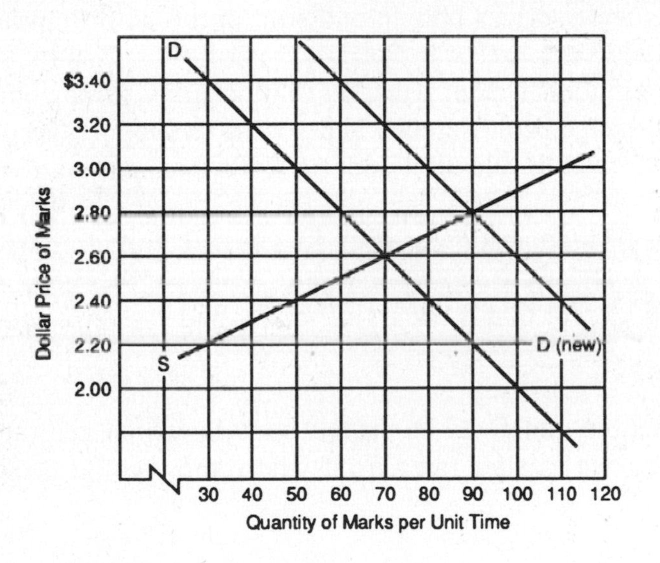

2. a. A decrease in the demand for British pounds will occur if world tastes change away from British-made goods, the British price level rises relative to the world's, world income falls relative to British income, and/or British interest rates fall relative to world interest rates, among other reasons.
   b. A surplus of British pounds, a British balance-of-payments deficit.
   c. depreciate

PROBLEMS

1. a. -, 11181; b. (1) 710, 10475, -4 (any order) (2) +, 11181
2. 0.25, 4
3. a. 0.25, 4; b. (1) 400 (2) 100; c. (1) buy, 160 (2) sell, 170
4. a,c,e

CASE STUDY

1. It would seem that the protectionist argument would lack much of its force if its main fact turns out to be incorrect.
2. We should be sure that a problem really exists before we attempt to solve it.

GLOSSARY TO CHAPTER 34

Appreciation An increase in the value of a domestic currency in terms of other currencies. In a fixed exchange rate market, appreciation cannot occur spontaneously; it must be done officially. Then it is called revaluation.

The balance of payments A summary record of a country's economic transactions with foreign residents and governments over a year.

Balance of trade The value of goods and services bought and sold in the world market.

Currency crisis A situation in the international money market that occurs when a country no longer has the wherewithal (foreign exchange, gold, credit, and so on) to support the price of its currency. A currency crisis brings forced devaluation under a fixed exchange rate system.

Depreciation A decrease in the value of a domestic currency in terms of foreign currencies.

Devaluation The same as depreciation except that it occurs officially under a regime of fixed exchange rates.

Dirty float A system in between flexible and fixed exchange rates in which central banks occasionally enter foreign exchange markets to alter rates from where they would be with no such intervention.

Fixed exchange rates A system of exchange rates that requires government intervention to fix the value of each nation's currency in terms of every other nation's currency.

Foreign exchange market The market for buying and selling foreign currencies.

Foreign exchange rate The price of foreign currency in terms of domestic currency. For example, the foreign exchange rate for francs is 20 cents. This means that it takes 20 cents to buy one franc. An alternative way of stating the exchange rate is that the value of the dollar is five francs. It takes five francs to buy one dollar.

Freely floating (or flexible) exchange rates Exchange rates that are allowed to fluctuate in the open market in response to changes in supply and demand. Sometimes called free exchange rates or floating exchange rates.

Gold standard In its purest form (which is only hypothetical), an international monetary system in which gold plays a prominent part. Nations fix their exchange rates in terms of gold. Thus all currencies are fixed in terms of each other. Any balance-of-payments problems could be made up by shipments of gold.

International Monetary Fund (IMF) An institution set up to manage the international monetary system. It came out of the Bretton Woods Conference in 1944, which established more or less fixed exchange rates in the world.

J-curve A situation following a depreciation in a country's currency value internationally. After the depreciation, there is a worsening of the country's foreign trade deficit and only some time later an improvement in its foreign trade position. The tracing of the movement of net exports resembles a J.

Par value The legally established value of the monetary unit of one country in terms of that of another.

Purchasing power parity (PPP) Exists between two currencies when on average changes in the exchange rate reflect only relative changes in the price levels in the two countries.

Revaluation The opposite of devaluation.

Special drawing rights (SDRs) A reserve asset created by the International Monetary Fund that countries can use to settle international payments.

CHAPTER 35

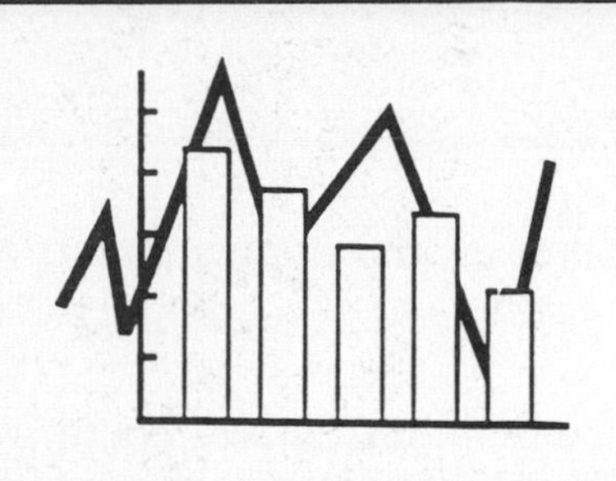

DEVELOPMENT ECONOMICS

PUTTING THIS CHAPTER INTO PERSPECTIVE

Chapter 35 is concerned with the analysis of economic development-- how nations increase their material standards of living. Be advised that much of the material in this chapter lends itself to emotional and ideological bias. Those on the left of the political spectrum tend to think that developing countries are poor because they have been exploited by advanced nations. For them the solution is massive transfers of money and capital from advanced nations to the developing countries. Those on the right of the political spectrum tend to stress that most developing countries violate many sound economic principles (as developed in your textbook) by violating property rights and by extensive governmental interference with markets. It's a safe bet that the topics in this chapter will generate controversy in any group discussion. Many people tend to have strong opinions about economic development. Indeed, many hundreds of books have been written on that important topic, but a consensus of opinion does not seem to be emerging.

You should realize that any definition of a developing country is arbitrary. Perhaps the best way to classify nations is according to their socioeconomic characteristics--life expectancy, infant mortality, literacy, expenditures on education, and so on.

Chapter 35 is interesting because it explores several myths concerning less developed countries (LDCs) and economic development. One such myth is that LDCs suffer from overpopulation or excess population growth rates; there simply are too many exceptions to this notion. An even more serious myth is that advanced nations have more abundant resource bases than do developing countries. Moreover, while it is true that developed nations have a greater capital stock than do developing countries, it does not follow that giving or selling capital to developing countries will generate economic growth. Apparently capital accumulation makes sense only when it is *profitable*. Furthermore, some developing countries would be better off economically if they specialized in agricultural production rather than trying to industrialize.

Another myth is that foreign aid transfers from developed nations to LDCs can help the LDCs significantly. In practice this has not occurred. Often the LDCs become too dependent on foreign aid or the foreign aid is used nonproductively by corrupt developing governments. (It is important to keep in mind that any *productive* investment project in a LDC will be financed by world capital markets.)

One relatively underrated approach to economic development is to expand property rights in developing countries. Not only would such a policy encourage foreign investment, but it would also induce residents of such countries to be more productive.

LEARNING OBJECTIVES

After you have studied this chapter you should be able to

1. define industrial advanced countries, newly industrialized countries, developing countries, vicious cycle of poverty, and modern economic growth.

2. identify characteristics of industrially advanced countries, newly industrialized countries, and developing countries.

3. recognize the socioeconomic characteristics of developing countries.

4. enumerate at least three theories that attempt to account for economic development.

5. list at least three barriers to economic growth in less developed countries.

6. recognize the main characteristics of modern economic growth.

CHAPTER OUTLINE

1. Some nations deal with the problems associated with being relatively rich, while many others struggle to remain economically viable; there doesn't seem to be much agreement as to why some nations are rich and others are poor.

2. Some people divide the world into three categories of nations.
   a. The industrially advanced countries (IACs) include the industrialized noncommunist countries of the United States, Australia, New Zealand, Canada, and Japan.
   b. The newly industrialized economies include members of the Pacific Rim: Singapore, Hong Kong, Taiwan, and South Korea.
   c. The developing countries include the many less developed countries.
   d. The concept of the developing countries is rather vague because it lumps together countries that are very different in cultural, economic, political, racial, and ethnic terms.
   e. Socioeconomic indicators of the level of economic development include life expectancy, infant mortality, and literacy.

3. In general, the world's nations with the fastest-growing population are in the developing countries.
   a. The world population growth rate has fallen and in some countries there has been a dramatic reduction in population growth.
   b. On an international level there is little relationship between poverty and population density, and rapid population *growth* does not necessarily create poverty.

4. One theory of economic development stresses the need for *balanced growth*, with industry and agriculture given equal importance.
   a. With notable exceptions, one characteristic of developed countries is their high degree of industrialization.

b. The development of modern rich nations seems to have occurred in three stages: agriculture, manufacturing, and services.
c. Although many developing countries have a comparative advantage in farming, many developed nations subsidize their farmers and restrict imports from developing countries; such a policy reduces worldwide incomes and encourages developing countries to turn to industrialization, for which they do not have a comparative advantage.

5. Although many people believe that a large natural resource base is necessary for economic development, in practice no high correlation exists between resource base and economic development.

6. Developed nations certainly have a larger capital stock than do developing countries but it is not easy for the latter to import capital (or to receive it in grants) and use it productively.
   a. In order for a nation to develop its own capital stock, it must save and invest those savings profitably.
   b. Even households in developing countries save; they save in ways that are not readily apparent.
   c. People, and nations, at all income levels must save for the future--and they do.
   d. Developing countries have imported the technology and the means to reduce death rates and to reduce infant mortality which, in the short run, leads to increased population; in the long run it could lead to decreased incentives to have children.

7. The more certain private property rights are, the more private capital accumulation there will be; enforced private property rights, at the very minimum, will induce foreign investment, which will increase living standards.

8. Various routes to economic development include trade with the outside world, human attitudes and aptitudes (and incentive structures), and political institutions which are conducive to development.

9. The Marshall Plan, which transferred capital to already developed nations, does not seem to be the correct model for helping developing countries.

10. Modern economic growth (MEG) is characterized by productivity growth, population growth, sweeping structural changes, and the application of science to the material satisfaction of wants; there are advantages and disadvantages to being a latecomer to MEG.

KEY TERMS

Developing countries
Newly industrialized economy
Industrialized advanced economies

KEY CONCEPTS

Balanced economic growth
Development economics
Modern economic growth

COMPLETION QUESTIONS

Fill in the blank or circle the correct term.

1. The nations of the world can be classified into three groups, based on status of development: ________, ________, and ________.

2. Socioeconomic indicators of development include __________, ____________, and __________.

3. The stages of economic development seem to be ________________, ______________________, and ________________________.

4. A natural resource is something scarce occurring in nature that people can ________________________.

5. In order for a developing country to accumulate capital, it must ________________ and ______________________ profitably.

6. The more certain property rights are, the (less, more) private capital accumulation there will be; developing countries discourage foreign investment in their country when they _________________ domestic industries.

7. Various routes to economic development include ___________, __________, and __________.

8. Modern economic growth is characterized by sustained increases in per capita ______________, by (decreases, increases) in population, and by (slight, sweeping) structural changes; the driving force of MEG is ________________ advancement.

TRUE-FALSE QUESTIONS

Circle the **T** if the statement is true, the **F** if it is false. Explain to yourself why a statement is false.

T F 1. It is very difficult to define or to categorize a nation as a developing country.

T F 2. Some countries that are not industrialized actually have very high per capita incomes.

T F *3. The per capita income of a nation is sufficient to classify its level of economic development.

T F 4. The populations of industrially advanced countries tend to grow less rapidly than those of developing countries.

T F 5. Excessive population growth is clearly the main cause of poverty among developing nations.

T F 6. Rapid population growth does not necessarily create poverty.

T F 7. In most cases developing countries would be better off if they abandoned agriculture and introduced heavy industries such as steel and automobiles.

T F 8. For a country to develop economically it must have a large resource base.

T F 9. Foreign aid has successfully transferred capital from developed countries to developing countries.

T F 10. People in developing countries are too poor to save anything; therefore capital accumulation is impossible.

T F 11. Programs that reduce malnutrition can help contribute to economic development.

T F 12. Generosity by developed countries has contributed to high population rates in developing countries.

T F 13. Religious, military, and government monuments in developing countries are evidence of past saving.

T F 14. Developing countries often use foreign aid or foreign loans nonproductively.

T F 15. Latecomers to economic growth often attempt growth before preconditions exist.

T F *16. Even if every dollar of foreign aid were used productively by developing countries, such aid would not contribute greatly.

T F 17. Latecomers to MEG have tremendous advantages, and few or no disadvantages.

MULTIPLE CHOICE QUESTIONS
Circle the letter that corresponds to the best answer.

1. Which of the following helps to classify a nation with respect to its economic development level?
   a. per capita income
   b. life expectancy
   c. infant mortality
   d. All of the above

2. Which of the following statements is probably true?
   a. On an international level, there is a strong relationship between poverty and population density.
   b. Rapid population growth does not necessarily create poverty.
   c. A nation needs a large resource base to develop.
   d. Foreign aid can transform a developing country into a developed nation.

3. Which seems to be the final stage in a nation's economic development?
   a. manufacturing
   b. services
   c. heavy industry
   d. agriculture

4. Which of the following can help developing countries significantly?
   a. elimination of farm subsidies in developed countries
   b. foreign aid
   c. transfer of physical capital to them
   d. nationalizing private industries in developing countries

*5. Which of the following is most *unlike* the others, regarding a nation's economic development?
   a. foreign aid
   b. nationalizing domestic industries
   c. enforcing private property rights in developing countries
   d. giving physical capital to developing countries

6. Which of the following indicates developing country past saving?
   a. religious monuments
   b. government monuments
   c. military monuments
   d. All of the above

*7. The maximum contribution to development by foreign aid
   a. is small, even if it used productively.
   b. is enormous, if only it is used productively.
   c. is zero.
   d. must exceed the interest rate charged to the developing country.

*8. Which of the following countries has *not* experienced significant economic development over the past 25 years?
   a. Taiwan
   b. North Korea
   c. Japan
   d. South Korea

9. Which of the following occurs in a nation that has experienced modern economic growth?
   a. Increases in per capita productivity.
   b. Increases in population.
   c. Application of science to production.
   d. All of the above

10. Humanitarian foreign aid
   a. can help developing nations if it reduces malnutrition.
   b. may harm recipient country farmers.
   c. may reduce incentives to be productive for recipient countries.
   d. All of the above

11. Loans to developing countries
   a. were not used productively, by and large.
   b. are mostly owed to private Western banks.
   c. have mostly been restructured, to avoid default.
   d. All of the above

MATCHING

Choose the item in column (2) that best matches an item in column (1).

(1)	(2)
a. developing countries	f. highly developed service sector
b. newly developing countries	g. low literacy rates, high population growth
c. industrially advanced countries	h. Pacific Rim
d. MEG	i. application of science to production

CASE STUDY

There is a shocking lack of awareness on the part of students and the general public, as to who benefits from the process of capitalistic development. Many people believe that economic development benefits only the rich and causes the distribution of income to become even more skewed in favor of the rich.

The late Harvard economist, Joseph Schumpeter, long ago pointed out that capitalistic development mostly benefits the poor. He noted that the essence of capitalism is mass production, which (after all) is production for the masses. Modern working people enjoy services previously unavailable even to kings and queens. To name but a few: modern medicine and dentistry, clean water and sanitation facilities, safe meat and other food from all over the world.

Who benefits from the speed of travel due to the automobile and the bus? Royalty? Schumpeter notes that even electric lighting is no boon to royalty, who could afford candles and servants to tend to them. He further noted that Queen Elizabeth owned silk stockings and that the capitalist achievement does not consist in providing more silk stockings for queens, but in providing them to factory women and secretaries--and at prices requiring steadily decreasing amounts of their labor time. Thus, it is cheap cloth (cotton, and synthetic) as well as mass produced shoes, shirts, autos, televisions, radios, and so on (and on and on) which benefit the poor. Indeed, increased leisure and freedom from the drudgery of much factory and housework are also capitalism's achievements which mostly benefit the lower and middle class (the latter probably owes its very existence to capitalism).

1. Does the U.S. experience indicate a more uneven distribution of income over time?

2. Are there any costs to capitalistic development?

ANSWERS TO CHAPTER 35

COMPLETION QUESTIONS

1. industrially advanced countries, newly industrialized countries, developing countries
2. life expectancies, infant mortality, literacy
3. agriculture, manufacturing, services
4. use for their own purposes
5. save, invest
6. more; nationalize
7. trade, changing attitudes and aptitudes, helpful political institutions
8. productivity, increases, sweeping; scientific

TRUE-FALSE

1. T
2. T
3. F Life expectancies, infant mortality, and literacy rates are important too.
4. T
5. F The evidence is mixed.
6. T
7. F Numerous countries have a comparative advantage in agriculture.
8. F A large resource base is neither a necessary nor a sufficient condition for economic development.
9. F This has proved to be a difficult problem.
10. F They can and do save; they must use their saving in more economically productive ways.
11. T
12. T
13. T
14. T
15. T
16. T
17. F There are disadvantages: tremendous pressure to "catch up" leads to impatience and a willingness to adopt radical solutions.

MULTIPLE CHOICE

1.d; 2.b; 3.b; 4.a; 5.c; 6.d; 7.a; 8.b; 9.d; 10.d; 11.d

MATCHING

a and g; b and h; c and f; d and i

CASE STUDY

1. The pre-tax, pre-transfer distribution of incomes has remained relatively constant; after considering those two the distribution of income is more even. Hence capitalistic development has improved the lot of the masses without generating more income inequality.
2. Costs include disrupted lives (as changes in tastes, technology, and comparative advantage have occurred) and increased pollution levels.

GLOSSARY TO CHAPTER 35

Industrially advanced countries (IACs) Canada, Japan, the United States, and the countries of Western Europe that have market economies based on a large skilled labor force and a large technically advanced stock of capital goods.

Modern economic growth (MEG) The theory of economic growth in which growth is characterized by increases in per capita output accompanied by increases in population and driven by the application of science to the problems of economic production.

Vicious cycle of poverty A theory that low per capita incomes are an obstacle to realizing the necessary amount of saving and investment that is required to obtain acceptable rates of economic growth.